DESIGN OF MY JOURNEY

AN AUTOBIOGRAPHY

———

DESIGN OF MY JOURNEY

AN AUTOBIOGRAPHY

―――――

Hans Kasdorf

A JOINT PUBLICATION OF
CENTER FOR MENNONITE BRETHREN STUDIES/
VERLAG FÜR THEOLOGIE UND RELIGIONSWISSENSCHAFT
2004

DESIGN OF MY JOURNEY

Copyright ©2004 Hans Kasdorf

All rights reserved. With the exception for brief excerpts for reviews, no part of this book may be reproduced, stored in a retrieval system or transmitted in whole or in part, in any form, by any means, electronic, mechanical, photocopying, recording or otherwise without prior permission of the copyright holder.

Published simultaneously by the Center for Mennonite Brethren Studies, 1717 S. Chestnut Ave., Fresno, CA 93702 (http://fresno.edu/affiliation/cmbs), and VTR Publications, Gogolstr. 33, 90475 Nürnberg, Germany (vtr@compuserve.com, http://www.vtr-online.de)

This book is part of the series edition afem - mission specials, ed. by Klaus W. Müller, Bernd Brandl and Thomas Mayer.

Publication Consultant: Kindred Productions, Winnipeg, Man.
Cover Design: David Kasdorf.
Printed in the UK by Lightning Source

Library of Congress Cataloging-in-Publication Data

Kasdorf, Hans, 1928-

    Design of My Journey / Hans Kasdorf
      P.   cm.
    Includes bibliographical references.
    ISBN 1-877941-10-7
    1. Kasdorf, Hans, 1928-
        I. Title II. Series
    BX8143.K37 2004
    289,7'092 – dc21

Bibliographic information also published by Die Deutsche Bibliothek.
Die Deutsche Bibliothek lists this publication in the Deutsche Nationalbibliografie; detailed bibliographic data are available at http://dnb.ddb.de.

To
my wife Frieda:
treasured partner and companion;
and to
our children and grandchildren:
Dianne and Steve with Maren,
David and Julia with Amelia,
Evelyn and Don with Natalia and David
with
love, affection, and gratitude

Contents

Foreword ix
Vorwort xi
Recognition with Gratitude xiii
Introduction xv

Part I: Providence and Provision (1928-1930)

1. The Land That Rocked My Cradle 3
2. The Year of Great Turning 9
3. Escape from Slavgorod to Moscow 15
4. Under Siege in Moscow 20
5. From Siege in Moscow to Safety in Mölln 28
6. Developments in Germany 35
7. Voyage Across the Atlantic 43
8. By River Rail and Road to Our Destination 51

Part II: Formative Years of Childhood and Youth (1930-1949)

9. The Place Where I Grew Up 61
10. A Profile of Our Jungle Land 71
11. Pioneering Ventures on a Jungle Farm 78
12. Insights from Old Letters 88
13. Former Dwellers and Foreign Settlers 97
14. Shaping Influences in Early Years 101
15. Memories from the Lighter Side 108
16. On the Ordinary Edge of Daily Life 114
17. Dogs and Cats and Snakes and Rats 120
18. Of Birds and Butterflies 125
19. Valleys Deep and Mountains High 131
20. Customs and Culture Colony Style 139
21. Christian Celebration with Tradition 149
22. My Youthful Dreams in Jeopardy 157

23. When Lightning Struck Our Village	164
24. Modest Tributes to My First Mentors	171
25. Farewell, *Heimatland*, Farewell	177

Part III: Learning the ABC of My Life's Mission (1949-1962)

26. First Months in Canada	188
27. Winkler Bible School	193
28. Beyond the Prescribed Curriculum	199
29. Two Are Better Than One	207
30. Winnipeg and Chilliwack	212
31. Long Road to Blumenau	218
32. Back to Serve My *Heimatland*	224
33. Rewarding Missional Service	234
34. Mission Interrupted	241

Part IV: Detour in Academia (1962-1976 [1978])

35. Summer School and Tabor College	248
36. University of Oregon	255
37. Facing an Alluring Crossroad	262
38. College Teaching and Seminary Studies	268
39. Lengthening the Service Cords	276
40. Deepening Missiological Stakes	284

Part V: On the Missiological Service Road (1973-2003)

41. Full-Time Seminary Teaching	296
42. More Studies While Teaching	304
43. The Seminary Decade of Mission	311
44. Committed to Servanthood in Mission	319
45. The Rite of Passage Called Retirement	325
46. Giessen and Frankenthal	332
47. Concluding Reflections	339
Selected Bibliography	345
Glossary	349
General Index	352

Foreword

Fredrick Buechner writes in *Telling Secrets,* "Maybe nothing is more important than that we keep track, you and I, of these stories of who we are and where we have come from and the people we have met along the way, because it is precisely through these stories in all their particularities...that God makes himself known to us most powerfully and personally."

Hans Kasdorf has enriched us humanly and spiritually by telling us his story. I have followed the broad outline of his story for the past fifty years and now he has filled in the blanks for me. Fifty years ago, Hans enrolled as a student at the Mennonite Brethren Bible College in Winnipeg. I had never met him previously, but after having him in my classes for several years, I found in him a kindred spirit. He had come from Brazil a few years earlier to study at the Winkler Bible School in Manitoba. Here he met his future wife, Frieda Reimer, whom he married before coming to Winnipeg. (Frieda was an excellent typist and she typed a Masters' thesis for me.) Our student/teacher relationship was gradually transformed into friendship. It was a friendship such as C. S. Lewis describes in *The Four Loves:* "The best sort of friendship consists of a few people absorbed in some common interest."

Although the Kasdorfs left Winnipeg after graduation, we followed their movements from a distance. We were delighted to see Hans broaden his academic training in preparation for future ministries. His deep desire to participate in the missionary endeavors of the Mennonite Brethren Church found expression in several missionary ventures in South America, including his native land, Brazil. Along the way, Hans discovered that he had teaching gifts and so he decided to continue graduate studies in modern languages. He then went on to earn a doctorate in Missiology and, later, a doctorate in Theology.

After teaching for a number of years at Fresno Pacific College, he accepted the call to become Professor of World Mission at the Mennonite Brethren Biblical Seminary in Fresno. It was here that our paths merged once again, when I was asked to become Professor of New Testament at the seminary. We were now colleagues, and our friendship deepened over the years. My wife, Lena, and I always enjoyed our association with Hans and Frieda, especially when we visited each other in our homes.

What always impressed me was Hans's diligence. He gave himself completely to the work of God's kingdom and would not allow frivolous distractions deter him from his divine calling. On focusing his energy and his gifts on the area of his expertise and passion, he made a profound impact on his students. In spite of considerable accomplishments both as teacher and a writer, Hans has always been modest and even self-deprecating about his contributions to the work of the church. Like Paul, the apostle, he has always insisted, "by the grace of God I am what I am."

His kindness to others was recognized by both students and colleagues. By taking a genuine interest in the life of his students, he became an effective mentor for them. He had a special niche in his heart for foreign students. Both in seminary chapel and in church on Sunday Hans could be seen quite regularly, sitting beside his deaf colleague, Dr. D. Edmond Hiebert, writing down what the speaker was saying and passing on notes to his colleague. After doing this myself on several occasions, I realized what a labor of love this was.

With all his devotion to his calling, his striving for godliness, and his rigorous work habits, Hans remained delightfully human. He never lost his sense of humor. Like many of God's saints, Hans and Frieda also experienced physical pain; but in spite of disappointments and sad moments in their lives, they were able to laugh at the droll and the incongruous experiences which public ministries provide in rich measure.

After officially retiring from seminary, Hans had an open door for the exercise of his gifts and his expertise in churches and theological schools of Germany. On his 70th birthday, the Free Theological Academy of Giessen honored him with a fine Festschrift: *Die Mission der Theologie*.

As I reflect on Hans's life, the words of William Inge, Dean of St. Paul's, come to mind: "It does not seem to me that clever books and brilliant sermons have done so much for me, as those chance glimpses into characters far above my own." It is with great delight that I recommend the following chapters from Hans's pen, in which we get such "chance glimpses" into a life well lived.

David Ewert
Professor Emeritus of Biblical Studies
Canadian Mennonite University
Winnipeg, Manitoba

Vorwort

Diese englische Erstausgabe ist ein gemeinsames Unternehmen zwischen dem Center for Mennonite Brethren Studies (CMBS) in Fresno und der edition des Arbeitskreises für evangelikale Missiologie im Verlag für Theologie und Religionswissenschaft (VTR) in Nürnberg. Als sein Nachfolger als Fachbereichsleiter an der Freien Theologischen Akademie (FTA) in Gießen komme ich gerne der Bitte entgegen, dazu ein Vorwort in Deutsch zu schreiben.

Dass Hans Kasdorf nun seine Autobiographie vorlegt, ist ein Geschenk für alle, die ihn durch persönliche Kontakte und durch seine literarischen Werke kennen—und die ihn nun noch besser kennenlernen werden.

Professor Dr. Hans Kasdorf hat gleich nach seiner Pensionierung in den Vereinigten Staaten vier wichtige Jahre in Deutschland an der Freien Theologischen Akademie den Fachbereich Missionswissenschaft und Evangelistik aufgebaut. Jede seiner Vorlesungen an der FTA war handgeschrieben, neuformuliert und durchdacht. Dabei arbeitete er bis kurz vor dem Gang in den Hörsaal daran, änderte, ergänzte, diskutierte mit Kollegen einzelne Kriterien—obwohl er sie selbst schon in der Tiefe durchgedacht hatte: Professor Kasdorf sagte seinen Studenten an der Freien Theologischen Akademie nicht nur, er sei ein Lernender, er praktizierte das.

Er hat deutlich gemacht, dass es nicht nur Theologie der Mission gibt, sondern auch eine Mission der Theologie. Zwar hat die Mission in der Theologie ihre Wurzeln, die Theologie aber hat in der Mission ihre Frucht. *Die Mission der Theologie* hat sich als Fazit seiner akademischen Arbeit so in der Freien Theologischen Akademie geprägt, dass die Herausgeber die Formulierung als Titel für eine Festschrift zu seinem 70. Geburtstag aufnahmen.

Hans Kasdorf stand als Ermutiger eher im Hintergrund, doch wenn es darauf ankam, hat er spontan und mit klaren Worten Farbe für die Mission bekannt. Er begleitete den Aufbau des Arbeitskreises für evangelikale Missiologie und lieferte Artikel für dessen Zeitschrift, *evangelikale missiologie*. Als er vor etwa 30 Jahren gebeten wurde, die Leitung für eine Ausbildungsstätte für Missionare zu übernehmen, lehnte er mit der Begründung ab, es gäbe einheimische Fachleute dafür, die Verantwortung für Deutschland tragen sollten. Hatte doch hier die Missionswissenschaft mit Gustav Warneck vor der Wende zum 20. Jahrhundert begonnen!

Kasdorf hat die Schätze und Werte des Anfangs der deutschen Missionswissenschaft an der School of World Mission des Fuller Theological Seminary in Pasadena studiert. Dort habe ich ihn 1976 kennengelernt und war vom ersten Moment an beeindruckt. Er ist einer der wenigen amerikanischen Missiologen, die Zugang zur alten deutschen Literatur hatten, sie prüften und das Gute in ihre wissenschaftliche Arbeit integrierten. Nach Gustav und Johannes Warneck hat er auch Schätze deutscher Missionswissenschaft bei Keyßer, Freytag, Hartenstein, Vicedom und Gutmann erschlossen. Natürlich setzte er sich auch mit den aktuellen Missionswissenschaftlern auseinander, stritt jedoch nicht mit ihnen, zog aber deutlich seine eigene theologische Linie. Er hatte mit seiner ersten Dissertation eine Reihe von Forschungsprojekten eingeleitet, in denen junge evangelikale Wissenschaftler die kirchlichen Missionen und deren Vertreter aufgearbeitet haben. Dass er ein Lernender blieb, stellte er in seiner fleißigen akademischen Arbeit unter Beweis. Es war ihm wichtig, den kontextuellen Bezug von Kultur, Religion und Evangelium gründlich aufzuarbeiten. Man findet bei ihm exakte Wissenschaft, grundlegende Theologie und angewandte Praxis auf dem gemeinsamen Nenner der Mission.

Die deutsch-mennonitische Mentalität mit ihrer ethischen Geradlinigkeit, tiefer persönlicher Frömmigkeit und ihrem intellektuell transparenten Denken wird in seiner Persönlichkeit deutlich reflektiert. Der Gottesbezug und die Liebe zur Heiligen Schrift sind für ihn Maßstab seiner Forschung; sie durchziehen seine Literatur, Vorlesungen und Gespräche, die wie selbstverständlich Gedanken um Mission enthalten.

Ich bin Hans Kasdorf — dem persönlichen Freund, dem Bruder im Glauben, dem Fachkollegen — sehr dankbar für seinen Einfluss in meinem Leben und Dienst für die Mission. Der Dank gilt nicht zuletzt seiner Frau Frieda, die seine Eigenschaften verstärkt und ihn immer begleitet, damit in seiner eingeschränkten physischen Kraft sein überaus wacher Geist zum Ausdruck kommt. Auch ihre Kinder und Enkel haben sicher manchmal schmerzlich auf den Vater und Großvater verzichtet.

In der Einheit von Leben und Glauben der Persönlichkeit und des wissenschaftlichen Arbeitens von Hans Kasdorf wird deutlich, was Gott durch einen Menschen machen kann, der sich ihm zur Verfügung stellt.

Klaus W. Müller
Dozent und Professor für Mission
Freie Theologische Akademie — Gießen (Deutschland)
Evangelische Theologische Faculteit — Leuven (Belgien)

Recognition with Gratitude

In the course of writing I have received many encouraging words to guide my hand across the page with greater ease. Now that the pages are filled, I feel constrained to recognize with gratitude some of the many people who have so graciously touched me along the way, as well as those who generously granted permission to use copyrighted sources, assisting me in my attempt to fashion out of life's season a *Design of My Journey*.

Ingrid and Hans Wittke, our friends and former neighbors in Gießen, secured the photograph of the ocean liner *Monte Olivia* with Copyright [2003] by the *Reederei Hamburg Süd*. The maps, "Barnaul (Slavgorod) Colony" and "Mennonite Settlements in Brazil and Uruguay" are from the *Mennonite Historical Atlas*, 2nd edition, Copyright 1986 by Springfield Publishers. Unless indicated otherwise, Scripture quotations are from the New International Version of the Bible, Copyright 1986 by the Holman Bible Publishers. I gratefully acknowledge permission to use these references for my book.

Paul Toews, director of the Center for Mennonite Brethren Studies (CMBS) in Fresno, was the first on this side of the Atlantic to raise the question about having my autobiography published by the Center. Since I have spent the major part of my life serving the Mennonite Brethren Church, I was sympathetic to his idea without disregarding other options. Among them was Thomas Mayer, general manager of the Verlag für Theologie und Religionswissenschaft (VTR) in Nürnberg. Long before I had completed the manuscript, he wrote me that there was interest in publishing the book in Germany. From these and other possibilities has evolved a joint project. Kevin Enns-Rempel, archivist and editor of the CMBS, assumed editorial responsibility and together with Thomas Mayer was helpful in working out details of a copublication between the CMBS and the VTR. That in itself is a rather novel venture for which I am grateful. Marilyn Hudson of Kindred Productions in Winnipeg was always ready to answer questions about the mechanics in the process of preparing the manuscript for the press.

Our daughter-in-law, Julia Kasdorf, professor of creative writing, waded through one of the early versions of my manuscript in its raw form. Only after she returned it with kind comments and suggestions did I become aware of the next to impossible task she had undertaken to give shape and form to a chaotic pile of pages printed on both sides. Phyllis Martens, author and teacher of English; Wilfred Martens, university professor of English language and literature; and Albert Pauls, instructor of business, read later drafts of my manuscript. Each time I reviewed the feedback they gave me, I felt enriched as if I had been in a profitable English class; it was truly a learning experience. I express my heartfelt thanks to these professional women and men for their constructive comments.

Special words of appreciation to my esteemed friend, former college professor and seminary colleague, David Ewert, for his gracious "Foreword" in English. The same is due to Klaus W. Müller, another dear friend and a competent successor in the Department of Missiology and Evangelism at the Freie Theologische Akademie in Gießen, for his kind "Vorwort" in German. Frieda and I have been blessed by these men and their wives, Lena and Ulrike, at different times in our lives. We treasure their friendship.

I thank God for His grace and goodness in blessing me with a wonderful and supportive family. Our son David has invested his talent in integrative arts to make the cover design. As I already mentioned, his wife Julia gave me some helpful points how to "tell the story" of that journey more effectively. Our daughter Evelyn and her husband Don have been a constant source of encouragement, urging me to write about my life for them and for their children. Our daughter Dianne has come to my rescue—countless times. Whenever my computer had me all confused, I called her by phone, and she was usually able to put me back on track. Her husband Steve maintained enough confidence in me that I would eventually finish and said, "I want to read what Pop is writing." She also made several trips from Salinas to Fresno to scan the pictures with captions into the book.

Finally, Frieda has not only helped when I needed help the most, she was at my side throughout the long process of writing and revising and rewriting again; she read each revision and assisted in a thousand other ways. I can neither measure in weight nor express in words what I would like to say; I simply have no adequate language to express my indebtedness to her and the children, except two words of virtue my parents taught me at the very beginning of my journey: Thank you!

Introduction

My earthly life had its beginning long ago and far away. Now the time has come to give an account of the road I have traveled from my cradle in Siberia to retirement in California. The road has been long and sometimes rough. As I stop and look over time and distance, I see a certain design only God in His foreknowledge could have drawn. It is like a compass, giving direction through all my days and a measure of wisdom to discern my steps in His ways. "How precious to me are your thoughts, O God!"

Motive

When the people of Israel were freed from slavery in Egypt, crossing the Red Sea into the desert, they were instructed to observe the Passover meal as a commemoration of their freedom (Ex. 12:24-27; Lev. 23:4-8). As they reached the end of their journey, crossing the Jordan into the promised land, they were told to take twelve stones from the river and put them into a pile as a memorial to God's faithfulness (Josh. 4:1-9). Somewhat like the Passover meal and the heap of stones, my story is a memorial to God's grace and goodness in my life.

When children ask, so the biblical injunction goes, their elders should respond. My children have asked. These pages are a modest attempt to respond. I must also mention that my wife Frieda—partner, helper, and the mother of our children—has encouraged me not only to write, but to write *now*. She reminds me that "to wait may prove to be too late." She is right. Procrastination is no virtue and can have unwelcome consequences. She knows my fragile frame all too well. For two score years and more she has been the companion of my pilgrimage, walking the road with me from one land to the next—ever faithful, always true, willing to forfeit comfort and leisure, instead of insisting on ease, vacations, and pleasure.

Sources

My first recollections about my own life come from oral tradition. I remember sitting on my father's lap with my brother Nikolai and sister Katja next to him listening to stories from Russia. Occasionally, Mother and my older siblings would add some details to enrich the tales. I treasure those childhood memories.

Over the course of many years I have collected a variety of written sources both published and unpublished. My task now is to sort them in a manner that will create order from disorder. In doing so, I have spent considerable time studying primary records and secondary literature at the *Kirchenarchiv* in Mölln, Germany, and at the Center for Mennonite Brethren Studies in Fresno, California. Most of the sources, however, are part of my private library collection. They include books and records from Peter Pauls, a dear friend since our pioneering years in Brazil; personal papers from Peter Isaak, for many years business manager of the co-op in Witmarsum where I was working in the 1940s; some writings of the late Katherine Nickel, my mother's first cousin, of Reedley, California; a copy of "Documents Relevant to the Wiebe Family Reunion," prepared by Peter Penner, Emeritus Professor of History of Mount Allison University and grandson of my mother's sister Katharina, married to Peter J. Wiebe of the Slavgorod Colony in Siberia. Our families escaped in 1929. The Wiebe family got visas for Canada, my family emigrated to Brazil.

Another source of information is a fourteen-page questionnaire completed by my siblings in Brazil and my collection of personal and family letters. These include letters from my mother's parents, siblings, and kinfolk in Russia, as well as letters from my parents written to Jakob and Anna (my grandmother's sister) Nickel in the United States, covering the years 1882-1942. Arnold Nickel, my second cousin (grandson of Jakob and Anna), has preserved many of these letters and made them available to me. In addition, I have the correspondence with my parents from 1949-1955, and with my father until he went to be with the Lord in 1968. With few exceptions, the photos used in this book are from my personal collection.

Genre

"Every person has at least one book in him, the story of his own life. Every life is filled with incidents and quiet heroism, with struggle and joy." These words quoted by my college professor David Ewert in his book, *Honour Such People,* reenforce the fundamental conviction that, indeed, I carry within myself incidents and experiences that deserve to be expressed. The question, however, is how best to do that. I do not want to write an academic piece of work; much less do I desire to write a romantic novel for mere entertainment. I have no thesis to prove, no problem to solve, no single plot to develop, no suspense to build. All I have is a story to tell of my life that unfolds in terms of events in time and space.

I confess that I find this kind of writing extremely difficult and ask the reader for leniency in critiquing my literary style and method. One of the dilemmas I face is that there are many mini-stories within the main story; they, too, call for explanations and reflections and thereby tend to disrupt the chronological sequence of the narrative. Thus the tale I am telling is not strictly narration of a story; it is rather a kind of "postmodern genre" that transcends boundaries by blending narration, meditation and reflection, making use of rhyme and rhythm, history and geography, and whatever form seems best to fit the context. Such themes as providence and provision, faith and freedom, courage and ambition, suffering and celebration are important segments of my story and legacy woven into a tapestry of a thousand threads that give shape and meaning to life.

In his history of the Winkler Bible School, *A Place Called Peniel,* my former Bible teacher, George D. Pries, captures essential elements of the kind of genre I am dealing with. He writes,

> The ability to remember is one of man's unique endowments. Man can remember and thus he acts today and hopes for tomorrow in the light of his past experiences which he has assimilated and which have become a part of him. In telling his personal history, man discloses who he is and gives evidence of a true self into whose life-story diverse and countless impressions have been woven toward a life pattern.

By telling a personal history one is inevitably faced with the question what impressions and incidents to include and which to withhold without either magnifying or diminishing the elements needed that give "evidence of a true self." That is an issue every biographer must seek to resolve.

In his autobiography, *A Journey of Faith,* my friend and former colleague, David Ewert, asks, "How much self-revelation is appropriate when one writes for a wider audience?" He goes on to say that "there is an inner sanctum in every person which should be guarded against invasion and over-exposure." The point made by Ewert is, indeed, valid and calls for literary circumspection.

My story is a rather simple tale fashioned from examples and experiences of life; it is like a personal conversation of things that now are with things that have been. The major components of that conversation revolve around the providence of God to which I owe the fulfillment of my mother's prayer from the time she dedicated me to God when I was a child in Siberia. That particular incident is a piece in miniature within *God's Design,* to borrow the title of a book on Old Testament theology written by my colleague Elmer Martens. For the most part I have chosen to tell my story in the first person. After all, I was a participant in the events that transpired in the course of my life. Even as a child I was there and lived through them.

My story is not merely the record of a tourist, but the account of a pilgrim. The difference is significant and cannot be overlooked. The attraction for the tourist lies not so much in the journey itself, as in its destination: the place of pleasure promised in the travel plan. As soon as the sightseeing and entertainment are over, there is only one thing left: return home and talk about the fabulous experience. Not so for the pilgrim, whose delight lies more in the journey itself than in its destination.

A pilgrim journeys with purpose, always facing challenges and tasks that give meaning to life *en route*. Thus it is not only the natural beauty of God's creation or the great works of art produced by humankind, however glorious these may be, that make the journey of the pilgrim rich beyond words. A pilgrim who desires to know the Creator himself must transcend the realm of nature and human achievements, and be prepared for a detour now and then. That means, as C. S. Lewis reminds us, leaving the hills and the vales, the woods and the wilderness and going back to our studies and our Bibles, to our church and to our knees.

Detours may be a nuisance to the tourist, but they are the very soul of a pilgrim. A pilgrim is always *on the road*, so to speak, and thus not able to describe the destination, at least not from experience. That is why my story will remain incomplete until my Lord writes the conclusion.

Purpose

My first objective is to transmit to my children and grandchildren not only events and experiences from my personal life, but also cultural and spiritual values and virtues that I have come to treasure. They are like the warp and the woof woven into the fabric of my being; they have contributed to the process of becoming a follower of Jesus; they have formed my worldview and shaped my understanding of the essence of life and the purpose for living.

In the event that others with whom I share a common legacy of faith outside of my family—be they Anabaptist or Lutheran, Mennonite or Reformed, Puritan or Pietist—should find in my chronicle some nuggets of value and encouragement, I shall consider their interest an honor and their actual reading of my story a special reward for having written it.

What one biblical writer wrote generations ago is apropos to my story: "Not to us, O LORD, not to us but to your name be the glory, because of your love and faithfulness!" (Ps. 115:1).

Wisdom

I grew up not owning much, as my parents had neither luxury nor wealth. But we never lacked work and had no cause to be bored. True, we had hardships to overcome and tensions to deal with. I have never been fond of either, yet I look at them as experiences that contribute to the formation of sterling qualities in a person's life. After all, the Christian life is defined neither by material things, nor by circumstances but by precepts and principles set forth in the Scriptures and by treasures of collected wisdom.

I am moved, therefore, to conclude my introductory remarks with "a lesson for life." My children will know what I mean. They remember that in my wiser moments I tried to teach them lessons for life. In fact, they remember that expression so well that they have humorously proverbialized it and used it on me—sometimes in season, sometimes out of season. They know that I am still a learner, but also a teacher. I pray that they will be the same—with one difference: learn wisdom sooner in life than I did. That is why I end my preliminary comments to my story with an authentic word of wisdom spoken by a seasoned wise man millennia ago. It is, indeed, "a lesson for life" which they, while still young, can apply to their own way of living and then pass it on to their offspring. Here it is as recorded in *Proverbs 4:1-5*:

> *Listen, my sons [and daughters], to a father's instruction;*
> *pay attention and gain understanding.*
> *I give you sound learning, so do not forsake my teaching.*
> *When I was a boy in my father's house, still tender,*
> *and an only [youngest] child of my mother,*
> *he taught me and said,*
> *"Lay hold of my words with all your heart;*
> *keep my commands and you will live.*
> *Get wisdom, get understanding;*
> *do not forget my words*
> *or swerve from them."*

PART I

Providence and Provision (1928-1930)

From Siberian Steppes to Brazilian Jungles

If God is for us, who can be against us?... Who shall separate us from the love of Christ? Shall trouble or hardship or persecution or famine or nakedness or danger or sword?... No, in all these things we are more than conquerors through him who loved us. For I am convinced that neither death nor life, neither angels nor demons, neither the present nor the future, nor any powers, neither height nor depths, nor anything else in all creation, will be able to separate us from the love of God that is in Christ Jesus our Lord.
– The Apostle Paul in *Romans 8*

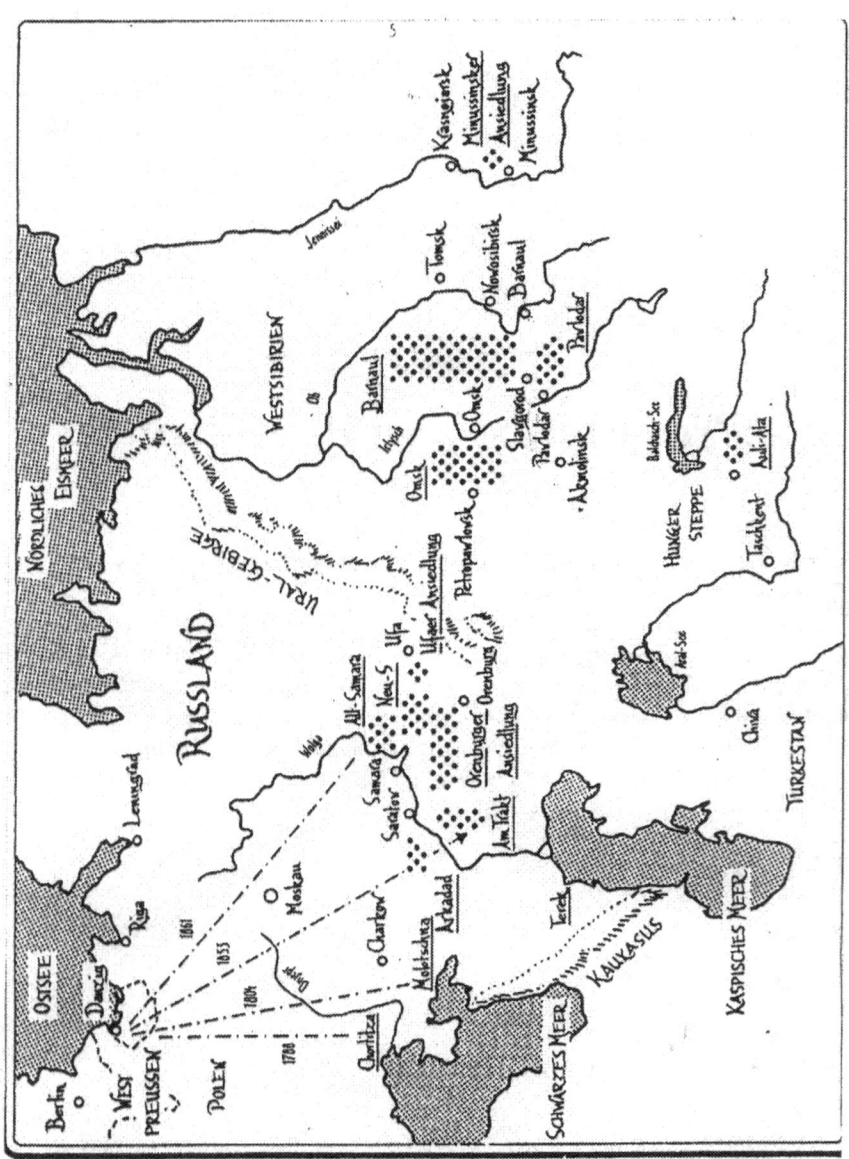

Mennonite settlements in Russia during the 1920s
Source: P. M. Friesen, *Alt-Evangelische Mennonitische Brüderschaft in Russland (1789-1910) im Rahmen der mennonitischen Gesamtgeschichte*. Reprint edition by the Verein zur Erforschung und Pflege des Kulturerbes des Russlanddeutschen Mennonitentums e. V., 1991.

1

The Land That Rocked My Cradle
(1928)

> *My frame was not hidden from you*
> *when I was made in the secret place. . . .*
> *All the days ordained for me were written*
> *in your book before one of them came to be.*
> *How precious to me are your thoughts, O God!*
> –King David in *Psalm 139*

I was born 27 July 1928 in Slavgorod, Siberia, as the youngest of nine children. Because I have no personal recollection of either the time or place of that event, I must rely on oral accounts given to me by my parents and older siblings, who seemed to remember every detail of it. If I should follow my inclination, I would let my mind run ahead of the cradle and talk about things and events which I personally do remember. That would mean, however, taking a big leap from the land of the Siberian steppes where I took my first wobbling steps to the land of the Brazilian jungle where I learned to run with determination.

"Siberia" is the English designation for the immense geographical expanses comprising the northern third of Asia. For centuries, the Russians have called it *Sibir´*, a word borrowed from the Tatars, as Peter Rahn explains. *Sibir´* is a compound noun derived from *sib* (sleep) and *ir* (land). The Tatars may have called it "the sleeping land" because it had remained undisturbed since the days of creation and never felt the smarting cuts of plow or harrow on its unspoiled surface.

In the fourteenth century the Tatar people had established their kingdom on flat and open land on the Irtysch River, and in the 1580s Cossack Yermak, a band leader of independent Russian Cossacks, conquered the tribal Tatars and established Tobolsk as the capital of the region. When Peter the Great took control of Russia, he annexed the entire Siberian land mass to his empire. The early Tatars, with their predominantly nomadic culture, were still roaming throughout the region when the Mennonites and other Germans settled there in the late nineteenth and early twentieth centuries. Siberia contained within its boundaries the potential for atrocity as well as prosperity. My people experienced both.

In *A History of Twentieth-Century Russia*, Robert Service writes that Siberia became the choicest land mass for *en masse* resettlements. In fact, it became a dumping ground for all the peoples that incurred Stalin's suspicion. Russia's own intellectuals like Dmitri Volkogonov, Aleksandr Solzhenitsyn, and Edvard Radzinsky agree that in no other single region in the world have so many people been coerced to die under violent conditions as in Russia's *Sibir'*. Many of my family's kin were among those forced into a violent final sleep in that ancient sleeping land where they will rest until that great resurrection day when sea and land will give up their dead.

Gerhard Fast, a young school teacher and family friend who moved to Siberia at the same time my family did, makes a telling observation in his book, *In den Steppen Sibiriens:* "*Sibirien!* This mysterious land with its expansive steppes, towering mountains, and giant streams; with its immeasurable riches in gold, silver, coal, and iron ore; with its wolves; with its places of exile and banishment; and with its colorful mixture of peoples is about to become [our new] homeland." Fast wrote those words as he reminisced on the time when the Mennonites from various colonies were in search of new land for their young and growing families.

The first Mennonites settled in Asiatic Russia as early as 1882, founding four villages in Aulie-Ata (Dzhambul) in Turkestan. Some isolated families moved there in the 1890s. The massive migration, however, in which my family took part was set in motion after the construction of the Trans-Siberian Railroad,1892-1905. In 1906 word came to Mennonites and other peasants throughout European Russia that large areas of farmland east of the Ural Mountains, including the hitherto uncultivated and desolate Kulunda Steppe, were becoming available. The news spread like prairie fire in the drought of summer. Enthusiasm flared among landless and landed alike. They responded promptly.

In February 1907, several teams of experts from various Mennonite settlements were on their way to explore the land in Siberia. Some went as far east as the Amur on the China/Manchuria border, where another Mennonite colony was eventually established. The majority, however, were overwhelmed by the endless open fields and meadows of the Kulunda Steppe. Before long, large segments of Mennonites were again on the move, this time crossing continental boundaries to establish numerous settlements around or near Omsk, Pavlodar, Barnaul, Slavgorod, Novo-sibirsk, and other cities.

By the time my family moved in 1910 from Zagradovka to Slavgorod and settled on the Kulunda Steppe, government surveyors and engineers had already designated certain sections for villages where the newcomers would live. Initially, the government designated fifteen *desjatina* (about fifteen hectares or thirty-eight acres) of land, including a plot for a homestead, to each male member of a family. In his book, *Die deutschen Dörfer in der westsibirischen Kulunda-Steppe*, Manfred Klaube notes that the Mennonites considered such inequity of land distribution unfair. After some negotiations they received permission to assign an equal parcel of fifty *desjatina* to each household. According to an outside observer, writes Klaube, the Mennonite villages were generally as similar to one another as one egg is like the next. A distinct feature on each side of the road were rows of aspen that looked like forest groves, behind which were the houses and barns, fruit orchards and vegetable gardens. Everything was clean and orderly, a unique trait of Mennonite villages in many lands.

Those Mennonites who settled in the Omsk region established their villages north and northeast of Pavlodar, and north and northwest of Barnaul, with Omsk being their primary commercial and civic center. Those who settled more in the heart of the Kulunda Steppe made Pavlodar their major post for trade and civic transactions. After the completion of the Trans Siberian Railroad and simultaneous with the massive Mennonite migration to Siberia, Czar Nikolas II sponsored the building of a new city called Slavgorod. It was strategically situated northeast of Pavlodar, west of Barnaul, and south of a major concentration of Mennonite and other German villages in the very heart of the Kulunda Steppe. Pavlodar was a harbor city on the Irtysch, 240 kilometers southwest of Slavgorod, while Barnaul on the Ob lay 500 kilometers northeast of the new steppe settlers.

The christening of this group of over fifty villages (known as *"Die Fünfziger Dörfer"*) as one single colony appears to have been a difficult process. Since the steppes had undefined boundaries, the settlements and villages were collectively referred to as Barnaul, situated in the general vicinity of that ancient city and within the limits of a region by that same name. That made the search for an identity in the endless steppe all the more urgent. Thus, as Klaube points out, the Mennonites organized themselves in 1909 into five church parishes that included their own thirty-six villages and a number of other German settlements. Eventually they were grouped together as one colony named after Slavgorod, that new city west of Lake Kulunda and northeast of Pavlodar.

As Slavgorod grew in fame and prestige, the Mennonites made it their center for trade and commerce, legal transactions and civic recordings. The vital records of six of my siblings as well as my own may still be in the files of Slavgorod—unless they have in recent years been moved to the archives of Pavlodar or Barnaul. In the 1920s there were numerous larger and smaller Mennonite and other German settlements in Siberia, but Slavgorod was the largest.

At the time the Mennonites bought land there they did so by the rule. The head of each household had to draw a lot, which indicated both the village and the homestead where the family could build and live. Father's lot showed that he would settle in Alexandrovka, village No. 16, quite centrally located. That is where he built the family home and where we lived for nearly twenty years. That is also where six of my eight siblings were born: Heinrich (1910), Truda (1912) Tina (1915), Margaretha (1917), Katja (1920), and Nikolai (1924). It was also the place where Grandfather and Grandmother Kröker and two of my sisters, Truda and Tina, died and were buried.

My uncle Peter Wiebe, who was married to my mother's sister Katharina, remembers the beginning years in Siberia as "hard, very hard." Yet "through tenacious diligence, trust in God, and united efforts," the Mennonite pioneers were able to master their difficulties. They built for themselves an environment and a culture in which their material, social and spiritual needs were met. Within a few years, Uncle Peter adds, "we were able to live a life of relative ease, contentment, and peace."

In the fall of 1909, the early pioneers celebrated their first *Erntedankfest* (harvest thanksgiving). The men put up a huge tent, constructed seating facilities, and gathered green and fall-colored branches to decorate the place. The women baked *Bulktje,* a tasty white bread baked and eaten only on special occasions. In addition, they baked *Tweeback, Pluschtje,* and *Plumiplautz.* Plenty of it. On an embankment a short distance from the tent, the young men dug holes in the ground for ten huge cast iron cauldrons in which to cook *Borscht,* a typical Russian/Ukrainian soup, upgraded by the Mennonites with cabbage, potatoes, meat, onions and spices. There was plenty of everything for everyone to eat two full meals: *Meddagh* at noon and *Faspa* before going home.

The first of September was a beautiful Sunday. People came from every direction. The scene in the village was as festive as the mood of the participants was grateful. They came to celebrate God's grace and goodness, His greatness and glory. "It is God," they declared in words of Psalm 67, "who has been gracious to us and blessed us. He has brought us to this land. We have cultivated and worked, sown and planted, but God has watered and given the harvest. Now we are bringing in the fruit. May the peoples praise you, O God, may all the peoples praise you!" With thankful hearts they celebrated from morning until evening.

At that time they still saw nothing on the political, economical or spiritual horizon which in any way suggested that the time would come when celebrations such as this would not be tolerated. In 1913 there were more than ten thousand Mennonites living in the Slavgorod/Barnaul colony looking with optimism and hope into the future. Even when the war broke out, followed by the revolution, my people always believed and hoped for better times ahead. And, indeed, they continued celebrating harvest festival year after year for about two decades.

The Land That Rocked My Cradle

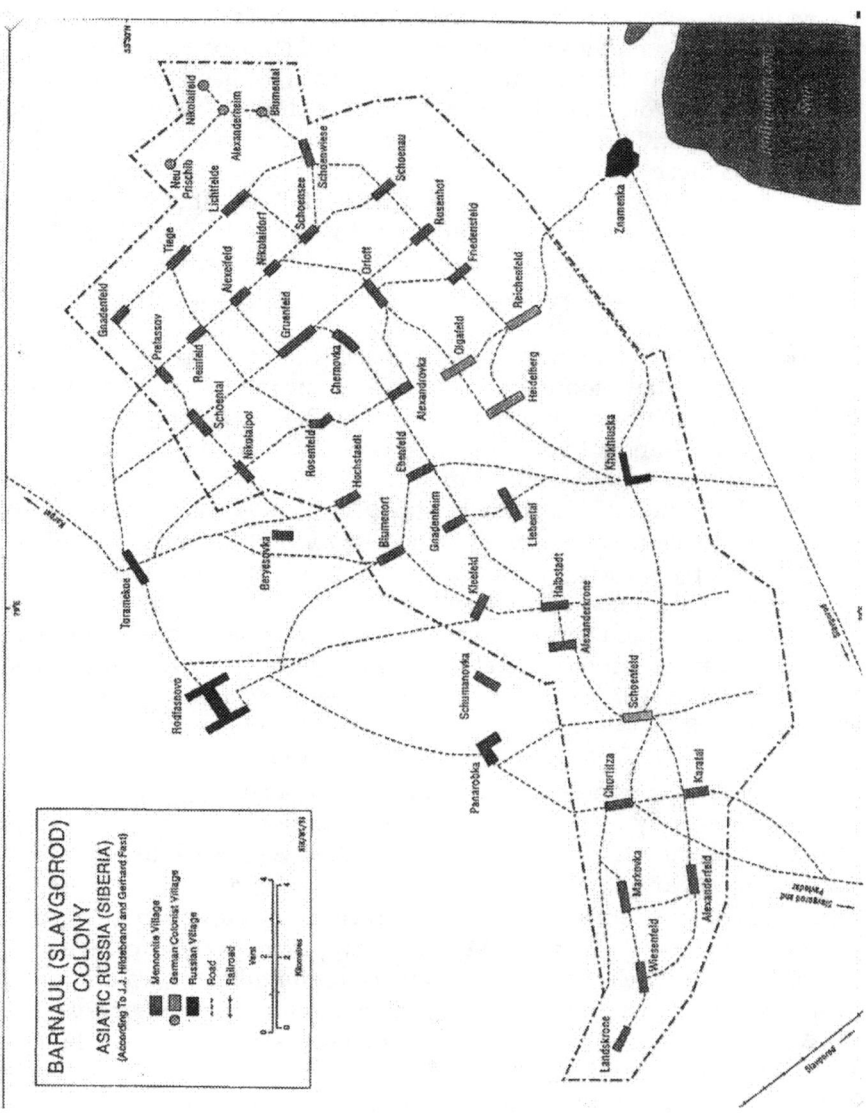

The Slavgorod/Barnaul settlements in Siberia, with Alexandrovka, village of my birth, in lower center.
Source: Schroeder and Huebert, eds., *Mennonite Historical Atlas*, 2nd. ed., 1996.

In September of 1929, they were about to celebrate again. But they did not because of events that had transpired in the meantime. All across Europe bombed-out craters lay still stained with the blood of First World War victims. Following the war, Imperial Russia was plunged into an unprecedented era of revolution, civil war, anarchy, political chaos, and famine. The years from 1917 to 1922 were turbulent years with consequences just as fateful as those of the great war. My ancestors and their progeny were caught in the midst of those turbulent times. Nikolas II (1868-1918), the last Czar of the Romanov's "mighty empire," was dethroned in March 1917. After months of imprisonment and humiliating treatment, the entire family was mercilessly executed in the darkness of a Siberian cellar in that even darker *Ipatiev Night* of 16 July 1918.

The Russian monarchy was annihilated, never to rise again. Russia was on the way to becoming the Marxist-Leninist version of a socialistic state, known as The Union of Socialist Soviet Republics, or simply Soviet Union. While Imperial Russia had much blood on its hands, Soviet Russia drowned its very soul in the blood of innocent millions. All this bloodshed crushes the heart with grief, says the Russian playwright, Edvard Radzinsky, as he rehearses the history of "the imperial twilight and the red dream." My parents experienced only the first decade of that red dream, while most of their siblings went through seventy years of infernal conditions on earth. Clearly the beginning of the great woes had come. Peace and prosperity together with religious liberty had been taken from the people. The next thanksgiving celebration in which my family participated after 1929 was in a different land, a land far, far away.

When I was four months old, I came down with diphtheria, a childhood epidemic common in those days. A number of children in our village had already been snatched out of their mothers' arms; their days were too few, their life-span too short. Death is very cruel. In those days it was always close to home, lurking at the doorsteps of many families. While children were the parents' most precious treasure, they seemed to be death's most favorite prey. My maternal grandparents, for instance, buried five of their eleven children. When Grandmother writes about that to her sister in the United States, she does not minimize pain and loss. But she considers herself fortunate when she tells of a close relative who had given birth to sixteen healthy children of whom only four survived. My mother also knew the pain caused by death in the family.

Such, then, was the land and place that rocked my cradle for a mere sixteen months. Metaphorically speaking, it turned out to be a violently rocking land.

2

The Year of Great Turning
(1929)

The harvest is past, the summer is ended
and the fruit-gathering over,
yet we are not saved.
– A Lament of the People, *Jeremiah 8*

Much like the people of Israel, my people escaped slavery and oppression, though in a different way. Again, like the Israelites, the Mennonites journeyed through a "wilderness" of sorts, not knowing where the road would lead or end. Then, too, like the people of Israel, my people went through severe tests and trials, some to the utter limits of their endurance. But unlike the Israelites, my people went by faith and hope alone, without any promise of either land or liberty. Only about one third of them saw their hopes realized. For the other two-thirds, all hopes were shattered. Many of them, especially the teachers and preachers, were executed or sent to concentration camps in Siberia and elsewhere. There was also the loss of all they had achieved: their land and labor, their hearths and homes, their kin, culture, safety and security.

The year 1929 was a terrible year for the average person in the Soviet Union. It has been recorded in the annals of Soviet history as "The Year of the Great Turn." It was so designated by Stalin himself, as Edvard Radzinsky points out in his biography of Stalin. The reason was not that in that year thousands upon thousands, including my family, tried to escape to freedom. The reason lay much deeper: this was the year when Stalin reached two irrevocable decisions. First, to eradicate religion as incompatible with socialism. To begin with, he ordered to close 1,400 churches and religious training institutions, be they Orthodox, Lutheran, Baptist or Mennonite. Second, to liquidate "the kulak as a class," be they Germans, Russians, Ukrainians or any other ethnic peoples within the boundaries of the Soviet Union.

In his personal account, *Gebt der Wahrheit die Ehre,* Karl Fast refers to this enforced religious and socioeconomic revolution of 1929 as *"ein jäher Umsturz,"* a cataclysmic change. Stalin's strategy was to replace faith in God by submission to the Soviet system and to replace private property by government owned land and industry. In his book *Mennonite Exodus*, Frank Epp has aptly summarized the situation by saying that those parts of the Soviet plan which affected the Mennonites most deeply "were collectivization of agriculture, the renewed attack on religion, and the policies of education and indoctrination by the state." Conditions became unbearable. This plan not only intensified the already prevalent terrifying fear throughout the land, but also deprived my people of hope for survival, let alone peaceful living.

In April of that year, the Soviet authorities issued a document that destroyed the very basis of religious existence for the Mennonites in Siberia and elsewhere. It said, in effect, that all religious organizations are forbidden to exist and must cease to function anywhere in the land. By way of summary, the new law stated that the Mennonites and other religious groups were under no circumstances permitted to (1) provide mutual aid to the needy; (2) establish any type of cooperatives for economic purposes; (3) give material support to church members; (4) hold meetings for children, youths, women, and men; (5) have prayer meetings, Bible studies, sewing circles, and religious instruction; (6) organize hospitals and medical assistance; (7) arrange for excursions or any kind of entertainment for children; and (8) make available libraries or any kind of reading material. In short, our people were placed into a total spiritual and religious vacuum with the intent to suffocate their souls, starve their minds, and thereby crush their human will and spirit.

To bring about socioeconomic equality, the kulaks were so heavily taxed that they had to give their last cow and pig and chicken and every piece of furniture to the government. Worst of all, every bushel of grain was taken away as a "payment of debt" to the Soviet State. Some had to borrow money or merchandise to deliver what was demanded, lest they be sentenced and banished to Stalin's labor camp system, known as the *Gulag,* where inmates were interrogated, starved and often tortured and executed. These orders involved not only the Mennonites in Siberia, but all Mennonites, Germans and Russians who did not fully comply with the authorities.

Service writes that Stalin successfully redrew Lenin's original blueprint and finalized his own version of the New Economic Policy (NEP), which included the following parts: (1) Replacement of the private farmer called *kulak* by the communal *kolkhoz* (collective farm) as an inseparable part of the NEP. This meant dekulakization on the one hand and collectivization on the other. (2) Exchange of the agricultural peasantry for the industrial human machinery driven by mandates from Moscow. This meant a shift from a private agricultural enterprise to a communist industrial economy. (3) Prohibition of religious practice based on faith in the transcendent God. This meant that belief in the true and living God,

Creator of the heavens and the earth, was ridiculed as obsolete whereas loyalty to the Bolshevik Party was made mandatory and absolute.

How, then, was the spiritual nature of the soul to be nurtured? Radzinsky answers that question by pointing out that Stalin, a former seminarian, created a "biblical language" for the Communist Party. By using biblical metaphors, Stalin stated emphatically that he was "born not of woman, but of the Party" with the resolve "to become a god." And thus, writes Radzinsky, "A Bolshevik Trinity, a triune godhead, was emerging. Marx, Lenin, and himself (Stalin). Gods of the earth." Even though Marx and Lenin were no longer living, Stalin had absorbed their ideology and become the continuing embodiment and incarnation of their spirit. Thus he and he alone represented a self-appointed trilogy of gods on earth. In *The Wolf of the Kremlin*, the biography of Lazar Moiseyevich Kaganovich, "the Soviet Union's architect of fear," Stuart Kahan [Kaganovich] speaks of an updated Soviet Triumvirate, made up of Zinoviev, Kamenev and Stalin. Stalin knew that the Russian people needed this kind of substitute for the true Trinity. This perception of himself and his two most trusted comrades as a "trinitarian deity" led Stalin to demand from every citizen of the land unquestioned agreement with his economic philosophy, total submission to his demands, and unconditional obedience to his mandates.

After all, he thought of himself to be the god of the land, imminent and visible among his people. Every effort on the part of the Mennonites, individual, corporate or united, to resist the Party's process of dekulakization and collectivization ended in failure. More and more leaders were apprehended and executed, adults in ever larger numbers were arrested and sent to labor camps, and children were forcefully removed from their parents and put into atheistic schools and day care centers. "We must inflict a really annihilating blow on the kulaks," S. Kosior instructed the members of his commission, while Sergei Kirov wrote of "columns of tractors digging the kulaks' graves." Radzinsky goes on to say: "Train after train after train transported peasants in cattle wagons. There were floodlights on the roofs of the wagons and guards with dogs inside." My people interpreted these signs as impending disaster for everyone who would either voluntarily choose not to escape or be forced to stay. In either case, the consequences would be annihilation of the peasantry. History has proven them right.

In an earlier chapter I described the first Harvest Thanksgiving of 1909 in Slavgorod as a great celebration. Twenty years later in 1929 it should have been even greater. But it was not. The only crops people were able to harvest were hunger and terror, neither of which are conducive for celebration or thanksgiving. Thus it was a "Harvest of Sorrow" instead of thanksgiving. By this time my parents had already sold their *Wirtschaft*— their land and everything they had. But the family was still there and participated in the events of the season. As the people in the villages were ordered to bring in the grain, which under normal circumstances would have been the twentieth Thanksgiving, there was a feeling of increased ambivalence in the Siberian atmosphere. There had been uncertainties the year before, but this year the conditions were even worse. Were they hoping against hope to have enough food for another year? Many remembered 1909 when for the very first time they had put the plow into the ground to prepare the innocent soil for the seed; they thought of those crisp, clear spring days when they had walked with measured steps across those harrowed fields to spread the seed to sprout, take root in the ground, and grow to yield its fruit at harvest time. They also remembered their first official harvest festival in those difficult, yet hopeful pioneering years.

In those early days, one writer observes, they had read the words of Psalm 67. They had uttered prayers of thanksgiving. Now in 1929 they were reading and reciting the same prayer in the words of the same Psalm. But this time the mood was one of supplication rather than of praise, saying: "May God be gracious to us and bless us and make his face shine upon us. . . . Then the land will yield its harvest and God, our God, will bless us." The Lord, Creator of heaven and earth, had blessed and sustained them through the years. They wanted to be confident that He would do so now. Gratitude and hope, faith and charity had filled their hearts and souls then and, they hoped, that it might be so again.

But things were very different now in that fateful "Year of the Great Turn." Conditions of the times caused the people to wonder. They were struck by wariness. The virtues of gratitude and faith, hope and charity, while still present, were mixed with frustration and fear. Doubt, even despair, hung in the air. They knew what the imposition of Stalin's first Five-Year-Plan held in store for them. They had been given to understand in no uncertain terms what it meant. For all practical purposes they were not harvesting their own grain at all; they were harvesting a crop from the fields which they had sown on their own land; but it was no longer their land, it was not their harvest, it belonged to the Soviet State. Whatever the peasants did not surrender "voluntarily," government agents deprived them of everything, down to the unharvested wheat still out on the field.

This shift was hard for my people to understand. It took time and mental energy to process a totally new way of thinking. The realization that they had been dispossessed by the state and themselves become a possession of the Soviet system had a numbing effect on their ambition and motivation. They were no longer respected or treated with any kind of dignity. They had become a mere commodity that could be discarded at will. This made Mennonites, other German colonists, and even Russian peasants exceedingly restless and fearful. And thus, instead of celebrating the Harvest Thanksgiving together as a village or a local church, many found themselves journeying westward from Slavgorod to Moscow. This journey was brought about by a collective *Angst;* a terrifying fear had gripped young and old alike. Entire villages were being deserted and whole districts depopulated. The situation is reminiscent of Oliver Goldsmith's poignant lines in his lengthy poem, *The Deserted Village,* penned in 1770:

> Ill fares the land, to hastening ills a prey,
> Where wealth accumulates, and men decay!
> Princes and Lords may flourish, or may fade;
> A breath can make them, as a breath has made;
> But a bold peasantry, their country's pride,
> When once destroyed, can never be supplied.

Farming had been rapidly collectivized and entire villages communized. Not only the big or average farmer, but every farmer with any amount of land was by this time treated as a *kulak* and deprived of voting rights. However, the worst blow was the attack on religion. Because mothers had to work in the fields, children were placed into day care centers in custody of atheistic babysitters and homes of godless caregivers. Teachers in school ridiculed belief in God and made fun of all religious practices of home and church in front of the pupils. This was going too far for Christian parents. Many had endured dekulakization; they had accepted deprivation of all material possessions to the point of abject poverty; but they were not about to give up their Christian beliefs and values. They refused to betray their spiritual convictions and historical legacy. They were determined not to sacrifice their children to atheistic Bolshevism. Many saw escape as the only option.

The Soviet state increased its pressure. To make sure that the policies were being carried out, notes David Schartner in *Bibel und Pflug*, the government sent such tough communist comrades as Gekel (a former German prisoner of war), Bapkow (Babkow), and Schatochin to the colony to enforce the new rules. While these men in our villages were ethnic Germans, they had embraced the ideology of Communism. They operated by the rule of absolute totalitarianism: they tolerated no resistance, no opposition, not even the slightest indication of disagreement. They replaced at will the Mennonite teachers and preachers and other village and civic leaders with men of their own stripe. Gerhard Fast reports that Stalin also sent such powerful figures as Marshal Symyon Budenny (Budjennyj) and Comrade Kliment Voroshilov from the Central Committee in Moscow to control and oversee the overseers in Siberia. They became the taskmasters of our people in Slavgorod. Whoever dared to oppose or resist their demands and orders was psychologically humiliated, physically mistreated, or in other ways brutally penalized in the presence of friend and foe, family or neighbor. Those who were sentenced to appear before the firing squad were considered lucky by those who had to endure extended periods of torture.

In my judgment, no one has depicted the chronicle of inhumanity more graphically and scientifically than the Russian literary genius Aleksandr Solzhenitsyn in *The Gulag Archipelago*. His main focus in the First Part is on the prisoners behind barbed wire labor camps where he himself shared in the incredible suffering. The chapters on "Arrest" and "The Interrogation" alone describe in minute detail what my parents told us in simple and shorter versions of the experiences of our people in the late 1920s. *The Gulag Archipelago Two* is a brilliant analysis of the consequences following "The Year of the Great Turn."

That was also the year of the greatest turn in my family's life: the year of escape from Slavgorod to an unknown destiny. But what, I am inevitably moved to ask, became of the place we left behind? Only history can answer that question.

3

Escape from Slavgorod to Moscow
(August 1929)

Our Father who art in heaven, Hallowed be Thy name,
Thy kingdom come, Thy will be done
On earth as it is in heaven.
Give us this day our daily bread.
And forgive us our debts, as we also
have forgiven our debtors....
—Jesus Christ in *Matthew 6 (NASB)*

Conditions continued to deteriorate on every level of existence. People who had little to eat today knew that they would have less tomorrow. Many had nothing. My parents seem to have had a foreboding of coming events as early as 1924 when they wrote of "dark clouds on the horizon" coming toward their settlement. Two years later they wrote that the people were restless everywhere and talked about moving away. By late fall of 1928 they reached the nonnegotiable decision to escape. Thousands of others came to the same conclusion that the future was as unpromising as the present was uncertain. Taxation had come to the point of extortion. Religious oppression had become the order of the day. In fact, everyday life was made intolerable, every move was under watchful eyes—sometimes familiar eyes from within the village itself, sometimes eyes of strangers from unknown quarters. Their presence and purpose was clear to everyone: spy on people and report to authorities. The times were completely out of joint and there was no one to set things right.

Our people knew that the time to take to the road and run was now or never. It was as though an irresistible force was driving them to sell what had not yet been taken away, or to give away what they knew they could not keep. There were obstacles: First, there was the sick baby. Mother was particularly apprehensive about my condition. Moreover, there was the problem of letting go of house and farm. They began to realize how much they had become attached to their possessions. It was emotionally and materially difficult, simply to abandon what they had come to love. Furthermore, they were overcome by uncertainty and fear. Aware of our plans to escape, the authorities watched every step my father took and put roadblocks in the way wherever possible. At about this time a number of families had escaped from Siberia and made it to Moscow. They had high hopes of getting visas to emigrate to another land. Some succeeded, others did not. My father knew that chances for escape would be slim. But try he must to save the family. And try he did.

In April 1929 he was able to sell the farm, even if only for a fraction of its value; but the times were such that Father was grateful he could sell at all. Now came the challenge of leaving the farm behind for an unknown destination. Everyone foresaw problems ahead, particularly in Moscow, if and when they ever got there. Yet the people were determined to flee despite potential danger, possibly even death. They had little else to lose, except life. By faith they hoped that they had much to gain.

As I reflect on old letters and reports from the late 1920s as well as on recent books and articles about those times, I see two underlying irresistible forces moving our people to escape: fear and faith. One was driving, the other pulling. "Terror is the rule of people who themselves are terrorized," Engels is quoted to have said. In *The Wolf of the Kremlin*, Stuart Kahan reminds us that the early Soviet regime very skillfully fashioned those ten words of Engels into the most powerful tool to accomplish its end. No one knew that better than Stalin. He adopted these tactics of terror not only for his enemies, but also for his friends, as David King persuasively documents in his pictorial history of the Soviet Union, *The Commissar Vanishes*. Even the population at large had to be terrorized, says Radzinsky, to give the authorities total control and ultimate victory.

Terror and fear became Stalin's most successful weapon to carry out his plans of total conquest of the human spirit. My parents knew it intuitively, and trembled. *Wie haudi emma sitjhissi Schizh* (we were always terribly afraid), as my father put it. The terror of being imprisoned or banished to labor camp or shot without trial was present in every household. True *Angst* (fear mixed with distrust) weighed like lead on their minds and hearts. It was that kind of fear that kept people from talking to neighbors about plans to escape. They understood what Jesus meant when he spoke of a time in which people would betray and hate each other (Matt. 24:10). Some left their homes in the night when friend and foe were sleeping. That is a tragic commentary. It shows that faith and trust had been replaced by fear and suspicion. On the one hand, it seemed that fear had fractured the resiliency over faith. On the other hand, there remained a fragment of faith pulling our people into the unknown.

Between April and August 1929, our family tried numerous times to escape. First, we went from Alexandrovka to Slavgorod, hoping to get from there by train to Moscow. But that was not to be. Father rented temporary housing and the family shifted back and forth between the city and the colony. We stayed in Slavgorod for several months and then moved to

Pavlodar. But there, too, we were detected and detained by the police. Again, we went to Slavgorod—praying, believing, hoping. This went on over a period of several months. What was supposed to be the last attempt to get from Pavlodar to Moscow ended in another disappointment. Again we were turned back to Slavgorod.

In his notes Father does not specify how many times this happened. But he writes that on 11 August, our prayers were answered and our hopes realized. With the exception of my sister Susanna with husband Kornelius Funk and their daughter Antoinette, our entire family became part of a mass movement set in motion to leave for Moscow in August 1929. The journey began with a team of borrowed horses hitched to a carriage leaving the village for the train station. What a journey that must have been! It was the last time in Siberia that we as a family would ride in that familiar fashion: a wagon drawn by a team of horses driven by my father. Father described it as "the most difficult trip" he had ever taken—a trip into the unknown.

Yet there was one known factor in all of this: Father knew that the time had come to let go and say farewell to everything he had labored and lived for all those years in Siberia. My three sisters and two brothers were sitting on bags and trunks in the back of the wagon. Mother sat on the driver's seat next to Father. I was sitting on Mother's lap covered with a large shawl haphazardly, but deliberately, thrown around us. There was much more than Mother and child hidden under that cover. There were emotions of deep sadness, of grief and pain endured in profound silence.

Our family was only one of many. Even without either passport or visa, people embarked by faith on the long and ominously hazardous journey. Some drove one hundred kilometers, others as many as three hundred, to find a train station where they could purchase tickets for the capital. The government had given strict orders not to sell train fares to any Germans, be they Lutheran, Catholic or Mennonite. Thus they had to go to regions where ticket agents did not recognize them as fugitives. I cannot recall if Father ever said exactly from which city or town in Siberia we eventually left for Moscow.

My parents sometimes spoke about that trip. Groups could generally not stay together in one train car. Families were frequently forced to travel in different trains. For some, the trip took six days, for others even longer. The meals on the way from Slavgorod to Moscow were simple. There was little variety and no surplus. Our people had to plan ahead and prepare food for the journey. Somehow they had managed to bake *Tweeback,* plenty of them. That is what my mother, and many other mothers, had done. How they did it, I do not know. Our family had already been uprooted since we sold the farm in April. Now it was August. We had not had our own place to live in for about four months, nor could we harvest our own grain for flour or fruit from the garden.

Nonetheless, here we were on the train to Moscow, supplied with several burlap sacks filled with *jireeschte Tweeback*. These double-layered toasted rolls can be stored for months without a trace of spoilage. They were a typical staple when people traveled or worked on the field away from home. That is what kept us alive on the escape route from Slavgorod to Moscow. Some families had managed to take smoked sausages and ham with them. But like the Israelites of old who left "their fleshpots and garlic" in Egypt, most of our people had left theirs with the Bolsheviks in Slavgorod or elsewhere.

Whenever the train stopped, the men stepped out with empty containers, fetched boiling water from the steam engine of the train, and brought it back to the cars in which their families were. The women then made hot tea. As soon as things were ready, entire families rose to their feet and stood with hands folded and heads bowed, while one of the fathers prayed in German (not Low German): *Unser Vater in dem Himmel! Unser täglich Brot gib uns heute* . . . . ("Our Father in heaven, . . . Give us this day our daily bread. . ."). Sometimes he prayed the Lord's prayer, sometimes a prayer in his own words. At other times the group or family sang a table song. After saying grace, they all sat down, drank tea and ate *jireeschte Tweeback,* or whatever they had with them for the journey.

Our escape was literally at the eleventh hour. While the goal was Canada, no one knew what our destination actually might be. No one had the slightest idea that the trek from the flat and fertile fields of the Kulunda Steppe in Siberia would eventually lead us to the mountainous and inhospitable jungles of subtropical Brazil. Of course, not everyone chose to or had to go that route. But my family did.

There is something admirably mysterious about human nature. The people of Israel soon seem to have forgotten about their hardships in Egypt, but they remembered the "fleshpots." My parents spoke much more often about *dee goodi oolli Tiet* (the good old times) than about the hardships in Siberia. And they did so with deep emotions mixed with pain and passion. I remember getting angry as a child when they told us of the bad things. I even cried out of pity for my parents that they had lost so much. I also wept for all the relatives who had stayed behind. But then my father in his wisdom would tell a story from the good times, especially about the long winters when the children played in the snow. My older siblings talked about the sleds Father had made for them, and about the fun they had had, especially when their friends and cousins had joined them in a competition of sliding down the hard-frozen, snow-covered manure pile. I found that comforting and reassuring.

As I think back, I marvel at the positive attitude my parents maintained, at least for the most part, when they spoke of life in Siberia. I don't recall that either Mother or Father ever expressed anger or complaints. And yet there were times of profound sadness, especially when an occasional letter from Russia reached us in Brazil. The change from their way of life in the open Kulunda Steppe to that in the closed jungle must have been much more traumatic than I could understand at the time.

Only in retrospect have I begun to understand the kinds of mixed emotions that attach themselves to farewells and goodbyes. I have not been forcefully deprived of earthly possessions or suffered religious oppression, as my parents had. Yet I, too, have moved numerous times between continents and countries. Each time I had to say farewell to family, relatives and friends; that in itself was hurtful enough. Each time I experienced a certain loss of identity, a sense of insecurity, a painful feeling of loneliness. Such feelings are best described by the German word *Heimweh*. The English term "homesickness" is not a fitting equivalent, but may be the best we have. In addition, there is the inevitable culture shock that touches every fiber of nerve and emotion. And with it comes a lingering longing to return from whence one has come without being able to explain why.

But there is also a redemptive factor in all of this: namely the hidden sense that things can never be the same as they once were. And thus one comes to terms with reality, finds a measure of emotional equilibrium, and begins to adjust to new conditions and circumstances. When I ruminate about the times I experienced cultural transitions, I think of my parents and siblings. How must they have felt when we came from Siberia to Brazil? I realize that my own experience is inadequate as a comparison, but I am using it for the purpose of trying to understand what their feelings must have been like. Quite often, I must concede, I have an unrealistic wish to discuss these questions with parents and siblings. But they are no more. Their journey as earthlings, a journey far more eventful than either the one from Slavgorod to Moscow or the trip from Moscow to Brazil, is over. They have made the final transition; for me it is still to come.

4

Under Siege in Moscow
(Aug-Nov 1929)

In my distress I called to the LORD;
I cried to my God for help.
From his temple he heard my voice;
my cry came before him into his ears.
– King David in *Psalm 18*

In the *Deutsche Geschichte im Osten Europas*, Volume 10: *Rußland*, it is reported that from the beginning of September 1929, through subsequent months of that year, 100 to150 refugee families arrived in the suburbs of Moscow every day. Many of them, like my family, were Mennonites from Siberia. It was truly a mass movement. Fearing a colossal loss of prestige in the foreign press and worldwide public opinion, Party leaders became exceedingly nervous and irritated with the situation. Their primary concern was to stop the one-way flow of German peasants to the Soviet capital. But how? They found a way.

Since the Soviet authorities were unprepared to deal humanely with the masses to save face in the international media, they initially tried to ignore reality. When that failed to bring desired results, they resorted to other measures. As more and more refugees arrived at the gates of Moscow, they became a people under Soviet siege without being fully aware of it. Secret service agents were everywhere. Their order was not to protect the refugees, but to prevent their escape. It soon became apparent to the atheistic authorities that they had to do with a people who trusted God for deliverance. The record has it that Stalin ridiculed such simple faith, saying, "Your God will first have to perform a miracle before you will be permitted to leave Russia." To make sure that he, and no one else, would determine their fate, Stalin put his most trusted comrade, Mikhail Ivanovich Kalinin, assisted by like-minded henchmen, in charge. Not only that, he also gave strict orders that "this garbage, this German pest," as he called the refugees, be cleaned up immediately. That meant elimination.

As a former peasant, Kalinin had been elevated by Stalin to the powerful position of Chairman of the Central Executive Committee. Along with Kliment E. Voroshilov and Vyacheslav Molotov, Kalinin played a major role within the troika of Stalin's "obedient and loyal servants," as Radzinsky calls them. To ensure that all the bases were covered to make escape impossible, the Kalinin triumvirate enlisted Grigorii (Grigory) Zinoviev. Lenin himself had hand-picked Zinoviev as one of his closest lieutenants and delegated him to attend the October 1922 session of the All-Russian Central Executive Committee in Moscow. With that background, Zinoviev knew the history as well as the goal of the Bolsheviks, and also had achieved credibility within the present Central Committee. Even Stalin was pleased with the arrangement, at least for the moment. He was fully satisfied that the fate of the refugees was as secure with Zinoviev as in his own hands.

Just as Pharaoh of old did not want to let the people of Israel go, so Stalin, this man of steel, with the full support of his comrades and cohorts, had no intention of ever letting our people out of Russia. They had too much to tell the world. There were too many experiences and stories foreign reporters were eager to hear. The stakes were simply too high for the Soviets to ignore the situation. Thus they took every measure to prevent our escape, except one: they failed to count on God's intervention. No human organization, regardless of prestige and power, can deter God from performing a miracle. The thoughts and deeds of the Lord Most High are infinitely higher than the intentions and determinations of any human being, including those of Stalin and Kalinin and their loyal comrades in high office. In this case, God overruled all human measures and performed a miracle of exodus for thousands of our people. Sadly, though, about twice as many remained in Soviet hands and were crushed.

I should explain that very few, if any, of the refugees went to the central station in Moscow. They disembarked at smaller stations in villages such as Djangarovka, Perlovka, Kljasma, and Puschkino some twenty or thirty kilometers outside the capital. Thus the whole drama did not take place directly on the stage in Moscow, but at the proverbial "Gates of Moscow."

One of the refugees' first tasks was to find a place to live and food to eat. Clad in leftover army coats from World War I or in coats made from sheepskin, and with the high Russian fur hats on their heads, the men rushed into the village to find lodging for their families. The women wore large warm kerchiefs wrapped around their heads and shoulders and the usual black Sunday aprons tied around their waists. Many carried babies in their arms. The women and children stayed with their belongings at the station, waiting in hope that their husbands and fathers would soon return with the good news that they had found a place to live. The locals immediately identified them as strangers and soon learned of their plight. Some offered to help in whatever way they could. Others saw their chance to make a few extra rubles by charging exorbitant rent for inadequate housing.

The only shelters available in the villages were either *datschas* and summer cottages of the rich vacated for winter or temporary barracks built for the Soviet army. These places had no heating and next to no furniture. Most people slept on the floor. In order to save on rent some families shared a single room that served as bedroom, living room, storage room, and kitchen.

As soon as our family had taken possession of our rented dwelling, we became aware that we were not alone; but neither were we in good company. The place was infested with lice, fleas, and bedbugs. They had been there before us, hiding in every crack and crevice. No sooner had we spread our beds than they scurried in fierce competition for the blood of their invaders. While such pesky insects were not uncommon in Russia, as my brother-in-law Bernhard Esau recalled with minute detail, our family had never experienced anything like this before. Never had they seen such a mix of bloodsuckers in one place. However, we, like most others, were not in the position to rent an apartment or house of better quality.

There was reason for mounting anxiety. No one knew how long we might have to stay until we would get our visas—if we would get them at all. Where should or could we go? No country was willing to take us in. Many of the refugees, including my family, stayed nearly three months on the outskirts of Moscow. Some stayed even longer. My older siblings were able to find work and earn money for food. My brother Nikolai recalls how he and two of my sisters went to the surrounding woods and pastures to collect firewood and dry steer manure commonly used in stoves for cooking and heating. Father was preoccupied with securing exit visas and spent much time in the capital.

The situation grew more critical with each passing day. The icy winter was upon us. Food supplies diminished. The visas were not forthcoming. Threats of being sent to Siberian concentration camps or to prisons or back to where we had come from hung over us day and night like a drawn sword about to pierce its target. The likelihood that that could happen any time was real; fear made everyone tremble. There was much praying and sighing in the camps.

It became evident from the very beginning that the refugees would have to organize themselves into groups within their respective camps. Leadership and direction beyond the immediate family circle was as crucial as food and shelter. They were painfully aware of this need, lest they lose all sense of direction. They also knew that the best leaders are not necessarily the ones chosen or elected; they are often the ones who emerge because they are needed for the moment and trusted for the task. So it was within our group in Moscow.

One day the men gathered in a small forest near the capital, besought God for guidance, and formed a rather loose organization and a strategy on how to approach the authorities as a united front with petitions, letters, and hundreds of signatures. In the course of the discussion, several men were asked to take leadership. Among them was Heinrich Martins, small of stature, but big for the occasion. He was outgoing, assertive, and fearless. Gifted with diplomatic skills and a relentless sense of perseverance, he demonstrated courage and valor in a time when these qualities were most needed, yet hard to find. Fluent in Russian, German, Low German and a conversational English, Martins became the leader of a group of about 327 persons, who later journeyed from Moscow to Kiel and eventually to Mölln. Initially, our family was part of this first group, but did not remain in it.

As my father and other heads of families negotiated with the authorities to obtain needed documents for leaving the country, they went to every travel agent and tried their luck at every door in the Kremlin. They approached every officer they met. They pleaded for help to get out of Soviet Russia. It is reported that they even staged a demonstration. The idea to do so came from a high-ranking officer of the Communist Party. His name could not be disclosed. During the time in Moscow, Heinrich Martins had gained the friendship of the Tolstoyans (followers of Tolstoy) who were particularly sympathetic toward the Mennonites and even held to some of the teachings of Jesus found in the Sermon on the Mount. One of the Tolstoyans introduced Martins to an influential Party member. "For about a month," writes Martins, "I visited this man every night under the pretense of teaching him English." In the course of time this man told Martins what Stalin and his immediate comrades were planning to do with the refugees. "The situation is grave," the officer confided. He then suggested that the people stage a mass demonstration. They followed his advice.

Mothers with children and women of all ages organized in groups and marched to the Office of Internal Affairs in the Kremlin, hoping to get a hearing. Some even dared to approach Soviet leaders like Mikhail Kalinin and Grigorii Zinoviev, Stalin's hand-picked comrades who held the fate of the refugees in their hands. But neither one gave them a single ounce of hope to get permission to leave. The conversation between the Mennonite women and Soviet immigration officials went something like this:

"Please, give us the needed visas so that we can leave."

"Go back from where you have come. Go home."

"We have no home. We have no place to go. Everything has been taken away from us."

The officials responded in honeyed words of promise: "Listen to us: we will give everything back to you. We will meet all your needs. Just go back."

Similar scenes were staged day after day. Running out of patience, one of the officials demanded to know who their leader was. Obviously, he was of the opinion that the whole drama would come to an end if only they could identify, apprehend and eliminate the group leader. But to the credit of these refugee women, no one was coward enough to betray their leader.

After repeated demands and mounting pressure by the authorities, one brave mother volunteered: "Do you really want to know who our real leader is? Should I give you his name?" Every soul was silent, except some restless children.

The officials were delighted. "Please, let us hear it," they urged. A hush of terror filled the atmosphere in the Kremlin halls. No one knew what to expect. Tension tightened to the breaking point. Every refugee feared the worst consequences. Then the elderly mother stepped forward and calmly said to the Soviet atheists: "It is our loving God. He is our leader."

It goes without saying that the officials were stunned and the women with their children relieved. It was like a victory in a melodramatic performance, even if by untrained players. The mere thought of trying to visualize Mennonite women from peasant villages in Siberia and elsewhere staging a demonstration inside the waiting room of Kalinin's office within the Kremlin walls of Moscow would have been enough to move spectators to tears and to laughter at the same time. There they stood. They were our mothers holding us, their children, securely in their arms. Some were silent. Others sighed in desperation. Many prayed in faith with hope. All of them pleaded either by their presence or with spoken words. They pleaded without ceasing for their exit visas. It was a scene pathetic enough to move the stones of the Kremlin into action.

But it would be a betrayal of faith to interpret this particular scene of that drama in Moscow as merely a human demonstration. It was much more than that. God Himself was the director of that stage, using comedy in seriousness to demonstrate His power by confirming the simple faith of the actresses in the presence of atheistic authorities. That left no one in doubt that, indeed, God was in charge of the situation. The mother I quoted earlier was right when she said: "Our loving God is our leader." He could be neither apprehended nor eliminated by the Soviets.

As I analyze the historical intricacies and reflect on all that transpired in Moscow in 1929, I can only marvel at God's design for our people, including my family. It was nothing short of divine leading that we as refugees gained compassion from such influential persons as the Friends of Tolstoy. Among them was Yekaterina Pavlovna Peschkova-Vinaver, first wife of Maxim Gorkii. Gorkii himself had become a trusted supporter of the Revolution and had won the confidence of Stalin. In fact, Radzinsky credits him for coining Stalin's famous motto of operation: "If the enemy refuses to surrender he must be destroyed." History has demonstrated a thousand times that Stalin's philosophy of operation was guided by that principle.

Why, then, I am compelled to ask, did Stalin and his comrades not destroy all the refugees? Were they not the enemies of the state who would not surrender to the demands of the Party? Why, then, did the authorities allow about one third of them to escape to safety? Why was my family—and why was I—among those fortunate ones who did eventually get out of the Soviet Union? There is only one answer—the one given by that valiant Mennonite mother in Kalinin's waiting room: "It is our loving God. He is our leader." I can only see it as divine providence.

But that acknowledgment does not answer every question in connection with the drama at the gates of Moscow. Was God not also the leader of those who were later apprehended and sent back, only to perish along the dreadful journey from Moscow to Siberia, or in the death camps, or the Gulag, or within such dreaded prison walls as those of Butyrki and Lubyanka in Moscow? I have no answer to those questions, except to say that human beings have the capacity to nurture simultaneously two spirits within themselves: one divine, the other demonic. Goethe puts it succinctly in *Faust I:*

> Two souls, alas, are housed within my breast,
> And each will wrestle for the mastery there.
> The one does cling with passion, crude for lust
> And hugs the world for power in its rage.
> The other longs for pastures fair with trust
> And leaves the murky world for loftier heritage.

I want to believe that there may have been a spark of the divine image and a trace of human compassion, even within such hardened Party members as Maxim Gorkii and Mikhail Kalinin. From my own interpretation of things, it does appear that Gorkii was in the position to speak a decisive word in upper political circles and that he housed a compassionate soul within his breast. When, for example, his wife Yekaterina, who headed the Political Red Cross at the time, approached the authorities on behalf of the refugees, she actually was able to persuade them to postpone the decision to arrest our group leaders in the fall of 1929. As a result, they were permitted to continue negotiations for exit visas. My father was one of the negotiators.

Day after day, for weeks on end, they explored every avenue to acquire visas for Canada. There were, in fact, occasional indications that the Canadian authorities in Ottawa might soften and grant the needed visas. Hopes were particularly high whenever larger numbers were allowed to appear at the Canadian Embassy for medical tests and interviews. In the screening process, however, those hopes soon dissipated. The Canadian authorities turned out to be highly selective. Those with the virus-carrying eye disease known as trachoma, or with the slightest physical disability were disqualified. My father, for instance, had a "lazy eye" (presumably caused by amblyopia in early childhood) which was functionally blind. In his other eye, however, Father had very good vision to the end of his life. Then there was my brother Nikolai. As a toddler he had been struck by a colt which left him with a broken arm. While the bone had healed, the elbow had remained slightly tilted. Neither Father's vision nor my brother's arm was ever a noticeable handicap in their work, but it did disqualify our family from securing visas to Canada. We were not the only disappointed ones. Families in which there were several young girls and the father was the only male were disqualified on grounds of an "insufficient work force."

Prior to the change of parties in Ottawa from the Liberals to the Conservatives, the Canadian Embassy in Moscow had issued a total of 1,036 visas (not counting the seventy families mentioned earlier) in a rather short period of time. But as history has demonstrated a thousand times over, politics operates by power, not compassion. The change of parties in Ottawa evidently also effected a change of heart within the Embassy in Moscow toward the Mennonite refugees on the outskirts of that city. The books were closed. The gates were locked. No more visas were being issued. That meant that my family and many others would not be admitted to "the promised land." A few more families with either children or parents already residing in Canada secured visas while in Germany so that families could be reunited; but those were exceptions.

The consequences of parliamentary rulings in Ottawa were far-reaching. Thousands of refugees whose application for visas were turned down were deeply disappointed. Infinitely more serious was the fact that the immigration policies sealed the destiny of those still in Moscow. Unless some other country would soon offer to receive them, they were in imminent danger of being disposed of as a perishable commodity along the railroad tracks or dumped in the concentration camps of the Siberian mines and forests. Such well-known Canadian Mennonite diplomats as David Töws, B. B. Janz, and C. F. Klassen interceded for their brothers and sisters in Moscow and pleaded with the authorities in Ottawa; but their pleas fell on deaf ears at both ends. They found little more compassion in the hard heads in Ottawa than in the "man of steel" in Moscow.

Meanwhile, Professor Benjamin Unruh of Karlsruhe, himself a Mennonite from Russia, and Professor Otto Auhagen, a diplomat of the German Embassy in Moscow, continued working around the clock on behalf of the refugees. Dr. Auhagen visited the refugee camps and promised to do everything to turn the attention of the world to their tragic situation.

Before too long the case became a hot topic in the global press. The *New York Times* chided in bold headlines: "Canada Declines Admission to Mennonites. Germany Is Undecided, and the Soviet Union Sends them Back to Siberia." People in the Moscow refugee shelters prayed and pleaded, wept and waited. They seemed to get no answer. There was much fear; there was little hope for change; there was still faith in God.

Martins now instructed the men to gather the signatures of all the people in the camps, appealing for permission to leave the Soviet Union. Their efforts paid off. In two days they had six times the number of signatures needed to get a hearing. This first group had created a kind of model for others to follow. Leaders throughout the camps began to form groups to expedite the documentation process. Initially, each group consisted of one hundred families. Within a short time they had formed many different groups with a total of more than ten thousand persons. The result was that an envoy brought this message: "Permission to emigrate granted." At least some were eventually permitted to leave. Once again, God overruled the Soviet policy of destruction.

For whatever reason, my father seems to have changed his intended departure from the first to the second group. That meant that we would not take the train to Leningrad with the "Group of Kiel" under the direction of Heinrich Martins, the first group to get out of Moscow to Germany, but wait for the "Swinemünde Transport," as the second group became known.

5

From Siege in Moscow to Safety in Mölln
(November-December 1929)

> *The LORD is my rock,*
> *my fortress and my deliverer;*
> *my God is my rock, in whom I take refuge.*
> *He is my shield and the horn of my salvation,*
> *[He is] my stronghold.*
> —King David in *Psalm 18*

The atmosphere at the gates of Moscow remained tense. The outlook improved only for those permitted to leave. Many groups, some larger, others smaller, eventually got from Moscow to Mölln. I will limit my brief observations to two groups: the Group of Kiel and the Swinemünde Transport. The first was routed over Leningrad and Kiel (near Hamburg, Germany), the second over Leningrad and Swinemünde (near Stettin, Poland, formerly East Prussia). Before long, however, all the groups that got out of Moscow came to the refugee camp in Mölln.

The Group of Kiel was successfully forging its way ahead of all other groups. Some historians have been rather critical of this group, arguing that Mr. Martins acted too independently, giving insufficient consideration to the welfare of the rest. It is also said that this group of 327 persons circumvented the regular channels of negotiation in order to get certain advantages ahead of other groups. That may or may not be so. I am in no position either to pass judgment or to clarify possible misunderstandings. Negative interpretation of the actions of the Group of Kiel may have been the reason why my father decided to wait for a second opportunity to leave Moscow for Leningrad, even if that increased the risk of staying behind.

It was late at night on 28 October when the heads of households of the Group of Kiel received orders to get ready by early morning. "There was chaos and excitement in the camps," Father recalled. "But we were also terribly afraid of what might happen to us and our families. Many fathers and adult sons had already been apprehended by the police and no one knew where they had stayed," Father explained.

The next morning a special train, guarded by armed police and secret agents, waited on the tracks. The huge steam engine made a groaning noise, emitting its huffs and puffs as though it was signaling urgency to get moving, lest the engineers would receive orders from Party officials to call off the trip. With crying babies clutched in their arms, the mothers were ushered in first. Older children followed, holding their younger siblings tightly by the hands. Men and women assisted the aged or otherwise handicapped persons to make sure they would not stay behind. The rest carried boxes and bundles with family belongings, stumbling helter-skelter after them onto the train. As the whistle ripped through the cold air, the guards and agents scattered quickly; inconspicuously as they had been trained to do, they took their place among the refugees. All doors were locked and the first group was on its way to safety, so they hoped. They were sure of what they were leaving behind, but not so sure of what might lie ahead.

"October 29 will remain unforgettable in the mind and memory of many," wrote Heinrich Martins in his "Erinnerungen an Moskau 1929," in the book *Vor den Toren Moskaus*. "For it was on that day when early in the morning a train was standing ready for the first group of the thousands of refugees gathered near Moscow to board the train for Leningrad." From Leningrad they hoped to get to Germany and from there to Canada. The group did reach Germany, however less than 20 percent had Canadian visas.

My father stood thoughtfully and watched, wondering when our turn would come. Did he regret that he had voluntarily chosen to let the first opportunity for escape go by, not knowing if and when a second chance would present itself? But I am certain that Father knew the risk he was taking, and that the consequences would affect his entire family.

Under normal circumstances the journey of 650 kilometers from Moscow to Leningrad (St. Petersburg) would have taken ten or eleven hours; but for the Group of Kiel it took three or four days with many stops and interruptions along the way. Nobody knew why. "Many, many prayers ascended to our Heavenly Father," recalled the late Peter Friesen, an old friend of mine whom I visited in Curitiba for the last time in 1995. The possibility of being shipped to a labor camp in Siberia was still very real. "After all," Friesen went on to explain, "the human cargo was labeled by the Communist authorities as *kulaks*. For all practical purposes that word meant that we were enemies of the country, betraying Stalin's new order and trying to run away from it." And, as I mentioned earlier, Stalin's motto was that, if the enemy refuses to surrender, he must be destroyed. This was no empty slogan.

The Group of Kiel was fortunate. Its stay in Leningrad was only one night. The only regrets some of the more adventuresome young men may have had, as Peter Friesen remembered, was the fact that they had no time for sightseeing. Even sixty-five years later Friesen felt deprived of a great opportunity and lamented on behalf of the Group of Kiel, saying:

> We wanted to see at least the Czar's residence, but they would not let us. There we were in Rome and could not see the pope, as the proverb goes. Already the next day we were ordered to board the new and clean Russian steamer built by a British engineer. It was a freighter with facilities to accommodate a fairly large number of passengers. The ship was christened *Felix Dzerzhinsky*, in honor of a high-ranking Party member by that name. This was the ship's virgin voyage, on its way to England. The captain and personnel were friendly and kind, the food was plentiful and tasty, and the scenery past Finland, Sweden, and Denmark simply spectacular. The four-day journey from Leningrad to Kiel was like an oasis in the midst of an emotional desert. There were no more threats. The danger of being sent to Siberia had become history. The heavy atmosphere of fear and tension gradually gave way to a more relaxed and hopeful mood.

Yet underneath the surface of gratitude and jubilation there lingered the gnawing question of the Kiel Group's action: had its leader been too hasty? Had he run ahead of God's timing? Assuming the group had acted rather independently and bypassed the diplomatic channels pursued by Unruh and Auhagen, the records contain at least a partial justification for its action. Unruh concedes that the alleged irregularity may have been a blessing in disguise. It may even have been providential. What he means is that the Group of Kiel may, in fact, have helped the German government in Berlin to look at the plight of the refugees from an entirely different perspective than might otherwise have been the case.

I believe Unruh is right. For it was only after the unexpected arrival of this group at the harbor of Kiel that the local authorities, the government in Berlin, and the German people as a whole began to prepare for the arrival of thousands more. Even more important is the fact that German newspapers began to print headlines in bold letters, saying: **The Fate of One German Is the Business of Every German.** These words appeared under the auspices of the German Red Cross, various mission agencies, and a host of other goodwill and welfare organizations throughout the land. Another article carried as its heading the name of a newly-formed organization called "Brüder in Not!" (Brothers in Need!). The article reads in part:

> A catastrophe has come over the Germans in foreign [Soviet] lands. By hunger, disparaging economic and political conditions of the times thou-

sands of German farmers [including Mennonites] in Siberia have been driven from house and land. A migration of the starving Germans has begun in Russia. Robbed of every chance for a continuing existence, ten thousand German peasants have gathered in the vicinity of Moscow in order to escape via Germany to a foreign country. Hundreds of them, poor and destitute, have already arrived in Germany.

The last sentence is a direct reference to the Group of Kiel consisting of 327 (other sources say 320 or 329) persons who landed in the harbor of Kiel on 3 November 1929.

As the Group of Kiel was leaving the station at Perlovka, a second group of 291 persons, referred to as the "Swinemünde Transport," became anxious to take the next train to Leningrad. Father had registered our family with this second group. He recalled:

For the next minutes that seemed like hours, our people were standing there, staring with a sense of misgiving and uncertainty after the train until its rumblings and clattering on the endless tracks and the echo of its ominous whistle disappeared into the distance. The police who were standing by ordered our people back to their quarters. "Get ready for tomorrow," the officers commanded, assuring us that the next day at 12 o'clock midnight another train would be ready for us.

My father and other heads of families cleared their accounts with the landlords. People packed their meager possessions and returned to the station to wait for the appointed time. But there was no train. Since they could not return to their quarters, and since space inside the small station was limited and overcrowded, only a few mothers with small children were allowed to stay inside. The rest scrambled for a place under the open sky on the cold and windy platform along the tracks. After a wait of over forty hours, a train finally pulled up. It was 31 October, 7 o'clock in the evening. Everyone was eager and ready to get on board. This time even the guards and police were unusually kind and helped them with the baggage.

As the train moved away from Perlovka, people noticed that it was going in the direction toward Moscow. It stopped on a side track near the city. No one knew why. There was no one to ask. All doors were locked. No one was allowed to go anywhere. Evidently, our siege in Moscow had not yet ended. People were cold, hungry, and apprehensive.

Four days later (4 November), two men came on board. They inquired what we were doing and ordered everyone to leave the train within three hours. Then they left. Of course, we had no place to go and were still there when the officers returned. Now they demanded rent for the use of the train. They kept on harassing us in many other ways until a third man came and told us that the train would leave momentarily for Leningrad. And so it did. What a relief. Walter Quiring calls it *luck,* Abram Löwen speaks of it as a *miracle*. My father refers to the episode as "the leading of God that we were able to get from Moscow to Leningrad. It was an answer to prayer."

On 6 November we arrived in Leningrad. Like the Group of Kiel before us, we were transferred to buses and taken to the so-called *Sovtorgflott*. The third floor of the headquarters for the Soviet fleet of overseas shipping and trade served as a kind of guesthouse for foreign travelers.

The experiences in Leningrad were far from a pleasure fair and our stay there by no means a retreat. Yet Father loved to talk about this phase of our journey with a sense of pleasure. We children, especially the younger ones, loved to listen to that story. It was always a time of laughter at our house. Even if the event as a whole was rather serious and dangerous, there were segments of the story that Father told in a humorous fashion.

> After the authorities had taken away every rubel we still had, we were given something to eat. It was actually a very appetizing meal. Right after eating we were ordered to clean up. To begin with, we were ushered into shower rooms to take a shower. That was a blessing, especially after months of refugee life in Moscow under rather primitive conditions. But the special disinfectant soap they gave us had a foul odor that lingered on our bodies for days. It was supposed to kill all insects we might carry with us. Then we had to slip temporarily into a kind of pyjama or nightgown provided by the hosts while our own clothes were being baked for several hours in a preheated oven. The reason was to make sure that we would be free from fleas and lice and bedbugs which we had picked up in Moscow. That was all fine and good. The problem was, that the quarters we stayed in were infested with the same pesky little creatures we were trying to get rid of. The only difference was that the ones we had brought with us had been raised in Moscow, whereas the ones we would take with us had been nursed in Leningrad. If there were those among us who might have been clean upon arrival, they had a lean chance that they would be free of lice when leaving this place.

The gowns we received were apparently all the same size for adults and children. Father described in detail how some adults could cover themselves only partially while the children were quick to discover that they could step on their own sleeves. That in itself created outbursts of laughter in an otherwise somber mood. It is amusing that even in the midst of the seriousness inherent in refugee life, God allows unscheduled comical scenes to emerge that lighten and brighten the heavy atmosphere.

Things went well for a week. We had three meals a day in a dining hall and straw to sleep on in a dormitory. But Leningrad was not our goal. We wanted to move on to Germany. Yet no one could or would give us information if and when that might happen. Besides, we were locked in. No one was allowed to go out and no one was able to come in.

On 13 November there was a sudden change in the daily routine. We were not called to the dining hall for breakfast, and did not get anything to eat all day. Children were hungry and began to cry. When our elders asked for food, they were told that the kitchen personnel had used up the money they had taken from us and we would be on our own, unless we could come up with additional funds for food. When our leaders explained that the authorities had taken every rubel, even the last *kopeke,* from us, they were told to write their relatives and friends to send them more. They knew, of course, that their suggestion was foolish, impossible to realize. There was absolutely no understanding and no compassion.

As the situation became desperate, five of our men were granted special permission to leave the premises to find a solution. They sold their watches and rings and whatever jewelry they had and traded in their musical instruments, items of clothing and bedding for bread and other things to eat. By the time our people were finally allowed to leave, some of them did not have even the most basic apparel needed to continue their trip. Others were quick to share what they were able to spare.

Meanwhile, three or four of the men were called to the office downstairs. When they returned they had alarming news to tell: First, on 17 November the Soviet government had begun a massive repatriation exercise, shipping refugees from Moscow to Siberia. Second, Ottawa had cabled a final and conclusive message that no further visas for immigration would be granted. Third, Germany was not prepared to take in any more refugees—not even on a temporary basis. Fourth, since there was no country willing to receive us, and since we could no longer stay in Leningrad, there was only one alternative: "We [the Soviet government] are forced to send you back to where you have come from. The process will begin tomorrow." Those were no empty threats. A Soviet declaration of such grave nature shot fear and trembling through each member of the Swinemünde Transport. "We were overcome by a sense of terror that no words can describe," writes Löwen.

Our leaders decided to draft one more appeal to the German government. Several of the men personally took it to the German Consulate General in Leningrad. He, in turn, wired Berlin immediately and got the reply: "Let them come." It was clear to the refugees that the Lord had once again answered their cry for help.

On 27 November, after three full weeks of waiting and suffering, both physically and emotionally, we were allowed to board the Russian steamer,

Alexey Rykov. It proved to be no smooth sailing, however. Two hours after leaving the Leningrad harbor, the ship ran aground. Tugboat after tugboat pushed and pulled, but to no avail: the ship stayed stubbornly stuck in the sand and would not move. It took several days of hard work before the steamer was again seaworthy and afloat.

Finally, on 2 December our ship entered the Port of Swinemünde at the mouth of the River Swina, not too distant from the city of Stettin (Szczecin) in Northeast Germany (actually, northwest Poland at the time). The area that was formerly known as Pomerania was acquired by Prussia in 1772. Thus when our forebears emigrated to Russia in the late 1780s and after, they were for all practical purposes leaving Prussia with its German people. After World War I, however, large portions of West Prussia were given back to Poland, though the inhabitants were still German. Thus when in 1929 we entered the harbor of Swinemünde of Northwest Poland, we were back in the general region from where our ancestors had emigrated to Russia some 140 years earlier. It was as though we had been on a long journey and were now back home. However, the "homecoming" was no more than a short dream. Neither Swinemünde nor any other place in Germany would ever again become our home. Our destination was still unknown. So was that of thousands of other Mennonites still in Moscow: their fate was still in the iron grip of Kalinin and his heavy-fisted comrades.

6

Developments in Germany
(1929-1930)

> LORD,
> *you have assigned me my portion and my cup;*
> *you have made my lot secure.*
> *The boundary lines have fallen for me in pleasant places;*
> *surely I have a delightful inheritance.*
> –King David in *Psalm 16*

The city of Kiel, where the first group had landed, provided temporary accommodations only for that one group. German soldiers helped them unload their belongings and settle for the night in a large empty harbor warehouse with neither beds nor partitions. They brought loads of hay and straw to sleep on, hundreds of folding chairs to sit on, and enough tables to eat at. Unlike the Swinemünde Transport who were forced to sell bedding and other articles in exchange for food in Leningrad, most people in the Group of Kiel had been fortunate enough to keep their pillows, sheets, and blankets that added comfort to sleeping on straw.

And there they were: a huge family in one room large enough to host 327 persons, old and young, big and small, male and female, friend and foe. Every day for three weeks the government provided soup and bread and butter for the strangers from the Soviet Union. Even if that was not a menu with great variety, it was infinitely better than what they had lived on during the journey from Slavgorod and other colonies via Moscow to Leningrad. After three weeks in the warehouse, they were moved to nearby army barracks with living conditions much improved. There they stayed for three more weeks. Then they were told to move to Hamburg, about 120 kilometers south of Kiel. Once again, the hope of getting visas for Canada flared up in the camp, this time higher than ever. But not so. Ottawa had spoken and would speak no more.

Meanwhile, our group on the *Alexey Rykov* had also reached the northeastern shores of Germany. "Upon landing in Swinemünde, 2 December 1929," Father writes, "we were graciously treated to a generous meal and then transported to a refugee camp in Hammerstein." Abram Löwen writes in his memoirs that "many of our brothers and sisters from Russia had already found temporary shelter" in Hammerstein and others in Prenzlau. Everyone knew from the outset that these shelters would be temporary, Father explained; the German government had made that unmistakably clear. All refugees from Russia would have to leave Germany as soon as some country somewhere opened its doors for permanent residency.

While the Germans were hospitable and sympathetic, it was not within their power to change our status. The Soviet authorities had forced us to turn in our birth certificates and other documents. We were now *personae non gratae* in a foreign land. As undocumented aliens, we were homeless, stateless, and for the most part moneyless. Our elders became painfully aware of the biblical reminder that on this earth there is no enduring dwelling place, be that house or land, country or city.

Those of us who ended up in Brazil remained stateless for decades to come. We had neither right nor privilege to citizenship; we simply had no identity papers to prove that we even existed. Yet God has endowed the human spirit with a tenacious hope for better times ahead. For the moment, however, our highest aspirations were to be free and to live out our faith somewhere in this world. As I look back, I cannot help but wonder whether we have not long since replaced those humble wishes with a sense of greed beyond our basic needs.

During our brief stay in Germany we were living between the times and between two worlds: On the one hand, our experiences of the immediate past in the Soviet Union lingered with us day and night; no one wanted to go back. On the other hand, our immediate future was shrouded with uncertainties; no one had a clear view of what lay ahead. Things happened so fast and furiously that decisions had to be made before options could be properly weighed. That made it especially hard for our elders and leaders. I recall from meetings held in Brazil some years later that our people would blame their experiences in our new land on decisions our elders had made while still in Germany. In some instances the "accuser of the brethren" succeeded in raising the tempers far above the already high tropical temperature. Others again expressed different views, urging their brothers to nurture an attitude of gratitude rather than giving vent to discontent.

In addition to other difficulties, there was a serious outbreak of diphtheria and scarlet fever in the camps. It reached epidemic proportions, particularly in Hammerstein where our family was staying. Löwen describes the tragedy as *ein großes Kindersterben* (a massive dying of children). At least 288 children died within days. Reports indicate that they had become so emaciated and weak during weeks and months of refugee life that their immune system had been nearly destroyed. The situation must have been similar to that in biblical times. At least on two occasions there was "lamentation, bitter weeping and great mourning," to paraphrase slightly a prophet of ancient times. "Rachel was weeping for her children and refused to be comforted, because her children were no more" (Jer. 31:15; Matt. 2:16-18).

To Germany's credit it must be said that the people in charge had become cognizant of the refugee crisis and were committed to improving conditions and alleviating suffering as fully and expeditiously as possible. They invested an enormous amount of money and labor to sanitize, renovate, and equip a huge *Unteroffiziervorschule* (a preparatory school for officer training) in Mölln. This school had been used during World War I but was now vacant.

Mölln is situated at the northern end of the famous *Lüneburger Heide*. A medieval city with quaint architecture, old churches, cemeteries and beautiful parks, it is today an attractive tourist city with fountains and spas and many family-operated hotels, restaurants and coffee houses. One of its major cultural attractions is centered in the roguish jester of *Til Eulenspiegel* who is said to have lived there in the fourteenth or fifteenth century. Built around several natural lakes and lush forests, the city lies about fifty kilometers east of Hamburg.

During my years of teaching and preaching ministry in Germany, I wrote to the mayor of Mölln, explaining briefly my interest in researching my family history, including the episode of Mennonite refugees in his city nearly seventy years ago. In a courteous response he assured me that I would have liberal access to any archival materials relevant to my quest. A few days later I received a letter (5 August 1999) from Mr. Lopau, the city archivist, giving me specific information about records housed in the church archives covering the period from 1929 to 1933. He also sent me an essay he had written on "Das Flüchtlingslager für die Rußlanddeutschen in Mölln (1929-1933)," in which he describes that phase of our history in some detail. Within days, writes Lopau, a total of forty freight cars loaded with materials and provisions marked "URGENT" rolled into the Mölln train station. Every truck, big or small, every wagoner with a team of horses, and every light wagon that could be pulled by hand was put into action for transporting goods and materials from the station to the school where the refugees were to be housed. Men and women by the hundreds worked in shifts from 6 o'clock in the morning to midnight. By 21 December the school was ready to be occupied.

On 22 December our people from Hamburg, Hammerstein, and Prenzlau began to converge in Mölln. For many it was a happy reunion; for others it was a bitter disappointment when they discovered that their loved ones were not among the arrivals. My father recalls how we were warmly greeted and welcomed by Mayor Gerd Wolff and his wife. "In addition," says Father, "we received gifts and toys for the children to celebrate Christmas. We were free people, even though we were still in a refugee camp. We experienced much goodwill, love and compassion from the people in Mölln that we shall never forget."

At one point in December of 1929, there were 2700 refugees in Hammerstein, 1600 in Prenzlau, and 1200 in Mölln. Eventually, all were moved to Mölln. The two eastern camps were closed in April 1930. Only Mölln continued to operate until 1933. The quarters were adequate, the food was excellent, and the overall treatment, including spiritual and medical care, better than could be expected.

For Christmas Eve, the Refugee Commission had prepared a program to celebrate the birth of Christ. Everything was festively decorated. When my wife Frieda and I were in Mölln in 1999 to see for ourselves where I had been as a small child, I found in the church archives an original copy of the Christmas program dated 24 December 1929. It contained thirty-three items, listing title and presenter for each. The Christmas story was presented in a variety of forms: children, young people and adults sang Christmas songs and carols in choirs and small groups; many recited poems and Bible passages; others presented short skits and narrations to rehearse the events in Bethlehem of long ago. The children received gifts and special treats that had been given by local people. My brother Nikolai, who was almost six at the time, remembers the thrill of Christmas in Mölln. I was too young to remember.

While the spirit of the refugees was high at the moment, their mood was not unmixed. They could not erase from their memories the past Christmas celebrations in Russia. Nor could they forget their relatives and friends who had shared with them the flight from Siberia and the experiences in Moscow, but had been apprehended and forcibly sent back. Then there was the thought of Christmas next year; no one knew where and under what circumstances that might be. But the message of the angels to Bethlehem's shepherds helped to reassure them that the Prince of Peace was the center of "peace on earth and good will to men" — even for pilgrims on a refugee trail with a stopover in Germany. By this time our people had been on the road for at least four months. Mölln was to be the last stop before our final destination. But no one was sure, no one yet knew when and where our journey would finally end. The only consolation was that we were out of the Soviet Union. We were free people.

As hopes of getting visas for Canada vanished, my people began to look at the options open to them at that time: Brazil or Paraguay. The Mennonite Central Committee (MCC) entered the negotiations, urging all Mennonite refugees to go to Paraguay rather than Brazil. The reasons either expressed or implied were the following: first, in 1926 and 1927, Paraguay had taken in about 1,800 Mennonite immigrants from Canada who had settled on the arid land of the *Gran Chaco*. Theoretically, they should be able to assist newcomers in their transition from frigid Russia to tropical

Paraguay. Second, the Paraguayan government declared its willingness to accept any number of Mennonite refugees, regardless of their medical condition. Third, Paraguay guaranteed full military exemption to all Mennonites.

Despite these appealing arguments and the promise of support from the MCC to those who went to Paraguay, a large number decided to go to Brazil instead. Unfortunately, that decision fractured the relationship between our Mennonites in Brazil and their brothers and sisters in Anglo America for years to come. Although this chapter in the history of my people was not unknown, it was more or less kept away from the printed page until the Paraguayan historian Peter P. Klassen was asked to write the "official" history of the Mennonites in Brazil, entitled *Die rußlanddeutschen Mennoniten in Brasilien*. Klassen has documented that missing chapter in great detail.

While my father did not regret his choice to go to Brazil, he was saddened by the apparent rift caused by that choice. He explains how that choice was made. During our time in Mölln, our people learned about available land in Brazil. Within days they began to talk about buying land from the Hanseatic Land Association or Colonization Agency. Friedrich Lange, an agronomist by vocation and a representative of the German government by appointment, was in charge of the legal real estate transactions. He made the deal attractive. This totally unspoiled land in the "virgin forests" of southern Brazil, so the potential buyers were told, was situated in a valley along the *Rio Krauel* in the interior of the state Santa Catarina. It sounded much more idyllic than the actual jungle with its high hills and steep *serras*, its deep gorges and ravines, turned out to be. But having been rejected by Canada, declaring their reluctance to move to Paraguay, and knowing that our temporary time in Germany was running out, our people decided to purchase land by proxy—land unknown and unseen. My father wrote that the decision had been hard. Yet after discussing the question with Mother and the older children, they agreed as family to buy land and move to Brazil. Humanly speaking, the purchase seems to have been less than prudent, though it may have been providential.

It is important to bear in mind that German authorities were the first of any foreign dignitaries to turn a listening ear to our cries of desperation. Just as Martins and some of his right-hand men in Moscow had worked hard and long on behalf of the earliest refugees, such as the Group of Kiel, so Professors Benjamin Unruh and Otto Auhagen continued to labor tirelessly on behalf of all known refugees, regardless of where they came from or to what faith they belonged—Mennonite, Lutheran or Catholic. What they needed in order to accomplish anything of substance, was the undivided support and cooperation of the highest political echelons in Moscow and Berlin. In the meantime, Ottawa and Washington, Rio de Janeiro and

Asunción had also become political players, holding the destiny of thousands of refugees in their hands.

No matter which country would eventually open its door for permanent immigration, everyone looked to Germany for a solution of the immediate present. While some refugees had already been given exit permits, many more would have to be released if the Bolsheviks wanted to save face within the international community.

On 25 November 1929, *Reichspräsident* Paul von Hindenburg in Berlin made the bold declaration that Germany was prepared to grant temporary asylum to all German refugees. That put him and other leaders in the position to put pressure on Moscow to let the people go. Subsequently, the Soviets granted exit visas to several thousands more refugees still in the suburbs of the capital. The last group forged its way through bolted gates and iron curtains, leaving Moscow on 10 December of that memorable year of escape. And then the Gates of Moscow were locked with stone and steel, keeping the would-be refugees behind the darkening shadows of the Iron Curtain.

The significance of 25 November cannot be overemphasized. For it was on this day that more than five thousand men, women and children were released from bondage to freedom. In an article describing the historical episode at the gates of Moscow, Walter Quiring writes that of those who found temporary safety in Germany, 2,529 eventually emigrated to Brazil, 1,572 went to Paraguay, and 1,344 received visas for Canada. Frank Epp gives the same statistics in *Mennonite Exodus*. In his 1995 essay, "Let My People Go! A Catastrophic Episode in German/Russian Emigration: 1929," Peter Penner reverses the figures for Paraguay and Brazil.

I will never forget a youth meeting in our Krauel colony in 1947. Johannes Janzen, one of our esteemed leaders and preachers, talked to us about the frightening experiences of our people at the gates of Moscow. As he reviewed in some detail the events of those months, Mr. Janzen pointed out the historical significance and challenged us to keep alive the memory of those days when God used different people, especially the German government, to intervene on our behalf. "But gratitude in words alone," he underscored, "is inadequate. It becomes meaningful only when it is translated into action. Our Brazilian reality offers ample opportunity to show our gratitude by our deeds and by the way we live among the people of our adopted land." That lesson on our own history made a deep impression on me and other youths. I began to understand the importance of 25 November. It has become our true "memorial day," a day of thanksgiving for our freedom and a day of intercession for multitudes still in captivity throughout the world.

I conclude this chapter with a comment or two on conditions for the refugees in Germany and a personal experience that enhanced my understanding of the situation. Our people experienced joy and sorrow during their stay in Mölln. On the one hand, they fulfilled the biological mandate given to Adam and Eve, "Be fruitful and multiply": forty-eight children were born there to Mennonite families. On the other hand, they also experienced death. As the cradle normally produces joy, so the grave produces sorrow. More than three hundred bodies, mostly children, are buried in the German cemeteries of Prenzlau, Hammerstein and Mölln. They were transferred, as it were, directly to eternity without ever seeing their new home in a strange land. In the *Alter Friedhof* (Old Cemetery) of Mölln stands a monument erected on an elevation under an old oak tree in memory of those who died there. Its epitaph reads: *Hier ruhen 30 Russlanddeutsche Flüchtlinge 1930.* (Here are resting 30 Russian-German refugees, 1930.) My niece Toni Funk, first child of my sister Susanna and her husband Kornelius, is one of them. When my wife and I were there in August of 1999, the cemetery director pulled from the shelf a big ledger, turned the pages and showed me the names of the people. One of the pages he xeroxed for me contains the following note about my niece: "Funk, Antoinette Dorothea 3. 4.2.1930." She was three years old.

With some exceptions, the German people as a whole treated us with respect, generosity, and kindness. Public officials, medical doctors, kitchen personnel, and pastors were helpful in meeting every need. When I stop to think that they cared for 1,000 to 1,200 men, women, and children on any given day in Mölln alone, I can only marvel at the kindness we received from the Germans.

It has always been my desire to go back to my birthplace in Siberia, to the suburbs of Moscow where we spent time as refugees, and to Mölln, the refugee camp in Germany. I have given up on going to Siberia. But in May 1998, Frieda and I visited our children in Moscow and saw much of the city. Even if I had no way of identifying the place we stayed at in 1929, just being there helped me to visualize much better what the wait at Moscow's gate must have been like. In August 1999 we also spent a few days in Mölln, together with our friends from France, *Pfarrer* Günther and Rosemarie Moll. As we stood on the parking lot, looking at the imposing multistoried building where we had been given shelter nearly seventy years earlier, Frieda said: "I wonder from which window your mother and you were looking out when you were here as a baby."

Just then a gentleman drove onto the parking lot where we stood. I introduced myself and explained our reason for being there. With German courtesy he introduced himself as "Herr Ullrich Heimann, instructor of military law at the *Bundeswehrverwaltungsschule*." He explained that the building, which he called *der alte Kasten* (that old box), had been built during World War I to train military officers. He went on to say that since then it had served many different purposes, but had more recently been converted to function as a national defense administration school. No doubt, Herr Heimann noticed my curiosity and offered to give us a tour of the building and premises. That alone was worth the trip to Mölln. We took a number of pictures, thanked our kind host, exchanged our farewells and good wishes, and left for the church archives.

To give a tangible expression of gratitude to the German people in general and the city of Mölln in particular, the refugees collected money and hired a professional wood sculptor to design and fashion a plaque with the words of Jesus in Matthew 11:28-30 engraved in solid oak. To this day the plaque hangs in the foyer of the main sanctuary of the old *St. Nikolas Kirche*, which our people attended. In translation the text reads:

> *Come unto me, all you who are weary*
> *and burdened, and I will give you rest.*
> *Take my yoke upon you and learn from me...*
> *For my yoke is easy and my burden is light!*
> *Gratefully dedicated by the*
> *Russian-German Refugees*
> *A. D. 1930.*

7

Voyage Across the Atlantic
(Jan 16-Feb 7, 1930)

*When the ship was caught
by a wind of hurricane force,
we took a violent battering.
And when the storm continued raging,
we finally gave up all hope of being saved.*
– Paraphrased excerpts from Acts 27

We knew by now that the journey we had started in the Kulunda Steppe of Siberia in August 1929, was to end in the jungles of southern Brazil. While no one could see the end from the beginning, everyone would see the beginning from the end. These would be two different worlds with lands and waters in between. It became progressively clear that these worlds would be as different as day is different from night. We soon would be looking back on weeks and months of travels on roads and rails, on waterways and narrow trails. And should we stop to recount our steps, we would quickly discover that we had traversed thousands of kilometers by crossing plains and mountains, seas and rivers; that we had come through fields and forests, hamlets and cities; that we had traveled on two continents (Asia and Europe), moving toward the third across the Atlantic. Our hopes and aspirations, mixed with uncertainties and fears, were still hanging in suspense, not knowing what might come next.

On the Ocean Liner *Monte Olivia*

The time of departure for the first group came closer with each passing day. From available records it is possible to trace the route from our camp in Germany to our colony in Brazil. At about 8:30 in the morning of 16 January 1930, we boarded a special train that took us from Mölln to the harbor on the Elbe River in Hamburg. Once more, many relatives and friends were separated without certainty about the destiny of either those who left or those who stayed. To express our common sentiments it seemed appropriate to join our hearts and voices in singing a favorite hymn written by Paul Gerhard, based on Psalm 37:5: "Commit your way unto the Lord; trust also in him; and he shall bring it to pass."

> Commit your ways—confiding, when trials will arise—
> To Him, whose hands are guiding tumultuous seas and skies.
> When clouds and storms are raging, He has their paths assigned.
> In Him—His powers engaging—each shall safe refuge find.

In Hamburg we had to undergo one more of the medical inspections that had become routine since leaving Slavgorod five months earlier. From the passenger halls of the harbor in Hamburg we were ushered to board a small ship (H. Martins speaks of a "motor boat") that was to take us on the Elbe River to the ocean liner Monte Olivia. From the records I have it is not entirely clear whether we boarded the Monte Olivia in the same harbor or in the famous Steubenhöft Cruise Terminal with its three-hundred-meter-long *Hapag-Hallen* of Cuxhaven where the waters of the Elbe are absorbed by the North Sea. Be that as it may, this relatively new luxury liner had taken thousands of the rich and famous on pleasure tours across the seas. Now that same ship was given the task of transporting destitute Mennonite refugees from a harbor of northwestern Germany across the Atlantic to southeastern Brazil.

By 6 o'clock in the evening the foghorn signaled that it was time to move. By 11 o'clock that same night we were supposed to arrive in Cuxhaven, but did not. Even the next morning we were still floating on the Elbe. It seems that dense fog delayed our journey for fifteen hours before we got to the open sea.

According to the passenger list compiled by Mr. Martins on board the ship, our group consisted of thirty-three family heads and a total of 179 persons. Six of these families came from Orenburg, one from the Crimea, three from Omsk, and twenty-three from Slavgorod, including my family. The majority settled in our village Waldheim, the rest in Witmarsum. As I grew up, I got to know all of these people and now find it interesting to review the names of the passenger list and then visualize the precise homestead where each used to live. The record also has it that on two subsequent trips the Monte Olivia took Mennonites together with other passengers to the same destination in Brazil.

Since our ship had more space than passengers, several families were lucky enough to get first-class state rooms in the center of the vessel where the swinging and swaying was less noticeable. The majority, however, traveled in second-class compartments located at each end of the ship. Even those cabins would have been more than adequate, had it not been for the discomfort of motion sickness that affected some more than others. Fortunately, that happened only periodically when the winds hit the waters with such force that the billows rocked the boat from side to side and up and down like a piece of driftwood. While seasickness is generally not deathly, it can make one feel more like dying than living. For the most part, the great Atlantic was calm and serene, and the journey itself was peaceful and pleasant.

Our vessel made a scheduled stopover at the Canary Islands near the northwest coast of Africa. It anchored just long enough to replenish its fresh water supply. During those few hours the passengers became engrossed with the deep-sea divers surrounding the ship. They were not professionals, but hopeful breadwinners for themselves and their families. With great eagerness they retrieved every foreign coin that passengers dropped into the sea, and regarded each as a treasure with which to buy basic necessities of life; at least so we were told. As we crossed the equatorial line to the south of the Canary Islands, the crew put on a festive celebration with sea gods and mermaids on center stage. Some of our people found the show offensive and sacrilegious. Others were fascinated with this traditional flair that is unique to ocean travel.

In his memoirs, David Schartner remembers 2 February 1930, as a very happy day on which his half-sister was born to his mother and stepfather, the Kliewers. When the parents named her Anna, the ship's captain protested, explaining that the family had ignored an important ancient tradition. "It is a captain's prerogative," he demanded, "to choose the name for the first child born on an ocean voyage." He insisted in no uncertain terms that she be called Olivia, after his ship. The parents compromised and called their little daughter "Anna Olivia." That satisfied both, the captain and the parents.

The name reminds me of an incident from my early days in school. When I was in grade one, I thought that Anna Olivia was the most beautiful girl in the world, worthy of a special gift. But I had not much to give except one precious little item which my brother Heinrich had given me: an empty revolver cartridge. I carried it in my pocket at all times and used it as a whistle. When I blew into it, it made a piercing sound. I treasured that thing beyond words. Yet I was about to make the biggest sacrifice I had ever made. I remember how I stood by the open window in our one-room school. I would whistle just once more, I told myself, and then let it drop at Anna's feet. I whistled. Other children looked up with admiration. But then something happened deep within my soul: right then and there perished the thought of sacrificing my treasure for Anna Olivia. Thus ended my love affair.

On 4 February land was in sight. We had come to Rio de Janeiro. The *Pão de Açucar* (Sugar Hat Mountain) and the magnificent *Corcovado* (Statue of Christ) were in clear view. The natural beauty of the first and the astoundingly marvelous construction of the second inspire awe in anyone who sees them for the first time. These first impressions which our people got of the land they would soon call their homeland were simply breathtaking.

After unloading and reloading freight for about ten hours in the harbor of Rio, the ship again set out to sea and moved southward along the eastern coast of Brazil. The next day we reached Santos, a major harbor in the State of São Paulo. Most of the French, Portuguese, and Spanish passengers disembarked, cargo was loaded and unloaded, and we were again on our way toward the harbor next to our destination in Santa Catarina.

According to David Schartner's recollections written up in *Bibel und Pflug*, 6 February1930, was recorded in the annals of our journey as the most memorable day. While the passengers were enjoying their dinner in the dining room, the captain called over the loudspeaker, apologized for the interruption, and then made a terse announcement saying that the Monte Olivia had orders to anchor immediately, that all passengers should be at ease and not panic, and that alternative transportation would be provided to take them to the next harbor.

Such unexpected event caused much consternation and anxiety among the passengers. Before long, we learned the reason: an SOS cable had signaled that another ocean liner had had an accident on the high seas. A German ship had evidently drifted off course, struck a coral reef, and was rapidly sinking. The vessel already engaged in the rescue operation had inadequate equipment and was in desperate need of help. The Monte Olivia received orders to stand by her sister ship. That meant that all passengers with their belongings had to transfer to another vessel. As soon as the other boat arrived, the sailors lowered a floating bridge to connect the two vessels. The crew unloaded our baggage, and the passengers were instructed to transfer immediately. Bidding farewell to captain and crew of the Monte Olivia raised the emotions of the passengers once more to the point of spilling over, especially as the ship's orchestra accompanied their departure by playing the dramatic tune of "God be with you 'til we meet again."

Pulled by a tugboat, our "new vessel" was nothing more than a huge barge, ruggedly structured and designed for cargo, not for passengers. The belly of this monstrous canoe was so deep and its sides so high, recalls Schartner, that no one could look over the sideboards to see either land or water. The only bright spot at that moment of our voyage was the clear southern sky above. Nonetheless, within hours of that same day of 6 February, we were towed into the harbor of São Francisco in the State Santa Catarina. Here we stepped onto truly Brazilian soil and were bidden a hearty welcome, not by Brazilians, but by two German gentlemen, Friedrich Lange, whom we had met in Mölln, and Bruno Mekien (Meckien; Mekin). Both were representatives of the Hanseatic Land Association.

There we were, dumped like cargo in the sweltering heat of São Francisco. But we were more than cargo. We were human beings, all 179 of us, big and small, old and young. Some were sitting, others standing; some were resting, others restless. Some were weeping, many simply waiting to move on; all were watching their few earthly possessions. There are times in life when even the most menial articles are valued like treasures. That's how we felt about our few belongings. As I have stated earlier, we had been dispossessed in the Soviet Union, stripped of things we considered basic for existence. Few in number were the items my family had managed to salvage. Among them was a wicker travel trunk. Besides some clothing it contained two very precious items of great sentimental and some monetary value. One was a Kröger wall clock which our parents had received as a wedding gift from Mother's parents. The face was quite ornamental, yet simple. It had an hour and a minute hand, a brass pendulum, two heavy and two light brass weights, each on a chain to regulate time and chime. The second item was a silver samovar which my mother treasured dearly In addition we had a few canvas handbags with personal effects. We also had received some clothing and utensils needed for survival in the jungle, given to us in Mölln by generous people from Germany and Holland.

And thus we were once more possessors of possessions. We were again the proud, yet humble owners of two or three enameled mugs, a cast iron frying pan, some cooking pots and enameled dinner plates. We had forks and spoons—at least one for each family member—and two or three knives. In addition, each household had an ax and a hoe plus such tools as a *foice* and a *facão*. These are as indispensable in the jungle as a tractor is for today's farm on the prairies. "Nobody can function without them," we were told. That is why we guarded these gifts lest they, too, should be "collected" from us while we waited to continue our journey.

On the Coastal Steamer *Max*

The wait seemed endless. Finally, something came into sight. *Max* appeared on the glassy, glaring surface, visible against the horizon. At first it was no more than a mere speck on distant waters, but soon we saw that it was a ship. What a relief, especially for mothers with small children and for sisters who had to watch their younger siblings. My sister Margareta, for instance, did her share in taking care of me. And, I almost hesitate to admit, I gave her a hard time. I certainly lived up to the reputation I had gained among the passengers: they called me *"dee schlemmi Hauns."* That is the kind of a nickname one neither takes pride in nor bothers to translate. Suffice it to say that it was no compliment. The name goes back to Siberia when I was quite young, and it has followed me to adulthood. Even many years later when I preached in Brazil, Paraguay, Canada, and

Germany, once even in the United States (in Madera, California), I have heard people ask and remark: *"Es daut nichj Kausdarps Hauns, waut emma schlemmd? Nu haft't doch noch waut von dem jijaeft."* That is to say that *"dee schlemmi Hauns"* has come a long way and made something of himself. Actually, it was more God's doing than mine.

The cargo of this modest coastal steamer was unloaded in short order, and our few boxes and bundles of belongings were loaded just as fast. The ship was equipped with only a few primitive cabins, short on cleanliness and comfort. These "state rooms" were reserved for women and children. The menfolk had to find a spot on the open deck to put down their heads. That might have been all right, had it not been for the tropical downpour on *Max* that night.

We had barely left the harbor when the sailors pointed to the horizon where black thunderclouds were rolling and rising out of nowhere, towering ever higher, coming ever closer. Since none of our people understood Portuguese, the sailors used body language to explain what we should expect. They made wavy motions with their hands, swayed sideways and backwards and forward with their bodies, put fingers in their mouths, and in a forward-bent position made distorted facial expressions. They were trying to tell us that ocean waves would come and play havoc with the ship, and that we would get seasick. They were so right.

In a matter of minutes blinding lightning ripped through the clouds and deafening thunder rolled through the air. It was an ominous scene. The sailors put a heavy canvas over the deck to keep us from getting wet, but to no avail. The storm was so violent and the downpour so intense that the spouts along the edge were too few and narrow. The water could not run off fast enough and in a short time we had a literal flood on deck. In a recent book, *Brasilien: Heimat für Heimatlose,* Peter Pauls quotes from the journal of our group leader, Heinrich Martins: "Dreadful night. Terrible winds. Thunderstorm. Rain. Life in danger. Nearly everyone sick." Worse yet, the ship was tilting sideways to such depths that we were in danger of tipping over at any moment. People were terror-stricken. Children clutched any adult that happened to be near. Many cried for fear and prayed to the Lord in despair. Some asked as the disciples once asked, "Lord, don't you care that we perish?" My father recalls how a number of strong and sturdy men and women locked their arms together to form a human chain of unity and then sang in melodious harmony the song written by the nineteenth-century German poet-evangelist, Ernst Gebhardt: *Meister, es toben die Winde.*

> Master, the tempest is raging! The billows are tossing high!
> The sky is o'ershadowed with blackness, no shelter nor help is nigh;
> Carest Thou not that we perish? How canst Thou lie asleep

When each moment so madly is threatening a grave in the angry deep?
The winds and the waves shall obey my will!
Peace, be still! Peace, be still!
Whether the wrath or the storm-tossed sea,
Or demons, or men, or whatever it be;
No water can swallow the ship where lies
The Master of ocean and earth and skies;
They all shall sweetly obey my will;
Peace, be still! Peace, be still!

Bruno Mekien, who welcomed us upon arrival in São Francisco, was also on board. A seasoned seaman himself, he ordered the captain to steer the ship away from the shore against the waves back onto the high sea. As he did that, the steamer regained its balance; and after several more hours of charging the waves, *Max* was again able to move toward our destination. It took us nine hours instead of the scheduled four hours to get to the next harbor. "We gave thanks to God for answered prayers," recalls Father, "by singing the last stanza of the song." The Lord had brought us through the stormy waters without loss of life. We finally landed in Itajaí, the last ocean harbor of our journey across the Atlantic to southern Brazil.

For a variety of reasons the mood of our people was less than optimistic. Unreasonable custom officials who demanded that every bag and box be opened and emptied heightened the anxiety of the weary pilgrims. Besides the trauma of the past and the uncertainties still facing them, they had two other concerns. For one thing, they were ambivalent about our land purchase. My people had bought land before—in the Molotschna, in Zagradovka, and in Slavgorod. Each time they were about to do so, they sent trusted experts to investigate the geographical location, quality of soil, type of vegetation, marketing facilities, climatic conditions, and many other things. This time it was different: they had negotiated a land deal while still in a German refugee camp without having the foggiest notion what the land might be like. Of course, they had seen pictures and heard speeches presented by representatives of the Hanseatic Land Association, but it is not now nor was it then the custom of a realtor to say more than is required to market the property. The seller must make the product so appealing that the potential buyer is converted into an actual buyer. In our case there was no choice.

Another factor was the loss of our identity. While we were grateful to be out of the Soviet Union, we began to realize that we had become displaced persons. We had lost our fatherland and had been deprived of our citizenship. The Bolsheviks had first dispossessed us, then disowned and rejected us, and finally even stripped us of our identity. We had become *personae non gratae;* we were diplomatically declared unwanted and unwelcome. We had become a people with no land to live in, no law to turn to, no documents to verify our existence. Germany had received us, but only as temporary transients. Brazil was graciously granting us asylum and a place to live, but only as "stateless aliens" without any national identity. We were unsure what that would mean in years to come. We soon found out. Today I know. I had countless legal problems when crossing international borders until I finally became eligible to secure Canadian citizenship thirty-three years later.

Our six-months-long journey from the Kulunda Steppe in Siberia to the jungles of Brazil was literally "a journey of pilgrims and strangers."

8

By River Rail and Road to Our Destination
(8-12 February 1930)

> *The angel of the LORD encamps all around*
> *those who fear him and delivers them. . . .*
> *The eyes of the LORD are on the righteous,*
> *and his ears are attentive to their cry.*
> – King David in *Psalm 34*

Itajaí was then as now an important harbor city in Santa Catarina. It is situated in the bay where the Itajaí River flows into the Atlantic. For the next twenty years, during which we lived in the Krauel Colony of the interior, Itajaí was our nearest ocean harbor for trade and business with the outside world. We took most of our agricultural and industrial products there by road; they were then transported by ship to Santos in the State of São Paulo, and Rio de Janeiro, the capital of Brazil at that time. I have vivid memories of Itajaí and the route that leads from there some two hundred kilometers inland to our colony on the Krauel River. But before I write about that, I must complete the account of our first expedition.

After clearing customs in Itajaí, we continued our journey: from Itajaí to Itoupava Secca, a suburb of Blumenau, by river; from Itoupava Secca to Ibirama by train; and from Ibirama to Alto Rio Krauel by horse and wagon, oxcart, and on foot.

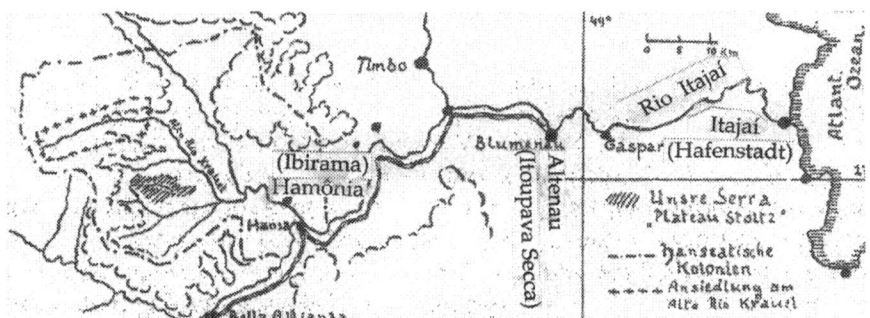

Map of German Settlers in Santa Catarina. Route we traveled in 1930 from Itajai to the Krauel in the interior.
Source: Original map by David Enns, with monor modifications. Personal library collection.

By River Boat with Paddle Wheels

After hours of waiting in sweltering heat with heavy, humid ocean air blowing hard across the unsheltered harbor platform, the passengers were exhausted, thirsty, and hungry. Some were disoriented with weariness. What preoccupied our fathers and mothers more than anything else was the kind of vessel that would take us from the harbor of Itajaí along the river. They were worried about this waterway toward the rapids near Blumenau, where navigation would end and other means of transportation would have to be found. It was a valid concern, indeed, especially after the frightening experience on the steamer *Max*.

It was on 8 February in the afternoon when a fairly big river boat named *Blumenau,* powered by a steam engine with a huge paddle wheel on each side docked like a dwarf next to giant ocean liners resting in the harbor. Some of the refugees, my father wrote, preferred going to Blumenau by land, but the majority went by boat, as did our family. The crew helped us load our belongings. As soon as that was done, our people were ushered on board and instructed to find a spot to sit or stand. It became evident at once that we were not on a luxury liner. Concern for safety continued to rise.

The paddle wheels were put into gear and we were again on our way, moving upstream along the Rio Itajaí. The water was muddy and unusually high, overflowing the banks and flooding much of the flat but narrow delta on both sides. The flood was caused, we were told, by heavy downpours in the interior. The Itajaí is known for its angry current which alternates between rapids and cataracts and quiet, lake-like *poços*. Along its entire length of 250 kilometers from its source in the *serras* until it releases its water into the Atlantic, the river has to squeeze and wind its course through numerous valleys and mountains. Only the distance of approximately eighty kilometers between the cities Itajaí and Blumenau is navigable. The valley is flat and low, rising only slightly above sea level. The massive torrents of water from the mountainous interior on the one hand and the slow runoff in the shallow valley on the other, create perfect conditions for flooding. When Frieda and I lived in Blumenau, we saw the water of the Itajaí rise far above normal, spilling its muddy contents in all directions. The record has it that ten to sixteen meters (thirty to fifty feet) of flooding is not uncommon. Such floods were always catastrophic for the peasants living in the shallow delta of the narrow valley, as well as for the people living in cities along the river. Blumenau was often hit very hard, resulting in great destruction.

Just beyond the narrow flats on each side of the river bank the terrain was generally rugged. The rocky cliffs and mountains with occasional waterfalls and dark ravines visible from our boat were an indication as to what we could expect once we reached the land we had bought while still in Germany. At places the water passage was so narrow that a vessel the size of ours could barely pass through without scraping its sides. Hidden sandbanks and jagged granites posed a constant danger to navigation, particularly during flooding when the waters were deep and murky and the banks at places were not visible.

By sunset of that day we had reached Itoupava Secca, where the river's navigability comes to an abrupt halt because of rapids. That is where the first phase of our journey ended, a journey I have called

River Route Review

From the ocean harbor winds a quiet river deep into the land.
Boats of wood glide slowly forward as they watch for rocks and sand.
Swaying, halting. And their human cargo from a distant shore
staring, searching, spying for familiar sights: — they are no more!

Jungle crowns are rising like an arrow, piercing the clear sky;
and the passengers are asking, puzzled, where this leads, and why.
River banks are lined with flowers. Clusters — yellow, red and blue,
dropping petals, dripping nectar, radiating pleasing hue.

Wonderland? This virgin forest? It looks ominous! Unsure!
O dear God! You're its Creator. You're our Guardian. Are we secure?
Lo! Those mountains! Ancient *serras:* solid granite with deep caves
that gave shelter to the natives who once dwelt there with their braves.

Mighty waters thunder from the rocks into cataracts below:
Tumbling. Twirling. Turning round and round in search of exit flow.
Whisp'ring springs emit the freshest water, bubbling from the ground,
forming brooks that gently murmur, moving, splashing, ocean-bound.

Crystal clear their droplets sparkle as they spill across the rocks,
quenching thirst of beasts and humans, satisfying birds in flocks.
One must hear and smell and see and touch and taste this jungle flair
with its humid, rising mist; its scorching heat; its clammy air.

In the distance — hear the craters? Roaring like the *Iguaçú!*
We are passing smiling people on their barges and canoe.
As our boat crawls slowly onward, coming to its resting place:
waterfalls — creation's wonder — blocking every sailing space.

Hush! The captain's voice is calling, "We've arrived. 'tis journey's end.
Disembark and find your lodging. 'Altenau,' I recommend."
Friendly people bid us welcome, give us supper; what a feast!
They provide us with night lodging for the greatest and the least.

Then the fathers and the mothers and their children, big and small,
raise their voices to their Father up in heaven, one and all:
"Thank You, Lord, for Your protection, thank You for Your guiding light.
Grant us rest for soul and body, keep us safe throughout this night."

Short the hours and brief the sleeping, barely had we closed our eyes
when the children started weeping, asking questions: countless "whys"?
Dogs were barking. Cats were howling. Roosters crowed. The night is gone.
They announced that day was dawning. Weary pilgrims must move on.

The Second Phase by Rail

The residents of Altenau (Itoupava Secca) had been notified of our arrival; they were prepared to receive us with the kindest hospitality. They served us a delicious supper, provided clean night lodging, and told us that we should get ready to travel on the next day after breakfast. And travel we did, setting out on another phase of the journey, this time by rail.

The day was February nine, nineteen thirty was the year.
And on that early morning an "iron horse" was standing near.
Our family fathers, thirty-three, trunk and suitcase on their backs,
were hurrying toward the train that waited there on narrow tracks.
Our mothers and our siblings, our youths and children in the hall,
were rushing after them; some stumbled, as they heard the porters' call.

With their black caps and snow-white gloves, their uniforms prim and slick;
they were courteous, ever helpful—these friendly gentlemen—so chic.
The jungle steadily got deeper, denser and intensely dark.
Up ahead appeared an opening, where we had to disembark.
The place was called *Hamonia* with an office for our land.
We ate. We rested. We moved on. It was hard to understand.

The train ride from Itoupava Secca to the station Hansa near Hamonia (renamed Ibirama) was nothing short of a treacherous venture because of the excessively curvy road along the river that winds its way through the mountains. In a distance of about eighty kilometers there were thirty-nine intersections where the tracks crossed the road. This made travel by road and by rail extremely hazardous, and collisions of trucks and trains were common. In later years I have frequently traveled this route and seen wreckage scattered on the side of road and track, sometimes rolled into the ravines. Fortunately, today most of those crossings have been eliminated by improved engineering and construction of both the highway and the railroad.

The Hanseatic Land Association had its headquarters in Ibirama. That is also where Bruno Meckin, director of the Association, Dr. Lange, the official representative of the German government for the colonization project and its settlers in Brazil, as well as Johannes Aurich and the Association's professional surveyors, Mr. Dudi and Mr. Weber, had established their homes. They had prepared temporary lodging for our entire group of thirty-three families. Some were housed in a new tobacco shed, others in a warehouse.

The understanding was that many of our people would have to stay in Ibirama until the administration could make the necessary arrangements for us to move to our land about sixty kilometers farther inland. The land had to be surveyed and divided into colonies or farms. With few exceptions, each colony would consist of either fifteen or thirty hectares (thirty-seven and seventy-four acres, respectively) of jungle land. Dudi and Weber, together with their team of surveyors, had the responsibility of finding or building some kind of primitive shelter, referred to as "Sommerkamp Barracks," until we could construct our own, more permanent dwellings. That is what all of us were longing for—a place to settle down.

The Last Leg of Our Journey

When we began our journey in Slavgorod six or seven months earlier, we set out with horse and wagon and then traveled by train to Moscow. Now we ended as we had begun: we traveled by train from Itoupava Secca to Ibirama and from there with horse and wagon or with oxcart and on foot to the Krauel, our final destination.

We could not all move at the same time since there were not enough wagons or other means of transportation for people and baggage. That meant that many had to walk, especially the men and boys. This was truly "the last leg" of our journey. The first fifteen kilometers or so we traversed along a gravel road, which was advantageous for the wagoners, but disastrous for bare feet. "We felt relieved and grateful once we reached the dirt road," my old friend Peter Friesen recalled. At places the road was not much wider than a deer path. The Brazilians called it *picada* or *picadão*. Downpours were frequent and heavy, causing a *picada* to become next to impassable. Even on foot it was difficult to move ahead. The trek through the jungle seemed endless. Now and then there was a clearing with a house, a barn, and often a tobacco shed. The occupants were German colonists who, a generation or two ago, had also bought land from the Hanseatic Land Association and had already established themselves as "progressive" peasants, as Friesen records in his autobiographical notes. These colonists considered the Krauel, particularly the upper area, to be one of the remotest places in the region. That is where we were headed.

In 1995 I was in Curitiba, Brazil, speaking at a missionary retreat sponsored by the *Deutsche Indianer Pioniermission* and the *Marburger [Brasilien] Mission*. That is where I again met my dear friend Friesen, whom I had known since childhood. After the retreat we took time to visit together and review some of our experiences during those pioneering times in the Krauel. Friesen was now a widower in his nineties, yet his mind was as sharp and his humor as delightful as ever. He loved to talk about our journey from the Soviet Union to Brazil. He verified for me what I had read in his autobiographical reflections about the way we made it into the interior of the jungle. I will tell the story in the form of a rhyme as I reflect on the context of that memorable journey.

> Zig-zag up and zig-zag down, shoving, pushing on our trail.
> So the trek keeps slowly moving, not much faster than a snail.
> Two steps forward, one step backward; three and four, we try again.
> "It's a game," someone is calling. Others laugh to ease the pain.
>
> On a hillside works a peasant who's for years been living there,
> growing sugarcane, tobacco, beans, mandioca with great care.
>
>> "Where you come from?" he enquires.
>> "Are you Germans? Russians? Poles?
>> Where you going?" he's demanding.
>> "We've got land for hardy souls."
>
> Peter Friesen, as our spokesman, does explain whence we have come:
> "We are refugees," he tells him, "and in search of a new home.
> But this trail seems rather endless, leading nowhere, it appears.
> We are weary, hungry, tired, somewhat anxious, filled with fears.
> Gracious sir—if I may ask you:—How far is it to the Krauel?
> Can you tell us how we get there, how much farther must we crawl?
> We must get there, lest we perish 'ere we reach our journey's end.
> The Krauel is where we're told to settle, make a living with our hands."
>
>> "Can't be true," the peasant mutters,
>> but he does not dare to speak.
>> He is chewing his tobacco,

> storing juice between his cheeks.
> "Phew, the Krauel?" The old man's spitting,
> spewing out that liquid tar.
> "Let's see—the Krauel," he says while sitting.
> "Just keep on walking, it's still far.
> You will find it yonder *serras*—
> yonder *serras*, dark as mold.
> 'The devil's grandma does reside there',
> goes the tale that's being told."

Friesen and his friends are shaken, shaken to the inmost core.
Not expecting such an answer, they keep silent, ask no more.
Dusk and wet the narrow pathway through the jungle curves along.
One hears hardly any laughter; only faint the pilgrims' song.
Weary wand'rers caravanning with their ox carts, mules, on foot.
Suddenly the guides are calling: "We take leave now. You stay put."

And put we stayed. We had come to journey's end. It had been a long and tedious journey from the Siberian steppes to the Brazilian jungles. "As God was with us there," Father tried to reassure himself with confidence, "so He'll be with us here."

The land surveyors of the Hanseatic Land Association had been instructed to prepare temporary lodging in a jungle clearing made by German colonists who had moved there in the 1920s. Several families in our group found shelter, at least so they thought. They made themselves "comfortable" in what appeared to be an empty pig barn with mud floor and no walls. There were similar shelters known as "Sommerkamp Barracks," so that all of us had at least a roof over our heads. On the bare dirt floor lay corn straw to sleep on. While such beds were neither soft nor comfortable, we did not have the luxury of choice and were grateful for what good people had provided.

During our first night in this breezy castle, a heavy tropical rainstorm moved through the area. Within minutes, everything was just as wet and muddy under the leaky roof as the earth was under the open sky. Two young men were particularly shaken up by the fierceness of thunder and lightning. "We feared for our lives," writes David Schartner in *Bibel und Pflug*. In a serious conversation his friend said to him: *"Weetst Du waut, Doaft, hia woa wie nijh lang laewi. Wie woari ons blooss motti betjhieri, daut wie dann nijh filoari goani."* Those are meaningful words, saying: "You know what, David, here we won't survive very long. But we'll have to get saved so that we will not go lost."

PART II

Formative Years of Childhood and Youth (1930-1949)

Aspirations with Restrictions Growing Up in the Jungle

To those who through the righteousness of our God and Savior Jesus Christ have received a faith . . . make every effort to add to your faith goodness;
> *and to goodness, knowledge;*
> *and to knowledge, self-control;*
> *and to self-control, perseverence;*
> *and to perseverence, godliness;*
> *and to godliness, brotherly kindness;*
> *and to brotherly kindness, love.*

For if you possess these qualities in increasing measure, they will keep you from being ineffective and unproductive in your knowledge of our Lord Jesus Christ.
— The Apostle Peter in 2 *Peter* 1

Brazil in relation to its neighboring countries
Source: *Mennonitisches Jahrbuch für Südamerika 1968-1969.*

9

The Place Where I Grew Up

*Each person needs a little place, and be it ever small
of which he says, "Look what I've got; it's mine, and that is all.
Here I can live. Here I can love. I need no more to roam.
It is a place of peace and rest, a place to feel at home."*
— A rhyme from childhood memories in translation

When we settled in Brazil we had traveled from a land of long winters covered with ice and snow to a land of long summers known for humidity and heat. It was as though we had come to a different planet. Our point of departure in Siberia was situated longitudinally eighty degrees east of the meridian and latitudinally fifty-two degrees north of the equator, whereas our destination lay forty-eight degrees west of the meridian and twenty-six degrees south of the equator, just below the Tropic of Capricorn. The distance in a straight line between the two points is approximately 8,800 miles or 14,000 kilometers, crossing the meridian time line from east to west and the equator from north to south.

The precise place was known as *Alto Rio Krauel* or simply *Krauel*. The Krauel is only a small river of approximately forty-five kilometers from its source in the high *serras* to the point where it merges with *Rio Hercilio*, a major tributary of *Rio Itajaí*, which in turn empties into the Atlantic Ocean. Only the upper part was referred to as *Alto Rio Krauel*. Prior to the coming of any European settlers in the area, the Krauel was known as *Rio dos Indios* (River of the Indians), suggesting that indigenous peoples had inhabited that region at one time. In 1903, the name was changed to *Rio Krauel* in honor of Richard Krauel, the German ambassador to Brazil. Driven by a sense of responsibility and concern for the German settlers between the *serras* and along various rivers, Dr. Krauel came to visit them in those isolated parts of the world. It seems safe to assume that his interests may also have been connected with the German Hanseatic Land Association (HLA), from whom the earlier colonists from Germany had bought their land. Now the Mennonites and other Germans from the Soviet Union had also bought land from the same source.

The connection between the German government and the HLA is also implied in a 1930 article in the *Kölnische Zeitung*. The writer is critical of

Krauel and Stoltz-Plateau, the original Mennonite colonies in Santa Catarina (1930-1953) and additional settlements in Paraná and Rio Grande do Sul.
Source: Schroeder and Huebert, eds., *Mennonite Historical Atlas*, 2nd. ed., 1996.

the fact that the German-Russian wheat farmers had been transplanted from the open Siberian steppes to the dense Brazilian jungles. He infers that the push for such a move may have come from diplomatic sources rather than from the settlers themselves. The journalist may have a point, but it does not change reality. The fact is that we had come there, believing that God had his hand in our move. It was now up to us to learn how to survive there, and to discover our purpose and mission in that particular part of God's creation. I knew it only as *Krauel*, the place where I was growing up.

The transition from one land to the other was for me a mere "small step," but for my parents and adult siblings it was "a giant leap." The jungle was the only world I learned to know. I grew up there and loved it. But for my parents it was very different. They had experienced another world, had known another land, a land they had loved at one time. They had vivid memories of Zagradovka in the Ukraine and of Slavgorod in Siberia. They could make comparisons, I could not. My vision and worldview remained amblyopic, adjusted to circumstances that were as narrow as the valley where I lived. Opportunities to expand my horizon were limited. We had no radio, no newspaper, no books, save two: a Luther Bible and a Mühlheimer New Testament. Yet deep down I never ceased to dream of other worlds somewhere beyond the horizon, outside my field of vision. Although those dreams remained hazy because I could not even intelligently talk about them, they did not go away, except for a brief season in my teenage years, which I will explain later.

There is something about the Krauel that always intrigues me. I cannot identify it, yet it is there. Even today the mere mention of the word *Krauel* unleashes a thousand memories and perceptions. Most of them are pleasant and positive—not in the sense that everything was so wonderful, nor in the sense of idealizing the past as though it had been a bed of roses without thorns. To make such claim would be neither realistic nor true. Yet there was something about our way of life in general and my experiences in particular that moves me to a sense of genuine gratitude for the people I lived with and the experiences we had in common, including the many hardships. During my early teens I was often reminded of Father's words upon arrival at the Krauel: "As God was with us there [in Siberia], so He'll be with us here." Perhaps it was that consciousness of divine presence combined with the resilient faith of my father in the midst of adversities that made my formative years in the Krauel so rich and meaningful.

Upon visiting the Mennonites in Brazil, Harold S. Bender wrote of our settlements in Santa Catarina as "an almost criminally impossible location." Perhaps few, if any, could have understood Dr. Bender's words better than my parents. They knew from experience, particularly during those first pioneering days, that the mere effort to exist placed high

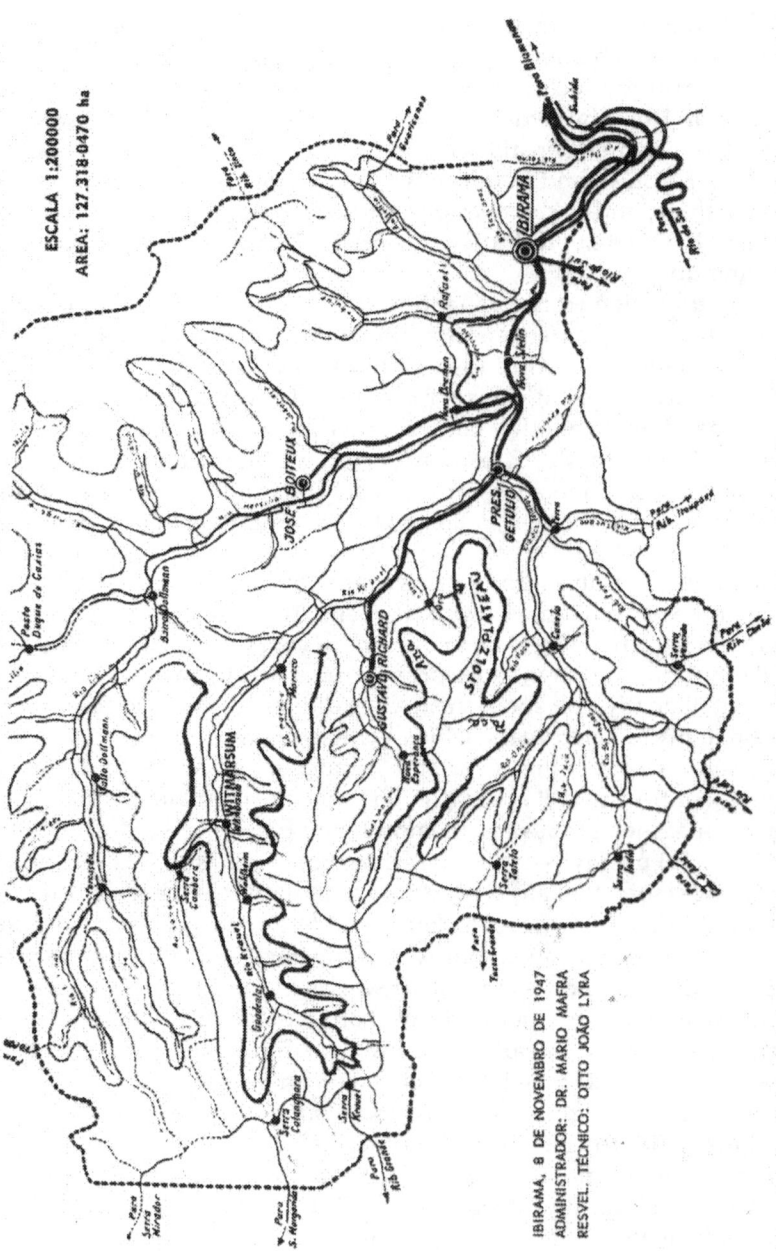

The Krauel Colony with the villages Witmarsum, Waldheim and Gnadental in the center of the large land area settled predominantly by German colonists.
Source: Peter Pauls., Jr., *Mennoniten in Brasilien 1930-1980.*

demands on body, soul, and spirit. Their immediate future must have appeared like a maze in a dark tunnel with the potential to threaten even their faith. Not until my later teens did I ever sense the crushing burden of survival that must have weighed heavily on the shoulders of my parents and oldest siblings during the early years. In those times of transition and adjustment they must have asked a thousand questions to which there were no easy answers. I can best verbalize it this way:

Reflection on Transition

"Is this the land where we shall settle, shall settle here to stay?
No freezing storms of ice are drifting, no snow where children play?
Is this the land that has no seasons: summer, winter, spring and fall?
A land where lynx and tigers quiver when wild boars grunt and call?
A land so old, and yet so new; a land exotic, foreign, strange?
A land so different from *Sibir'*. Will we survive this change?"

        Thus they conversed within themselves,
        raised questions without end.
        They contemplated night and day,
        were trying hard to understand.

"Take heart, my soul; my soul, take heart! Thank your almighty God!
He rescued you through Moscow's gates—far, far from Slavgorod.
Come now! It's time to build a dwelling where we can sleep and eat;
a place where we find shelter for weary bodies, tired feet.
A place where we together sit and rest and talk and pray;
a place where parents with their children can laugh and sing and play."

        They went to work, to work they went.
        They went and tackled the unknown.
        They went with courage, not despair.
        They went with God, went not alone.

Four tree trunks serve as corner posts, one with roots still in the ground.
Four beams are laid across the top, still green and natural and round.
The walls are made of split palm trees tied with vines to keep them tight.
The cracks between the halves remain, letting in fresh air and light.
The roof is made of grass and palm leaves to keep the inside dry,
to shelter people in their beds from giant bugs and bats that fly.
In the center of the earthen floor, twelve stones are neatly piled.
The fire's lit for cooking meals; its smoke mosquitoes keeps exiled.

> Such was our home for parents,
> children, relative and friend.
> A home to live. A home to love.
> A home to share in our new land.

During the time we built our house, we were still living in the Sommerkamp Barracks about three kilometers downstream from where our land was located. There was no road, only a narrow *picadão* along the river. To begin with, Father and my brother Heinrich first constructed a primitive one-room shack with a thatched roof and split palm walls, hidden in the forest. It provided temporary shelter and a place where Mother could cook black beans and rice over an open fire. The men cut bamboo culms, palm trees and timber, split logs into planks and boards, and made shingles for a more permanent family dwelling. Mother and my two sisters— Greta, twelve, and Katja, nine—were helping to clear the underbrush. My brother Nikolai at age six was helpful in his own way. The best I could do was to observe the family at work. My sister Maria had stayed in Ibirama, working as a maid in the Meckien household to earn some cash for the family.

As soon as the house was far enough along to be occupied, we took our belongings from the Sommerkamp Barracks and the temporary shack, and moved into our first house on our own piece of land. This house was truly the family's handiwork. We lived in it for eight or nine years. Each time I think about all the experiences we as a family shared in that house, I become quite sentimental. I have seen a thousand houses since then. Some of them were merely shacks along the riverbank, others were like spacious palaces. But none have I seen as attractive as the one we built as pioneers in 1930. By "attractive" I mean neither architectural design nor esthetic beauty. That house never felt the stroke of a paint brush. Neither do I mean interior amenities of luxury and comfort. I simply mean a place we could legitimately call "our own." It was truly the family's handiwork. We had built it with raw materials garnered from the jungle and had done so with our own hands. Not the slightest burden of a mortgage was pressing on our minds. It was the centerpiece of our family during those pioneering years on the Krauel. It was *our* new house. We were thankful for it; I was proud of it.

The house was ten meters (thirty-three feet) long and eight meters (just over twenty-six feet) wide with a lean-to two-and-a-half meters (about eight feet) wide along the lower side. This open veranda with a dirt floor served as kitchen, dining room and sitting area. Since the house was built on the side of a hill, we had to go up four steps into the *groote Schtoaw* (living room) and sleeping area. There were three bedrooms: one for the parents, one for the girls, and one for the boys. Each room had a window with a wooden shutter, but no glass. In the corner of the living room connected to the bedrooms, Father built a stove of sod bricks that served as a closed-in fireplace during the cold, rainy season. That is where we sat when the parents told us stories about life in Siberia and where we had family Bible reading and prayer.

I knew that house like the palm of my hand. I knew every corner of every room and every piece of furniture Father had made by hand—the wardrobe and chest of drawers, the beds and benches, the tables and the stools. As a small boy, I observed every move he made as he measured, sawed, planed and chiseled to fashion handsome masterpieces from crude pieces of wood. I asked a thousand questions in the process. I also knew every crack in the floor and every crevice in the wall. On hot summer days, I lay on my stomach and looked through the crannies in the living room floor to the open space below. That's where the roosters and the chickens and the mother hens with their chicks gathered to rest in the shade. With their beaks ajar, they lapped up the breeze that occasionally moved from one end to the other underneath the elevated floor. It was fascinating to observe how even the tiniest chicks knew their mother by her clucking tone.

Another fascinating place was the attic. We called it *Bähn*. Father made a simple ladder leading from the living room floor to the upstairs. That is where Nikolai and I had our private "tannery," of sorts; that is where we stretched, pinned, and dried the skins of animals we trapped. That's also where we children played on rainy days. My favorite toy was a doll named Isaac, fashioned from what may have been papier mâché. The tragedy was that my dear Isaac had lost part of one leg from the knee down. He was getting old, and his head was beginning to wobble. I remember the sad day when his head fell off and I nearly lost mine out of grief. Enough. Suffice it to say that our first house was a wonderful place—"a place to feel at home." So was our village, as well as our colony with its surrounding wilderness and wonder.

Our colony consisted of three villages extending approximately twenty kilometers along the upper Krauel Valley. Our homestead was in Waldheim, situated between the other two Mennonite villages: Witmarsum to the east and Gnadental to the west, where the river plunged down from the *serra* into a narrow bed meandering eastward through the valley. Waldheim was made up primarily of families who came with the first transport on the Monte Olivia. Each individual tract of land was called a "colony," and the owner of each colony was referred to as a "colonist." In a similar way, the entire settlement was collectively designated as a "colony." Thus our Krauel settlement was actually a colony of colonies owned and operated by colonists.

It seems imperative to clarify a frequent misunderstanding. Some writers, for instance, tend to substitute "Witmarsum" for "Krauel," as though they were identical. While Witmarsum was the commercial and civic center where most business and legal transactions were processed, it was not the name for the Krauel Colony, only for the first of the three villages. When the Mennonites deserted the Krauel Valley between 1949 and 1953, they dissolved the entire settlement in Santa Catarina. One group (including my parents and several siblings with their families) moved south and established *Colônia Nova* near the city of Bagé in the state Rio Grande do Sul. The remaining group moved north, took the name "Witmarsum" with them, and called their colony near the city of Palmeira in the state of Paraná by that name. In the meantime, Witmarsum in the Krauel has become a municipality of the region with the original village as the political center for the municipal offices. It is an interesting phenomenon of history to find in the interior of southern Brazil a municipality with a small city named in memory of Menno Simon's place of birth in the Dutch province of Friesland, even though the present inhabitants have no ethnic, cultural, and religious connection whatsoever with the Menno tribe.

Initially, the Mennonites established two colonies or settlements in Santa Catarina: The Krauel Colony with 150 families, and Stoltz-Plateau with approximately 100 families. This settlement on the high plateau was also called *Auhagen* in honor of Otto Auhagen, the German diplomat who was a key player in helping our people get out of Moscow. Connected by a winding road, the two colonies were about forty-five kilometers apart, but only half that far if we walked via a *picada* through the forest across the *serra*. On such festive occasions as Thanksgiving, the churches often celebrated together. Parents with smaller children took the longer route by wagon, the young people usually walked. That event was always like a picnic for us. Unfortunately, the settlers of Stolz-Plateau saw no hope for survival. Within less than ten years that colony was abandoned, leaving a small remnant of the hardiest souls behind.

These two Mennonite colonies, Krauel and Auhagen, made up only a small part of the larger German colonization project undertaken by the Hanseatic Land Association. The majority were Lutheran and Catholic. We became well acquainted with such colonies as Neuhoffnung *(Nova Esperança)*, Neu Breslau *(Presidente Getulio)*, Dona Emma, and Ibirama. We felt a special kinship with the people in Neuhoffnung. They too had come from the Soviet Union in the 1920s; thus we had a common background. We also shared a common faith with them. Even though they held some convictions with regard to eschatology that differed from ours, there was a strong spiritual affinity that drew us together. From time to time our preachers even exchanged pulpits. We as young people got together to compete on the soccer field, or to visit on such special occasions as Easter, Pentecost and song festivals.

In 1934, thirty-five families with a total of 176 persons came from China to Brazil. They were part of a larger contingent of refugees who had crossed the Amur River to Harbin around the same time that we managed to escape via Moscow to Germany. Some of them had found refuge in the United States in 1932 and others in Paraguay in 1934. While most of the Harbin group settled in Stoltz-Plateau, a number of families came to the Krauel. Initially, they lived with other families until they were able to buy land and build their own homes. The Johann Willemses with their three children lived with us. I was six years old at the time and remember the evening when Father brought them to our house. Mother had prepared a welcome meal and arranged for lodging: the parents slept in the living room, my sisters took Truda Willems into their room, and my brother Nikolai and I shared our room with the boys—Johann and Aaron.

The two families had much in common as they talked about experiences in the Soviet Union, even though they had lived far apart. We were amazed and sometimes saddened by the stories the Willemses told about their flight over the Amur and how they had been able to survive in China. I was particularly moved with compassion when they spoke of incredible hardships along the way: how they suffered starvation, cold, and sickness, and how they had had to bury the dead in the snow, and then keep on moving. Our friendship with the Willems family lasted until they moved to Curitiba.

All along the Rio Krauel were smaller tributaries. The land along these streams was also divided into individual colonies. Witmarsum had three such tributaries: *Tucano Anú, Cambará,* and *Tucaninho*. Our village had only one small tributary called *Tucanobóia* (or simply *Boi,* ox) with four or five single colonies wedged between two *serras*. When my sister Margareta was married to Peter Krüger in 1938, the young couple lived there until the whole Krauel Colony was dissolved in the early 1950s. Gnadental had three tributaries: *Feliz, Catangara,* and *Jacabemba*. I became particularly enamored with the *Feliz*, and that for a special reason.

My brother-in-law Bernhard Esau, who was married to my sister Maria, had an admirable entrepreneurial disposition; he liked to sell and buy or trade and move. When I was about eleven years old he bought a colony at the upper end of the *Feliz*. In his ingenious way, Esau built a modest sawmill and a flour mill. He operated the whole enterprise by a water wheel run by power harnessed from the stream. The place was enclosed by *serras* on three sides; one could not go anywhere, except whence one had come. That far corner became the Esau domicile for a few short years. The place still lingers like a video with sounds and images in my memory bank. I always loved to go there, even if it meant walking at least ten kilometers, regardless of rain or shine.

The *Feliz* was a mere rivulet, originating in a fountain right there in the hollow of the *serra*. Esau's house with a thatched roof and dirt floor stood on the edge of the riverbank next to the mill. The bed of the stream below the dam was rocky, the water shallow, crystal clear, and cold. That was where I loved to play with my niece and nephews, even though they were younger than I. As soon as we were soaking wet—which did not take very long—we had to come and sit around the fire to get dry and warm. Sometimes my sister would bake biscuits from corn flour, stone-ground in their own mill, and brew *mate* (a native tea) or make hot chocolate. Was that ever a treat, especially when she served *Thjarpswrenj* (squash jam) with those fresh biscuits. That gave me enough energy to make it home in about one and a half hours, except in rainy weather or on dark evenings when it took longer.

The social, civic and economic structure of our colony was patterned closely after the system our people were used to in Russia. We had one man known as *Siedlungsleiter,* the equivalent of the *Oberschulze* in Russia or a mayor in the United States and Canada. He represented the interests of our colony at the government level. Of equal importance was the person in charge of our colony cooperative business ventures. It was his job to find markets to sell our products and buy needed merchandise at prices affordable for such a modest peasant society as ours.

Then, too, each village had its own *Schulze.* His responsibility was to look after such village needs as road maintenance and school functions, and to represent common concerns at the colony level. The role of the elder and preacher was not one of authority and power; his duties were preaching, Bible teaching, and caring for the spiritual welfare of the church. Our elders in Brazil were more the servant type, never rising to the prestigious position of the Mennonite elders in the Russian context. We also had our own primary school in each village with instruction from grades one to four. In the early years, the school buildings were used for church services and other meetings. Only in the late 1940s, after a dynamic renewal movement in which many young people and older persons were converted, baptized, and joined the church of their choice, did each of the two major church groups build its own meetinghouse.

——— 10 ———

A Profile of Our Jungle Land

O LORD my God, you are very great.
You make springs pour water into the ravines;
They give water to all the beasts of the field;
The birds of the air nest by the waters;
You water the mountains from your upper chambers;
You make grass grow for the cattle,
and plants for man to cultivate,
bringing forth food from the earth.
—Adapted from *Psalm 104*

Our colony was situated in a narrow valley extending some twenty kilometers along the meandering Krauel, which forges its path about midway between two mountain ranges called *serras*. The designation for that type of mountains is derived from the Portuguese word for "saw." From a distance these mountain ranges look like a gigantic saw with its teeth pointing upwards. The two *serras* by which the Krauel River and valley are hemmed in are, in fact, a row of giant teeth nature has formed, protruding from the jaw of a much, much larger *serra*.

What makes the geography of Santa Catarina both peculiar and unique are its jungles and its mountains. Wedged between the states of Rio Grande do Sul to the south and Paraná to the north, its massive jungles cover the entire distance from the Atlantic Ocean in the east to the Argentinian border in the west. The other phenomenon is the direction in which the *serras* are situated. While the colossal *Serra do Mar* in Rio Grande do Sul and Paraná runs parallel to the Atlantic coast, in Santa Catarina it breaks up into two ranges: *Serra do Mar* and *Serra Geral*. Both serras curve sharply eastward and descend rapidly toward the Atlantic, except for the last eighty kilometers nearing the eastern shore of the Atlantic. The Rio Itajaí is navigable for this entire distance, and the land along both sides of the winding riverbed is quite flat. That also makes it extremely prone to flooding. The geography of Santa Catarina makes the interior accessible only from the direction of the Atlantic Ocean, and even then not without difficulties.

At the time we moved there, the Krauel Colony was a rather tiny and isolated piece of earth on our planet. Situated between latitudes 25° and 30° south of the equator, the Krauel has a subtropical climate. While the change in the seasons is negligible, there are noticeable differences between summer and winter. In winter the temperature occasionally drops to freezing. I recall those cold winter months of July and August when the temperature dropped far below the comfort range. The sun hid behind the clouds for weeks on end, unable to penetrate those dark heavy floating blankets or radiate a few degrees of warming comfort on those shivering barefoot pilgrims below. No matter how we longed for a warm spot, it was hard to find. Our houses had only single walls with many cracks. Very few had any kind of interior heating. At times it was so cold that our bananas, oranges, and tangerines suffered severe frost damage. Even such staple crops as sugarcane froze in the field, causing serious feed shortage for our livestock.

But in summer it was different. Temperatures ranged for weeks from 35° to 40° C. (about 95 to 112° F.) with a humidity frequently above 90 percent. Quite often we went to bed tired and wet with perspiration. Since the nights seldom cooled off, we rose in the morning nearly as tired as when we had gone to bed. What made the climate periodically bearable, even quite pleasant, were the tropical downpours with thunder and lightning that made our houses rattle and the beds vibrate. On a typically hot and sultry afternoon we sometimes had two or three thunderstorms, with rain pouring from the water-laden clouds with such force that a flood could come within hours. This was particularly hard for the farmers. Since most of our fields were on hillsides, these tropical rains caused irreparable erosion and damage to the land.

During our later years as missionaries in Blumenau I usually called on people in the afternoon, either in their homes or at their workplace. My means of transportation was a bicycle. Whenever I saw thunderheads towering upward from behind the *serras,* I knew that I had only fifteen to twenty minutes to find shelter before rain or hail came down with a fury. Many times I was caught in the storm, got soaking wet, and was forced to ride home without accomplishing my mission. In the hot summer months, in both the Krauel and in Blumenau, these tropical rains went as fast as they came.

As I think about the years at the Krauel, the first image that appears on the screen of my mind is the jungle with all its charm and attraction. That is where native vegetation grew in its original and organic best. It was also where insects and reptiles, birds and beasts in multifarious varieties found their food and shelter and their needed rest. When I was in the second grade, we had colored charts and maps, showing the wildlife of Santa Catarina. I saw many of those birds and animals in real life and was so mesmerized with those pictures that I was determined to make a drawing of each one of them, particularly those beautiful birds. Unfortunately, a mandate from the government forced our school to be closed the following year. That ended my formal education in Brazil; but it did not quench my thirst for further learning nor my desire to expand and deepen my acquaintance with the plant and animal life of the region. While that interest has never disappeared, it has been overshadowed by other ambitions and thus remained largely unrealized.

In later years I often traveled by bus or car along the modern roads and highways which by then had been built through jungle lands across the deep ravines and the high *serras* of Santa Catarina and neighboring states. Never have I ceased to marvel at the variety of trees and underbrush that line each side of the road like a thick, dark green wall. The sight always brings back memories of the years I used to live there with my parents, sisters, and brothers. I always had a paradoxical feeling of dread and admiration, an ever-present sensation that never vanished from the time we arrived there in 1930. It always seemed that the dark, dense shroud was concealing a thousand mysteries which had to be explored.

In his history of the Mennonites in Brazil, Peter Klassen quotes from Maria Kahle's *Deutsche Heimat in Brasilien* in which she writes of the "immensity and gloominess of those mysterious jungles of Brazil." I know firsthand what she means. I know what jungle is and looks and smells like. I even know what it feels and tastes like. Each one of my God-given senses has been aroused and tried by living there.

One has to bear in mind that a Brazilian jungle is not like a European or North American forest, no matter how lush and green and thick the forest growth may be. The only likeness the two have is color. Anyone approaching the rim of a jungle can easily be overcome by the frightening hostility with which those nontransparent walls seem to stare at every intruder who dares to cross its mysterious threshold from the outside. Such were the first impressions we had when we got to the Krauel. "We had no idea," my parents said, "what the real jungle would be like." My father had worked for nearly seven years in the Russian forests, both in the Ukraine and in Siberia, but "never have I seen anything resembling the rain forest of our colony at the Krauel," he explained.

There is the thickness of the undergrowth with its thousand thorny tentacles straining in every direction and vying for the tiniest piece of space cracked open by the light of the sun. There are the creeping and crawling vines and the climbing, twining rope-like woody lianas winding themselves around each tree and shrub within reach. There are also the strangest-looking, root-like tentacles, thick as a man's arm and strong as a cable. Some of them are rooted stocks draped like stalactites from upper branches in the trees to the ground below. Similarly, there are the lianas dangling in the air like a disarray of tangled ropes with a fibrous network of roots firmly nestled in a parasitic plant that thrives on sap which it takes from a branch high up in a tree. As soon as such hanging roots reach the ground they throw out their own new rootstock, become firmly anchored in the soil, and then venture out on a second phase of growth. In this aggressive process they begin their lethal action of wrapping themselves in an upward direction around the trees that stand close by. Even the biggest jungle giant cannot ward off the slow but steady strangling, squeezing, sucking force with which such mighty parasites go to work until their host is overcome by the relentless choking pressure. It may take a hundred years or more; time is of little consequence for such ancient jungle growth.

The density of growth and foliage reduces the amount of sunshine to a twilight, allowing just enough illumination to penetrate the darkness, and sufficient heat to sustain life and promote growth in the humid, broiling atmosphere below. At ground level the jungle appears equally impenetrable. Such domestic animal as a horse, mule, sheep or steer, will intuitively not venture into the jungle on its own. It knows the danger and potential harm that lurks behind those dense walls of nature. Small wonder that explorers of the region sometimes called it the "green hell."

And yet there is something enchanting and charming about all that. I always found jungle growth most captivating. As far back as I can remember, I was charmed by it. It had a natural beauty and enchantment, an appeal all its own. It provided for us children and teenagers opportunities for exciting exploration and fun. The vines and lianas which I just mentioned are a case in point. We used them for climbing up to the branches of trees we could otherwise not reach. We looped and knotted selected vines to make trapezes and swings. It was an exhilarating thrill to grab a long, strong vine and swing across a ravine. Admittedly, such flights could be hazardous, depending on how we landed on the other side.

Equipped with a bow in my left hand and a quiver full of arrows, a *funda* (a slingshot made from two equally long and strong rubber straps with a leather pouch at one end and the other tied to a forked twig with a handle) and stones in my pocket, a *facão* in a sheath on the left side, and a dog as companion and guardian, I spent countless hours roaming and exploring. I knew my way around and usually found what I was looking for. I soon learned that the *picadas* of such animals as *cutias, pacas* and *pacaranas* (small, but desirable game in the region) were relatively easy to find and to follow. Such *picadas* were fairly safe and nearly always led to a brook or fresh water fountain. That is where animals and some of the most exotic birds in their splashing feathery color came to drink. Occasionally, a spectacular drama unfolded, especially when the birds engaged in a flirtatious ceremony, displayed plumes of incredible beauty. Others, in

A Profile of Our Jungle Land   75

laying claim to their territory and demanding exclusive rights, had to fight off the intruders. I found those bird fights delightful. The feathers they lost in the process became a prized treasure for wearing on a Sunday hat or on the left lapel of a Sunday jacket.

I was also utterly fascinated by the common black monkeys called *macacos*. They lived in large groups, stayed high up in the trees, and held together as though they belonged to organized families or clans. They seemed to be a kind of migrant "monkey society," traveling long distances without ever touching the ground. Only when they wanted to add corn or squash to their diet of wild fruits and leaves did they come down from their elevated abode. Whenever that happened, our crops suffered severe damage and we, the farmers, great loss. As a rule, however, they stayed in the jungle network. I often watched them jump and swing from tree to tree, play and fight, shriek and whistle as though trying to outdo each other. The only time during the day they became completely silent was when the great white Brazilian eagle circled overhead, mimicking the whistling sound of the monkeys to a perfect pitch. Once that predator had surveyed the territory, it pulled in its wings and came swooping down with the speed of lightning out of the sky toward one of the young sitting by itself on the periphery of the monkey clan. An eagle's attack always gave rise to unusual excitement and great lament over the loss of one of their family members.

Then there were the big, brown monkeys, commonly called "howling monkey." They were more sedentary and often lived as entire families in the huge *figueiras* with enormous branches and a rich supply of fruit. Unlike the smaller black monkeys, these larger primates bellowed in a chorus-like manner. Although their songs clearly lacked melodious finesse, at least to the human ear, the "singers" seemed to know what they were doing: they started and stopped all at the same time. What I found particularly interesting was how they disciplined their mischievous young. They actually spanked them with their hands while uttering a series of scolding complaints. As soon as they finished the disciplinary action, the elders took their hurting children into their arms and held them against their bodies.

Of course, the jungle was also teeming with insects: wasps and bumblebees, horseflies and mosquitoes of all kinds and sizes—including the malaria-carrying mosquito. They were most annoying, to say the least. But to watch the rare display and drama of exotic birds and butterflies, or the monkey families in the trees above and the lonely three-toed sleeping sloth hanging on a branch below, all in their natural habitat, was partial compensation for the discomfort caused by nasty insects. Another thing I enjoyed on my excursions was picking wild fruit or berries and engaging in "primitive hunting." Seldom did I return home empty-handed. My mother was somewhat apprehensive when I stayed away for hours on end and always glad when I returned unharmed. She was also pleased when I came back with a bush hen or two attached to my belt. She welcomed such spoils as a supplement to our meager diet—except once.

The only time Mother complained about my prey was when I brought home two or three *sabias,* worm-eating birds, resembling the North American robin. For the first time in her life Mother cooked sabiá soup. It was also the last time. To give the soup more content and flavor, she added some rice and the usual herbs from field or garden. The soup had more flavor than expected, a distinct and pungent flavor; but no one in our family considered it a gourmet dish. The Brazilian *sabiá* is known for its beautiful singing and colorful feathers, but hardly for its good taste. If the *sabiá* were mentioned in the Bible, it would certainly not be listed among the clean birds kosher for human consumption. I never brought home another *sabiá* with the intent of having it cooked. I did, however, gather wild fruit in bamboo containers to take home.

The most common fruits, nuts, and pods in our area were the *pinhão, pitanga, jabuticaba, maracujá, ingá, araçá,* and *curitiça*. The *pinhão* is a nut of the *pinheiro* and grows in clusters the size of a medium-sized soccer ball. As soon as the cluster matures, it falls to the ground and breaks open, and the nuts can be gathered in large quantities. We ate them either boiled or roasted. The *araçá* is a tree fruit resembling a small yellow plum. It is delicious, but not easily accessible. Monkeys and birds were tough competitors. Once they had garnered the fruit, there was little left for us to glean. We had better luck with *jabuticaba* and *maracujá,* which grow on shrubs and vines respectively. These fruits are not only delicious for eating when freshly picked, but also excellent for baking and for making jelly and marmalade.

In retrospect, I recognize that some of those sights, sounds and smells I found so fascinating must have seemed truly ugly, odd and strange to any foreigner who ventured out to visit the Krauel; but for me they were nothing more than common, ordinary aspects of the environment that made up my life. It was a place that offered me solitude for silence, and all the ingredients needed for an introspective, sentimental young mystic as well as for a restless visionary with the aspirations of an idealist. (Of course, I knew nothing about either of those movements in history.) There was something about that place that bound me to its very soul. As far as I was concerned, it was truly "a place to feel at home." That may have been sheer naïveté on my part, but I was growing up a man committed to the Krauel with its simple way of life. I value that place and cherish those years. To borrow a phrase or two from C. S. Lewis, I would say that my homey-sentimental feeling for the Krauel was a genuine "love for home [and] love of old acquaintances, of familiar sights, sounds and smells."

More than fifty years have passed since I left that place in 1949. Since then, I have been exposed to immeasurable influences and forces that have reshaped and restructured, remade and remolded my perception and understanding of the larger *kosmos*. It has been a total intellectual and cultural metamorphosis. I suddenly found myself in an environment that was as different from that of the Krauel as night is different from day. My world had to become bigger; my horizon had to expand. If I wanted to survive and be useful in the kingdom of God, then my worldview had to become grounded in a nonnegotiable core of biblical and theological truths as the trustworthy norm for living the life of Christian discipleship in any given culture. That has remained my ongoing challenge. Yet those twenty years of living in the remote jungle of the Krauel Colony have remained an inestimable phase of my life for shaping my understanding of service and ministry in later years. I am profoundly grateful for that experience.

11

Pioneering Ventures on a Jungle Farm

So the LORD God said to Adam,
"Cursed is the ground because of you.
It will produce thorns and thistles for you,
and you will eat the plants of the field.
By the sweat of your brow you will eat your food
until you return to the ground , since from it you were taken."
– Adapted excerpts from *Genesis 3*

The charm and enchantment of the jungle, which I truly loved, was somewhat diminished by the fact that the jungle land was also our farm land on which we depended for sustenance. Hidden in its dark, green growth lingered destructive elements that reduced rather than increased both quality and quantity of our potential harvest. If "thorns and thistles" are a sign of God's curse after the Fall of Adam and Eve, then the ground on which we had settled bore all the marks of our Creator's displeasure. That is why domesticated livestock would rarely venture into the jungle. For thorns and thistles grew everywhere. Some were harmless, except for the pain caused by the prick or the sting. Others were poisonous and caused severe infections. Yet there was also the promise that mankind would "eat the plants of the field," even if "by the sweat of the brow." My parents were able to compare pioneering in Siberia in 1910 with their experiences several decades later in Brazil. The differences were decidedly greater than the similarities as I will show by delineating four areas related to pioneering ventures on a jungle farm.

It was no simple task to convert a piece of jungle land into a cultivated field for planting and sowing in the hope of a harvest. The natives called the initial stages of that process *roçar mato,* which means to "raze the forest." The German colonists in the region spoke of it as *Waldschlagen.* Since in those pioneering days very few of our people knew Portuguese, and not many Mennonites used High German outside of the church context, we devised our own expression and talked about *Wold schloane.* A literal translation would be "hitting the forest" or jungle. That implied demolition of the forest in preparation for cultivation and planting.

Our implements to clear the jungle consisted of three basic hand tools: the first was the *foice,* which we called *Feistel*. This was a sharp steel instrument made in the shape of a question mark. The cutting blade was seven to ten centimeters wide and twenty-five to thirty centimeters long, attached to a wooden handle approximately one meter in length. Then we had the *machado*. That was similar to any steel ax used in Europe, the Americas and other parts of the world, except that the cutting edge was sharp as a razor, wide and rounded in the shape of a new moon; it could be lethal in the hands of an inexperienced woodsman. We also had an *enxada,* a hoe. While we did not use the hoe for clearing the jungle, it was useful for planting, weeding and cultivating. Everything was done by manual labor.

Perhaps the hardest part was *Wold schloane,* or hitting the jungle. And hit it we did with a vengeance. In doing so, we were not only destroying underbrush and trees, we were also unsettling the natural environment for wildlife in the area. However, our alternatives were few: either we cut down the jungle to plant for harvest, or we starve. We chose to survive and took on the jungle with our own hands. I will put it this way:

Wold schloane

Now go to work! This jungle has been standing for a thousand years.
Face the challenge, grab your tools and leave behind your fears.

That's how duty calls and urges, urges them to move with haste,
lest the rainy season stop them and their crops will go to waste.

How those ancient giants tremble from the roots to crowning height
when the valiant foreign stranger swings the ax with all his might.
Hundred vassals strung together with a net of creeping vines,
each of them must crack and falter when a giant king reclines.
They come down with crashing thunder. Awesome is their splitting fall!
Birds are flying, reptiles fleeing, insects fluttering, big and small.
Even snakes are slithering slowly from their secret habitat:
jararacas, anacondas, vicious vipers, slim and flat.
In defiance they are hissing, moving, striking in despair.
But their venom is quite harmless as it sprays into thin air.
Look, a porcupine comes rolling on its sharp, erectile quills;
rolling fast and ever faster down the mountains and the hills.
Lo, the bullfrogs. How they're jumping! Like balloons they do inflate.
Yet as tree and branch are crashing these poor creatures are too late.

Thus these foreign settlers labor—labor hard to clear their land.
And the tools which they are using cause them blisters in each hand.

Finally, it's time for planting on this rough and rugged field.
In faith and hope they wait and pray for a modest harvest yield.

There were at least four or five phases in making a *roça*, i.e., preparing a piece of jungle land for planting. First, we carefully staked out the area that was to be cleared. The choice was determined by the type of crop we wanted to plant. For *mandioca* or *aipim* we chose areas that were not on steep mountain sides, lest the tuber be laid bare by erosion and cease growing. Corn was less sensitive in that respect.

Once we had decided on the area to be cleared, we cut down all the underbrush, such as wild shrubbery and young trees, the thorn bushes and a thousand different kinds of vines and creepers and every variety of bamboo before tackling the bigger trees. That was tedious work, often done with the help of women and of children old enough to handle a *foice*.

The third phase was cutting down the trees with an ax. That was hard work and dangerous besides. I have records that speak of trees thirty to forty meters high, reaching five to six meters in diameter. We had some giants on our land that were about forty meters high, but not that thick. Very often the branches of those big trees were entangled with vines and creepers, strong as nylon rope. Even if we had cut them off at ground level, they were still wrapped around the branches and held an entire grove of trees entangled in their snares. The woodsmen had to calculate rather carefully, cut every tree at a certain angle, and then throw a giant against the whole entangled grove, hoping that all the trees would fall simultaneously. The danger was always real. Branches often tore off and catapulted in unexpected directions. Accidents happened, but relatively few fatalities. It usually took ten to twelve days to clear one hectare of land.

The next phase consisted of drying and burning. Once the forest was cut down, it was left lying for weeks to dry. As a rule, we lacked neither sunshine, nor hot weather and wind. On a hot afternoon when the wind was not too strong, the neighbors came together for the event of burning the *roça*. The fire was set along the edge. At first the tiny flames flickered as though hesitating to take on the challenge of burning up the huge area of fine shrubbery and big trees with all their branches that lay prostrate on the ground. Yet it is in the nature of fire to generate its own wind and heat. Those feeble, flickering flamelets quickly gained sufficient energy to charge with a fury and fervor awesome to behold. The dry, hollow bamboo tubes not only intensified the heat to the level of an inferno, but also unleashed explosive sounds that were more like gunshots on a battlefield than the fire of a *roça* surrounded by the quiet, peaceful jungle. The problem was that only the dry leaves, some undergrowth, and the lighter branches were consumed by the fire; the tree trunks and heavier branches remained intact.

Finally, when the fire was burnt out and the blackened *roça* had sufficiently cooled off to be walked on with bare feet, we chopped off as many branches from the bigger trees as possible, gathered the smaller logs which we could manually move, made huge piles, and set them on fire to make room for planting. Such woodpiles burned for many hours with glowing coals remaining under the ashes for days. These ashes posed a real danger, as I once discovered in a *hot* experience that I will tell later. The stumps and trunks remained immoveable. Some of them eventually decayed; others seemed to be indestructible and lay on the *roça* for years. We simply planted between and around them. This was not to my father's liking. He always took pride in planting perfectly straight rows in every direction. He could do that on the open fields of the Kulunda Steppe in Siberia, but not on the rugged terrain of the subtropical rain forest. Here one could not plant in straight rows, only in patches.

As my parents had done in Siberia, so we as family did now in Brazil: we always planted in hope for a harvest. Because of the generosity and compassion of the Red Cross of Germany, the Mennonites of Holland, and Mennonite benevolent organizations in Europe and America, we received financial assistance to buy the most needed supplies until we had our first harvest. Before we could even think of planting, however, we had to come to terms with the fact that it would be neither wheat nor rye, barley or alfalfa. Our staple crops, at least that first year, would be *batata doce* (a starchy sweet potato), *feijão* (black beans), and *milho,* a kind of corn that grows giant stocks but seldom produces more than one small ear on each. *Milho* is what we used as feed for domesticated animals and for grinding flour for our baking needs. In subsequent years we also grew other varieties of beans, tubers, sugar cane, tropical fruits, and vegetables.

As we were soon to discover, the land that had produced a luscious jungle, that no one ever harvested, refused to produce equally luscious crops for needy peasants. Once foreign settlers had stripped the original vegetation and planted agricultural products of their own choice, the soil seemed to close its fertile womb and to withhold from the peasants their due reward for hard labor. That was partly due to the fact that we did not know the makeup of our land from the river to the *serra*. The soil near the river lacked the quality needed to grow corn. The closer we came to the *serra*, the thicker was the layer of humus retaining moisture and the more productive the ground proved to be. Initially, our people did not know that and planted corn where they should have planted *aipim*.

Now and then there was a year in which the crops turned out quite well. Much depended on the quality of seed we used for planting. Weather, wind and water also played a significant role, as did the amount of work we were able to invest in controlling weeds and destructive animals and birds. Such rodents as mice and rats were particularly clever, sniffing their way from plant hole to plant hole and feasting on the tender kernels as soon as they began to sprout. The jungle population in general had little concern for the peasant and could strip the fields bare before the fruit was ripe. There were hosts of competitive harvesters that intensified our already intense concern for survival. We simply had to accept the reality that competition with the new environment was as fierce as the soil was frugal: the jungle farm would probably never deliver extraordinary treasures into our nearly empty baskets. That knowledge, however, offered little relief. Our primary concern remained that the land would yield sufficient food for the family table in the kitchen and the fodder trough in the barn. Anything above that basic need was a special bonus. I recall how my father so fervently prayed for daily bread, how he gave thanks to God for each meal, and for a good harvest of *aipim* and black beans.

Aipim or *mandioca* was on the average not only our best crop, but also a versatile product with many uses. The plants are from one to two meters high, depending on the variety. Each plant has three to five single stems branching out on top. The foliage is tender and desirable for feed. Each plant also produces tubers of varying sizes, weighing up to three kilos (over six pounds) per tuber. One drawback was that it took at least two years for a crop to mature. That meant that we did not harvest any *mandioca* the first two or three years. Our first black bean harvest, however, was good. Yet neither man nor beast can live on beans alone. Some of our people became discouraged and wondered if they would make it. A few families gave up and moved away. But Mennonites are resourceful people, even in the jungle. Before long they discovered improved seed varieties. Some new types of *mandioca* were especially delicious when cooked, fried or baked. Next to black beans with rice and cornmeal, *aipim* was the staple food for the colonists as well as for their fowl and domestic animals.

Already the second year was considerably better. On 21 June 1931, the church in Witmarsum, and on 5 July the same year, our church in Waldheim held their first Harvest Thanksgiving celebrations in their respective village schools. From that time forward Harvest Thanksgiving was always a special day for young and old. Each family brought samples of products to the school house as a token of what God had allowed to grow on their land. That included such common items as squash, cucumbers, black beans, and corn. We also learned to grow such exotic tubers as *cará*, which renders a soft, slimy-looking starch used as a cohesive ingredient for baking breads and biscuits from corn flour, the huge *yama* tubers to feed our pigs, and the smaller *taya* roots for human consumption. These never gained the reputation of a favorite dish, but they provided variety.

Thanksgiving celebrations always reflected a mood of joy and gratitude. The preachers challenged us to see God's greatness in creation and his kindness in provision: the land had yielded its fruit to meet our basic needs. The choir sang jubilant songs of harvest and thanksgiving. Children and young people recited poems and Bible verses related to the occasion. Already the day before, the menfolk set up tables and benches and the womenfolk baked and prepared the best they had under prevailing conditions. Food was simple, but enough for every guest to share a common meal as part of the celebration, just as our people had done in Siberia a few short years earlier.

In the afternoon the mood of celebration was somewhat different from that of the forenoon: much time was spent in intercession and prayer for those who had stayed back in the Soviet Union. There was hardly a family who did not have immediate members or close relatives who either had chosen to stay behind, hoping that conditions would improve, or who had been apprehended in Moscow and transported into the unknown. While the news of their plight in prisons and labor camps was sparse, whatever information we did receive was less than encouraging. In fact, it was heartbreaking, a sobering reminder of what might have happened to us if we had not been able to escape. Now we were free to plant and to harvest and to celebrate God's goodness, whereas our people in Russia had nothing—except a harvest of suffering, sorrow, and starvation.

Our pioneering experiences on the jungle farm were not without major hardships; yet we were fortunate to grow food to eat and felt compelled to count our blessings. A fascinating element of jungle vegetation we had to cope with was the variety of bamboo native in our region. As I grew up I learned to know the usefulness as well as the nuisance of the different kinds on our land. Bamboo added a unique aspect to jungle growth I found especially attractive. Hardly ever did I find a stock growing in isolation. Bamboo tends to grow in patches with hundreds of culms solidly lodged in a root system that invades large areas of soil below the surface. Most culms are hollow; some are woody and solid. They grow so closely together that only the smallest and slimmest animals, mostly the rodent and reptile types, can squeeze in for shelter.

In later life I read books on bamboo and was not surprised to learn that botanists and biologists have identified more than 1,200 varieties growing around the world. Some scientists spend a lifetime studying these peculiar jungle grasses. After saying everything they know, they are still confused about this giant jungle grass which they call "a plant of mystery and wonder." What leaves scientists no less baffled than it left us perplexed was in the early 1940s when we experienced the flowering cycle which I can best describe as bane and blessing of blooming bamboo.

The three main varieties of bamboo on our land were *bambu imperial* or *taboca gigante*, *bambu japonés*, and *bambu azul*. The gigantic imperial bamboo often reached thirty-five meters (120 feet) in height. Its green and shiny culms consisted of hollow internodes of various lengths joined by hard, solid nodes complemented by decorative foliage. Since the joints were thick and sturdy and the space between them long and hollow, the tubes could be used for storing different products. Natives used them even for cooking by placing them on heated stones away from direct flames. Some of the giant tubes could also be cut to size and used as drinking cups, resembling modern mugs without the handle. People often split the culm in half, shaved out the nodes and used it as an open water line to lead water from a natural fountain to drinking troughs for cattle or even into the house as running water. This type of bamboo thrived best near the *serras* where the layer of humus was quite thick. The *bambu japonés* with its thin, smooth and solid culms could be used to build chicken fences and a host of other structures on the farm. Then there was the *bambu azul*, the most common in our area. We used it in many different ways: as building material, for basket weaving, making traps, and much more. The phenomenal aspect of this particular species was its heavy seed-bearing capacity: only once in thirty to thirty-six years. That was truly a mystery and wonder.

German and Polish colonists who had lived in Santa Catarina much longer than we predicted a harvest of bamboo seeds for the early 1940s with potentially serious consequences. They were right. I recall how apprehensive they were when they talked about the coming "bamboo catastrophe," as they referred to it. We found it hard to believe what some of those seasoned colonists said, nor did we understand what they meant. We soon found out. While I do not recall the exact time, I do remember the event. It takes at least three years for the *bambu azul* to complete its seed-bearing cycle. A year or two before the blooming season actually started, we noticed unusually vigorous growth. The foliage turned dark green and luscious. The underground root system spread in all directions, developing new rhizomes and throwing out new shoots everywhere. After a relatively short blooming season, heads appeared, looking like wheat ears, only shorter. It seemed as though there were no tares, only full ears for a rich harvest. However, there was no one to bring in the crop, except the birds and rodents and other jungle creatures, that must have multiplied more than a hundredfold within a year or two. We used as much seed as possible to feed our livestock, but only until it fell to the ground. Then came the aftermath of a crop wasting away on the humid jungle floor.

Pioneering Ventures on a Jungle Farm

We learned rather quickly what our seasoned peasant friends had meant when they spoke about serious consequences. On the one hand, the great abundance of bamboo seeds engendered a dramatic increase in the rodent population of the area; on the other hand, we noticed a corresponding increase in poisonous snakes that fed on the rodents. Obviously, neither the one nor the other was particularly beneficial to our existence. On the contrary: rodents and other types of wildlife that had multiplied during the blooming season were running out of food and began to starve en masse, causing an unbearable stench in some areas of the forest. In addition, they invaded our barns, even our homes, in search for food. When we began planting corn that year, these creatures claimed every kernel we put into the ground, and the snakes became increasingly aggressive. It was like a plague, reminiscent of the plagues in Egypt. But there was a blessing in all of this: blooming bamboo came only once during our time in the Krauel.

As soon as the bamboo plants had shed their seeds, they began to dry up. Within about six months every stock of every larger patch throughout the entire region had wilted, dried and died. Even the roots decayed and eventually turned into mulch. *Bambu azul* is extremely combustible when dry. The mature culms contain expandable fumes in their hollow internodes between the joints and can turn into virtual powder kegs. Although we had frequent fires during this time, they were usually restricted to areas of thick bamboo growth. The rest of the forest remained unaffected because of the green foliage and the prevailing high humidity. That must be seen as nothing less than a remarkable balance of nature put in place by our Creator.

I must also mention that there was much more than thorns and thistles and innumerable bamboo groves that made "the densest, darkest jungle in the Brazilian wilderness" both mysterious and enchanting. In the process of razing the forest in preparation for planting, we discovered wood of worth and wonder. This wood turned out to be a redemptive factor for our existence.

Since we had bought land from the Hanseatic Land Association, and since we had the reputation of being trustworthy people, the German government was willing to advance the money for our fare in order that we could embark on the long journey across the ocean. The agreement was, as I understand it, that Germany would settle the account with the shipping company and, together with Holland, would initially subsidize our living costs, so that we could establish our homes, work on the land, build roads, and become self-sufficient as soon as possible. It was also understood and agreed that we should be able to generate adequate funds from the crops we would harvest to repay the government its generous loans toward ocean fare and land purchase. The major resource to do so, we were led to believe, would come from the jungle itself: we were to harvest special wood, including precious and semiprecious varieties, and sell it on the market for export.

The intention on our part to pay our debt was genuine; but the outcome for the real estate agency must have been disappointing. The only extant record shows that in 1938 our people, collectively, made one payment on the ocean fare. With the outbreak of World War II the books were closed, though some continued to make payments on their land. My father was one of them. Even if he may have paid only a portion of the ocean fare, he did everything possible to pay in full the thirty hectares of jungle land we had bought.

The most desirable wood for sale value came from such trees as the *imbuia, jacarandá, peroba, canela prêta, canela sassafrás,* and *cedrão (cedro).* The *cedrão,* a broad leafed cedar that yielded beautiful red and pink patterned wood used for fine furniture, was always in demand. Every cedar we found on our land, Father delivered to a special mill owned and operated by the Eichinger family in Ibirama. After receiving his money, he immediately went to the office of the Hanseatic Land Association and made another payment.

I vividly recall the occasion when Father made the last payment (I believe it was in 1945). He had taken a load of cedar logs to the Eichinger Mill in Ibirama where the Hanseatic Land Association had its headquarters. That was about sixty-five kilometers from our village. The roads were extremely poor. In fair weather the round trip took two full days with two, three or four horses pulling the wagon bearing a load of one or two logs, depending on size and estimated weight. It was completely dark by the time he came home. My brother and I unharnessed the horses, gave them water and feed, and went to the kitchen where Mother had prepared a hot meal. Before we sat down to eat, Father broke the news with a big smile on his face: *"Fondoag hab etj de latzte Laundschuld betoalt."* (Today I have made the last payment on our land debt.) What a relief that was for all of us.

The most common tree in our area to yield large quantities of soft lumber for building material was the *pinheiro* or *araucária.* A mature *pinheiro* with a trunk of at least one meter in diameter standing straight as a plumb line, was delightful to behold. These towering giants surpassed all jungle growth as though they wanted to show off their huge, evergreen umbrella-like crowns to the other more humble species. I clearly remember the fate of one such *pinheiro* on our land.

My father and brother Heinrich had cleared the jungle from our house all the way to the river. About three hundred meters from the house they carefully cleaned the debris around a giant *pinheiro* to save it from the fatal blow of the ax and potential damage by fire when burning the *roça.* Standing all by itself on an elevation, this tall tree was a majestic sight. Father wanted to save it for the time when my brother would get married; he calculated that this giant would render enough lumber to build a modest house for Heinrich, with some left over for sale. But what no one had counted on was the destructive force of nature. Lightning struck, sheared off all the branches on one side, and tore a huge slab out of the trunk from top to bottom. As we stood there the next morning bemoaning damage and loss, my brother-in-law, Kornelius Funk, thoughtfully said, "We can only thank God that lightning did not strike our homes. We live so close by."

12

Insights from Old Letters

God is our mighty fortress,
always ready to help in time of trouble.
Nations are in a rage! Kingdoms crumble!
God raises his voice and the earth itself melts.
The LORD All-Powerful is with us.
The God of Jacob is our fortress.
—My paraphrase from *Psalm 46*

The contents of a letter become more lucid when one knows something about the person who wrote it and the context in which it was written. That is especially the case with letters from generations past. In the 1920s and 1930s my parents corresponded with close relatives, including some who lived in the United States. In 1879 my mother's aunt, Anna Bärg, sister to my maternal grandmother, Maria (Bärg) Kröker, emigrated together with my grandparents from Zagradovka in the Ukraine to Buhler, Kansas. Before long, Anna fell in love with Jakob Nickel, also a recent immigrant from Russia. The two got engaged. When my grandparents moved back to Russia in 1881, Anna decided to stay in the United States and marry her dear Jakob. As I have pointed out in the introduction, the Nickel family corresponded with my parents, first in Russia, then also in Brazil. Arnold Nickel, grandson of Jakob and Anna, inherited an impressive volume of old letters, some written by my parents. When we moved to Fresno in 1968, we became friends with the Arnold Nickels, who were anxious to have us read those old German letters neatly written in the Gothic script. I have translated several of those that give authentic insight into my own experiences during our pioneering years in Brazil.

Two Letters from My Parents, 1932

Both letters are in one envelope addressed to Jakob and Anna Nickel, Buhler, Kansas. Although each letter is written on a separate sheet of paper, there is only one signature for both. Father begins and Mother concludes. I will first present the letter from Father.

Waldheim, 13 July 1932.

Dear Uncle and Aunt! For quite some time I have wanted to write to you and your dear children. Yet nothing has become of it until today. I have actually no good reason for not writing sooner, but I do have excuses. For one thing, we are here always very busy. To settle in the jungle takes a great deal of effort, much energy, health and hard work. Besides that, I must admit that I am lethargic when it comes to writing letters. But the opposite is true when it comes to reading letters. The letters we receive are being read over and over again.

But now before I continue I want to wish all of you out yonder good health for body and soul, which we together with our dear children are enjoying to this day. Thanks and praise be to our God.

We have received your letter as well as the card with the invitation to your golden wedding anniversary. Thank you very much for both. We really appreciate it that you have thought of us and invited us. Even though the invitation came late, we would have loved to be there. Of course, that is impossible. But we would be very happy to see a photograph of your family.

Now I would like to tell a little bit about the things we are doing out here. We are here in the midst of winter. June, July and August are our winter months. In July we are already hard at work on the land and in August we begin to plant. In some areas people begin planting in July, but that is too early for us. Even in August we can still get frost which is very harmful for the young corn plants. We are still hard at work clearing some more jungle. In a couple of days we will have cleared 2.5 hectares (5.5 acres). Then we wish for dry weather so that we can burn the *roça*. The more we can burn of the fine underbrush and tree branches with all their foliage, the less work we have to clean up what we have chopped down. A strong fire also kills some of the wild seeds in the ground and helps to control the weeds, but enhances crop growth. At present we have a lot of rain. The rainfall is generally quite heavy in our area. But that is what we need. If the summers are dry, then everything we have planted suffers greatly. Last year we had a fairly good corn crop, but not enough for bread and feed. The wild pigs have destroyed much of our crop. They always come in large herds. Once they know where the corn is, they come back again and again. The parrots, too, never miss out on a good meal in our fields. They also take more than we want them to take.

Planting season begins in August and goes right through until Christmas. In September we already have to hoe every day so that the weeds don't grow over everything we have planted. For as soon as it gets warmer the weeds grow unbelievably thick and fast. That makes life extremely busy—day in and day out from early morning to late in the evening. In Russia it was not like that, especially not in Siberia where we lived for the last 20 years. By the time when the first snow came in October or November we had everything cleaned up and were ready for winter. And yet we are glad that we can be here together with our dear children, and not in Russia—even if it is very hard. Here we can have church service and Sunday school every Sunday. We also have our own schools with good teachers, so that our children will be able to get a good education.

When we read the reports in the *Rundschau* and the letters about conditions in Russia—things are simply terrible. And yet we can do nothing about it. We are helpless. We cannot even send them anything because we don't have money. And besides that, our milreis [Brazilian currency] has no value on the international market. But one thing we can do: We can pray that the Lord would set them free from their slavery and that He would keep them firm in their faith until their final redemption.

At present our situation is also difficult and hard. We need nearly everything. Yet we are free and live in hope that things will gradually improve and life will become easier. If we only could harvest enough corn we could begin raising a few pigs. That would help to get some cash. There always seems to be a market for pork, even if the price is low. Currently it sells for 16 to 18 milreis for one *aroba*. [Note: One *aroba* has 15 kilos, about 33 pounds. The exchange rate at that time was about 13,75 milreis to $1.00. That means, a peasant could get approximately $4.90 for a 100-pound pig. HK.] We [as colony] have also built a milk processing plant. If we could have three or four cows, that would also give us a little income. Unfortunately, the cows out here produce on the average very little milk. We have two cows which together give only two to three liters per day. If we had the means, we would buy a young cow. For the time being, however, we have no chance to do so, even though cows are not that expensive. Yet we don't have what it takes. We do have a wagon with a team of horses and have been able to earn enough to pay for it. But now that more and more people have their own transportation, our income becomes less and less.

Accompanying Father's letter is one from Mother. Although she gives no name of an addressee, the content makes it clear that she, too, wrote to the Nickels.

I too will try to write something. We should have written sooner. We were truly surprised when we received an invitation to your golden wedding. Please, accept our belated thanks. You have often been in our thoughts, especially on your golden anniversary. We felt as though we were right there with you and consider you very fortunate to be surrounded by all your children and grandchildren.

When I think about how scattered we are, then I am overcome by painful homesickness. My brother is suffering in Siberia, stripped of everything. Sister Greta is still in the south where her husband has a job. As far as we know they still can buy some bread now and then. But there are days when they get nothing. About [Sister] Liese I only know that her husband has been arrested, but I do not know where she and her two sons are. The Wiebes [Sister Katharina and her husband] are in Canada and we are here in Brazil. His [Wiebe's] siblings have all stayed in Russia and suffer greatly from hunger. It is terrible the way all our loved ones have to live there. O, that God would keep them from despair. What a peculiar fate has befallen us! We are scattered in all directions. Many of our loved ones were also on the road to flee and get away, just as we were. Despite the fact that we here are living under conditions we have never experienced before, we are glad that we do not have to be in Russia. Granted, it is very difficult. Yet in Russia we also had to work hard. Some even have left their health there. [This is most likely a reference to her own fragile condition of which she writes in a subsequent letter. HK.]

It seems as though one has to have the physical strength of a giant in order to vanquish the jungle. For it is no simple matter to turn jungle into useful land, especially when those parts which one has cleared do not burn off properly. In such cases one cannot do anything with the land. That is what happened to us with one hectare [cleared] jungle. We had so much rain that it did not burn and so we could not use it. Now we have cleared some more and hope for dry weather. But again, the frequent rains are not a good indicator. But we thank God for health. Even if I have heart problems and headaches they have so far always subsided sufficiently that I am able to help out.

[Our daughter] Mariechen has worked out for some time. But she came home on 1 August, because there is so much to hoe and the land where we harvested last year's crop has to be prepared for planting. That means that all the weeds will have to be cleared with the hoe. Then there is the new piece [of land] where the jungle has been chopped down. That must now be burned off, and the smaller trees and branches have to be put into piles before we can plant anything. I would like to send you a picture of a freshly burned *roça*. It is quite something to behold. We have become used to it by now. The main thing is that it burns well, so that we can clean up the smaller shrubs and branches and use the land for planting. The work in itself is enjoyable, even if one gets covered with black soot from head to toe. The good thing is that we have plenty of water for bathing and washing; the bad thing is that it is hard on clothes which are difficult to come by. Not because they are not available, as it was in Russia, but because we don't have money to buy them.

Again, we are grateful that we don't have to be in Russia anymore. We had good times [in Russia] when we had everything we needed. We often think of our full bin of [wheat] flour. Here we have to learn to get along with corn flour. We can manage that as long as we have the *cará* root. That is a starchy tuber which we grind up and mix with corn flour to hold the dough together. But to make *Tjielktje* [favorite Mennonite pasta], noodles, pudding, *Bobbat* [a yeast dough baked with smoked sausage or ham], or bake *Zwieback* for a change is impossible without wheat flour. But wheat flour is too expensive for us to buy. Yet we have hope that things will improve.

We have two cows, but they give very little milk. One should calve in October. We paid 590 milreis for the two together. That may sound terribly much. In today's rate of exchange that amounts to about $46.00. We also have five pigs and two litters of four and five each. Then we have about thirty chickens. The problem is that they are always in danger of being caught by jungle dogs and tiger cats that love to devour them. In the garden we have constant trouble with deer. They have again eaten all the tender heads of cabbage. And yet we can't seem to catch them. The wild pigs are also very destructive, always coming around in large herds. We hope that with time things will get better.

Now I must conclude for today. I covet for you all the best and wish you good health as you get older. May our dear God bring all of us to that eternal home in heaven. With greetings and best wishes from all of us to all of you. "May there be peace within your walls and security within your citadels." Ps. 122:7. [Signed] Heinrich and S[usanna] Kasdorf.

A Letter from Mother, 1934

This letter gives day and month when it was written, not the year. However, from the description of certain events with references to specific dates it becomes evident that the year was 1934.

10 November.

To Uncle and Aunt Nickel: Peace to you! We received a wonderful letter written by you. It has been a long wait. We had nearly, yet not totally, given up on getting an answer to our last letter. It has made us truly happy that you have once again sent us such a precious letter. After all, you are our only close relatives who write in such a manner.

My mother [Mrs. Nickel's sister] has told me much about you. I would really love to chat with you and tell you how things are. Since I am no longer able to hoe in the *roça*, I spend most of my time alone in the house. In such times it would be so nice to visit with Mother. I thank God for a healthy family and that we have enough to eat and drink.

Last year I had to spend the entire time from February until Pentecost in bed. Was that ever a difficult time! But our dear Savior has heard our prayers. I have been able to get up once more. Yet I cannot do anything heavy. I would like to help, but I cannot. I want to be satisfied if only I could do the most essential work in the house. I am thankful to God that He provides needed health; without that it is hard.

My husband has two young workers with him [on the field]: Greta and Katja. Greta is seventeen years old and has a lot of stomach problems. Katja turned fourteen on 1 November. She is light and thin, and should actually still be in school, but she is needed at home. Nikolai is in school. He is ten years of age. Hans is six and is supposed to go to school after Christmas. [Due to rheumatic fever I had to skip one year. HK]. Mariechen and Heinrich are both married. Mariechen is twenty-six and Heinrich is twenty-four years old. Both are living nearby. Mariechen's wedding was last year, 23 [or 22?] November. Weddings are different here than in Russia. Yet it was quite a nice wedding. After the ceremony we had a modest meal of coffee and baked goods made from corn flour. Then there was a lot of singing and playing. In the evening we had such a heavy rain that the guests had a hard time going home.

You will probably wonder what we can make from corn flour. Well, we take some cara root which we mix with the flour, add sugar, cocoa and certain kinds of extracts [i.e., vanilla, peppermint etc. HK] and then we bake without wheat flour. (Of course, I would occasionally like to make noodles for a noodle soup, but for that I need wheat flour which we rarely can afford to buy.) So much for that peripheral comment.

Mariechen's husband is a Bernhard Esau. Heinrich's wedding was 26 June of this year. His wife is Lena Hübert. She seems to be a lovely child. Our children, the Funks [Susanna and Kornelius] live a few kilometers from our place. He is a teacher in Witmarsum. They have two children — Arthur and Alice. Funk has already learned the language of the land and passed the examination [in Portuguese]. He gets a fairly good salary. Both have committed their lives to the Lord. Yes, even here we must say that the Lord is mindful of us and blesses us. There are quite a few who have given themselves over to the Lord and praise him for salvation. At times it seemed as though the Lord did not hear our prayers and we tended to be discouraged. There were so few who were coming to Him. O, how we now rejoice that so many are praising the grace of Christ, even those of whom we least did expect it. The Lord willing, we shall have a baptismal service on 25 November, but I do not know how many will be baptized.

What more shall I write? If you could ever come here and see how things are going, then you would get a real picture of what it takes to settle in the jungle. We are putting our trust in the One who has said that we should cast all our cares on Him. He has always given us direction and help when things got difficult. We still have clothes to wear and enough to eat each day. Every time we think of our loved ones in Russia we are moved to gratitude for all that we have.

I wish you a joyous Christmas and a blessed new year. Heartfelt greetings with song Nr. 344 in the new *Glaubensstimme* [Voice of Faith]. Please convey also greetings to all your dear ones. Thank them for their greetings to us. With love, Susanna.

Letters from Mother and Father, 1937

Father's letter is dated 23 April without giving the year. Mother's letter is undated, but in the same envelope. The postal stamp shows that the letter was processed through the post office in Florianopolis, Santa Catarina on 13 May 1937, and in Dinuba, California, on 8 June the same year. The letter is addressed to Arnold Nickel and his Aunt Katharine who, by that time, had moved from Kansas to California. First, excerpts from Mother's letter, which opens with a greeting without specifically stating to whom it is written.

> Greetings with Psalm 37:4-5. With great interest we read your letter. It was a great surprise to hear from you. . . .
>
> You want to know how large our family is. Three children [Susi, Mariechen, and Heinrich] are married, four are still at home. Susi married a Funk. He is a school teacher. He has already learned Portuguese and teaches in the Portuguese language. Mariechen married an Esau. He is a harness maker and farms on the side. Heinrich married Lena Hübert. They have a small farm next to ours. Heinrich usually works for others, helping to build houses. He earns up to 6 milreis per day. [The Brazilian currency was called milreis at that time. 15 milreis was equivalent to US $1.00. HK] The other four are still at home. They are Greta, Katja, Nikolai and Hans. The two boys are going to school—Nikolai to middle school [*Realschule*, grade 5] and Hans to [second grade] primary school.
>
> You also want to know how we are making our living here. . . . We are able to make our living off the land, but it is not easy. We are used to hard work from Russia. But here everything is so very different. Before we have even a small plot of land in the jungle ready to plant anything at all, we have to work long and hard. The thick underbrush has to be cleared first, then the trees have to be cut down with the ax. After weeks of hot drying weather we burn as much as possible before planting with the hoe. It takes years before we can plow a little piece here and a little piece there. Yes, even the table [food] is very different from what we know

from Russia. Bread, for example, is made from corn flour. But it can be prepared in a way so that it is quite tasty. Things change with the seasons of the year. [This means that our diet was seasonal, depending on what we were able to grow and harvest at various seasons of the year. HK] According to letters we get from relatives in Canada, our way of raising pigs and poultry is much simpler than theirs.

I have given you a brief report about many different items. If you have more questions, please ask again. It would even be better if you would come here and visit us in person. . . .

I have to close for now. We commend you to the Lord. All of us greet you from the bottom of our hearts.
[Signed] H[einrich] and Susi Kasdorf

What follows is Father's letter to Arnold Nickel, written at the same time (10 November 1937) as Mother's. Father fills in several items omitted by Mother and adds other information to answer all of Nickel's questions.

Dear Friend and Brother Nickel!

We received your letter unexpectedly. But we were very happy for the occasion to read a letter from California. We can see from it that conditions there are also hard in different ways. It is comforting to know that life is not only difficult here in the Brazilian jungle. We have had to change our way of life completely. Everything was totally foreign to us [when we got here]. It is a warm region, yet there is no arable land, only a giant jungle, so that things looked rather gloomy at first. But thanks be to God, things have gone better than we had imagined. Up to this point we have generally been in good health and able to work. Anyone who is well and willing to work can have enough to live on.

As you know, we came out of Russia to Germany without any possessions whatsoever. The little money we had when we left Siberia was taken away by the Russian customs officials [in St. Petersburg]. When we got to Germany, we had nothing, yet the German people received us very warmly. We stayed there for six weeks and then had to move on. Our desire was to move to Canada, but when we saw that the doors were closed we decided together with our children to go to Brazil. And we are still content to be here. As we read letters from relatives and acquaintances we conclude that there are hardships anywhere in the world. It appears that the situation [in Russia] gets increasingly more oppressive. Despite the fact that humankind endeavors to improve the world, we see the dark thunderclouds rise steadily higher.

Now I would like to answer your questions. Actually, my wife has already answered some of them. Yes, land is still available around here, even in our immediate vicinity. There are always people who are looking elsewhere to find something better. They want to sell their farms. Only the future will tell whether or not they will find something better than what they have here. The Hamburg Company [i.e., the Hanseatic Land Association] is still selling land for 60, 80, and 120 milreis per hectare [approximately 2.4 acres]. One can buy different parcels of land from 15 to 50 or even up to 60 hectares each colony [farm]. But it is all jungle. The exchange rate is 15 milreis for 1 dollar [$1.00]. But one does not have to pay cash. When one buys a full colony [60 hectares], one usually has to make a down payment of 500 milreis. The rest can be paid within seven years at 7% annual interest. A good cow costs from 300 to 400 milreis. A horse costs the same. A new wagon costs between 400 and 500 milreis and the complete harness for a horse is 150 to 220 milreis. My wife has already written about the cost of other items. Feed for farm animals has to be planted.

Before we can plant anything at all, we have to clear the jungle by cutting down the underbrush and then chop down the big trees. That has to dry for quite a while before it can be burned. Once the finer stuff is burned, we cut off branches from trees, throw them in piles and burn as much as possible. Only then can we plant corn and beans and mandioca between and around the stumps and tree trunks. You see that this is a totally different method of farming from the way we did things in Russia. Surely, it is also much different from the way you are farming in California. Now I would be curious to hear from you what you think about Brazil.

Please give greetings to your parents, grandparents, and siblings from your relatives Heinrich and Susi Kasdorf.

P.S. If you cannot come here personally, we would very much appreciate at least an answer to our letters.

That ends Father's letter, but I have no record whether or not Arnold Nickel ever responded. Arnold does not remember either.

13

Former Dwellers and Foreign Settlers

> *I, the LORD ... will come to their rescue.*
> *I will not forget them.*
> *I will make rivers flow on mountain peaks.*
> *I will send streams to fill the valleys.*
> *Everyone will see this and know that*
> *I, the holy LORD God of Israel, created it all.*
> —From *Isaiah 41*

Neither the German colonists nor the Mennonites from the Soviet Union were the first human beings to settle in the Krauel Valley. Decades prior to our coming, so we were told, the Brazilian government had ordered these indigenous people to vacate the entire region and make room for foreign settlers. The stories that were floating around about them when I grew up seemed more fictitious than factual; they kept me mystified, but curious.

In the 1930s our people made an agreement with the Hanseatic Land Association to build a road along the Krauel River as partial payment for the land. The project was under the engineering supervision of a certain Mr. Trappke. I remember the man mainly because of his interesting leather cap that gave him a unique, outright comical appearance. Trappke was small in stature, but tall with words. He could speak for ten, as those close to him used to say. Besides that, the workers knew him better for his indulgence in brandy and other spirituous beverages than for diligence and engineering expertise.

The Land Association had put him in charge of a *turma* for road construction. A *turma* was a crew of thirty men working in three units of ten in each on a common project. My brother Heinrich and other young men from our colony were working as a *turma* under Trappke's supervision. Each weekend we younger boys took food and other supplies to some crude barracks the men had built for temporary shelter. The terrain was rugged and rocky, with huge granite boulders protruding from the ground. All drilling and blasting and digging and earth-moving was done manually. Our men did not even have the assistance of a humble donkey or an ox to move the earth, only homemade wooden wheelbarrows. It was no easy job.

On one occasion Heinrich took us with him to a nearby elevation from which we could overlook the valley some kilometers down river. "Look over there," he said. "That strip of light green growth along the Rio Krauel is an old, abandoned Indian road. Those Indians used to make good roads." The tone of his voice indicated admiration for the way those former dwellers had managed to construct a road for their transportation needs. "They rolled some of the giant rocks into ravines and built bridges that can still be used. If we could only get to the opposite side of the river, it would be easy to build our new road along the pathway of the old."

When I saw how hard our men had to toil with pick and shovel and crowbar to hack a passable path through rugged terrain, I too gained great admiration for those Indians who had managed to construct a road without the benefit of any iron tools. To think that they had manually moved those huge rocks into ravines as a foundation for a bridge seemed like superhuman accomplishment. But they had done it. Our valiant men learned from them and performed similar feats.

I was truly excited about this information and wanted to know more about those original people who once lived where we had settled. What did they eat? How did they live? Where had they stayed? Since there were no ruins of man-made dwellings and no visible evidence of jungle clearance for agriculture, had they not planted anything? If the old road which Heinrich had shown us was built by the original inhabitants of the area, could the skeletal remnants we discovered in caves and the arrowheads we found on our land belong to the same people who had lived there at one time? If so, was I then walking on the same ground, fishing in the same river, and climbing the same wild fruit trees as the primeval inhabitants had done? I found these ideas intriguing. Only many years later did I find some answers to my questions about those former dwellers of the Krauel.

In his ethno-historical study, *Os Indios Xokleng: Memória Visual*, Sílvio Coelho dos Santos carefully unravels the quasi-mythological saga about the peoples who inhabited the jungles of Southeastern Brazil in pre-European times. Best known are the ancient *Guaraní*, who make up much of the current Paraguayan population, but their ethnic cousins, the *Xokleng,* were once living in the area where we settled. In fact, along with the *Kaingáng (Caingangue; Caingáng)* remnants of the *Xokleng* inhabit areas of Santa Catarina, Paraná and neighboring states to this day. According to the Wycliffe Bible Translators' *Ethnologue*, they belong linguistically to the *Ge* or *Jê* family along the Atlantic. The *Xokleng* were regionally known as *Botocudos* by their tribal rivals and as *Bugres* by the Europeans. Anglo

American sources still speak of *Botocudos* whereas Brazilian anthropologists seem to prefer the designation *Xokleng*.

The *Xokleng* were nomads, dominating large and undefined areas of the South Brazilian mountainous jungles where food was plentiful. They hunted a variety of animals and birds, collected honey from wild bees, gathered fruits and nuts from the trees and roots from the soil. Writing in the *Handbook of South American Indians*, the eminent anthropologist Robert Lowie adds that the *Botocudos* or *Xokleng* "did not disdain even toads and lizards." That, of course, was not an uncommon diet for any of the indigenous societies. But when I read that they delighted in "cooking worms that live in a bamboo, both for flavor and the marvelous visions they produced," then my mental reflexes automatically shut down my senses to spare me from dwelling on the wriggling, writhing whitish creatures with their red rim around the neck. I remember too well what bamboo worms looked and smelled like. I need say no more, except a word of thanks to my Maker for sparing me from the *Botocudo* diet.

According to the record, there was a clear division of labor between females and males. After each major hunting expedition the men replenished their supply of bows, arrows, spears and other artifacts needed to sustain their way of life. The women took care of the children and immediate needs of the clan. They extracted and treated the fibers from stinging nettles to weave blankets and covers for cold winter nights; they made clay pots and *taquara* baskets for storing food; they cleaned and dressed the animals and birds hunted by the men.

One of the ongoing struggles faced by the *Xokleng* was the territorial conflict with the *Guarani* on the one hand and the *Kaingáng* on the other. The battle was over the *pinhão*, one of the major food supplies for humans and animals alike, especially in the large *araucária* groves where the nuts were plentiful. As soon as the nuts fell to the ground, wild life of all kinds came there to feed on them. The natives came for both: gathering nuts and hunting animals and birds. The tribal wars over the *pinhão* are said to have been fierce, sometimes engaging entire tribes; at other times they agreed to fight it out in a duel. Silvio dos Santos notes that even the natural elements were often against them, and concludes with a sobering thought:

> The world of the *Xokleng* was no paradise as one can well imagine. It was a world of stiff competition and interdependence between themselves and nature. Their success was measured by the results of their individual and collective efforts based on the wisdom developed through the generations on how to utilize to their advantage the ecological space best suited for their habitat.

The situation for the *Xokleng* changed drastically when the Brazilian government placed the indigenous peoples on reservations. That happened many years before we settled on the land they once had occupied. The story of the coerced resettlement of the *Xokleng* is as tragic as the accounts about resettling native peoples in Anglo America. By the time we arrived in 1930, the number of these people, according to dos Santos, had been reduced by two thirds. That is one side of the tragedy. The other is that apparently no significant effort was ever made to bring the whole Gospel of Jesus and His Kingdom to them until the twentieth century. By that time their culture and social structure had to a large degree been destroyed and the population decimated.

But there is also a positive side to the story. In 1995, while teaching at the seminary in Giessen, Germany, I was invited to speak at a missionary retreat in Curitiba, Brazil, sponsored by the *Deutsche Indianer Pionier Mission* (DIPM) and the *Marburger [Brasilien] Mission*. It was there that Frieda and I met a number of German and Swiss missionaries who were working with different tribal peoples in Brazil and Paraguay, including the *Kaingáng* in Paraná. We were told that this tribe shares cultural and religious traits with other tribes, such as the *Xokleng*. One common visible feature is the finger-sized wooden pin or peg the men wear in their pierced lower lip.

Ruf aus dem Urwald, a book published by DIPM (1987), chronicles present efforts to assist these peoples to improve their way of life. Through an integrative approach of proclamation, health care, education, agriculture and marketing expertise, committed Christians are working with and among them to reconstruct a wholesome socioreligious way of life for the present with hope for the future. I was delighted to meet several Mennonite missionaries whose parents and grandparents I knew from the Krauel. Here they were, the third generation, working together with missionaries from Germany, Switzerland and Paraguay to improve the living conditions of the least fortunate peoples in Brazil. Since some tribal groups can no longer be identified by their original names, I am not sure whether the *Botocudos* or *Xokleng* are included in these efforts, but related tribal societies, such as the *Kaingáng*, are.

When the missionaries in Curitiba presented us with a genuine bow, several arrows and two spears (one for spearing fish and one for hunting deer) made by the current *Cacique* (chief) of the *Kaingáng*, my respect and admiration for these ancient people was renewed. I had made many bows and arrows during my teenage years, but they were poor imitations. None bore even the slightest resemblance to these genuine artifacts. Since such "weapons" are not items one takes across international borders, we donated them to the *Associação Menonita Beneficente* in Witmarsum, Paraná. My friend Peter Pauls, founder and director, was glad to accept these articles as designated "first fruits" for a proposed museum of the *Associação*, a local mission agency.

14

Shaping Influences in Early Years

*Think of what you were when you were called:
Not wise by human standards,
not influential; not of noble birth.
God chose the foolish and weak.
No one has any ground for boasting,
except in the Lord.*
--- Adapted from 1 Corinthians 1

From the day we are born our lives are being influenced and shaped by people we meet, places we live, decisions we make, and experiences we have. Some are positive, others negative. Seldom are they neutral, not always are they lasting. I will record three or four incidents that made a lasting impression on my life when I was young. They may not be profound. Yet I reckon them to be major pieces that have shaped a larger spiritual mosaic without which my chronicle would be incomplete.

When Elders Prayed for Mother

We had been in Brazil barely three years when church elders came to our house to pray over Mother, who was critically ill. She had a heart condition and also suffered from serious injuries she had sustained during the early years in Siberia. At the very beginning of World War I, Father was conscripted for the second time and sent away for three and a half years to work in the forests of northern Siberia. Mother had to stay alone with small children and take care of the family and the farm. One day while hauling straw for heating the house, the horses got spooked and began to bolt, totally out of control. Before they finally stopped in the barnyard, the load of hay lay scattered along the road, the wagon had partially disintegrated, and Mother had been hurled off along the way, resulting in permanent injuries in her left side. Neither her heart problem nor her injuries were ever properly treated and caused her excruciating pain.

I recall from the early years in Brazil when I was about four or five years old how Mother sometimes went off by herself, pressed both hands against her side and groaned audibly: *"It deit oaba so seea wee"* (it is so very painful), she would say to herself, weeping. In a letter (10 November1934), she writes to her aunt and uncle in Kansas about her condition: besides dealing with her pain, she finds it particularly hard that she is unable to help with work on the *roça*. From February to the end of May of that year she had to be flat in bed. Since I was too young to work in the *roça,* I stayed with her and spent much time at her bedside.

One night her condition became critical. Father woke us children and said that Mother was very ill. My sisters went to call our married siblings. All gathered around Mother's bed expecting her to die. Father asked my sisters to stay with Mother while he and my brother Heinrich fetched a team of horses and put them to the wagon so that Father could drive to the opposite end of the village and call the elders of the church to our house. Meanwhile, my brother Nikolai and I caught twelve to fifteen giant fireflies to have light in the room when Father would return with Kornelius Ekk and Johann Regier. We often used fireflies in a clear bottle to create light in the darkness of night. Even if they did not glow continually, they did light up as soon as we touched the bottle.

At least an hour went by before Father returned. As he and the men entered the room, it seemed as though we were on holy ground. That had nothing to do with the elders but with the presence of God. The room was filled with an atmosphere of faith and hope that God would intervene. Father read James 5:13-16 and made a brief comment about its meaning for the occasion. The elders anointed Mother with oil and prayed over her. That was the first time I had ever witnessed anything like that. It was a sacred act. Those were also tense moments. We expected God to do a miracle; and he did. Not that Mother's illness was gone, but she had less pain and sufficient strength to get up the next day. She got well enough to live and see her children grow up under her loving care and faithful prayer.

Whenever in later years during my church ministry I have been asked to pray over a sick person, the scene from my childhood stands vividly before me. Yet the act of anointing someone with oil, laying on of hands and praying over that person has never been easy for me. On the one hand, one always has to deal with consequences of the Fall: sickness and sin. The passage in James is clear about that. On the other hand, the act in itself is sacred and delicate. In such moments I have always felt that I was dealing with life in the balance, with faith put to its ultimate test. At the same time it is a ministry in which one must step back in order that the holy will of God can manifest itself unhindered.

First Lessons in Prayer

Prayer played an important role in the life of my parents, and that not only at meal time. Every night when Father was home he read the

Bible, we often sang a song which we knew by heart, and then all knelt for prayer. Mother frequently prayed by herself during the day. After Father and my older siblings had gone to work in the *roça,* she retreated to her bedroom and prayed ever so fervently to God. I sometimes sneaked up to the outside window and listened. Much of the time she spent in thanksgiving, especially for bringing us out from the Soviet Union. Then she interceded for those who had stayed behind and were now suffering incredible hardships. What touched me particularly was when she prayed for each one of us children by name that we all would accept the Lord and follow him. At times she was audibly weeping, which moved me to tears as well. I was deeply touched by those prayers and convinced that God hears and answers prayers. But I never let her see or hear me in those hallowed moments she chose to spend alone with God.

When I was a small child I learned two simple German prayer rhymes. Every night I prayed one of these prayers before going to bed. In the first grade I learned a third prayer which was a little longer. I shall quote and translate each in that order.

> *Lieber Heiland, mach mich fromm,*
> *daß ich in den Himmel komm. Amen.*
>> Dear Lord Jesus, make me good (godly),
>> that into heaven come I could. Amen.

> *Ich bin klein, mein Herz ist rein;*
> *es soll niemand drinn'n wohnen,*
> *als mein Jesus allein. Amen.*
>> I am but little, pure is my heart.
>> It's there for my Jesus,
>> He owns every part. Amen.

> *Christi Blut und Gerechtigkeit,*
> *das ist mein Schmuck und Ehrenkleid.*
> *Damit will ich vor Gott bestehn,*
> *wenn ich zum Himmel werd eingehn. Amen.*
>> The blood of Christ and righteousness,
>> they are my pure and glorious dress.
>> Through them my path to God is clear,
>> when I at heaven's gate appear. Amen.

At the age of about twelve I experienced an answer to prayer all on my own. We had bought a pair of domesticated rabbits to supplement our meat supply. It is no secret that rabbits multiply "rabbitually" without interruption. Before long, we had such an abundance of rabbits—black and white and brown and grey—that we began to give them away. But there was one silver-grey bunny that was special. Its fur was super-soft and shiny. It became my very own pet. I named it *Schmock* (Gorgeous). I fed it. I held it. I brushed it. I spoiled it. It became the envy of my friends in the village.

One day *Schmock* did not show up. I searched and called. I prayed to God to let me find my rabbit. I looked everywhere, but found no trace of it. It was a real test for my childlike faith. God had answered when the elders prayed for my mother; why was He not answering my prayer to find my rabbit? I was convinced that either a wild dog or a wild cat had sunk its nasty teeth into the poor helpless thing. I felt crushed, visualizing my rabbit in the jaws of a jungle dog. Yet deep down in my heart I still had a glimmer of hope and continued praying. My friends from our village knew about my loss. When they came to our place the following Sunday, I must have felt as Job did when his three friends came to comfort him. But unlike Job's friends, my friends did neither weep nor sit speechless for seven days (Job 2:11-13). Instead, they came to admire our rabbits. And there, out of nowhere, my lost *Schmock* came hopping along as though he had never been away.

The first chance I had I told my parents that *Schmock* had come back. They were happy for me. Without many words and in his quiet manner, Father said: *Scheena Jung, dentj emma doaraun, daut de leewi Gott onse Gebaede heat . Doaweajen baed wie emma too am.* (Always remember, my dear boy, that the good Lord does hear our prayers. That is why we always pray to Him.) He was actually quoting words from Psalm 65. Every time I read that Psalm, I am reminded of that lesson on prayer in my childhood.

Regretfully, and to the sorrow of my parents, there came some teenage years when I did not pray. But the words of my father, "Remember, my boy, . . ." never left my mind until I began to pray in earnest. In the course of my life I have repeatedly become a witness to the great truth: Indeed, "the Lord does hear our prayers" (Ps. 65:3).

Hauling Sawdust with Father

What is so special about hauling sawdust? Nothing. But I was not only hauling sawdust. I was doing so *together with Father,* and that made it very special. Besides, we were able to earn some money, for we had to pinch pennies to make ends meet.

I was only ten or eleven years old. Our school had already been shut down by the government. My formal education had ceased before I could finish grade three—at least for the next ten or eleven years. In the meantime I worked at home on the *roça* and then in the cooperative store of the colony. Peter Isaak, the store manager, encouraged me to improve my

Portuguese and also to become more proficient in arithmetic. Fortunately, I loved both, was able to take informal private lessons and accomplished a great deal in a short time. Unfortunately, however, I was not able to improve my reading skills because I had no books to read.

One day during this time, Father took a sack of corn to the cooperative mill to exchange it for flour. Since money was scarce, the cooperative operated on a share basis. The miller took a certain percentage (I believe 20 percent) for grinding and handling the corn, and the farmer got the rest.

While Father was at the mill, the manager asked him if he would not want to use his horses and wagon and haul sawdust from the big pile next to the mill to a designated location in a field about three hundred meters away. When Father came home that day, he was all excited about the prospect of some income and asked me to help him. I was elated and felt very important to help him earn money. We started the next day. Father wanted me to take a small shovel, but I insisted on a big one. He let me have it, but cautioned me with one of his many proverbial sayings: *"De Längd drajht de Laust."* What he meant was that I would tire very soon, using that big shovel. He was right. I had miscalculated the weight of the sawdust and the limits of my strength. Before long, I traded my big shovel for a smaller one.

Since we were getting paid by the load, I would have liked to make the wagon not quite so full. By the end of the day, so I reasoned, we could have a few extra loads and get more money. I suppose Father knew what I was thinking. He had been clear from the outset that we would make every load rounded, rather than level with or lower than the sideboards. When he sensed the direction I was going, he asked me a simple question: "If you and I were to hire someone to haul sawdust for us, how would you like him to fill his wagon—rounded full, just even with the sideboards, or not quite to the top of the sideboards?" Thinking only of my benefits, and not of what Father was driving at, I was quick to answer: "Rounded full." He affirmed my response with another proverb: *"Doot kratjht so fea aundre, aus dee fea junt säle doone."* (In everything do to others as you would have them do to you.) That was a lesson Father not only taught, it was the way he lived.

Next to the sawdust pile lay several logs on which we put the fodder for the horses, our own lunch, and the wagon seat. On one end of the seat we had a pile of sticks. After each load Father asked me to take one stick and put it to the other end of the seat. That's how we kept count. At the end of the day Father counted the sticks. Both of us were proud of our accomplishments and of the fact that each stick represented a *rounded load* of sawdust we had taken from the mill to the field.

We did not work nearly every day, only as needed to keep the sawdust from piling too high next to the mill. During the time we worked there, Father told me much about life in Slavgorod and Siberia. He even talked about his former smoking habit. When he and my mother were married, he had promised to quit, but did not do so until he was converted to Christ some years later. Mother had been disappointed—even hurt. Father also told about his half-brother Johann who had been not only a heavy smoker, but also an alcoholic. Uncle Johann died of throat cancer, leaving his wife with small children behind. Father did not state that his brother's cancer could have been caused by his habits, but he said to me in a passionate tone: *"Etjh hoap du woascht niemoals schmäetjhe oda supe."* (I hope you will never smoke or drink.)

We had been working for about a year when something happened that brought our happy hauling to an unhappy halt. One early morning on our way to work we took several sacks of corn along for Heinrich Unruh, the miller, to grind some of it for flour, the rest for feed. I stood in the wagon and lifted the sacks onto the edge of the sideboards so that Father could take and carry them to the respective bins inside. With one of the heavy sacks (sixty kilos) on his shoulders, he tripped over the threshold of the door, stumbled and sustained multiple breaks in his right foot and leg as well as in the ankle and knee. The men in the mill helped to get Father onto the wagon and I took him to the colony hospital nearby. Doctor Dyck and his staff did what they could, but treating broken bones and limbs was not his specialty. Father stayed in the hospital for some time. It took many more months to recover at home. His leg never healed properly; it remained swollen and quite stiff. Father limped to the end of his life.

Digging Sweet Potatoes with Mother

The term *batata doce* can best be translated as "sweet potatoes." Like *mandioca,* the sweet potato was a starchy tuber to feed humans and animals. The vines of the potato plants, like the foliage of the *mandioca* plants, provided additional fodder for the cattle. One morning Mother and I were digging sweet potatoes for our noon meal, the pigs' supper, and the chickens' breakfast the next day. The field was on a fairly steep incline. Mother was standing on the higher level about two or three meters away from me. She paused for a moment, leaning on her spade, then asked me this probing question: *"Hauns, waut welst do woare wann du groot best?"* (Hans, what do you want to become when you grow up?)

I was sixteen years old at the time, working at the cooperative store. That was also the time that Jacob an Anna Unruh from Shafter, California, were missionaries in Brazil. On one of their early visits at our house I had made a decision for Christ. But by the time I was sixteen, I had left my childhood faith and was by no means a committed Christian. Instead, I lived in a state of spiritual apathy, giving little thought either to what I would do in the future or what the future would do with me. I had come to a phase of indifference and thrown away not only my faith, but also my earlier ambition of someday going to school to learn about the greater world. Never having read a book, nor having much hope of ever getting one, my horizon seemed to get narrower with each passing year. I was resigned to being hemmed in between two *serras*; and I did not care. My ambition was as low as my vision was short. What should I ever dream of becoming under those conditions, except eke out an existence on the unproductive *roça* on which I was standing? Mother was concerned about my spiritual condition. Her question jolted me and made me think.

But there was more that Mother said to me on the day we were digging sweet potatoes. She told me of an event in my early life in Siberia of which she had never spoken to me before.

> When you were less than one year old, [Mother began], the times in Siberia were hard. Food shortages were increasing and people began to suffer. Many children in our village Alexandrovka died of diphtheria. You were very sick and got weaker by the day. We had only faint hope that you would make it through the winter. One night even hope seemed to vanish. In desperation I wrapped you in a blanket and went outside. There under the open sky I dedicated you to God, saying, "Lord, you have given us this child. You know how much we love him and how much we want to keep him. You also know how sick he is. We have no remedy for healing, but you do. If you make him well, he is yours for life. If you let him die, he is also yours. Your will be done."

Mother went on to say that she had taken me back to the house and told Father what she had done. Then she added, "You gradually recovered and survived. I believe you are here for the purpose of serving God. That is why I asked you the question what you wanted to become." From that day on I knew the answer: I would some day serve the Lord, even though I did not know how and where. That morning on the field when I dug sweet potatoes together with Mother was clearly the day when I became aware of God's call in my life—even before I was a Christian.

15

Memories from the Lighter Side

"Oh, well, naturally,"
said the [twelve year old] boy with a big smile.
"Father doesn't know anything about that.
He is too old to remember his childhood."
–In *A 2nd Helping of Chicken Soup for the Soul*

As Frieda and I were recently visiting with our friends Alvin and Lona Pauls at the breakfast table, our conversation revolved around God's greatness in some facets of creation, particularly His marvelous masterpiece, the human mind. "What I admire most in a person is the intellect," Alvin observed. Only two days away from his eightieth birthday, he continued: "Just think of man's capacity to reminisce, recollect, remember and relate experiences and events that happened sixty, seventy or even seventy-five years ago."

Not everyone has the gift to talk about personal experiences and historical events of the past spiced with subtle wit and humor as Alvin does, yet his assertion is right: the human mind has a tremendous capacity to remember what happened long ago. But sometimes it needs a little jolt in the right direction to connect certain happenings to put things into proper perspective. That is my experience in the process of writing about my journey. I have reflected intensely on my childhood days and become overwhelmed as much by the *manner* in which things come to mind as by the *matter* that suddenly appears on my mental screen. The things I remember may not always entail any big subject or outstanding event to write about. Yet the lessons learned from some experiences became the ingredients that have gone into the making of my life and character.

In this chapter I intend to reminisce about personal experiences through my childhood and early teenage years in Brazil. I must be selective, however, leaving the rest for "Stories by Opa," which I am writing for my grandchildren.

Since I was the youngest in the family, my siblings sometimes tried to convince me that I had been spoiled by all the attention they had given me. They may have had a point. I have never been able to claim model behavior. Likewise, I have never disputed or doubted that I was born into a family where care and compassion as well as tenderness and love were combined with firm discipline. My parents were not wealthy. Yet they possessed the ability to use whatever they had, including nonmaterial resources, that gave me a sense of security and a feeling of belonging. I am grateful to God for godly parents who succeeded in building a home on a foundation of ethical and spiritual values. I treasure those memories.

We had some food to eat even before our colony had a grocery store or a butcher shop. Our table was lean at best. The fat of the land had not yet reached us. We already had bought two or three piglets, but they were of poor stock, small and skinny. As my parents talked about the urgent need for meat and lard, they agreed to buy a half-grown pig. That must have been in 1931 or early in 1932, before we had our own wagon. And there lay the problem: how would Father get a live animal home? Others faced the same dilemma.

Several men from our village teamed up and walked along a narrow *picada* through the jungle to buy pigs from the German colonists who lived in Neu Hoffnung on the other side of the *serra*. However, getting their purchase home proved to be more difficult than they had envisioned. One of them came up with a brilliant idea—at least so they thought. They had to improvise. They used *cipó*—a fiber extracted from the bark of certain trees for making rope—to tie their live commodity one to the other. The idea was to lead those pigs like pets on a leash along the path across the *serra*. They soon found out, however, that pigs are neither the fastest learners nor the most cooperative pets when tied on a leash. My brother-in-law Esau (not yet married at the time) was one of the buyers. When he came home he was as exhausted as the piglets. He exclaimed in exasperation: "Phew! Pig or no pig, but I will never try that again."

That experience was helpful to my father. He, too, was about to buy a pig, but did not want to repeat the same method the young men had used in getting it home. One morning he got up very early and left all by himself to face the adventure of the day. He made a wise decision: instead of walking across the *serra*, he went to the nearest colonists down the river, bought a young pig, tied its feet together with *cipó*, put it on his shoulder, and walked home. But a pig is a pig, whether it is tied on a leash or hanging across the shoulder of a man—it has no appreciation for either means of transportation. Father's pig turned out to be as pigheaded as the pigs on the leash had been.

It was dark by the time Father got home. We had been waiting for hours. It had been a long and hard day. When he finally returned, he was hungry, thirsty and drained of energy. He put the pig on the veranda floor, our dining room. He untied its legs and let it go. It struggled to get up, but could not walk. Mother gave it water to drink and something to eat.

We, too, were eating. Father was overtired and soon went to bed. The pig recovered and began to walk. We children were overjoyed to have a half-grown pig—a white one with a long snout. We looked ahead to the time it would be big and fat enough to yield meat and lard for a richer diet. Thus we began raising our own pigs. Some we butchered, others we sold.

One day I was playing with my nephews and nieces in the yard facing the west side of our kitchen. My parents were not home. House and kitchen were separate buildings, connected by an open breezeway. There we competed, throwing sticks against the only wall with a glass window. As a seven-year-old I was the biggest and strongest among my playmates. I was their hero, showing off. They were impressed by my hard throws and bent over laughing each time my stick crashed against the wall. The louder the bang, the heartier their laugh—except once. My last throw was by far the loudest as it hit the window and shattered one of the glass panes. Some pieces lay inside the kitchen and some outside on the ground. Nobody was laughing. The atmosphere had turned from fun to fear.

Glass was hard to come by in those days, and costly besides. What should I say when my parents got home? And what would the parents say? I was soon to find out. I was still standing in shock, speechless. At that very silent moment I heard the rattling of the wagon wheels and the stamping of the horses' hooves; and there were my parents. When they saw us standing there they knew that something was amiss. Then they saw the broken window.

They suspected one of the small children to be responsible, especially when I asserted my innocence. Without knowing the biblical warning, I had a built-in voice that told me as clear as can be: "Be sure your sin will find you out"—not the sin of the broken window, but the sin of lying about breaking it. Only moments had passed when two-and-a-half-year-old Trudie revealed the truth. Lifting her little innocent hand, she pointed at me, stammering in her baby talk: *"Onkel Hauns Fensta twei."* The phrase was incomplete, but not the message. It was crystal clear that I was the culprit; I had broken the window. I stood there as a liar before my parents. I was guilty and ashamed. What example was I setting for my nieces and nephews? No longer did I feel their hero.

I recall my mother's proverbial saying in German as clearly as I remember the incident of the broken window itself: *"Wer einmal lügt, dem glaubt man nicht, auch wenn er gleich die Wahrheit spricht."* (Whoever lies once cannot be believed, even if he speaks the truth thereafter.) I have never forgotten those words of my mother; nor can I ever forget the disappointment in her voice and the grief I saw in her eyes. I felt bad about breaking the window, worse for being dishonest, and worst about the bad example I had been to my nieces and nephews.

My two youngest sisters, Greta eleven and Katja eight years older than I, were special to me. They were my chief guardians outside the home, watching over me like angels, especially during the early years in Brazil. Whether or not they were as gentle as angels, I shall leave unsaid. But I will say that I did not always make life easy for them. Forever unforgettable are those Sunday afternoons when we walked barefoot along a road hacked through the jungle to the village schoolhouse in Waldheim, where we had Sunday school. Two incidents are vivid in my memory.

Peter Görtzen was our teacher. He must have had poor eyesight, judging by the thick, heavy glasses he wore. I could not bear the sight of his spectacles and let everyone know. As soon as he began to tell a story, I was overcome by a need for a drink of water. My sisters took turns, going with me to the veranda, where we had a pail of drinking water and an enameled dipper used as a common cup. The problem was that my perceived needs for a drink persisted longer than my sisters' patience. I did my best to test that virtue to its limits. But once their patience was depleted, I was in trouble. Each of them grabbed me by one arm and walked unduly fast past the water pail to the outside door. There they paused just long enough to fetch the *Struckbassim* (a crude kind of broom made from scrubby, dry shrub branches) used to sweep the school yard. The rest need not be told, except to say that my sisters had formed a good team and knew how to handle that broom like experts. It also meant that Sunday school was over for that day, at least for the three of us.

Then there was that long walk to the school house. The weather was as unpredictable as weather can be, especially in summer. One Sunday the road might be dry and dusty like the Kalahari Desert of South Africa, and the next Sunday it could be as muddy and mucky as the Okeefenokee Swamp of Georgia. Some of us small boys delighted in running ahead in the deepest dust, fine as powder. We competed fiercely with one another as to who could raise the biggest clouds with our bare feet in order to hide from view those who were coming behind us. On rainy days we competed in slogging through the deepest holes with mud and sludge. That's how we walked to and from Sunday school, three kilometers each way. The lesson I remember best is not what the teacher taught, but the ability of my sisters, especially Greta, to combine tender love with firm grips for discipline. They did not exactly use a smooth ladle or belt when they deemed the time for reckoning had come. They fetched a rough, scrubby stick or branch from the underbrush along the road, a painful memorable instrument that left visible marks on my skin. I would have preferred if they would have used a belt or a whip, but not that scrubby stick. Unfortunately, the choice was theirs, not mine.

My boyish pranks and obstinate behavior were no match for my dear sisters' swift actions which sometimes made me seriously doubt their tender love. When they had grown up and I, too, had reached a level of maturity, those Sunday school incidents filled moments of laughter and delightful conversation in our family circle.

I must add, however, that there were many Sundays on which I was unable to walk due to severe pain in every joint of my body, particularly from the hips down. Sometimes my sisters had to carry me home. We called those attacks *Rhietinjh*. Whatever it was, the pain was excruciating and debilitating. Decades later, when I had my first heart attack in 1976, I went to see Dr. Eliasson, a cardiologist in Fresno. After examining my heart he suggested that I may have had rheumatic fever in my younger years, causing a defective heart. Continuing heart problems may be a sign that his diagnosis was correct.

Everyone knows that carrots sticks and chicken mites do not have much in common. Those tiny, almost microscopic grey mites thrive best in the chicken barn, whereas carrots grow in the vegetable garden. But in this case, one makes little sense without the other. The story is as follows.

It was a glorious Sunday afternoon in late spring. I was eight or nine years old. My friends from the village had come to our place. We agreed to take the dogs and make an excursion to the *serra* where we wanted to explore some of the caves, looking for human skeletons left there by natives of long ago. I knew of one such cave on the land of my brother-in-law Esau, situated between our colony and that of his stepfather, Heinrich Dick. As we came closer to the *serra*, we made a detour along the *picada* through Esau's colony and came out on Mr. Dick's *roça*.

And there they were, the healthiest looking carrots we had ever seen. There were also other vegetables, but our eyes hung on the carrots. Instead of exploring the caves near by, we were tempted to explore the size of the young carrots. There we stood—getting hungrier by the second. We knew that stealing was wrong, and we did not want to sin. But could we not just taste them? My trusted friend Willi Hübert agreed that we could. I could always count on him when it came to playing tricks and pranks. He never let me down; he could also count on me. Willi's twin brother Franz warned us, not to steal. In the end, we did not only taste—we all ate those fresh, delicious carrots. In the meantime, it had gotten late, and we decided to walk back on Dick's *picadão*. As fate would have it, we were still chewing on stolen carrots when we met Mr. Dick coming in the opposite direction along the same *picadão*. I knew we had been caught, and I had a good idea of potential consequences. My brother-in-law Esau and my sister Maria were the first, my parents the second to learn about my carrot thievery.

When I came home from school the next day, Mother and I ate lunch together. Father and my siblings were working on the *roça*. That was a relief, but not for long. As I sat across the table from Mother, she did not look *at* me; she looked right *through* me and asked: "*Hauns, woa weascht du jistri nomeddag?"* (Hans, where were you yesterday afternoon?). I knew that she knew the answer to her own question. Mr. Dick had told my sister and she had told the rest of my family while I was away in school. Those carrots that had tasted so sweet on Sunday had a bitter aftertaste on Monday.

My mother sent me to the *roça* to talk with Father—and that in the presence of my two sisters and my brother. Father put down his hoe, sat down on a tree trunk, and I had to sit next to him. I feared the worst. And it came—not physical punishment; it went much deeper than that. Father impressed upon me the seriousness of stealing, quoting the eighth commandment: "You shall not steal." Then he told me to go home, tell Mother what he and I had talked about, then go to Mr. Dick and confess and ask for forgiveness. That was hard, but I had no choice.

By the time I got to Mr. Dick's house the afternoon was about to fade away. And then this: my sister Maria was standing by the house talking to her in-laws. I did not want her to see or hear me when I apologized. The only way out was to hide in the chicken barn and wait for her to go home. And that's where the mites get mixed in with the carrots. The number of these pesky microscopic bloodsucking critters that within seconds covered my body from head to foot was legion times legion. I could hardly bear the burning and itching sensation over my entire body.

Finally, my sister went home. I walked up to Mr. Dick and confessed my sin of stealing. However, I had the distinct feeling that our good neighbor, known as *Tjlieni Ditj* (Little Dick), could not find forgiving grace to match my remorse. I humbly walked home with a double burden: the sin of stealing carrots was harder to get rid of than I had thought, and the chicken mites with their thousand itching bites stuck to my body until I took them that same evening to the river for a drowning bath. That day I learned a lesson for life: stealing has painful consequences—even in childhood. Mr. Dick was henceforth known as *Jalmaere Ditj* (Carrot Dick) instead of *Tjlieni Ditj*.

16

On the Ordinary Edge of Daily Life

Every person lives in one of two tents:
One is called content, the other discontent.
The measure of joy in life depends on the attitude
one has living under conditions prevalent in either tent.
—Adapted from *Uncle Ben's Quotebook*

    The tropics and subtropics are known for their predilection for all sorts of pests and parasites. Neither man nor beast is exempt from these macroscopic as well as microscopic forms of life that are annoying at their best and deadly at their worst. We had such a wide variety of them that the list would be too long to discuss here, even if I should limit it to the ones we had to contend with in our own family. I am here not talking about poisonous snakes, scorpions, and spiders. We had them too—plenty of them. What I am referring to are the tiny and not so tiny creatures that infested our bodies. They inflicted not only discomfort and pain; they also caused debilitating weakness, illness, even death.
    During the first years before we had a doctor at the Krauel, my mother made herbal teas which everyone had to drink from time to time. That was a common remedy widely used by the colonists of the area to treat children and adults for worms of all sorts. We certainly did not drink those teas for good taste, not even to quench our thirst. We drank them simply to prevent, reduce or eliminate parasitic infestations. They seemed to be effective, at least to a degree. Those simple homemade remedies gave way to more sophisticated recipes and treatments when our colony was able to secure the help of a medical doctor and his wife.
    In 1934 a young Mennonite medical student, a refugee from the Soviet Union, completed his internship in Germany. His wife was a nurse. The couple was faced with several choices. Dr. and Mrs. Peter Dyck had permanent resident status to live and work in Germany. They also had visas to emigrate to Canada, where Dr. Dyck's parents and siblings had immigrated several years earlier. Then there was the invitation from the Mennonites of the Krauel colony in the subtropical rain forests of southern Brazil. Of the three options, the last had the least appeal. Evidently, they must have perceived their calling as from the Lord to leave their medical

practice in Germany, forego attractive opportunities in Canada, and instead come to our colony in the jungle to serve a people in desperate need of health care.

I remember the day in 1935 that Dr. and Mrs. Dyck came to the Krauel. Our people were greatly pleased. While there was yet no hospital in the colony, their coming raised hope for the eradication of a host of prevailing diseases and infections to which our people had little resistence. Motivation to build a hospital rose to an all-time high. The facilities were ready within a relatively short time, a professional staff from Germany and Brazil was recruited, and an effective medical program was in place.

Among the most common parasites were pinworms, tapeworms, hookworms, and the giant intestinal worm called *ascariasis,* as thick as a pencil and twenty centimeters (eight inches) in length. If not treated in time, *ascariasis* were known to get into the bloodstream, lungs, and even the brain. The first victim I personally knew was Mr. Stjopan, who came seasonally to live and work at our place. One year he got very sick. My father took him to the hospital for treatment. My mother also did whatever she could, but there was nothing that could save his life. The huge *ascariasis* had made their way into the man's head. He died within weeks and was buried in the Waldheim cemetery. The second victim was a fourteen-year-old Hiebert girl who had the same malady. Her mother sought medical help outside our colony, but her daughter died within months because of those beastly parasites.

It seems only natural that one of the first problems Dr. Dyck attacked was that of eliminating intestinal parasites. His campaign was systematic. With the help of Mrs. Dyck he made us aware of the need to improve sanitary conditions. He introduced a healthier diet, including vegetables, which some people called "rabbit food." Others took him more seriously and followed his suggestions. Most effective were the new remedies and the methods of treatments he used.

He urged everyone in the colony to undergo an annual *Wurmkur*. I remember our first trip to the hospital for *Wurmkur*. It was a family affair, an exciting event for my parents, two sisters, brother Nikolai and me. Father was the coachman. He and mother sat in front, my sisters on a board behind them, and my brother and I in the back on the wagon floor. It was as though we were driving to a special colony festivity. But it was no celebration, this worm cure. First, we had doctor's orders to fast the night before and the morning of the cure. It was the first fast for us children. We talked all the way to the hospital, wondering with suspense what the worm treatment might be like. Well, we were to find out soon enough.

I shall refrain from describing the details of the treatment. Yet I will say that the herbal tea my mother made was a delightful treat compared to drinking measure upon measure of Epsom salts—some pure, some mixed with other medications—and dosage upon dosage of pure ricinus oil. The procedure lasted from early morning until well into the afternoon. By the time we had downed our consigned portions, the paths between waiting room and outdoor privy looked considerably more worn than it did the morning we got there. When we finally got home, we were so exhausted that we had barely enough energy to do the chores. The procedure had to be repeated at home, although in a milder and less regimented form, to make sure that the microscopic larvae would meet the same fate as the parent parasites. Our people at the Krauel expressed thankful relief that the battle against intestinal parasites could be fought with decreased intensity, thanks to Dr. Dyck's professional approach to the problem.

In my later years I have often had the impression that neither we in the Krauel in Santa Catarina nor those who moved to Witmarsum in Paraná in the early 1950s have adequately expressed appreciation and gratitude for the services Dr. and Mrs. Dyck gave to our people for nearly half a century. During one of my itineraries in Brazil in the 1970s, I visited Dr. Dyck and his wife in their home in Curitiba. Mrs. Dyck was in her last days of life, but able to converse. It was at that time that Dr. Dyck shared with me some of the highlights of his medical career, as well as some of the low points. He was gracious in his assessment of events and placed everything into the hands of God. The biblical injunction to remember our leaders also applies to this couple: They served our people in Brazil as pioneers and leaders in the medical field. Having said that, I must return to my parasites.

Another kind of parasite that plagued us beyond words was what we called *Bizhworm* (derived from the German term *Bieswurm,* also known as *Dasselwurm*). A generic name in Portuguese is *bicho.* I have no word for it in English. Cattle, dogs, and humans were the favorite hosts of these *bichos,* which loved to reside in the flesh beneath the skin. They got there through the bloodstream. A large, hairy, extremely swift-flying fly (*Biesfliege; Dasselfliege*) laid its microscopic eggs on the surface of the skin. During their rapid incubation process, the larvae penetrated the skin and entered the bloodstream of the involuntary host. Once the parasite was mature enough to be mobile, it moved around to find a suitable spot near the surface of the skin (even in the mouth) and began to torture its victim. But its progress did not end there. As the worm got bigger, it grew one ring of bristles after another, sharp as needles—the tool with which it enlarged its dwelling. Within a week or so it began to turn and twist, carving out for itself an ever larger territory within the body of the victim, who was by now squirming with pain and distress. The spot where it would finally emerge through the skin became red and infected. Dogs showed their agony by erratic twisting and turning, wincing and whining. I always felt very sorry for them. The cattle in the pasture had a similar response: with their tails up high they ran in circles as though they were possessed.

By the time these *bichos* were mature enough to spiral their way to the surface of the skin, they emitted a flow of foul fluids, attracting flies without number. These flies bred maggots within hours, so that the danger of infection and disease was increased many times over. In those early years there was little we could do except brush some kerosene, creosote, or turpentine on the outer skin of the infested areas. I was four years old, small and skinny, when I had my first *Bizhworm* on my left shoulder. After that I have had many more. So have my siblings. We simply had to accept the discomfort and pain as part of life. Yet I must admit that to share my earthly *tent* with the invasive *bichos* demanded an extra measure of grace to remain a host who was *content*.

In many parts of the world, people are familiar with such blood-sucking critters as lice and bedbugs, ticks, chiggers, mites and fleas. But not everyone knows the kind of tick or *carrapato* that attached itself to the neck of dogs so firmly that it could not be shaken off. In a week to ten days these ugly yellow ticks had grown to the size of a marble and reproduced countless times. If we did not watch out for the dogs, they actually got very sick, became lethargic and useless. Horses and livestock were also prone to attract large infestations of other varieties of ticks and lice that caused suffering and sickness to our domestic animals. No matter how hard we tried, we never won the battle against these insects.

Another nasty parasite was the tiny black flea or *bicho de pé* that lived not on the skin like a normal flea, but under the skin. Like the giant *carrapato* and a host of other tick-varieties, these near-microscopic *bichos de pé* were native to Santa Catarina. They were more than a pest; they were a plague. We called them *Saundflieje* (sandflies) in Low German. That was actually a misnomer. While there was a great variety of tiny, stinging sandflies, these were not winged flies at all; they were wingless parasites that lived in dusty cracks and earthen floors. They jumped at and attached themselves to every moving object within their vicinity, human or animal. They rarely came as singles; they seemed to live in colonies and jump in groups. Within split seconds they found a place to hide from which they could survey and test their new habitat. As soon as their new host stopped somewhere to rest, they went to work, usually in the night.

The favorite place of these *bichos de pé* to dig for a permanent dwelling was under the toe nails. They drilled their microscopic wells through the skin between the toes, or they made their nests in the cracks of cal-loused foot soles, thick and hard from walking without shoes. These pests had the ability to inject a tiny speck of fluid which acted as an anesthetic so that they could dig themselves into the flesh without being noticed. Their first job was to create around themselves elastic tissue with an almost invisible opening for air, that served as both shelter and incubation center. These nests with countless eggs were perfectly round and expanded to the size of a small pea. If not removed, they caused severe itching, pain, and infection. I have had hundreds of them. Some of my friends in school had every toe and crack full of *Saundflieje*, often accompanied by prolonged oozing infections.

Then there were the feared invasions of the armies that ruled the jungle. When they came, they came by the thousands—no, by the millions—all at once. They were organized like the military troops of a great general, and were bent on absolute domination like a ruthless dictator is determined to create one great empire of the world. Their territory had no boundaries, their hunting ground no limits. They had their kings and rulers, their generals and commanders, their fighting soldiers and their common laborers. I have seen them at work, these "army ants," as they are commonly called. No insect can avoid their notice, not even in the safest hiding places; no smaller living thing on the ground or in the trees, except the most alert flyers, can escape their cutting shears and the needle-sharp stingers with which they inject a numbing poison into each cut to paralyze their prey for easy conquest.

The army ants in our part of the world were cruel, brutal, dangerous, ruthless. Their colonies were above ground, serving as rest areas, feeding stations and breeding places, but not as permanent residences. Army ants are carnivorous nomads, restless wanderers and aggressive hunters, hence the name. When their food supply was depleted and their young were mature enough for the next march, they would break up camp all at once. The big, yellow kings and rulers led the way with the giant generals, the angry soldiers and the dark brown workers following. As soon as they had advanced far enough into the jungle, the yellow leaders would branch out to the left and to the right, taking a host of followers with them on each path. The heaviest concentration of soldiers stayed on the ground and a lighter contingent settled in shrubs and trees.

Meanwhile, a heavy back-up troop marched to the point where the front leaders had made a fork. These latecomers, however, did not follow the path to the right and to the left, but instead spread over every inch of ground between the two forks. That was the moment when the battle cry was given, and one began to hear a rustling and hustling sound as if a wind was moving through the jungle. But there was no wind. The noise was created by the fleeing insects: the cockroaches and grasshoppers, spiders and scorpions, even the occasional frog and snake, and every other creeping, crawling creature within the encircled corridor. They all sensed imminent danger and ran for cover. But there was no escape. No matter where they turned, they would eventually be captured, cut to pieces, and carried away. That was an ugly sight to behold. Even if I lacked compassion for spiders and scorpions and other repulsive crawlers and creepers, I found no pleasure in seeing an invasion of army ants, especially when they invaded beehives, chicken barns, even our homes. When they came in, people had to move out. I remember only one such invasion in our house. It was a devastating experience, except for one thing: when they had completed their conquest and moved out, the house was free of pests, such as crickets and cockroaches. That was effective pest control by pests.

The invasion took a day or two, depending on the area and volume of defense they had to contend with. As soon as the battle was over, the commanders formed new paths to retreat to a new rest area. The soldiers and the working ants dutifully followed with their prey to provide food for the whole colony at a new place. That is where they hatched their larvae and raised a new generation of warriors for another conquest, larger than the one before.

17

Dogs and Cats and Snakes and Rats

It is not just as we take it,
This mystical world of ours,
Life's field will yield as we make it:
A harvest of thorns or one of flowers.
—Johann Wolfgang von Goethe

The "day of the rat hunt" at our house was always a great day for the dogs and the cats. They loved every minute of it. To us on the jungle farm domesticated dogs and cats were much more than pets; they were as indispensable as the ox or the horse. We could not have done without either. We needed cats to help us control the mice and rats. Even then, the kind of rats we had in our region were so bold and brazen that many house cats could not handle them without help. That is why we also needed dogs. They sniffed out every hiding place of the mice and other rodents around the house and in the field. Whenever they became too plentiful, we had to take time off from fieldwork to reduce their number. Fortunately, that was still in the days when no one had ever dreamed that rats could be an endangered species.

As soon as we got ready for combat, the dogs rallied around us as though they knew what we were about to do. Even the cats became excited. We followed a certain routine in our agenda for the day. My brother Nikolai and I knew every nook and cranny in the barn and the pigpen, even in and under the house, where the rats had made themselves at home. Their favorite hideouts were between double walls, in the overhang of a roof, and under piles of lumber, fenceposts or firewood. If we succeeded in disrupting their cozy habitat to make them squeak and squirm, we felt that we were making headway. The dogs and cats stood by and did the rest. It usually took the better part of the day to clear our place sufficiently to keep those gnawing, destructive, annoying beasts from their indiscriminate visits to the pigpen and the pantry, or wherever they found their best supply of food.

Our dogs not only hunted rats, but performed other duties as well. They were our guardians and protectors. We needed them to keep away wildcats, jungle dogs, and other animals that were after our chickens, and field lizards that were after the eggs. But their greatest usefulness was their keen sense of duty to protect us against poisonous snakes when we worked in the *roça*. Then, too, they were helpful in fetching a stubborn horse, or in keeping an angry bull at bay when we had to mend the fence or do other kinds of work in the pasture. I must list three or four of our dogs that were special.

Over the course of years we had Caro, Nero, Leo, and Lalla. With the exception of Lalla, all of them were great hunting dogs, especially Nero. He was black with white spots, big and strong and fearless. My brother Heinrich and Heinrich Harder from across the river often went hunting together, not as a sport, but to provide meat for the family table since in those days meat was rare. They went for the bigger game, such as deer, wild pigs, and the brown or black *anta*. A wild boar was not known for tasty meat, but as an easy target because he was usually on the outer periphery protecting his harem. The women of the household were always pleased when the two Heinrichs returned from their hunting excursion with at least one wild pig, even if it happened to be a boar. Mr. Harder also had good dogs, but none measured up to Nero. He was quick to find the animals' hideout and to chase them toward the hunters or the river. He got the highest rating as an exceptional hunting dog.

Occasionally, Nero went into the jungle by himself. He liked to hunt for a *cutia*, commonly referred to as the Brazilian rabbit. It was a fairly large rodent with bristles like a wild pig, not with fur like the northern rabbit. It had no tail, very tiny ears, and good meat. Intuitively, Nero must have known that whenever he caught a *cutia*, he did not have to share it with the family; it was his alone. But hunting on his own without human companionship was risky, especially if he should meet up with a pack of *quatis* or with a herd of wild pigs. These beasts can be very aggressive, particularly when they have a litter or two of piglets in the herd. Wild boars guarding the herd are powerful and extremely dangerous. The quatis are also dangerous animals. While they are not much bigger than a raccoon, they are swift and tricky movers, attacking their target from all angles with teeth sharp and lethal as daggers. In either case, Nero would have little chance to survive an attack by a herd of pigs or a pack of *quatis*. One day it happened: he came home looking as if he had been in a meat grinder. Within hours he bled to death.

Leo was also fairly large and very clever. His special skill was getting the cattle from the pasture into the barn. He always got the ox or horse we wanted, as though he knew each one by name. When we told him to fetch Strelo, he was off, and before long was at the gate with Strelo. Leo had a tragic ending. He was bitten by a *jararaca*, a deadly snake that was common in many parts of Brazil. We did what we could to save his life. Even Lalla lay down next to him and licked his wounds. But Leo never recovered.

Caro had a terrible ending. He died of hydrophobia, or rabies. This was a common and very frightening disease in our region, especially among dogs. It is caused by a virus that attacks the brain and the central nervous system. It is readily transmitted to other animals as well as to humans by the bite of an infected animal. Whenever a dog with rabies appeared on the scene, the whole village was alerted. It was common knowledge that everybody was to stay in the house with doors closed. Only the strongest and fittest of men, armed with pitchforks and clubs, were out to get the sick dog. One morning my father noticed that Caro made a wide circle around the pond by our barn, as if he was afraid of water. Fear of water (hence hydrophobia), a stiff neck, and foaming at the mouth are sure symptoms of the disease. Caro had all of these—he had rabies. Fortunately, Father saw it in time to exterminate the dog before he could run away and transmit this fatal malady to others.

Lalla was a brown female dog, quite small, but exceptionally intelligent. She was no hunter, but a life saver—and that in the true sense of the word. We must have had her for at least thirteen years. She stayed on the colony with my parents when I left for Canada in 1949. What made her so valuable was the way she surveyed the territory for snakes. In early spring we began clearing a *roça*, either with the *foice* or with the *enxada*, to plant a new crop. The weeds were high and thick; and that is where Lalla did her life-saving job. She was always some five to ten meters ahead of us, sniffing for poisonous vipers. Her particular target was the camouflaged jararaca, of which there were at least ten different varieties. All were deadly. As soon as she detected one she would utter a special bark, telling us to come to her aid. When she noticed that we were moving toward her, she grabbed the viper with her teeth, shook it violently back and forth, then dropped it to the ground and waited until we got there, as if she was telling us: "I have done my job, now do yours." The snake was by no means dead. It was still hissing with fury to strike; but its back was disjointed as a result of the violent jerk it had received from the dog. Thus it was incapable of jumping and its danger greatly diminished.

There were days when Lalla found up to five and six snakes in a single forenoon. But one day she evidently missed one or had not been alert enough. She was bitten and became deathly sick from the poison. Thankfully, she survived without visible aftereffects, except that her behavior was notably altered. After three or four weeks of recovery she was again anxious to go with us to the *roça*. We immediately noticed a change in her demeanor. She was much more cautious when entering tall weeds and grasses, especially where there were logs and tree trunks covered by the thicket, where the snakes liked to hide. The other change we noticed was that she would never again attack a *jararaca*, or any other venomous viper such as the coral snake or the rattlesnake. She would still alert us by a whining bark, leaving it up to us to find the exact spot where the snake was hiding. Despite her caution, she was bitten more frequently as she got older. However, she had built up sufficient immunity to lessen the pain that was never as great as the agony she suffered the first time she was bitten.

During all the years we had Lalla, I never went into the jungle without her. She also loved to accompany me in the evenings when I went to visit one of my married siblings or when I ran an errand for my parents. There was many a time when she alerted me to danger. Of course, she did that for any one of us in the family. What never ceased to amaze us was the manner and tone of her bark. She had different ways of letting us know what kind of danger or what type of animal or reptile she was smelling or seeing in the vicinity, and whether it was on the ground or lurking up in a tree. I could also tell if it would be a chase after a *tatú* or a *cutia*; or if it would be a snake hiding somewhere in a coiled position ready for the intruder to come near; or if I would have to prepare myself for a stationary encounter with a fearless creature, such as a giant *lagartixa*—a mini- crocodile up to two meters (over six feet) long, or a bullfrog. A bullfrog poses no great danger to humans, though when it is disturbed in its habitat, it protrudes its elastic "horns," then inhales so much air that it becomes twice its normal size, and can look fierce. But it stays put, come what may—it simply will not run.

On one of my hunting expeditions I had crossed the river and was walking ever deeper into the jungle. As I was ascending toward the *serra*, I noticed that Lalla was getting increasingly restless. Suddenly she made a sharp turn and disappeared in the thick underbrush. I knew by the rhythm and tone of her bark that it was neither a snake nor something up in the trees. I expected to encounter either a *lagartixa* or a bullfrog. I was wrong; it was neither. Instead, it was a near-black *cachorro do mato*, also known as *graxaím* (jungle dog, or wild dog). These *graxaíms* were a real menace to our fowl population, catching chickens on land and ducks and geese on water. They were also known for their aggression. In this instance, the *cachorro* was not afraid of Lalla, but obviously did not like me next to her. It tried to jump over the thick trunk of a fallen tree, but slipped back and turned towards me. With its upper lips raised to bare every tooth in its quivering jaw, the *cachorro do mato* stared straight at my face, positioned only about a meter in front of me. I must admit that I was frightened; so was Lalla.

Knowing that she was no match for this wild beast, I made no attempt to urge her to attack. The best I could do in that moment was to put a round stone into the leather retainer of my *funda*, aim at the animal's forehead, stretch the rubber straps with a firm grip on the forked wooden handle, hold it for a moment—and let go. The stone did its job. The wild dog lay before me with all four legs stretched out. Lalla instantly jumped at its throat as though she, too, had a job to do before she could feel a sense of victory. After I finished skinning my prey for its soft fur, I walked home to tell the family of the adventure. The praise I received was more for the fact that there would be one less *cachorro do mato* to destroy our chickens than for the prized furry skin for which I was particularly happy.

Not long before I left for Bible school in Canada in May 1949, I went to visit my sister Margareta and her family. They lived at the Tucano Boi at the time, about three kilometers from our house. Lalla accompanied me. After supper we noticed dark clouds rolling in from behind the *serra*. We heard rumbling thunder in the distance. Within minutes the whole sky was an ominous sight, unleashing blinding flashes of lightning, deafening cracks of thunder, and mighty downpours. The rain let up for a moment, but not the darkness. With Lalla beside me, I ventured out to walk home. The road was extremely slippery. Every hole and hollow was filled with water, as were the ditches along the curving road. I could not see my hand before my eyes. It was literally pitch dark. Lalla must intuitively have sensed my predicament and the danger of slipping into deep water next to the path. Whenever I came close to the edge, she would press against my leg, as if telling me to move left or right, depending on which side the danger was. When I finally got home safely, my parents were as relieved as I was.

This happened to be the last time that Lalla gave me such a remarkable guided tour in the darkness of night. Soon thereafter I left for Canada, and the dog stayed with my parents at the Krauel.

18

Of Birds and Butterflies

Little bird up in the tree,
Oh, so tiny, scant to see.
Yet the song it sings, and the peace it brings
Echoes in my ear. Echoes in my ear.
—Childhood song in translation

I have little book knowledge about birds and butterflies. All I have are the memories from personal observation and experience in the Krauel, where both were plentiful in their natural setting. Even as a small child I was fascinated by the brilliant colors of the flora and fauna in the region. At the time I did not think of it as something special; it simply was an integral part of the ambience in which I lived. In retrospect, however, I take it as God's design to compensate, at least to a degree, for the educational opportunities I did not have. The splendiferous radiance of God's creation as displayed in living birds and butterflies was nothing short of magnificent. Small wonder that, when the Lord laid the cornerstone of creation, "the morning stars sang together and all the angels shouted for joy" (Job 38:7). That is why I feel compelled to relate a few vignettes from that segment of my natural schooling with neither books to read nor walls to keep me in, only nature to observe. When I tell a tale or two about birds and butterflies I do so simply to remember my early years in Brazil.

I was always mesmerized by the visual and audible beauty in the world of nature, particularly the variety of birds. I never ceased to marvel at their cheerful chirping and soft singing. They produced a host of melodic tunes (and some not so melodic noises) which my pen cannot even begin to describe. The same is true of their nesting habits. Take *João de Barro*, for instance. While not much bigger than a common blackbird, it is a clever building engineer, cementing its family dwelling on the top of a high tree stump or a wooden pole, using a certain kind of clay mixed with mud and bulrushes. It has the gift for architectural design that could make a human craftsman envious. In the process of fashioning its construction, *João de Barro* made sure that the upper half was as perfectly round as any human being could make it without precision instruments. Not only that; this bird was also good in intuitive mathematics, carefully calculating the size to have enough space for built-in tunnels and dividers. These were like a maze to confuse potential intruders. Once the nest was finished and completely cured, it was nearly as hard and strong as bricks fired in a kiln. In such a nest upon a post, *João* and his *Juanita* were safe and secure to raise their young.

Just as ingenious as *João de Barro*, though very different in appearance and size, was that small, brown chirping bird with a bright blue chest and greyish-yellow wings for which I have no name. It may belong to the same passerine bird family as the finch or the sparrow, but with nesting habits all its own. We simply called it *Spetjafoagel* (thorn bird) because it built the outer frame of the nest from nothing else than dry twigs with thorns. This *Spetjafoagel* was no bigger than a barn sparrow, yet its nest, usually hidden among the leaves of thick underbrush, was at least eight to twelve inches in diameter with a thorny, curving tunnel two to three feet long used as an entry way. The interior of the nest proper was lined with clay to keep the moisture out and cushioned with fine moss and soft feathers to make a cozy and comfortable place in which to hatch their eggs and feed their young.

For prize-winning displays of glowing feather dresses I would nominate the big white-breasted *tucano* (toucan) and the yellow- and red-breasted *papagaio* (parrot), which at that time were still plentiful in our area. Their colorful beauty was most striking in short and slow flights as they moved from one tree to the next. While both were herbivorous birds, their feeding habits varied significantly. The *tucano* had a bright yellow, long and thick horny bill with sharp, serrated blades on the upper half to cut leaves and fruit to size for easy consumption. The *papagaio* had a short hooked beak, hard and sharp as a chisel to split the hardest nut to take out the core. Like the toucan, the parrot also thrived on fruit, but added nuts instead of leaves to its diet. Regrettably, as my friend Peter Pauls writes, some of those exotic birds I used to admire have during the last decades become rare, even extinct.

My parrot Rico of the *maracanã* species was an exceptional bird with an interesting history. When I say "my parrot," I actually mean our parrot. It belonged to the family. My job was to take care of it. We did not buy him from a pet shop, for there were no pet shops. We got him from the nest shortly after he was hatched and called him Rico, "rich." And rich he was, surpassing other parrots in beauty and intelligence.

Close to the edge of the jungle we had a *roça* of *mandioca*. At the time we cleared that part of the forest we left a giant *pinheiro* of the *araucária* family standing there to be harvested when needed. Little did we know that a pair of *maracanã*, one of the large varieties of parrots had selected this particular *araucária* to chisel out a hole with their razor-sharp beaks for a nest. One day in spring—I believe it was in October—Father said that we would have to cut down the big *pinheiro* for lumber. We could sell part of it, and the rest we would use to improve our barn. So my father, my brother Nikolai, and I took our axes and went to work.

As the huge *pinheiro* hit the ground with a mighty force, it broke open at the weakest spot—exactly where the parrots had carved out their nest. And there we saw to our amazement two young parrots. Only one was alive. It was tiny and completely without feathers, but it had a big head with a large beak. It looked ugly, totally out of proportion. We took it home and I began to nurse and feed it. I soaked dry cornbread in milk and with a teaspoon put some of it into its beak. Before long it swallowed the cornbread and wanted more. That was a good sign.

Rico thrived well and grew much faster than we had expected. Soon he got feathers—green and blue with yellow and red on his wings and his long tail. His cheeks were snow white with a brilliant red line above his curved upper beak. His eyes were light green with yellowish circles; they looked like two perfectly round, glowing jewels set in a white mounting with a red line crossing from one eye to the other. His lower beak was shaped like a dipper, but hard as diamond and sharp as a razor. He could crack the hardest palm nut, which could be crushed only with a hammer or a rock. However, no nut ever posed a problem for Rico. He simply picked it up, held it with the toes of one foot while balancing himself with the other, and then worked at it from every angle until it cracked open so that he could eat the kernel inside.

At times, Rico even cut the wire of his cage, made himself a hole and got out. Yet he was by nature a very charming, cuddly, and loving bird. He liked to sit on my shoulder when I walked around outside the house or when I sat inside. He groomed my hair and nibbled on my ears and neck. But he never bit me. The only time he got very angry and threatened to bite was when I teased him about his tail by trying to touch it while he was in his cage. He complained so loudly that the neighbors could hear him. The tail was his pride and joy which no one was allowed to touch. He always kept it shiny and groomed; every feather had to be in place with the bright colors visibly showing.

Rico learned to talk when he was quite young. He imitated the tone of our voices and the intonation of our expressions so exactly that Mother did not always know whether the parrot or one of us children was speaking. The dogs evidently had the same problem. He knew the name of each dog and seemed to take pleasure in playing tricks on them. Many times during the hot afternoons when the dogs were sleeping somewhere in the shade, Rico got the idea to call Lalla or Leo to get the cows from the pasture. He would not quit calling until at least one of the dogs showed up by his cage.

At other times Rico took pleasure in pounding with his special "parrot elbow" on one of the bars or boards in his cage, imitating a neighbor knocking on our door. Then he was quiet and listened for someone inside to say herein! (come in). He repeated that many times. If one of us responded, he was satisfied. But if no one answered, he knocked even louder and then responded himself by saying, *herein!* That usually was the end of his trick. He also loved to be part of a conversation, either when neighbors or friends came to our place, or all by himself. He knew how to change the tone of his voice, talked to himself, and then laughed as heartily alone in his cage as those of us sitting outside in the shade nearby.

My parrot was not only beautiful and intelligent; he also seemed to be content and happy. But he had a tragic end. When my sister Maria and her husband Bernhard Esau with their children decided to move to Curitiba, they implored us to let Rico go along with them. No one found it as hard to part with him as I did, but I consented. Not many months after their move, we received word that Rico had been poisoned by a neighbor. We have had other birds and parrots, but none ever measured up to Rico in beauty, brilliance, and intelligence.

The Krauel was home to a multiple variety of butterflies. The striking splendor of these insects fashioned by the Creator's hand defies description. The three most beautiful varieties in our area were the "Eighty-Eight" with a distinctive black-and-white display of the figure 88 patterned on the underside of their colorful hindwings; the "Owl Face" with large, intricately patterned eyespots on each outer hind wing, forming a perfect image of a staring owl; and the "Brazilian *Morpho*," the most desired butterfly for a worldwide market. The male of one particular variety of the *morpho* was distinguished by its brilliant metallic-blue wings which were used to make jewelry, serving trays, chess boards, and other artistic artifacts.

On the one hand, I see these beautiful creatures as a token remnant preserved by God in order to give us a glimpse of what paradise must have been like before the Fall, when cosmic design and order reigned in pristine glory. On the other hand, I also witnessed ample evidence of "Paradise Lost," that John Milton has so masterfully described in his epic poem. While Milton deals more with the moral and spiritual than with the esthetic and material aspects of Paradise, the one cannot be totally detached from the other. The thorns and the thistles as well as the pests and the parasites to which I referred in a previous chapter are obvious marks of the chaos, dread and dissonance that have entered the kosmos to disrupt peace and harmony in nature.

In those pioneering years we were always in need of money. We younger children did work at home on the roça, but not for wages. Even the idea of an allowance never came up in our home. Besides, Father had to save every penny for basic family needs. One day we heard that a certain Mr. Penner in the neighboring village had discovered a market for butterflies. My sister Katja and I got excited about the prospect of catching butterflies to make enough money for her to buy an embroidered handkerchief to fulfill the desires of her heart, and for me to buy the pocket knife which was at the very top of my wish list. I was six or seven at the time, Katja was eight years older. Father supported the idea and helped us make butterfly nets. Now we were equipped and ready for business. Our plan seemed perfect: we would catch butterflies, bring them to Mr. Penner, who in turn would sell them in Ibirama or Blumenau, and then pay us our due. That may sound like a slow process to reach our goal; yet we never questioned a positive outcome and were ready to work for it.

One hot and clear afternoon in the early summer in October or November we decided that the moment for a big catch had come. We took our new nets and proudly made our way along the picada toward the serra. There, we knew, was an open space in which humidity rebounded from the heat of the sun, and the wind was kept out by the surrounding forest. The place was like a giant basket nestled in the jungle. Butterflies of every size and color flirted and fluttered and performed their dazzling dances everywhere. It was a spectacle delightful to behold. As we stood there and watched their performance, we were so exuberant that we sang a happy jingle to the butterflies which in translation goes something like this:

> Butterfly, you jovial thing,
> Fetch yourself a mate to swing.
> Back and forth and to and fro,
> That's the way for you to go.
> Glisten, sparkle in the sun.
> Hurrah, hooray for number one.
> Up and down and to and fro,
> Hooray, hurrah for a great show.

We thought we had truly found the ideal spot for a rich catch. It could have been—but it wasn't, at least not for us that afternoon.

No sooner had we each found a perfect place on a fallen tree trunk over which the butterflies crisscrossed the open hollow than we heard a strange noise among the thorny shrubs along the edge of the forest next to us. And there he was: an anteater. Not one of the more common *tamanduá*, but one of the rarer giants with incredibly muscular front legs equipped with sharp and powerful claws. Its tail was as long as his outstretched body (over one meter; three to four feet) with uncombed and straggly hair draping to the ground. He poked his cylindrical head with his long, blanched-looking unsightly nose out of the bushes, lifted his heavy front claws onto a log, grunted and groaned as though he was saying that we were invading his territory, that we were not welcome, and that it would be wise for us to leave if we wished to forego the consequences. At least that was the message we perceived.

We were aware that this particular species was known for incredibly strong front legs with sharp and powerful claws to rip open beehives for honey and termite towers for larvae; but we did not know that they were totally toothless, using only their thirty-centimeters-long sticky tongue to lap up their soft and juicy diet. They do have a ravenous appetite for ants and bees and honey, though never for human flesh. It did not as much as occur to us that this hoary, toothless beast was an anteater, not a man-eater. Nonetheless, we left in haste. The butterflies, however, stayed with the anteater—at least those that settled in the lower weeds where he could lap them up.

This time we caught no butterflies and earned no money. Our desire for a handkerchief and a pocket knife did not go away until we tried again with some success for both ourselves and Mr. Penner. In addition to monetary rewards, whatever they might have been, Mr. Penner earned for himself the finest, exquisitely beautiful nickname in the entire colony: everybody called him *Flotta Panna* (Butterfly Penner).

19

Valleys Deep and Mountains High

The mountains that enclose the vale
With walls of granite, steep and high,
Invite the fearless foot to scale
Their stairway toward the sky.
—Henry van Dyke in Bennett, *Book of Virtues*

Life can have its ups and downs as well as its highs and lows. Some can be likened to euphoric peak experiences, while others may be more like shadows in the valley of death. I recall several such events along the pathway of my pilgrimage. They were experiences I did not choose, nor can I say that they were providential. I do not know how to categorize them. Yet they were real, they happened. For some, I am truly grateful. In other instances, I can only be thankful that God brought me through them and sustained my life beyond them.

Tender Feet in Glowing Coals

Tender bare feet of a little boy are no match for red-hot coals glowing under ashes. It happened during the Brazilian summer of 1930/1931, when I was two and a half years old. People were anxious to clear their land close to the river to plant *grama*, a tough perennial grass commonly used for pastures. *Grama* grows especially well in light, sandy soil. My brother Nikolai and I were playing close to our house, each with a pair of large snail shells we had found after burning a roça. We imagined these snails to be our oxen to pull logs out of the jungle, as we had seen Father and our older brother Heinrich do with real oxen. That was the only way to pull useful tree trunks to a safe place before the roça was set on fire.

"Fia! Tjhitjh doa! Woatjhentins brenni Rossi." (Fire! Look there! Warkentins are burning *roça!*) So my brother called out to me in decibels loud enough to split deaf eardrums. The fire was on the other side of the river where the Warkentins lived, at least a kilometer from our place. Before I could even see where it was, Nikolai was already far away, running toward the river to see the spectacular event from closer up. I ran after him. No matter how hard I tried and how loudly I cried, I had no chance of catching up with him—after all, he was over four years older than I. The main problem was that we had to cross a freshly burned *roça* on our own land between the house and the river. The piles of logs and tree branches had burned down, but under those ashes were still glowing coals. And that is where I got into serious trouble.

While my brother was smart enough to circumvent these huge ash heaps, my mind had not yet developed to the point that I could see the red-hot danger lurking under a blanket of silver-grey ashes. And so I ran straight into the first pile on my path. Of course, I stayed right there and screamed at the top of my strength. My brother was by now already standing by the river, looking across to the burning flames without the faintest idea that I was standing in a heap of glowing coals, roasting the flesh of my tender bare feet right to the bones.

Providentially, my sister Susanna heard me scream and was there in seconds. I remember as though it was yesterday how she grabbed me with both hands, took me into her arms, and carried me into the house where Mother was. Since there was no doctor and no medical help to rely on, Mother took over with the help of the "Great Physician." I have no personal recollections beyond that, not even of the pain. When Frieda and I visited my brother Nikolai and sister Susanna for the last time in 1995, we asked for the details of that incident. They confirmed that, indeed, the bones of my heels and toes had been plainly visible, and that no one had thought they would ever heal and be normal. But my feet have healed. That is nothing short of a miracle of God.

Under the Horns of Bull Prinz

Bull Prinz may have come from good stock, but he developed a violent temper. My father was never fond of inbred cows. He claimed that they were weak, susceptible to disease, and poor milk producers. He was right; yet that's all we had. Our first two cows together gave only three liters (about three quarts) of milk per day. So my father and several farmers in our village decided to get a bull calf from good stock, hoping eventually to improve the quality of our livestock. It was agreed that we would raise the bull to maturity, and then the other partners would take their turn in caring for this special animal.

Father and my oldest brother went to get the calf from a German colonist who lived a day's journey away. We younger siblings could hardly wait for them to return. Finally, they came with the young bull. All three were tired. The black calf with white spots was just a few weeks old, but fat, strong, and shiny. My brother named it Prinz because of its princely look. We all agreed that, because my sister Katja had a special liking for the calf, she should be given primary responsibility to care for

Prinz. She often took me with her when she fed, brushed and stroked him. Even I could occasionally stroke his neck and forehead; but it soon became evident that he did not like me.

Prinz grew much faster and thrived much better than anyone expected. Within three months he was quite big, strong, and fat. He was a beautiful animal. His sharp, pointed horns added authority to his bullish self-confidence. He looked almost elegant and became a conversation piece in the village. Every partner was pleased with the way Prinz was developing. But no one was as pleased and proud as Katja, who treated him with extra care and kindness.

As the bull got bigger and older, he began to act out his bullishness. He refused to be stroked, went at tree stumps with his horns, threw dust up into the air with his front feet, and made a bellowing noise that frightened even the horses. Job of old once raised the question whether an ox ever bellowed when it had fodder. Well, our Prinz did. He bellowed even during the night; he made the horses in the barn edgy with his angry roar. "It seems to me that Prinz is becoming a dangerous beast," Father cautioned Katja. "Maybe it would be better if I would take care of him instead of you." Katja insisted that she could do it and took a heavy stick with her each time she went to feed him.

One day when I again went along with her, Prinz looked up, lifted his nose, let out an angry roar, and came charging at me like a vicious dog. In a matter of seconds I was on the ground between a tree stump and his horns. Katja yelled and hit the bull with all her might, breaking the stick to pieces. In his rage, Prinz seemed neither to hear nor feel anything and kept on kneading me against the stump. Finally, he gave up and walked away, still bellowing with anger. He had really worked me over. I was badly bruised from head to toe and bleeding from my nose and mouth. That was the last time Katja and I ever went to feed that bull.

Father was right—Prinz had become a very angry and dangerous animal. For a while only my brother Heinrich with the help of our dogs could handle him. Before long the bull became so aggressive that we had to get rid of him while he was still fairly young. With time, our people got another bull and eventually succeeded in improving their livestock.

"Hauns Fesippt! Halpt!"

Our meandering Rio Krauel was not a big river, but it gave us a lot of pleasure—swimming, boating, fishing and much more. Generally, the river banks and bottom were sandy and firm, and the flow of water appeared quite normal. There were places, however, where the water rushed across rocks and rapids, and other places where the flow came to a virtual halt. These were sizable holes, too deep for safety.

We boys in the village made ourselves rafts out of bamboo or canoes out of wood to race in competing teams up and down the river. Some of the things we tried out were utterly foolish and extremely dangerous. Looking back on that time, I am amazed that not one of us drowned because of our daring stupidities. One Sunday afternoon when I was about fourteen years old, we again divided into opposing teams, each one trying to overturn the canoe of the other. In the course of that battle, I fell over the edge between the two canoes and was accidentally hit on the head with the oar by one of the boys. Apparently, nobody noticed. My call for help was completely drowned out by the yelling, screaming and laughing of the rest. My only thought was: this is it, I'm drowning.

But in the plan of God the number of my days recorded in His book had not yet run out; my time to go had not yet come. Johann Teichrieb, one of the big boys, suddenly saw my struggle and made a frightening yell: *"Hauns fesippt! Halpt!"* (Hans is drowning. Help!) That shocked everyone to silence, and in a split second Johann was next to me in the water. Others were quick to help in the rescue effort.

Johann Teichrieb never forgot that incident. Neither did I. While I expressed to him my thanks and appreciation for saving me from drowning, I could and should have done more. Six or seven years after the incident our ways parted—I went to Canada in 1949, and soon thereafter he moved to Colônia Nova in Rio Grande do Sul as part of a larger resettle-ment project. When I returned to Brazil in 1957, I had the chance to visit him briefly. He appreciated the visit, but our conversation was strained. He appeared to have more love for the things of this world than for the things of the Lord. Decades later he left word with my brother that he would like to speak with me if I happened to come to Colônia Nova. Was he now a drowning man waiting for someone to help him? He operated a business of some ill repute in the community. In 1991 I was there, but did not take the time to see him. When I returned again in 1995, Johann was no longer living. He had died a lonely man. I deeply regret that I did not visit him earlier and can only rely on God's forgiving grace for my neglect. There are urgent calls in life that demand immediate attention. I did not listen. A German proverb says: *"Was du heute kannst besorgen, das schieb nicht auf bis morgen."* An equivalent in English might be something like this: Whatever you can do today, do not postpone it or delay.

Life is Leaking out in Blood

My peers and I spent many a Sunday afternoon in the jungle. If we were not exploring some cave in the *serra*, we were picking and eating wild fruit or cherry tomatoes—a pastime as legitimate and harmless as it was enjoyable. But on this particular Sunday six or seven of us teenage boys decided to look for parrot nests in hollow trees, where parrots like to breed their young. So we took our *facões* and several *machados,* and off we went. As we marched along the narrow *picada* toward the *serra,* we made big plans: we would find young parrots, feed them until they had feathers and could eat on their own, and then sell them, divide the cash between us and have our very own money. In those days it was easier to talk about money than to get it. Our plans and intentions were not bad, but never realized. What happened instead was very different.

We were nearing the cliffs of the *serra*. The afternoon slipped by fast, and yet we found no parrots. Somewhat disappointed, we put down our tools and contemplated what to do next. Since it was getting late, we decided to go home before darkness set in. As foolish as teenage boys can be, we pushed each other around while collecting our tools. In the process, I stepped onto my own ax, which was leaning against a tree with the sharp edge turned outward. The resulting gash between my second and third toes on my right foot was over five centimeters (two inches) long. With nerves cut and veins severed, blood was gushing out like red paint from a pressure gun. None of us had any knowledge how to stop it. At first, I tried to walk on my own despite increasing pain. Each step aggravated the bleeding. Within about ten minutes I was too weak to walk. My friends took turns carrying me, two or three at a time. They helped me hold up my foot but that, too, became difficult. Second by second and dribble by dribble life was leaking out. I sensed it. And I knew it. My friends were as afraid as I was that the point of no return could be imminent. Finally, they got me home.

No one recognized the gravity of the injury as quickly as my mother did when she saw my greyish-white face. She told the boys to lay me down on my back outside in the yard with the injured foot in an elevated position. She tied a rag tightly around my leg above the knee. Then she lit a pile of rags and smoked my foot to sear the wound and stop the bleeding. Throughout that night Mother and Father held a vigil next to my bed and bathed my foot in a potassium solution. We called it *Kali* or *Kalium,* a blue powdery substance that acts as a disinfectant and healing agent when dissolved in water. While the wound healed many years ago, the scar is a visible reminder that life is fragile and that the Giver of life may have to use many different means to sustain it.

Each one of the personal rescue stories I have listed gives evidence that "my times are in your [God's] hand," as the Bible puts it (Ps. 31:15). He has brought me through the valleys and never withdrawn His guidance across the mountains of life. And God is still holding me in His hand.

My First Pair of Shoes at Sixteen

I had never owned a pair of shoes beyond babyhood in Siberia. In Brazil we either walked barefooted or wore crudely-made clogs. They consisted of a two- to three-centimeter-thick wooden base and a piece of cowhide covering the front end of the foot to protect the toes. We called them *Holtschlorre* in Low German or *tamancos* in Portuguese. Those are descriptive words for a type of footwear that one drags across the ground, making a slurring sound that is neither distinct nor melodious, yet quite audible, in the process.

In actuality, those clogs were fairly comfortable, except for running. And that is where we children had our major problem with those *Holtschlorre*. Since they had neither string nor buckle to secure them to our feet, they could easily be dropped and left without noticing it. I have spent much time searching for my clogs. I cannot help but wonder whatever became of those I lost in the jungle. But I never had to wonder about the consequences I faced when I "again" had lost my *Holtschlorre*. I had to walk barefoot until Father got around to making another pair.

In His foreknowledge and wisdom, our Creator has seen fit to allow us to go through different phases and rites of passage during our lifetime. When I was about fifteen years old, I went through a phase of vanity. I considered clogs to be ordinary and clumsy, whereas shoes became a status symbol among my peers, both boys and girls, in our village. My greatest wish was for a pair of shoes. Some of my friends already had them, and I wanted to be "with it," as my children said when they were teenagers. My parents had an understanding of my unfulfilled desire, but little money to fulfill it. I was at that time working as chore boy and clerk at our co-op store.

One day we got a small shipment of new shoes. Not a great selection; but there was one pair of black dress shoes with the famous brand name *Favorita*. Even today as I write these lines, my abnormally slow heartbeat increases its pace. I remember the strong desire by which I was overcome when I for the first time held those shoes in my hands. I looked at them with unspeakable admiration and not altogether innocent covetousness. Even the fact that one shoe was size 41 and the other size 42 did not bother me. I tried them on and was satisfied with the fit, which only intensified my desire to have them. What would the boys say? And what would the girls think? But where could I get the money to buy them? When I got home from work that day, I told my parents about our shipment of shoes at the co-op. They understood.

By that time I had never read C. S. Lewis—nor anyone else for that matter. I did not have the faintest idea that there was an ethical distinction between "likes" and "loves" or between, what Lewis terms "appreciative pleasures" and "need-pleasures." I simply did not think about life in such sophisticated terms. The other thing I did not know was that my parents, as only caring parents will do, had opened a kind of "savings account" for me in the business office of our co-op and each month deposited a small amount of my salary.

When my sixteenth birthday came up, my parents came to the store and bought me those shoes. Since it was not custom in our family to celebrate birthdays, the shoes were not a birthday gift; the purchase simply coincided with that yearly event. As I look at that first shoe-buying episode from today's perspectives, I have mixed feelings about it. On the one hand, I am satisfied to know that my desire for those shoes was prompted by "need-pleasure," as C. S. Lewis would see it, without ever diminishing my "appreciative pleasure." On the other hand, I cannot deny a feeling of selfishness and arrogance with a touch of "the pride of life." Nonetheless, I was so overjoyed with my first pair of shoes that even decades later, whenever I go to Brazil for a speaking engagement or on a church assignment, I buy myself *Favorita* shoes. But I always make sure that both shoes are the same size. They fit better that way.

My First Book at Eighteen

I have already mentioned that my schooling was interrupted soon after completing grade two. Fortunately, I had learned to read and write at that level. Unfortunately, however, I had no books to read beyond that. When President Getulio Vargas initiated his compulsory Nationalization Program in1937, our schools were closed soon thereafter by government orders and we became very much isolated from the rest of the world. With the outbreak of World War II the situation deteriorated from bad to worse. Our churches were shut down, correspondence with people in other countries was censured, German books, newspapers and other reading materials were destroyed, and we were forbidden to conduct any kind of meetings in German. Anyone caught speaking German was often mistreated, sometimes arrested and imprisoned.

All that changed after the War. In 1947 I received a small package in the mail. That in itself was a first. What was even more surprising was its content—a book; the first book I ever owned. Its title was *Erweckung gestern und heute* (Revival Yesterday and Today). It was written by Fritz Blum, a Bible school teacher in Switzerland. But the book did not come from Switzerland; it came from a German prisoner of war in Egypt. Inside the flyleaf was a short explanation: "This book was first sent to a German prisoner in Egypt. Now it goes to Hans Kasdorf in Brazil." That was a mountain peak experience.

The entire episode of my first book is wrapped up in the Providence of God, who works in marvelous ways his wonders to perform. That can be the only explanation of the way in which the book got to me and of the subject with which it deals. As I read this book, I was amazed to discover what God had been doing through the revival movements across the globe. This was for me another indication that He was preparing me to serve Him in world mission. For more than fifty years of preaching and teaching, I have always considered that first book as a confirmation of God's call to service in His kingdom.

Another interesting incident in connection with that book occurred in 1974-1975 when I was studying at the School of World Mission of Fuller Theological Seminary. There I met Werner Sidler from Switzerland who had been a missionary to Ethiopia for twenty-two years. Werner and I had each rented a room, but we shared a small kitchen in the same house. We often studied together and became good friends. When I mentioned my special book, he abruptly interrupted and exclaimed in surprise: "I know that book. I know its author. Mr. Blum was the *Rektor* of the *Freie Evangelische Schule Waldmannstrasse* where I was teaching before going to Ethiopia as a missionary." That encounter added another dimension to my amaze-ment of God's leading in my life. Frieda and I have visited the Sidlers near Lake Thun in Switzerland and have remained friends.

Title page of my first book.

20

Customs and Culture Colony Style

*Culture is the sum total
of learned behavior socially acquired,
not biologically or genetically transmitted.
That includes material and nonmaterial traits
which are passed on from one generation to another.*
—Adapted from Eugene Nida, *Customs and Cultures*

When I grew up in the Krauel, the word culture was not in my vocbulary. Only much later in life did I begin to understand the importance of culture as a powerful factor in the way we think, act, and react. Culture is a dynamic paradox, simultaneously mysterious and perspicuous. It is mysterious, because we do not see it; it is largely invisible in the manner we live. It is perspicuous, because its manifestations are evident everywhere; we live by them. While culture is pervasive and infusive, it is also restrictive and reductive—therein lies its power. In a certain sense each society creates its own culture, while at the same time being shaped by it. The outcome is its worldview—the way a society perceives the world.

Culture is a dynamic phenomenon. It always changes, demanding adjustments on the part of society. Such adjustments can bring with them serious tensions for Christians. Their challenge is to live out their faith within the context of the prevailing culture without forfeiting their theological convictions and moral principles which are based on abiding biblical norms rather than on the dictates of changing culture. What I am saying here about culture is not in a prescriptive, but rather in a descriptive sense. I am trying to show how things were, not how they ought to have been.

Learning Culture in Transition

My observations about culture colony style are in reality about a Mennonite subculture as I learned and experienced it during my years in the Krauel. Much of our learned behavior, the way we were thinking and doing things, had striking similarities to the way our forebears had lived in Russia. Many of the traits and traditions that had been near and dear to our people in Siberia had come with them across the Atlantic. This cultural transition from Russia to Brazil and the adjustment to a new way of life under a set of new circumstances proved to be extremely difficult. Some of the old customs simply did not fit into our new environment. Such factors as geography and climate alone were enough to throw our cultural and economic ways of doing things out of kilter. In Siberia, for instance, we celebrated Christmas in winter when the ground was frozen and covered with a heavy blanket of snow, whereas in Brazil we celebrated the same event of salvation history in sweltering summer heat with the temperature above 40°C (100°F) and 90 percent of humidity hanging heavily in the air.

Furthermore, in Siberia we lived on the open steppe with its endless expanse limited only by the horizon, which stretched to the farthest distance of our field of vision. But now we were squeezed into a narrow valley hemmed in by *serras* on every side with only one road to exit: the one by which we had entered from the Atlantic Ocean. Then, too, while the plow culture had dominated our agricultural enterprises on the flat fields in Russia, we now had to shift to a hoe culture, depending entirely on manual labor for subsistence. Nonetheless, certain aspects of our customs and culture remained with us requiring only minor changes and adaptations. One of them was the Low German language.

Onse scheene Muttaschproak

Growing up in a home where we spoke only *Plautdietsch* (Low German) and where the parents had a rich reservoir of stories in *dee scheene Muttaschproak* (beautiful mother tongue), I never questioned its worth and value. But I never understood why the preachers in church spoke High German, and why in school we learned Portuguese. Even though I was ignorant of the rationale behind our multilingual way of communicating, it never ceased to fascinate me. In fact, the phenomenon of language itself has always interested me. Decades later in graduate school I decided to devote time and energy to philology, language history, and linguistics. Not that I specialized in any of these disciplines; I simply wanted to learn about the origin, development, and extent of the large Indo-Germanic family of languages.

The particular form of German spoken by the Mennonites in the northern regions of the European lowlands, including Prussia, is only a small twig labeled *Plattdeutsch* (*Plautdietsch*) on the larger Indo-Germanic language tree. The Mennonites took their peculiar brand of Low German from Prussia to Russia in the eighteenth and nineteenth centuries, and from there brought it with them to the Americas in the late nineteenth and first half of the twentieth century. That is also how it found its way to

Brazil. With deep roots in other speech forms of the northern lowlands, our *Plautdietsch* has a much closer linguistic affinity to Dutch and English than to the more sophisticated High German that developed among the peoples of the highlands of southern Germany.

Regardless of where the Prussian/Russian groups of Mennonites have moved and lived, their *Muttaschproak* has linguistically remained fairly constant in that it has not been affected by the sound shift of the vowels which characterizes the *Hochdeutsch* (High German), the academic and literary language throughout German-speaking Europe. It is precisely this common linguistic basis which our Low German shares with the Dutch and English languages that proved to be a redemptive political factor for our Mennonites from the time of the Brazilian nationalization in 1937 through the period of the Second World War.

The significance of Low German for the Mennonites in Brazil can hardly be overestimated. I remember the day Father came home from a village meeting and reported to the family the information he had received there: "We are no longer permitted to speak German. Government agents have been sent to the colony to enforce the new law." This announcement caused no minor consternation throughout our colony. In view of what our people had experienced in the Soviet Union a mere decade earlier a threat of such gravity could not be taken lightly. Heinrich Martins and David Nikkel gathered signatures from heads of households, drafted a petition and personally went to Florianopolis to present the matter to the authorities. About a year later we received permission to use Low German instead of High German in our church services and other religious and social events.

In *Volk auf dem Weg* (June 1999), Alfred Pauls writes that the Low German language served us well during those difficult years. "Portuguese we did not know, German was prohibited and Low German was equated with Dutch." To verify that, the government agents sent to the colony tested our leaders by asking to give them the names of certain objects. For example: "What do you call a *vaca* [cow]?" they asked. The answer was *"Tjlemp"* or *"Tjresz."* The investigators knew that the German word for *vaca* was *Kuh*. But they had never heard of *Tjlemp* or *Tjresz*. Upon an extensive test the agents were perplexed. "There must be something about the language of these people from Russia that we don't understand," they concluded. They presented their findings to the authorities in Florianoplis and returned with the report that we were allowed to have our meetings in our peculiar language, which was thought to be Dutch. We gratefully complied, and henceforth spoke and sang and prayed and preached in our beloved *Muttaschproak*.

A fascinating feature of our Plautdietsch is its unique function as only one of three languages that made up our people's complete vehicle of communication. Many people can function with only one language. Not so the Mennonites—at least not for three or four generations in a new land. For more than two hundred years the Prussian/Russian Mennonites have been not only bilingual, but trilingual. Low German was always the language of the heart, spoken around the kitchen table in the family, in social and neighborhood circles in the village, and on the street. High German served as the predominant religious language, promoted and taught in private schools and spoken at most church events. But neither *Plautdietsch* nor *Hochdeutsch* was of much value for trade and commerce in countries other than Germany. Therefore, the national language had to be adopted: Russian in Russia, English in Anglo America, Spanish in Paraguay and other Hispanic speaking countries, and Portuguese in Brazil. It is interesting that the language of the heart has been the most tenacious and enduring language of our people in a foreign land.

While this kind of trilingualism has some inherent cultural and social benefits for the group, it also has distinct disadvantages. One major drawback is that the third language, namely that of the host culture, needs to be learned only by the leaders responsible for business and legal transactions on behalf of their people. The rest may never learn it and remain isolated within their subcultural island. That is how I experienced it at the Krauel. The first and second generation may be able to function quite adequately under such conditions. Sooner or later, however, language transition becomes inevitable. This may eventually lead to a loss of the *Muttaschproak* as the cherished mother tongue, as well as of *Hochdeutsch*, the treasured vehicle for religious expression. When that happens, the erstwhile trilingual society is being reduced to monolingualism as it did in Anglo America after World War II and as it is currently happening among my people in Brazil.

Another interesting phenomenon is the infusion of new words into our Low German in whatever country its speakers have lived. In Russia we adopted a host of native expressions and made them our own. The same happened in Brazil. While we continued using some expressions of distinctly Russian extraction, we accepted many Brazilian names and terms for objects and actions that were unique to our new environment. We simply adapted them to our way of speaking and never gave it a thought that we were actually speaking a Low German that our forebears of generations ago would have found difficult to understand. Yet we never ceased to maintain that we were speaking *onse scheene Muttaschproak*.

The Day on Which a Pig Died

Butchering a pig was not only a family affair; it was an occasion for neighborly participation and celebration in every village. Not the slaughtering itself, but the ritual accompanying it involved unique cultural practices which our people had brought from Russia.

Most important to us boys was the pig's bladder—yes, the raw bladder—just severed from the entrails of the animal. Let me be quick to dispel any thought that we treasured that particular organ as a food item. No, the bladder was not considered an exotic delicacy like the nose and ears and feet used to make *Siltfleesch*. We used the bladder exclusively as entertainment, for boys only. It was our "football." We took a straw to fill it with air, tied off the end as one ties a rubber balloon, and the ball was ready. So were we. That was the only football we could afford. Unfortunately, it was not very strong; but it provided a few hours of incredible fun. When it burst the fun was over and we waited for the next year when another pig would surrender another bladder.

I am amazed how quickly our people adapted to the new culture when it came to preserving the meat. Since there was no snow or ice, and we had no other means of refrigeration, we had to improvise, using different methods. One was smoking the ribs, some bacon, a ham or two, and sausages. The other was to cover selected pieces completely with ocean salt crystals. In each case we had to watch that the smoke would not subside during daylight hours—not even for one minute, and that the salt would not somehow shift to leave some parts uncovered—not even a tiny speck. If that ever happened the big blue flies were at it immediately, dropping living maggots on the meat. Within seconds these pests buried themselves and disappeared from sight. Only when we took the meat from the hooks or out of the salt did we discover the damage these despicable creatures had done at our expense. Sometimes this precious meat could be used only for making soap, but not for eating.

Soap-making was an art which my mother had mastered in Russia. I am not talking about soap with a delicate fragrance, the kind one buys in a drugstore. The soap we made was the product of everything inedible left over from the pig. These parts were cast into an iron cauldron hanging over an open fire. Mother added measured amounts of water and caustic soda and brought the unsightly conglomerate to a boil. We children had to take turns stirring the mixture for hours, until all particles were completely dissolved by the heat and the added chemicals. From time to time Mother came by to test the broth with its putrid odor. Each time she came to check how things were going, the one in charge of stirring the liquid mass at that moment had only one question: "*Ma, wannea kaun etj opheare met reare? Es it nijh aul foadijh?*" (Mother, when can I stop stirring? Is it not done yet?)

In our family, young children were not welcome at the initial stage of the butchering process. That was wise practice on the part of my parents. But once we boys were bigger, we were part of the whole affair. I thoroughly enjoyed it—until the one day that spoiled it for me. Usually, either my father, my brother Heinrich, or a neighbor was designated to make the kill. One fine day, however, the men decided the time had come for my initiation rite into "full manhood." That meant I was to stab the pig just the way it was always done. Well, I tried but failed the test. That was considered a serious matter: it showed lack of courage and bravery, if not outright cowardliness. Happily, I have long since discovered that there are more noble achievements to measure maturity and manhood than butchering a pig.

Wedding Rites and Rituals

I remember five weddings that took place in our own family between 1933 and 1947. I had the privilege of attending my siblings' weddings from the time I was five to the time I was nineteen. While I will not describe each of these weddings, I will use two or three as a point of departure to deal with the cultural aspect of wedding celebrations and rituals. When a couple agreed to get married, it was considered proper that the young man go to the parents of his beloved and ask for permission to marry her. That was not merely a matter of custom, it was a mark of courtesy. Only when both parents agreed to the marriage proposal could the couple become officially engaged in the church. Engagement was a serious event for the couple, their families, and the whole village. Thereafter came the wedding plans.

While I cannot remember any details from my sister Maria's wedding to Bernhard Esau on 22 November1933, I do recall an uproar at our house a day or two before the actual event. My brother Nikolai, who was then nine years old, did not want Maria to get married. Was it frustration, mere naughtiness, or something else? I do not know. But something drove him to take drastic action, thinking perhaps he could change our sister's mind. He picked up a pair of scissors, went into the room where she kept her wedding dress, and cut a hole out of the shoulder area. A big hole. The ensuing scenes were like a raging tempest of some duration, and not merely a bursting temper of the moment.

Since our arrived in Brazil (February 1930), Maria had worked as housekeeper at the Bruno Mekien family in Ibirama. She earned money to help the family get on its feet and to establish her own household. She had also bought fabric and together with Mother had made the wedding dress. And now this. Nikolai could not stop the wedding; he did, however, spoil much of our sister's bridal pride. I do not know exactly what happened after the incident, nor can I describe her wedding. Suffice it to say, she got married despite my brother's objections, and he survived the consequences, matured, and became as fond as I of our sister's husband

Bernhard. In a letter of 10 November 1934, Mother describes the wedding only as "different from the way we celebrated weddings in Russia. But it was quite nice. After the ceremony we had a meager meal, consisting of coffee and baked goods made from cornflour. Then there was a lot of singing and playing."

The next wedding in our family was that of my brother Heinrich to Lena Hübert, 26 June 1934. Mother writes about Lena, saying that "she seems to be *ein liebes Kind*," meaning "a loving child" or wonderful person. And that she was. I have fond memories of that wedding and of my late sister-in-law Lena. It was a double wedding. Lena's sister Anna got married the same day to David Schartner. Several of us boys were admiring the two couples, comparing their good looks and handsomeness. I remember saying that my brother's bride Lena was more beautiful than Anna. Willi, their six-year-old brother, who evidently did not want to argue about the beauty of his sisters, snapped back: "*Oaba Doaft sit schmocka aus Hein*" (but David is better looking than Heinrich). It strikes me as being rather humor-ous that six-year-olds—and boys at that—would engage in that kind of conversation.

Another thing I remember is that the wedding took place in a plain brick factory that belonged to Jakob Kliewer, stepfather of David Schartner. I still see between rows of drying bricks those long tables laden with food. The families of the brides and grooms as well as women from the village had baked and brought their best. There was no luxury, but there was variety and plenty. For us boys, eating was never a peripheral matter; it was central for life. Since we always had to eat in shifts at such occasions, we were sometimes shifty and tried to sneak in a second time. That happened particularly at weddings when the mood of the ushers was a bit more casual than at such celebrations as Thanksgiving and song festivals.

My sister Margareta (Greta) married Peter Krüger on 11February 1938. The wedding took place in our barn—not uncommon in those days. Katja and I helped Greta decorate the wedding hall with many palm branches, wild flowers and ivy wreaths, blocking off the part where we would have to feed and milk the cows in the evening while the wedding was still in progress. The groom and the big boys from the village made benches from logs and rough boards for the guests to sit on. The tables were set up outside under a canvas shelter in case of rain.

Weddings were at least a three-day affair. Greta's was no exception. The day before the wedding, women from the village brought such ingredients as lard, butter, tallow, milk, eggs and whatever else was needed for baking *Tweeback* and *Plautz*. The evening before the wedding was *Pultaowend*. The bridal shower might be a dynamic equivalent in the Anglo American culture; yet it is not the same.

The custom of a Mennonite *Pultaowend* has its origin most likely in medieval South Germany. Chroniclers tell us that the people of the village came together and made a deafening racket by smashing crockery or porcelain dishes to scare away evil and usher in good luck for the young couple. I must add that we did not break crockery or dishes, for we had none to break. Nor did we ever associate the event with either good or evil forces. Nonetheless, the evening was by no means silent. It was an occasion for a big party filled with fun and laughter, especially for the young people. We knew dozens of German songs by heart and sang in harmony like a big choir. We memorized and recited poetry and performed skits and dramas, sometimes of a lighthearted nature.

As a rule, the evening was quite meaningful. The couple sat behind a table, dutifully bowing and shaking hands with the guests as they placed a gift in front of them. The gifts were modest at best, consisting of such items as spoons, forks, knives, cups, plates, a pail, a baking pan and similar articles of immediate usefulness in a household. The party was a happy occasion, rarely ending before midnight.

While the wedding ceremony was usually in the afternoon, the celebration got off to a start by mid-morning. Family and relatives of the bride and groom were there for the noon meal. As soon as the tables were cleared and the dishes washed, guests arrived in droves and before long had filled the festively decorated wedding hall—wherever that was. The bridal couple sat on a pair of chairs tied together. The actual ceremony lasted about two hours, giving ample time for presentations by preachers, the village choir, other singing groups, and congratulatory speakers, as well as for recitation of poems and singing of hymns by the wedding guests. After the ceremony there was another meal, consisting primarily of such Mennonite baked goods as *Tweeback, Plautz, Pranitji* (probably a Russian type of cookie), and *Schnettji* served with coffee. It was not unusual for this meal to last up to two hours, depending on how many times the tables had to be cleared and reset.

Many guests had to go home in between to do chores, but returned for the evening program which at times was a rather somber event. It was not infrequent that family members of the bride and groom would sit and weep, especially the mothers and sisters. The meaning of those tears totally escaped me as a young boy. Later in life I became enlightened and learned that the evening of the wedding was perceived as an occasion to say farewell to a daughter or son, sister or brother. That made it an emotionally charged event.

The major part of the evening program was left in the hands of the young people. All the singing, playing, and reciting of poems was, for the most part, wholesome entertainment leading up to the climax: the moment when bride and groom had to give up the glamor of youth and cross the threshold into married life. The groom gave up his boutonniere with long white ribbons and the bride relinquished her bouquet as well as her tiara with the veil, and accepted in exchange a white bow pinned to the back of her hair by a married woman. This symbolized womanhood and submission to her husband, as understood in that cultural context.

The emotionally charged atmosphere of this particular phase of the ritual was heightened even further by more songs and poems plus farewell tears and hugs, creating a melodramatic effect of the evening celebration. On the one hand, the young people bade their farewell to a couple in transition from youth to adulthood. On the other hand, married couples gave the newly-weds a hearty welcome into their ranks. From *Urwaldpioniere*, a book by Peter Pauls, I have chosen one of the songs that was either sung or recited at this point in the program. It describes farewell and exit from youth, and welcome and entry into a new phase of life. Its major motif is tears of joy and sadness from the cradle past the altar to the grave. I do not know the author but will give a translation in my own words.

> Barely has one taken his first step in life
> when childhood tears appear, foreboding strife.
> But also tears of joy—what treasured bliss—
> when Mother greets her newborn with a kiss!
>
> As life matures betwixt its joys and pain
> the gift of love moves in, with tenderness to reign.
> A youthful heart may harbor secret fear
> when someone says, "I love you"—with a tear.
>
> How precious is each tear of the young bride,
> as her beloved tries to wipe it from each side.
> The two agree: one husband and one wife
> to join their hearts, share good and bad in life.
>
> And should the husband lose his cherished hope,
> the wife looks upward, knowing how to cope.
> She sees the stars shine brightly in the sky,
> and says, "Beloved, trust!" Then wipes his tearful eye.
>
> The man grows old. And, lo, the summ'ning bell;
> his loved ones all around him say, "Farewell!"
> A tear—in final moments—filled with pain,
> says its "good-by"—with hope—to meet again.

After this rather serious phase, the wedding ended in a jubilant episode. The bridal pair had to vacate the chairs on which they had been sitting for many hours and were told to mix with the guests. The bride was then blindfolded and turned and twirled around several times, to make sure that she did not know the direction she was facing. Meanwhile, the air was filled with suspense and anticipation. All eyes were fixed on the blindfolded bride and every guest was wondering to whom she would give her veil and crown. The girl she blindly selected and the boy to whom the groom gave his boutonniere became the focus for the concluding hour. (As human "foreknowledge" would have it, the couple was often selected because wedding plans were on the way.) The two were summoned to be seated in the empty chairs, given all the bridal paraphernalia, and ordered to sit still and hang on to each other. No sooner had they sat down than they found themselves hurled into the air by the strongest young men present. Under the applause of the guests, loud enough to lift the shingles off the roof, they were held in elevated position until they kissed each other to the satisfaction of the onlookers. The procedure was repeated two or three times. In the event that the chairs were broken in the process, they were hastily replaced. By that time no one could say that the night was still young.

The next day was *Notjhast* (after-wedding). This was reserved for family and friends who wanted to visit with the young couple, eat together once more, help clean up, and return all the dishes, pots and pans and whatever else had been borrowed from villagers and used before and during the wedding days.

— 21 —

Christian Celebration with Tradition

The mystery of our religion is a great wonder:
He was made visible in human form.
He was vindicated by the Spirit.
He was seen by angels.
He was proclaimed among the nations.
He was believed on throughout the world.
He was taken up to glory.
—Adapted from 1 *Timothy* 3

On a hot and sultry summer evening of 24 December when I was four or five years old, I was sitting on my father's lap, watching with rapt attention what was happening on the stage of our village school. My brother Nikolai and other "big boys" like him performed a play about Santa Claus. Only a moment after one of the boys announced that Santa Claus would come to school that night, the door opened and he walked in. He mumbled something to himself, carried a big sack on his shoulders, and a stick in one hand. Tradition had it that Santa Claus brought gifts in his sack for good children and used the stick to punish the naughty. I was totally engrossed in the event, yet not without a touch of fear. To my relief, Santa Claus made no use of his stick, only of his sack with a gift for each pre-school child sitting on a front bench or with a parent.

Since that memorable Christmas Eve celebration, many more have come and gone as an integral part of annual highlights we celebrated as Advent and Christmas, New Year and Epiphany, Good Friday and Easter, Ascension Day and Pentecost. Those events are the very hinges of salvation history. Some may be mixed with cultural and traditional symbols accumulated over hundreds of years. Yet when the outer layers are peeled away, the core remains, giving cause to commemorate the great salvation historical acts of God recorded in the Scriptures. After all, "there is truth to tell," as the late Lesslie Newbigin has put it. What better opportunity does the church have than to utilize these special days in the church year for the proclamation of the central truths? Quoting an eminent Scottish divine, David Ewert speaks about "the great landmarks of the Christian year." I treasure Ewert's book, *Proclaim Salvation: Preaching the Church Year*. It is a timely reminder of the wonderful opportunities we have to teach in our families and preach in our churches about the essential foundation of our faith and to herald to the world the message of God's great redemptive acts of self-manifestation in Jesus Christ and the Holy Spirit.

Few of our preachers at the Krauel were theologically educated. Only some had had pedagogical training in Russia. While none of them could be faulted for lack of faithfulness and godly living, their biblical expositions were often not more than lengthy homilies interwoven with stories and moral admonitions. But they knew the great truths of the Bible, held before us the salvific acts of God, and reminded us not to overlook the real meaning behind those theological landmarks of salvation history. There were then, as there are now, valid reasons for such reminders lest the central truths of the Gospel become hidden by peripheral aspects of culture and tradition. I can express only appreciation for the manner in which our family and the church celebrated the great events of the year, high points in the rhythm of life.

In our family tradition, the First Advent Sunday marked the beginning of looking for recipes and for Christmas songs and poems. Mother started to bake *Honnichskueke* (honey cookies) weeks before Christmas. They dried and hardened, but did not spoil in the hot summer months. She put them in small cotton sacks and hung them with a thin string from the ceiling rafters to keep them away from mice. She was not always successful—especially when two-legged "mice" climbed onto the table and picked at the sack until a cooky or two dropped out. Of course, we could never trick Mother. She knew the difference: real mice did not pick at the sack from the bottom.

Advent was also the time to start memorizing a "Christmas wish." This consisted of a simple rhyme addressed to the parents or, as odd as it may seem, to Santa Claus. School children got the poems from the teacher, preschoolers from their parents. We recited them on Christmas morning before opening gifts. While most of those rhymes and poems have escaped my memory, I still know some of them, and will include two in translation. The first I learned in Low German, the other in High German.

> Look here, Father; look here, Mother!
> I'm only still a little man.
> My wish list is short; I'll do what I can.
> But wait, when I'll be big and strong
> My wish list will be very long.

I imagine that my parents must have smiled with contentment and without fear that I ever would burden them with great wishes. Even if I said that I would wish more when I was big and strong, that wish would not exceed their resources—for these lines contain no wish at all, only words about a wish.

Every child of elementary school age also learned a poem or song, often concluding in a prayer. These items were selected by the teacher and kept secret from the parents until Christmas morning.

> In the glow of Christmas glory every heart is moved by joy;
> Every tongue recites the story—father, mother, girl and boy.
> "Sing Hosannah!" sung by millions near and far, in West and East,
> In the farthest zones and corners Christmas is the Feast of feasts.
> Here in shacks and there in castles, angels do good news declare:
> "Christ is born in Bethlehem's stable, joy and peace be everywhere."

While Christmas was always a season brimming with excitement and suspense, I also had to deal with a personal problem that caused some friction: I wanted to recite poems and wishes that were just as long and difficult as those of my siblings. My sisters called it being *grotsch*—arrogant.

In school we learned our plays and poems together as classmates. Next to our school playground was a swamp, and behind that was the jungle, totally unspoiled in its primeval pride. The boys of each class had their territory with special trees. As we climbed our very own tree, each had his branch to sit on. Now learning was in progress. The girls learned their parts by themselves, sitting on logs scattered along the edge of the playground. When the teacher rang the bell we all scrambled into our "hall of learning." That's where we practiced and rehearsed our dramas and songs and poems. The teacher made sure that diction, articulation and intonation were clear and correct.

Christmas eve at school was a great event. Everyone from the entire village who could possibly make it was there. The parents were proud of their children's performance, and the children were pleased to see the pride in their parents' faces. Singing took up a major part of the evening. However, there was a cultural irony in the fact that we sang such Christmas songs as *"Leise rieselt der Schnee"* and *"O Tannenbaum, o Tannenbaum .... du grünst nicht nur zur Sommerzeit, nein, auch im Winter wenn es schneit...."* Both songs speak of snow in winter; yet we had neither snow nor winter when we celebrated Christmas.

The highlight of the evening was the arrival of Santa Claus. Despite the sweltering heat, he wore a heavy coat, big boots, a Russian fur hat, and a long white beard. He announced in a low voice that he had brought some goodies to every child who had been "good," and then took out of his big sack small paper bags with some peanuts, candies, and a vanilla cookie for each child. Such treats were rare in those days. Whenever I think of that vanilla cookie from the *Sander Confeitaria*, I sense that the memory of my tastebuds is sharper than my mind. That cookie was so very special.

As soon as we came home from school, each of us children put a regular kitchen plate on the table in the living room and went to bed. The year before my brother Heinrich got married, he put out a bowl instead of a plate. I thought that he was terribly lucky and wished that I would soon be old enough to marry so that I, too, would have a chance to put out a bowl. My brother Nikolai and I usually lay awake for a long time and talked about the gifts we wished for. We also waited for the church choir to come by and sing those meaningful Christmas carols. As soon as I was old enough, I joined the choir myself. We often walked throughout the night singing songs of peace and joy at every home in our village. We felt specially rewarded when people asked us to come in for refreshments that included freshly baked Christmas goodies.

On Christmas morning we first did all the chores, then washed ourselves, changed into our Sunday best and rushed into the living room. The plates we had put there the night before were loaded with such good things as peanuts, candies, a chocolate bar from Saturno or Sander (famous chocolate makers), honey cookies that Mother had baked and glazed for the occasion, and a special gift item that was either covered with nuts and sweets or still hidden in the parents' bedroom.

After Father read the Christmas story and we children recited our Christmas rhymes, the parents surprised each one of us with a special present, such as a handkerchief, a comb or an item one of them had made. Two gifts stand out in particular. One year I got a little celluloid donkey. I treasured that toy beyond words. The material, however, was extremely susceptible to pressure and was easy to dent and crack. Before too long my donkey lost one ear, but never its charm. Another year Father had made a small wooden wheelbarrow for me. I was ecstatic and immediately went to my married siblings to give each of my nephews and nieces a ride. That was quite a treat for them and an adventure for me. We children also gave gifts to the parents—usually something personal or useful for the household.

On New Year's Eve we always had a year-end prayer meeting in our village hall. It was really a meeting of gratitude and thanksgiving for God's grace and faithfulness in the past year. Suitable songs and poems enriched every festivity; New Year's Eve was no exception. Since we had no song books, we relied on the reservoir of our memories. When we got home, we ate *Portzeltji* or *Niejoaschkueke* (deep-fried fritters) and drank home-grown green tea. In later years we sometimes had hot chocolate—a rare treat. My mother often wished she could have wheat flour instead of corn flour mixed with *mandioca* or *cará* starch so that the *Portzeltji* would hold together and be more fluffy. But to us children it did not really matter, as long as she made *Portzeltji* for New Year.

It was family tradition that we younger siblings went to our married brothers and sisters before the church service on New Year's morning. I recited a short poem in Low German about *Niejoaschkueke* and held out my hands in anticipation of a reward for my efforts.

> I saw your chimney smoking,
> I knew what you were making:
> New Year's fritters for the taking.
> You give me one, and I'll stay standing;
> You give me two, and I'll start walking.
> You give me three and four combined,
> Then I'll leave God's entire kingdom
> As my greatest wish for you behind.

Those fritters deep-fried in lard or tallow would not find their way onto a health food list today; but neither did a health food list in those days find its way to a remote Krauel kitchen.

The New Year's festivities continued throughout the day. In the morning we attended church service and in the afternoon we had time to visit family and friends. That, too, was a wholesome tradition. We younger children often ran ahead to the home of the host family. By the time the parents arrived we had already announced their coming, recited a rhyme or two, and received a small treat in return. Here is one rhyme I still remember.

Ektj koam vom Boij jerannt,	I come running from the hills,
Miene Bektjsi sennt jitrannt;	My pants are torn, have no frills.
Miene Fuppi sennt jibläwi.	But my pockets did not tear.
Woascht Du mie doafea waut jäwi?	Do you have something left to share?

In grades one and two I learned several meaningful New Year's poems. I will translate one of them in the form of a prayer as a tribute to parents:

> Once again a year has run its passage
> and a new one has begun this day.
> Who can count the hours in which God's message
> of His grace and goodness comes our way?
> Praise to you, O Lord, for all your mercies!
> You bore my parents with your powerful hand.
> And, me too, you guarded by your graces,
> from the first day to the very end.

Thanks to you with childlike praise and honor,
my dear parents, for your faithful hand,
always guiding, always leading onward
when I walk or sit, lie down or stand.
Thanks to you for vigilance and caring
and for nurture, always for my best.
Thanks to you for love and constant sharing
of your wisdom, patience—without rest.

And now, to you I lift my hands, O Savior.
To you I pray this New Year's day:
Bless both my parents—father, mother—
grant them your peace along the way.
Bless their efforts which they are investing
as they raise their child for you.
Keep my heart from foolishness in testing;
keep me faithful, brave, and true.

Thus we enter in the name of Jesus
bold and joyful into this New Year.
To my prayer, O Lord, please add your affirmation
and guide our steps to you forever more. Amen.

When we were finished reciting our poems and rhymes, both parents reached out their arms for a big embrace with a kiss for each. Our poems and recitations often brought tears to my parents' eyes. Father was especially susceptible to emotions during festive seasons. Not that he was particularly emotional by nature, but he was tender and compassionate.

The first session of the Annual Prayer Week was always held on the evening of 1 January. The week usually concluded on 6 January, Epiphany Day, which we called *Heilige Drei Könige*. Some people also commemorated the beginning of the Mennonite Brethren Church on this day.

With the approach of the Easter season, my parents often reminisced and talked about Easter celebration in Siberia. Perhaps that had something to do with the sharp focus of the Russian Orthodox Church on Easter as the most important religious holiday of the Christian year. We focused particularly on three events of Holy Week, ending the following week Tuesday. First, we observed *Jreendonnadagh*, or Maundy Thursday. Instead of school, we had church service in the forenoon. In the afternoon we got ready for Good Friday, commemorating the crucifixion and death of Jesus Christ. We referred to it as *Stelli Friedagh*, which literally means silent or quiet Friday.

On Saturday we prepared for Easter, a three-day celebration. We had to get enough feed from field and jungle for the cattle, sweep the yard, clear the weeds around the house, and bathe the horses in the river. Mother and my sisters did the baking and inside cleaning. By noon we were usually finished and spent a leisurely afternoon together. This included our customary *Faspa*, when we all tested Mother's *Paska* (Easter bread) and other pastries she and my sisters had baked. We also observed the custom of painting Easter eggs, provided the hens had been laying enough to do so. My sisters were the experts—so they thought; they extracted the paint from leaves and flowers that grew in field and garden. We boys had little to do with painting eggs but always participated in the Easter egg hunt. Occasionally, the parents had even bought a chocolate bunny for each of us children. Such special treats were truly special.

Every Saturday before Easter the big boys of the village put up a swing on top of a hill in our pasture. We called it *Jugendschockel* (youth swing). It was a huge construction, about ten meters (thirty-three feet) high, with a sturdy frame made of strong trees freshly cut in the woods. We borrowed chains from the villagers, secured them on the top crossbeam, and fastened a heavy plank of two to three meters in length at the lower ends of the chains. There was room for up to eight adults at a time. Two stood, one on each end, to keep the swing in motion. The others sat with their legs hanging down on one side or in a riding position facing the center, merrily singing and swinging. Just as painted eggs and chocolate rabbits are a purely cultural tradition with little or no spiritual symbolism, so did the swing have little or nothing to do with the real meaning of Easter. I have not been successful in my attempt to discover the origin and significance of the swing at Easter time. But it was great and clean pleasure, even if not without some physical danger.

The spiritual focus of Easter was on the resurrection of Christ, a hallmark of biblical truth, highlighted in the church and in the family. Every Easter morning members of the older generation exchanged words of greeting borrowed from the Russian Orthodox Church to confirm the resurrection of Christ: "*Kristos voskres!*" (Christ has risen!), the greeter said, to which the greeted responded: "*Voistinu voskres!*" (He has risen indeed!) A special highlight were the magnificent Easter songs and hymns sung by the choir. The Easter event usually was brought to a climax with a song festival on Tuesday, the final day of the celebration. The choirs from all three villages came together to exalt the risen Lord.

We next celebrated Ascension Day and, ten days later, Pentecost—the descent of the Holy Spirit on the church. The time was not only spiritually significant; it was also important because with it ended the fall season; winter had now set in. Pentecost marked the beginning of the cold season of the year. Let me be clear: "cold season" is a relative term. We never had snow, but occasionally the temperature dropped to freezing so that there were thin layers of ice on mud and water holes in the road. I dreaded those cold days. Most of us had no shoes and were only scantily clad. The school and our homes were unheated and often had large cracks in floors and walls. When the moist wind whipped through those openings, it chilled our flesh and blood right to the bones.

Two Pentecost celebrations stand out above all others: The one was when I was baptized on 25 May 1947, and the other was when Mother surprised the family with the first *Bulktje* in my memory. I was almost seven years old and had not yet started first grade. That year, Mother had a secret and would not tell us what it was. We suspected that it had to do with something to eat, but had no idea what. One day she gave us a clue by singing a familiar Low German rhyme:

Schockel, schockel scheia,	Swinging, swinging to and fro;
Oostre aet wie Eia.	At Easter time we're eating eggs.
Pinjste aet wie wittet Broot,	At Pentecost we eat white bread,
Stoaw wie nijh, dann woa wie groot.	We shall get big, if we're not dead.

This rhyme may not be very profound, but it conveyed in the context of tradition what Mother intended to communicate. On the one hand, it contained the secret to make us increasingly curious; on the other hand, it contained the solution, yet kept us guessing and wondering. We finally got the idea by reasoning this way: if we were eating eggs at Easter time, should we then be eating white bread at Pentecost? We knew about the custom of Easter eggs, but during the years in Brazil we in our family had never had white bread made from wheat flour. All we knew was corn bread mixed with *mandioca* or *cará* starch. This year, however, our co-op store had imported wheat flour from Argentina. Each family was entitled to buy a rationed portion. Father had bought some with Mother's knowledge. She was going to surprise us. And she did. That was the first *Bulktje* I remember eating. Mother was delighted that her secret had brought such an abundance of pleasure to the whole family.

22

My Youthful Dreams in Jeopardy
(1938-1947)

I, the LORD, I am your God, and there is no other.
I will pour out my Spirit upon all flesh,
and your sons and your daughters
shall speak of things to come;
your old men shall dream dreams,
your young men shall see visions.
–My paraphrase from Joel 2:27-28.

In a letter from 1932, Mother writes how grateful they are to be in Brazil where they are again free to live out their faith. She adds that the settlers have already built their own school, hoping that their children will be able to get a good education. I entertained that same hope. From my earliest years until my middle teens, I was hungry for knowledge and highly motivated to learn. I had dreams and visions about opportunities for education, which I perceived to lie somewhere on the other side of the *serras*. When in 1938 the government ordered our schools to close and confiscated all books, opportunities for nurturing the inquisitive mind were sharply diminished. But that did not deter me—at least not initially—from trying to learn as much as possible.

I went to some of our teachers and asked for help. From Kornelius Funk, my brother-in-law, I learned Portuguese grammar and poetry. Since we had no books, everything had to be memorized. Johann Penner, my former grade two teacher, gave me lessons in arithmetic and writing. I wrote down what he dictated and then did the work on my own. Addition and subtraction, multiplication and division became a mental game which I enjoy to this day. Several of my friends soon joined me in these learning ventures. A few years later Wanj Janzen taught me manners and skills as an effective sales clerk in our co-op store, where I began working as *Laufbursche* (errand boy) at a young age.

I marvel at the dedication of our teachers. Not only did they invest much time and effort, they also demonstrated that service to others demands personal sacrifice. Even more important was that they believed in us. They recognized the need to develop leaders for church and colony and saw in us the potential to fill that need.

But then came another blow. When my brother-in-law Funk died of cancer in 1940, some of my aspirations died with him. While I continued to learn from teachers Penner and Janzen, my personal ambition began to wane. Besides that, the spiritual needs of the colony were mounting, while resources to meet them were shrinking, leaving our most basic needs unmet. The result was a gradual loss of awareness of the seriousness of the situation and a diminishing sense of motivation to strive for something greater and higher. The material, cultural and spiritual resources of the colony were simply insufficient for normal growth and development. My worldview seemed predestined to remain as narrow as the Krauel valley, hemmed in by ancient *serras*. And, to carry the metaphor a step farther, as the rapids of the river caused its bed to become narrower and deeper, so the cliffs of the *serras* appeared to grow higher and steeper, reducing scope and field of vision to amblyopic levels. There came a time during my later teens when my motivation for learning reached a low point, bordering on discouragement, even pessimism. Thankfully, this phase was in my case relatively short, whereas others never recovered.

What was it, I have often asked myself, that brought about such a nonyouthful and unproductive outlook on life? What was it that put my former dreams and visions in jeopardy? Was it only that our schools were closed by the government? These questions have prompted me to look at that phase of my life from a distance in terms of both time and space. At the risk of oversimplification, I will try to identify three or four underlying causes, as I see them, that contributed to my gloomy outlook; those factors did not come overnight, but evolved over a period of years in the socioeconomic, "political," and religious context of our Krauel settlement. Not only did they impact me and other individuals personally; they created an ideological climate that was more harmful than helpful.

Because of the political leanings of a leading minority and the prevailing economic conditions of the majority during the early stages of development in the 1930s, the Anglo American Mennonite communities apparently were disinterested in becoming involved in our struggles. That made the situation attractive for the Germans to come to our aid; they took an interest in us and we in them. The relationship that developed between our people in Brazil and the emerging "New Germany" may have proved to be counterproductive in the end. Nonetheless, at the time some of our leaders saw that relationship as a solution to improve existing conditions. After all, the Germans had helped us get out of Moscow when no one else could or would; they had provided a temporary haven of refuge and cared for us in Mölln when no other country was willing to take that risk; the German Hanseatic Land Association had sold us the land on which we now lived; the German government had even assisted us financially in getting across the Atlantic to a permanent place in Brazil. Was it not only reasonable that they would again come to our aid? Many of our people seem to have thought so. My parents and other like-minded settlers, however, wisely cautioned not to jump onto a wagon without knowing where it was going.

I remember that several German representatives visited the Krauel as early as 1933 or 1934. One of the public meetings to which also the children were invited was held in the evening on the premises of the sawmill in Witmarsum. What impressed us beyond all else was the technological knowhow of these German men. Somehow they managed to harness electric power, either from the steam engine used to operate the mill or from a generator they had brought with them. I do not know the source they used. But I remember the occasion and the enthusiasm it generated among our people. One day after sunset we were seated in an orderly fashion on logs piled up near the sawmill under the open sky. There we listened to speeches and watched moving pictures about the economic boom and progress in Germany. We children were not only fascinated; we were mesmerized. Of course, we were as oblivious to any political motivation behind this kind of propaganda as we were ignorant of the rise of the Nazi movement in Germany at that time. History has shown, however, that our adults were not as ignorant as we children were. Yet a number of them were as captivated by what they heard in the speeches as we children were by what we saw in the pictures.

Other German visitors followed. One of them was Walter Quiring, a Russian-born Mennonite. He stayed in our village with the Peter Boschmann family. Two things I remember about Mr. Quiring's visit. First, he was going to write a book about our settlement. We boys talked about that and stood in awe of him. We envied the Boschmann boys for having the privilege of entertaining such a distinguished guest in their home. Then, too, Mr. Quiring took a special interest in the flora and fauna of the region. Perhaps he did it as part of his research, I am not sure. He trapped some birds and smaller animals and demonstrated how to preserve their beauty by stuffing and mounting them. Obviously, he had some skills as a taxidermist and was as anxious to teach this art to us as we were eager to learn it from him. Nikolai and I took every opportunity to pay full attention to what he was doing. We even tried our hand at it by stuffing a giant squirrel, but we soon discovered that taxidermy required more skill and knowhow than we possessed.

Dr. Quiring made one or two more visits to the Krauel in those years, conducting special meetings in our schools and reporting about the horrific conditions of Mennonites in Russia. That attracted our people to the meetings. But he also talked about economic progress in Germany. Everyone able to walk attended those meetings. In a personal conversation, the late Abrão Martens of Colônia Nova told me that, in his judgment the visits of Walter Quiring had left a positive mark on our people in the Krauel. Not everyone may have seen it that way.

Another result of our contact with Germany was the influence on the young people. I believe it was in 1937 when a German youth organization was formed in our colony. According to Abrão Martens, it was patterned after the *Deutschbrasilianische Jugendring* already in existence in cities like São Leopoldo and Pôrto Alegre with a high constituency of Germans. Contrary to some reports, the majority of our young people did not join this organization. The spirit of the movement, however, was clearly present in our colony, so that the *Jugendring* was endorsed by several influential leaders and teachers before it was organized. I recall how in April of 1936, we celebrated Hitler's birthday. Like a "midget army" we marched bare-footed back and forth along the dirt road in front of our schoolhouse in Waldheim, singing from memory the German national anthem *Deutschland, Deutschland über alles, über alles in der Welt* while the teacher marched ahead of us, counting *eins, zwei, eins, zwei* to hold us in line and step.

That brings me to my second point. Judging by the absence of recorded visits, I have come to conclude that outsiders (except from Germany) were rather reticent in coming to the Krauel to share their wisdom and counsel with us. Perhaps they feared that they would have too much to lose and too little to gain. That is also the impression I get when I read P.C. Hiebert's report entitled *Mitteilungen von der Reise nach Süd-Amerika*. If I am not in error, Dr. Hiebert was the first Mennonite from Anglo America ever to visit the Mennonites who had emigrated from the Soviet Union to settle in Brazil and Paraguay in 1930.

Hiebert came to the Krauel in 1937. I can still visualize how this tall, broad-shouldered man from North America stood behind the lectern in the Witmarsum school and opened the meeting with the words of Joseph: "*Ich suche meine Brüder.*" (I am looking for my brothers," Gen. 37:16.) Just as the patriarch Jacob had sent his son Joseph to look up his brothers and report back to his father, Dr. Hiebert went on to explain, so he had been commissioned by his church and by the Mennonite Central Committee to find out how their brothers and sisters in Brazil were doing. That was a familiar story and I could make connections. As a boy of eight or nine, I was much more impressed by his imposing personality and eloquent speech than I was as an adult by reading his written record of that visit.

While Hiebert describes the new settlement of Fernheim in Paraguay in great detail, using forty pages to do so, he devotes less than seven pages (plus some photographs) to write about the two Mennonite colonies in Brazil: Auhagen and Krauel. Most of what he writes revolves around his travels, giving minimal space and attention to the people themselves.

The one observation of substance in the entire report touching life and conditions of the settlers appears in his concluding statement:

> Here in Brazil, one can see how a people of the Steppe (*Steppenvolk*), due to circumstances, must prevail to become a people of forests and mountains. Indescribably hard! One admires their diligence, their courage, their performances, and their perseverance. The possibility to lead a simple, quiet, independent life in the fear of God seems to be given.

One can only wish that Dr. Hiebert had elaborated on the last sentence about the "quiet, independent life in the fear of God." What did he really mean with that loaded phrase? And what did he actually convey to his brothers and sisters in Anglo America about the spiritual and ideological atmosphere of our people in Brazil? In my view, those were precisely the areas of deepest need. This was, in fact, a time of major leadership crises and conflicts due, in part, to contacts with the New Germany and its influential ideology of Nazism. "The Brazilian Mennonite encounter with Nazis was distinguished by a lack of a distinct opposition, a weak youth movement, and lack of North American contact." So John Thiesen concludes his chapter on Brazil in the book, *Mennonites and Nazi? Attitudes Among Mennonite Colonists in Latin America, 1933-1945*. Thiesen is right about the "lack of North American contact." But he, too, fails to see the "distinct opposition." The opposition was not absent, only silent. Historians have seldom (if at all) been cognizant of this silent opposition; in my judgment they failed to understand the underlying reasons for that silence.

What we needed were not generalities about theoretical possibilities, but concrete words of encouragement spoken loudly and clearly so that we could be assured that we were not standing in isolation. We needed moral and spiritual support from outside sources, such as our Christian brothers and sisters in Anglo America could have offered. But such assistance was not forthcoming until after World War II. In the meantime the result was that the "quiet, independent life in the fear of God" was more quiet than independent and less in the fear of God than in fear of man. This feeling of isolation left its mark on the youths of my day, with consequences that have affected an entire generation.

A third factor was the radical nationalization program enforced during the presidency of Getulio Vargas. I have already alluded to the fact that the government closed our schools, deposed all German teachers, confiscated all books, and prohibited the German language, including its use in church services. I remember the occasion in 1938 when the doors and windows of the school in Waldheim were nailed shut by the authorities. This affected all of us like a candle extinguisher placed over a flickering wick, snuffing out the last glimmer of light. Or should I say hope? At any rate, that ended my formal education until my Bible school days in Canada. With our teachers and preachers under close observation by the authorities, the internal reservoir of our colony was nearly depleted, and we were no longer able to generate sufficient mental energy to motivate ourselves sufficiently to develop our God-given talents. That apathy has proven to be an irreplaceable loss for a generation or two in the cultural and spiritual development of our Mennonite society in Brazil.

I recall from family conversations that the interference by the government caused no insignificant restlessness among our people, whose experiences in the Soviet Union a mere decade earlier were still vivid in their memories. The Brazilian government did not deprive us of our property, as the Stalinist regime had done. Nonetheless, it did severely restrict our religious way of life and educational opportunities for children and youth by forbidding the use of the German language without providing a functional substitute in Portuguese. In isolated cases people were imprisoned and beaten or mistreated in other ways. The government also opened an office in our colony to make sure that we would comply with the new nationalization policies. The officer stationed there was Orlando Pamplona, holding the rank of army commander. Ironically (or was it by design?), his wife was of German descent and spoke the forbidden language flawlessly. Even Mr. Pamplona understood German.

As Providence would have it, the couple lived with my sister Susanna and her husband Kornelius Funk, one of the deposed teachers. Before long, there evolved an interesting drama. When the Funks spoke Low German to their children, the officer was utterly perplexed because he could not understand them. Believing that his mind was playing a trick on him, he told his wife to pay close attention to what was going on. She did, and was just as confused as he. This went on for about two weeks. The Funks were aware of their frustration, but decided not to initiate a conversation about it. Finally, the Pamplonas had to speak. And speak they did, not only to the Funks and colony leaders, but also to government officials who had placed them there. The outcome was that the Pamplonas actually became our friends and advocates. As I have noted in an earlier chapter, we were again permitted to hold church services and have family gatherings as long as they were conducted in Low German, which the Pamplonas considered to be Dutch rather than German.

These, in my judgment, were the major factors that over a period of years created an atmosphere of pessimism about the potential of improving one's life in the Krauel. My generation was caught in the midst of it, seeing its dreams and aspirations collapse like a shanty in a whirlwind. I too was in it—but only for a relatively short time. Thanks to two redemptive factors in God's design for my life, I was able to recover. For one thing, my parents were constant in their faith and sought to provide for us children a solid family atmosphere of unity and security. Despite the difficult years in the Krauel, they never ceased to be grateful for what we had, and to work responsibly toward improving existing conditions. I saw in their example the basic ingredients necessary for the development of a Christian work ethic and a meaningful life of service. Another factor was my conversion experience, which I will delineate in the next chapter. During the revival of 1947, I committed my life to Jesus Christ and decided to follow and serve him. That decision changed my thinking and outlook on life. I regained vision and hope for educational opportunities far beyond my original dreams and aspirations.

23

When Lightning Struck Our Village
(January 1947)

> *For if anybody is in union with Christ,*
> *he is the work of a new creation;*
> *the old condition has passed away,*
> *a new condition has come.*
> *This has all originated with God,*
> *for He through Christ has reconciled me to Himself*
> *and has given me the ministry of reconciliation.*
> —The Apostle Paul in 2 *Corinthians* 5 (Williams).

I could have entitled this chapter with the words of Christ spoken to the Apostle John on the island of Patmos: "I am making everything new." When I was eighteen years old I experienced that kind of renovation in a personal and spiritual sense. I am talking about my conversion following that particular Sunday in early January of 1947 when lightning struck our village. It was a sweltering hot day with matching humidity. The temperature remained high into the evening. That in itself was nothing unusual in the subtropics for that time of year. What was unusual, was the ensuing tragedy that night.

The young people of our village had agreed to get together in the front yard of the Johann Krüger residence. The Krügers owned the third colony at the lower end of our village Waldheim. They had a big house for a large family. Several of their children were in our group. We were determined to have a good time of games, singing folk songs, and other kinds of entertainment. The place was ideal. Nothing short of a Siberian snowstorm–which was most unlikely–could have hindered us from meeting that night. Heat and humidity were normal phenomena; even thunder and lightning could not have held us back. We could predict like a weather prophet, that within a day or two a thunderstorm would roll across the *serra*, pour out its fury over the valley, and the whole atmosphere would again cool down.

And so it happened. Our predictions came true sooner than expected. Before darkness had set in, we already saw a series of foreboding thunderheads appearing over the *serras* all along the serrated horizon. The clouds

When Lightning Struck Our Village 165

looked ominous. We knew that within an hour they would have to let go of their heavy weight of water, perhaps even frozen chunks of it, in order to move on. That's exactly what happened on that unforgettable January evening, as I shall detail it below:

> Just barely had the year begun, a brand new year of grace.
> Recorded in our calendar stood four digits in bold face,
> designed by hand and neatly crafted on a wooden plate:
> Nineteen hundred forty-seven. Eight syllables in lettered weight.

>> What will they hold or what contain?
>> Who, please, can tell us or explain?
>> Does no one know what is to come?
>> Does no one even dare to guess?
>> Does no one care that seven seals
>> hold anxious spirits in distress?

> We know the history, know not the mystery.
> We know what was, know not what is to come.
> There's only One Who knows it all: present, future, past.
> He knows what's hidden, knows what's sealed.
> He knows what is unknown; He knows the unrevealed.
> He knows whatever lies ahead: who will be living, who'll be dead.

> The second Sunday of the year had its beginning as every other Sunday did.
> And in a modest village dwelling six people played: "Make Me A Bid."
> The family had their Bible reading, how Christ the blind and ailing heals.
> The father of the house was leading as they prayed and ate their meals.
> They'd been in church with a dear friend; then did the chores and took a rest.
> How different was to be this Sunday's end, as the breath of life was put to test.

> And there we sat—some thirty youths, sat in another village house.
> merrily playing, cheerfully singing, then playing and singing combined:

>> "Let's sing it once, let's sing it twice.
>> Let's sing three times our youthful rhymes.
>> Let's sing once more to make it four.
>> Let neighbors hear our great encore:
>> How wonderful, this time of youth,
>> that sees the trivial things as cute:
>> We're free from care and free from frets.
>> We look past dangers, see no threats.
>> We have few worries, shed few tears.
>> How jovial, our youthful years"!

Thus we sing and thus we play as 'round and 'round we go.
Empty jesting, foolish laughing. Only youths can laugh that way.
As jokesters lead, vain heads proceed, yet everything's external show.
When hearts stay void, consciences seared, our burdens turn to lead.
There's premonition in the air, that causes fear and dread.

>   Suddenly, we hear it thundering.
>   We're shaken up; we're wondering.
>   Lightning flashes. Thunder thrashes.
>   God unchains the elements.
>   Serras rumble; jungles jumble.
>   Trees do squirm like a worm.
>   Shrubs are rattling; streams are clattering.
>   Torrential cloudbursts? It can't be!
>   Windows crackle in the turmoil,
>   streams of water, running free.
>   While we linger, ill at ease;
>   gone is every trace of peace.
>   In shock. Confused. No song. No play.
>   We'd like to leave. But we must stay.

We are still sitting where we sat before. Mr. Krüger's still awake.
His profession is to fashion tables, cabinets and chairs.
He's a master—skilled, creative—even coffins he does make.

>   Carefree? We? That's history!
>   Different moods now rule the room.
>   We're deeply shaken to awaken,
>   throw blank gapes, half dazed in gloom.
>   Deathly chillness reigns the stillness;
>   Our jests and laughter, all are gone.
>   Fearful, speechless we are asking:
>   How might end this oddest day?
>   Try decoding our foreboding:
>   Why, pray tell, we have to stay?

In that **other** village house a father struggles for dear life.
He cannot speak, can't say goodby to children and his wife.
A mother sobs, finds no relief; she stares at him in disbelief.
And one by one, three children sneak away and leave their places free.
The youngest follows in pursuit and slowly slides from mother's knee.
They all sang hymns, just moments past; but now all four are fatherless.

And here within the Krüger family dwelling,
we youths are nervous and perplexed.
But hush! What's that? What is he telling?
Do we hear whimpering noises vexed?

Horses trample. Wagons rumble.
Conversations—much aroused.
Loud lamenting. Painful panting.
There is chaos as in crowds.
Sudden knocking. O, how shocking.
Everything's most ominous!
Two hands groping, door does open—
And there he stands, this bearded man.
He wants to speak, but only if he can.
He stares at us with piercing eyes,
as though he looks right through us.
With faltering voice and sparing words
he speaks directly to us:

*"Mien Hauns es jroats vom Blitz erschlöagen.
We jie reed jewast, wann't hia jetroffen haud?
Daut mucht etj junt doch fröagen."*
(My John has just been struck by lightning.
Would you have been ready if it had struck here?
That is what I must ask you.)

The message in his dialect leaves everyone astounded.
It's most decisive, most direct; our innermost is hounded.
With searching eyes he looks again, then turns to Mr. Krüger:
"Make me a coffin for my son," he orders, and his mission's done.

In haste our host bids us "good night" and walks across the yard
into his shop with little light: his task this night is hard.

I will confess to some distress: That eerie Sunday evening
God's lightning struck. Struck every heart. We sat there, unbelieving.
Each one of us was flustered, numb, and stumbled to the door.
We rushed outside, said not a word. We barely touched the floor.
Our frightened mood was hard pursued by haunting echoes of those words:
*"We jie reed jewast, wann't hia jetroffen haud?'
"We jie reed jewast?"
—jie reed jewast?"
"—reed jewast?"
"—jewast?"*

On Monday was the funeral, the schoolhouse—filled to smother.
In every window someone sat—from one end to the other.
And whoever found no spot stayed on the hillside, sweltering hot.
Many leaned against the wall, others against post or tree.
Anxious was each one to hear, anxious each to see.
The choir songs lacked melody, the tunes were muffled, stiff.
Their voices shaken, words unclear, their message failed to lift.
Their choir leader was no more—he was beyond the golden shore.

"Our God is sovereign," preachers said. "He reigns. He's in control.
We do not always understand. But He's our comfort. He'll console."

All that God's servants spoke was right according to His Book:
His acts remain a mystery which we should never overlook.
God never acts haphazardly; His deeds be swift or be they slow.
He acts with purpose in His mind for human beings here below.

And as we at the graveside stood, God's voice was loud and clear:
"Repent, ye dwellers of the Krauel. God is calling. Don't you hear?"

> On Tuesday great awakening came,
> came sweeping through the valley.
> God's Spirit, loosed, knows every name
> in shack or house or alley.
> "God's cart of grace," the saying went,
> "is loaded with forgiveness."
> It moved along, paused here and there,
> brought joy and peace and stillness.

That's how it was when lightning struck, deep in our jungle village.
The family's grief did long remain—but hundreds did new life attain.

The Warkentin memorial service was held in the Witmarsum school, the largest meeting place of the colony. Whoever could make it was there, from all three villages. Businesses were closed that afternoon. The school was overfilled. A number of us boys were sitting in the open windows in a riding position with one foot in, the other out. Others were sitting or standing on the side of the hill along the west side of the school. I do not remember much of what was said, except one thing that had become the talk of the colony: "This is not an accident. This is God speaking." My parents shared that view. In my heart I knew they were right, but I tried to ignore what they said and resisted the Holy Spirit.

When I came home from work the next day I was told that Susi Fast, our neighbor girl, had become a Christian. She was the "first fruit," as Count Zinzendorf might have said, of a major revival movement that swept from end to end and from corner to corner of every tributary and village throughout the Krauel Colony. People confessed their sins and found forgiveness. Families and neighbors were reconciled. Never before in the seventeen years we had lived there had anything like it ever happened. The greatest impact seemed to be among the young people. Indeed, God was speaking. That also became the "hour of decision" in my life.

The week of the funeral I was under a tremendous conviction of sin. The question of the elder Mr. Warkentin, "If it had struck here, would you have been ready?" and the words spoken at the funeral, "This is God speaking" echoed in my ear every second of the day. At that time I did not know that, according to the words of Jesus, the Holy Spirit was at work, convicting me of "guilt in regard to sin and righteousness and judgment." By Friday evening I was so miserable that I felt like running away from it all, even if I had no specific plan in mind. As I walked out, my parents cautioned that I might be caught in a thunder storm. That was of little concern to me. I just wanted to get out on the street, hoping to meet some friends who had not yet been touched by that agonizing "revival fever." Perhaps they would come up with some idea that would give me relief. But God had a different plan for me that Friday night.

When I got to the road I decided to sit on the milk post and wait awhile. I had barely sat down when the rumbling of thunder was obvious. In twenty or thirty minutes it could be pouring. In disgust I went back to the house. I walked through the kitchen and tiptoed through the living room. There I saw the Bible on the table, but walked past to avoid the slightest noise, lest my parents should notice me. I should have known better. I overheard Mother say to Father: "*Hauns es tus. Hee's tridjjekoame.*" (Hans is home. He has come back.) Immediately she called and let me know that she had heard me sneak in: "*Etj frei mi, daut du tus best. Bute sitt it grulich ut,*" (I am glad you are home. It looks so ominous outside), she called from the next room. Parents have a sixth sense with a sharp ear, especially when they are concerned about their children.

I did not feel like talking to them. Nor did I want to get the Bible from the living room, let alone read it. But I had to. Something greater than my willpower drove me to it. I opened it at random and my eyes fell on Acts 2:38 which in the old Luther Bible was in bold print. In translation it reads: "Repent and be baptized, every one of you, in the name of Jesus Christ for the forgiveness of your sins. And you will receive the gift of the Holy Spirit." The word "repent" ("*tut Buße*" in German) bothered me. That's precisely what I resisted. And I knew it. So I randomly tried my luck with another verse. In His wisdom, God had chosen a hammer for me as I again looked at a bold-printed passage. It was Revelation 3:20 where the Lord says: "Here I am! I stand at the door and knock. If anyone hears my voice and opens the door, I will come in and eat with him and he with me."

That was it. Both Scripture passages were crystal clear. I knew what to do. I decided to run once more, but this time not away from God, not even into stormy weather outside; instead, I hurried to the next room where my parents were sitting. They were glad to see me. I told them of my miserable condition (as if they did not know!) and said, *"Etjh well mie betjhiere"* (I want to get saved). Within minutes we were on our knees, praying. I confessed my sins, received forgiveness, and committed my life to follow Christ. There was great rejoicing in our house. I had made the first step: I believed in my heart and also had made partial confession with my mouth, as the Apostle Paul puts it (Rom. 10:10). But the test was yet to come. I knew that I would have to tell my brothers and sisters as well as my friends and other people in our village. I would have to make confession wherever I had sinned. That scared me. But I did confess and became a free man; I experienced the words of Jesus recorded in the Bible, "So if the Son liberates you, then you are really and unquestionably free" (John 8:36).

As I look back on that experience, I am amazed at God's leading. Two events came together at that moment, reenforcing each other to confirm God's call in my life. One was the event on that cold November night eighteen years earlier on the Siberian steppe when my mother dedicated me to God; the other was now on that hot Friday evening in our remote village in the deep Brazilian jungle when I made a deliberate decision to commit my life to God and become a follower of the Lord Jesus Christ. The answer to Mother's prayer that I might some day serve Him was now visibly beginning to unfold. The determining point was my conversion to Jesus Christ, which changed my thinking and gave me a new direction in life. I regained those earlier aspirations and motivations for learning and serving. This time they came from a renewed heart, a changed mind, a fortified will, and the clarion call to rise above circumstances to new challenges.

24

Modest Tributes to My First Mentors
(1947-1949)

Stop acting from selfish ambition or vain conceit;
rather, in humility consider one another as superiors.
Stop looking after your own interests only;
instead, practice looking out for the interest of others as well.
—The Apostle Paul in *Philippians* 2.

C. S. Lewis in *Mere Christianity* states: "How monotonously alike all the great tyrants and conquerors have been: how gloriously different the saints." I am on the side of Lewis; I have no admiration for tyrants, but I do respect saints who follow Jesus as Lord. Such people have been my mentors and counselors, who enriched my life at different levels. To mention them all would require a book similar to the one by the Lutheran pastor Ernst Modersohn, entitled, *Menschen durch die ich gesegnet wurde* (people through whom I have been blessed). But my intent is not to write a book. I simply want to pay tribute to some of them who played a special role in my life by showing me what it means to grow in grace and knowledge of our Lord. While men like Johann Penner, Wanj Janzen, Peter Isaak and my brother-in-law Gerhard Giesbrecht, with whom I worked together in the co-op, influenced my life even before I became a Christian, I am limiting myself to the years immediately following my conversion.

My Parents: Guides by Word and Deed

My parents taught us children virtues by verbal expression and values by living example. Upon my conversion they became my primary mentors. They encouraged me to faithfulness, obedience, and perseverance in Christian discipleship. At the same time they also helped me to recover my earlier aspirations for learning and were instrumental to make it a reality. While neither one of them had ever gone to high school, they demonstrated a sense of contentment by serving humankind through deeds of kindness, goodness, and compassion. If they could serve God without special training then I could do the same.

Mother was sensitive to the needs of others, particularly the sick and lonely. She had always been that way and often reminded us children of the importance of helping people in distress. After my conversion, such acts of kindness as bringing food to a widow or a sick person in the village, or sewing articles of clothing for a needy family, took on new meaning for me. Father was most supportive, using Galatians 6:10 as a guiding principle: "We should do good to all people according to our opportunities, especially to those who belong to the household of faith." They made no distinction between believers and nonbelievers. That impressed me as I learned to walk the Christian way.

Another thing that impacted me as a young Christian was Father's quiet involvement in the life of the church. He was not a preacher or public speaker, but a perceptive, caring man. He seemed to know when someone in the church had spiritual needs. Quite often on Saturday afternoon when the fodder for Sunday was in the barn, the garden raked and the yard swept, Father would say to us: *"Junges, holt mie moal een Paet."* (Boys, fetch me a horse.) We got the horse from the pasture, put a bridle in its mouth and a sheepskin on its back and brought it to the house. Then Father would ride off to visit a sick person or a church member who had obvious problems in his walk with God. I am not aware that he ever confronted a person in a judgmental manner; he first sought to understand the problem before he offered a corrective. Depending on the situation, Father occasionally admonished people and always encouraged them to be consistent in their Christian walk. His visits were short and ended with prayer.

My parents became my model for serving the Lord with what we have. And if God wanted me to get additional education to serve Him more effectively, then I would go to school for that very purpose. That simplistic philosophy of service and education has stayed with me throughout my years of studies to this day. For a follower of Jesus Christ, the purpose of education, regardless at what level, is not to get a diploma or earn a degree or make more money or gain prestige in social circles or in the church; the purpose is rather to become equipped to serve the Lord most effectively in the church and in the world through whatever vocation that may be.

Kornelius Ott: A Watchful Deacon

I will never forget Kornelius Ott, a deacon in our village. He was an unusually tall, slender man with a bony structure and a long, thin face with high cheekbones. One Saturday evening after prayer meeting, several of us boys were standing in the open veranda of our village meetinghouse engaged in casual conversation. Suddenly I felt a big hand resting on my right shoulder. As I turned, I looked directly at the face of Mr. Ott.

"*Hauns,*" he said, "*hast du eenen Jonathan? Den mottst du habe.*" What he meant to say was that I needed a close friend like Jonathan, the friend of David in Bible times (1 Sam. 18:1-4). As providence would have it, his son Gerhard became my Jonathan. We shared our life's aspirations and spent time together in prayer.

On one of my service trips to Brazil in the early 1980s, I visited Mr. Ott for the last time. As I stood at his bedside, I took his big, bony hand and thanked him for the advice he had given me over thirty years ago. He remembered the occasion. Soon thereafter he went to be with the Lord. On another visit to Brazil in 1995, Frieda and I spent one afternoon with my friend Gerhard and his wife Mariechen. We reminisced about those earlier years in the Krauel. Shortly thereafter Gerhard, too, passed into eternity. The mark that Father Ott and his son have left on my life demonstrates the value of true friendship, which in turn reminds me of the words of Joshua Ben Sira in Sirach 6: "A faithful friend is a sturdy shelter: he that has found one has found a treasure."

Gerhard Schartner: A Humble Shepherd

Whenever I read John 10, where Jesus describes the character of a good shepherd, I am reminded of Gerhard Schartner. He was a man with a shepherd's heart devoted to guarding and guiding his sheep. His concern for the young people of our village and his love and labor for the church gave evidence of his unselfish commitment to Christ. Schartner was materially poor, and he may have been academically unschooled, but he was rich in wisdom and spiritual resources. He had been trained in the school of life. He demonstrated the essence of true servanthood. He knew that serving God does not depend on noble birth and eloquent speech. He was a great listener. No matter what questions we young people had or what problems we faced in our teenage years, Schartner was always there for us.

While his language was simple, what he said was often profound and always made sense. He radiated the love of Christ and demonstrated the fruit of the Spirit by his godly character and conduct. From him I learned that discipleship and servanthood are nonnegotiable, inseparable ingredients of the Christian life. Schartner symbolized for me what it means to wash the feet of others.

Jakob Regier: A Singing Reader

Jakob's father was a down-to-earth practical preacher with a mellow voice for speaking and singing. Jakob had inherited that same gift and used it to exalt the Lord. He directed our choir in Waldheim for years. But he was different from other choir directors I knew. He read each new song with clear diction and intonation and taught us to do the same. Then he engaged his soft tenor voice to sing the song into our hearts and minds. When he was finished, he asked: "Did you understand the words?" Of course, we did. "Did you also get the message?" he questioned. "The melody and music are the vehicle that carry the message, but its meaning is in the words. Therefore, tone, pronunciation and diction must be clear, so that the listeners can understand every word."

Jakob Regier also took time from family and work to read to us. Somehow he had been able to secure a German copy of Charles M. Sheldon's book, *In His Steps*. One evening a week the young people gathered in our village hall for a reading. I never missed a single session. I don't think anyone did. We were mesmerized by the author's poignant question, "What would Jesus do?" That was a timely question to those of us who recently had been converted. We were challenged to order our words and behavior accordingly.

I was also impressed by the manner in which Regier was reading the book. As I listened, it became clear to me that, even if I lacked Regier's mellow voice and musical skills, I needed to make every effort to pronounce each word correctly and distinctly. I have not forgotten that lesson when reading the Bible out loud, both in private and in public.

Gerhard Rosenfeld: A Teaching Preacher

When Gerhard Rosenfeld and his family came to Brazil, they settled in Stoltzplateau. As that colony dissolved in the mid 1930s, the family moved to the Krauel. My parents were delighted. They knew about Mr. Rosenfeld's effective ministry in Russia. He was a trained teacher, had a comprehensive knowledge of the Bible, was theologically well read and ordained as elder in the church.

The first visit of the Rosenfelds to our house is still vivid in my memory. Their two youngest sons, Adolf and Abram, came with them. Although somewhat older, they became our friends, especially for playing soccer. Adolf and my brother Nikolai developed special skills for that game. What impressed me on that first visit more than anything else about Mr. Rosenfeld himself was his striking appearance. He stood tall, straight and slender with a pair of piercing eyes below a rather high forehead; and he wore a full, silvery beard neatly trimmed with a center partition from the chin down. I was also struck by his friendliness. He never neglected to greet us children as part of the family they had come to visit.

In 1948, the year after the revival in the Krauel, Mr. Rosenfeld and Franz Fast conducted a church Bible school in Waldheim. Rosenfeld taught a course in general introduction to the Bible, which included Bible geography. I was overwhelmed by his erudition and convinced that he was the most knowledgeable man in the Krauel. He was also an eloquent public speaker. I loved to hear him preach. His messages were biblical, passionately delivered, and persuasive. They called for change in conduct and ethical living; this earned him no favor with some powerful leaders of our colony.

To be more specific, I can summarize Mr. Rosenfeld's impact on my life as a young Christian with three additional observations. For one thing, he taught me the ABC of Bible reading by emphasizing the importance of reading entire books, not only isolated passages or verses. Reading each text in the larger context has enhanced my understanding of the Scriptures. Furthermore, he took a vital interest in the young people of our colony. He encouraged and challenged us on a personal level. One Sunday afternoon when he and Mrs. Rosenfeld were visiting with my parents, he turned to me and said: "Brother Kasdorf, I see in you the gift of service in the church and would like you to preach next Sunday. Will you do that?" I do not know what I answered; I only know that I preached. My text was Hebrews 13:13: "Jesus Christ the same yesterday and today and forever." I received several compliments. But no one told me whether the compliment was for brevity or quality. I feel safe to say that it was the shortest sermon I have ever preached.

Mr. Rosenfeld was also instrumental in opening the way to Bible school in Canada. In 1948 he was delegated to represent our Brazilian church at the General Conference of the Mennonite Brethren Churches in North America where he inquired about possibilities for some of us to attend a Bible school. Upon his return he reported that the Winkler Bible School in Manitoba was open to accepting several students from Brazil, provided they would meet certain criteria. Four of us applied and began to correspond with the school. The process was slow and the outcome uncertain. In the meantime, my friend Franz Hübert went to study in Paraguay instead and the other two chose different vocations. With encouragement from my parents and other mentors, I decided to persevere and to pursue my goal. Admittedly fearful of the unknown, I ventured out into the big world—somewhere beyond the horizon of our narrow Krauel valley.

R. C. and Anna Seibel: A Missionizing Couple

During the revival of 1947, the Mennonite Central Committee sent two couples to the Krauel—the John Kaufmans and the Robert Seibels—as spiritual resource persons. They arrived in late March on a rainy Saturday afternoon with Abram Kröker in his horse-drawn coach. The roads were nearly impassable due to bad weather. As Mr. Kröker dropped off the mailbag at the co-op where I was working, R. C. Seibel came with him into the store, introduced himself, greeted the workers, and invited all of us to an evening service where he would preach. I was amazed by his boldness. Yet there was something about this man that impressed all of us. My brother-in-law Gerhard Giesbrecht, the store manager, remarked: "That man must be a real missionary."

The revival was still gaining momentum. The Spirit of God was at work from one end of the colony to the other. A genuine hunger for the Word of God was evident among the new Christians. Despite the rain and muddy roads, the meeting house in Waldheim where Mr. Seibel preached that first evening was filled to capacity. He spoke on Acts 4:23-31. The essence of his message was about confession, forgiveness, and commitment. It was a powerful message. The audience was visibly moved. After the meeting I said to my friends, "If I were not yet saved, I would become a Christian tonight," to which Franz Hübert responded: "I would too." His twin brother Willi had different ideas. With a smirk on his face he boastfully declared that the whole thing was something for weaklings, not for the brave and strong. But it did not take many weeks before my good friend Willi was overcome by One stronger than he, and he joined the rest of us "weaklings."

What impressed me most about Mr. Seibel was his love for people in general and his concern for the unsaved in particular. He seemed to know how to approach them and what to say to them without making them feel threatened. I learned much from his evangelistic preaching and the house visitations we made together.

Whereas the direct influence of my other early mentors discontinued when I left for Canada in 1949, the mentorship of Mr. and Mrs. Seibel continued well into the 1990s. From 1950 until1952, Mr. Seibel served on the faculty of the Winkler Bible School where I was studying. That is also where Frieda met the Seibels. During years of studies and ministry in South and North America our paths with the Seibels have crossed many times. On 10 January 1991, when relatives and friends celebrated Mr. Seibel's nineti-eth birthday at the Vinewood Community Church in Lodi, California, I concluded my birthday meditation by summarizing major aspects of his impact on my life, saying:

> Your evangelistic preaching was persuasive, your biblical teaching convincing, your friendship genuine, and your pastoral care-giving balanced. You once wrote to me, "Never be hasty in judgment. Be sure to see every side of the issue." I have endeavored to follow your counsel. You were also a prudent steward in financial matters. You had little use for luxury, but a tender heart for needy people and worthy causes. "Remember, obey, and greet your leaders." So said a sage to Hebrew Christians long ago. In that spirit Frieda and I salute you and Anna, our friends and mentors, with gratitude and appreciation.

25

Farewell, *Heimatland*, Farewell
(June 1949)

> *You then, my son, be strong in the grace*
> *that comes through union with Christ Jesus.*
> *The things you learned from me before many witnesses*
> *you must entrust to trustworthy men, competent to teach others.*
> *Take your share of hardships like a good soldier of Jesus Christ.*
> —The Apostle Paul in 2 *Timothy* 2

No father could have spoken more fitting words than those of Paul in 2 Timothy as a farewell message to his son. No mother could have quoted more appropriate words than those of Jesus in Matthew 6:33 to remind her son that the priority of a good soldier of Christ is to focus on God's kingdom, not on worries and concerns about "all these things." Those were compelling lessons I was about to learn; and I am still on the road of learning.

It was Monday, 6 June 1949. At dawn the rising of the glowing sun from behind the horizon announced the Lord's great love, compassion, and faithfulness for another new day. A cold, gentle breeze was blowing across the platform of the train station in Curitiba. My parents had accompanied me from the Krauel valley to the higher elevation in Paraná, where my sister Susanna with her children was living at the time. What I experienced there that morning was symbolic for each one of us. On the one hand, there were the unfailing mercies of our God. On the other hand, there were uncertainties facing my aging parents, now alone. Standing next to me was my oldest sister, widowed, alone. There we stood, waiting for the train that would take me to São Paulo. Alone. With those introductory notes, I will leave that scene for now and return to it at the end of this chapter.

Farewell to Everything I Knew

When I said farewell to the Krauel, I left behind everything I knew. I took with me only the things I knew: in sum total, very limited. That is one side of the story. The other is that I was also looking ahead to the unknown. I was eager to discover as much as possible of things I did not know: in sum total, unlimited. One of the benefits of being deprived of educational opportunities in my younger years was, at least theoretically, that I had ample storage space left to gather new information and knowledge. And, I confess, I am still gathering and learning. In his book, *On This Day*, Robert J. Morgan tells the story of the eminent seventeenth century Puritan preacher, Richard Baxter, who once wrote, "Study hard, for the well of spiritual knowledge is deep, and our brains are shallow." He is right.

The resources for learning are so incredibly plentiful and inexhaustible that I have barely touched the surface. But gathering knowledge must not become an end in itself, only a means to an end. I am reminded of *The Scarlet Letter* in which Nathaniel Hawthorne challenges the reader: "Preach! Write! Act! Do anything, save to lie down and die!" That is precious advice. During many years as a gatherer and learner, I have, by God's grace, also been able to teach and write and preach. Sharing with others what God has allowed me to garner from the abundance of resources is nothing more than living by the biblical principle of stewardship.

I am well aware of the sobering fact that I will never be able to say that I have made it, that I have arrived — not in this life. I am in process of becoming. That in itself is a satisfying, fulfilling discovery. It is a gift from Almighty God, my Maker and Sustainer. I am at peace to be a becomer until He will reclaim the breath of life He once gave to me. Until then I am His steward on the road of becoming what He wants me to become: a servant. Not more. Not less.

Farewell to My True *Heimat*

I have said earlier that the Krauel Colony was for me a place where I felt at home. That is not how it was for my parents, at least not in their early pioneering years. Their place to feel at home had been Siberia, not Brazil. But for me it was Brazil, especially that tiny hidden spot on the map known as the Krauel. That was home. I had grown up there. The Krauel meant to me everything that is contained in the German noun *Heimat* for which the English language has no dynamic equivalent. It is a word that defies description. The *Deutsches Universalwörterbuch* lists more than 150 entries of the noun, with a host of adjectival forms, to indicate the wealth of feelings, emotions, and sentiments associated with the untranslatable concept Heimat. Both the history of the German language and the amount of literature dealing with the concept give evidence to the extent to which the word has provided an almost unmatched reservoir for secular and religious poets and lyricists. They love to write and sing about motifs and ideas revolving around *Heim, Heimweh, Heimat, Heimatland,* and related expressions. Virtually everything one loves and knows about one's own culture and people is associated with *Heimat*. The word is not used to identify a peripheral cultural trait; it is part of the core itself.

Such Portuguese concept as *terra* or *patria* convey a similar meaning as the German word *Heimat*, although their contents are culturally determined. Their essence can be described as a place that is as much an integral part of oneself as the ground on which one lives; it is genuinely indigenous. The idea with all the nostalgic sentiments is best expressed in the lyrics of a Brazilian song by Antonio Gonçalves Dias which we sang as teenagers. It speaks eloquently of the place that was once so near and dear to me. For the benefit of my friends and kin in Brazil, I will quote the lyrics in the original and then offer my translation. The words *terra*, *palmeira* and *sabiá* represent tangible objects of my Heimat I left behind when I said farewell.

Minha Terra Tem Palmeiras

Minha terra tem palmeiras, onde canta o sabiá;
as aves que aqui gorjeiam, não gorjeiam como lá.
Nosso céu tem mais estrelas, nossas várzeas têm mais flores,
nossos bosques têm mais vida, nossa vida mais amores.
Em cismar, sózinho, à noite, mais prazer encontro eu lá;
minha terra tem palmeiras, onde canta o sabiá.

Minha terra tem primores que tais não encontro eu cá;
em cismar, sózinho, à noite, mais prazer encontro eu lá.
Minha terra tem palmeiras, onde canta o sabiá.
Não permita Deus que eu morra, sem que eu volte para lá,
sem que desfrute os primores que não encontro pro cá;
sem qu'inda viste as palmeiras, onde canta o sabiá.

My Homeland Has Palm Trees

The palm trees are my homeland's glory where the sabiá sings her song;
in other lands where birds are singing, their tunes are nothing but a gong.
The stars at home excel in brilliance, and the skies are azure-blue.
Those wild flowers! Oh, what fragrance fills the air with pleasant hue.
How my heavy heart is longing when, alone, I sleepless lie,
dreaming, dreaming of my homeland, the sabiá's song, the starry sky.

My Brazil has countless beauties, such as nowhere else I've found.
I keep on dreaming. Nights are lonely. I long for home; a piece of ground
where in the wind the palm fans rustle, in the woods the sabiá sings.

Her mellow tunes excel all others, are borne along by heav'nly wings.
The palm trees are my homeland's glory, the sabiá's song is my encore.
Dear God, I pray, don't let me die before I see that land once more.

Over the years I have often reflected on those words and come to realize how much it has shaped my patriotic thinking. By patriotic thinking do not mean nationalistic or ideological convictions. For good or ill, I have remained rather apolitical all my life. What I do mean, as I understood it at the time, is a homey feeling; a feeling of belonging and security attached to a certain place. In my case, it was the Krauel. I felt it especially when I took leave of family and friends, village and valley that had become a part of me.

All the patriotism I had developed was wrapped up in that small place, not in the giant country of Brazil. The reader may perceive my patriotism to be emotionalism rather than rational thinking. Yet at that time I identified with the sentiments of Antonio Dias. They gave me the impression of a limited horizon and kept my vision short. Yet somehow I always knew that my horizon would have to expand if I ever wanted to serve my Lord in the larger world. And there lay my fear. I was afraid to exchange my small place, my real *Heimat*, my *terra* with *palmeiras* and *sabiás*, for that larger world which I had envisioned but now feared to enter. When the time actually came, I dreaded to take leave and venture out into the big and unknown world.

Farewell at Different Stages

Krauel. Curitiba. São Paulo. Rio. Those four places bring back vivid memories of the four months, March to June of 1949, when I prepared myself mentally and emotionally to embark on a totally new experience in life. I had resolved within myself to pursue what I had envisioned as lying somewhere on the other side of the serras. Somewhere a world I did not know was beckoning me to prepare for a life of service and mission. Deep within myself I was aware of God's call and felt compelled to obey, whatever that would mean. My family and some friends encouraged me to venture out to new horizons, even if unknown. Others in the colony thought I was foolish and did not hesitate to say so.

The young people of our church in all three villages had become a close-knit group, especially since the revival two years earlier. Parties with rowdy games and dances had been replaced by gatherings in which singing of memorized songs, recitation of poems and folk music took center stage. These were always joyful occasions—except once: the Sunday evening of 29 May, when I said goodbye to my friends in the Krauel. All day had been difficult as I took leave of siblings, nephews and nieces. The day was filled with more goodbyes and farewells than I was prepared for. But there was no turning back.

The next day I found myself, together with my parents, sitting on a canvas spread over an open truck heavily loaded with huge sacks of *mandioca* starch and tapioca on its way to the harbor in Itajaí. (I should note, parenthetically, that the first part of that trip coincided with a historical moment for the Krauel: three men from there traveled with us—Peter Isaak, Peter Käthler, and Jakob Martens. They were delegated to investigate possibilities of a land purchase near the city of Bagé in the state of Rio Grande do Sul. As history tells us, they liked what they saw. Within two or three years my people moved to Colônia Nova near Bagé, while others moved to the state of Paraná, and the Mennonite colony in the Krauel was no more.) The sacks of starch were piled higher than the sideboards of the truck. Our only safety device against slipping or sliding off the canvas was a rope secured at both ends to prevent the sides from excessive bulging. We hung on for dear life as our driver, Jasch Boldt, skillfully maneuvered the four-ton Fargo truck along the narrow gravel road with a thousand curves, over *serras* and through gorges, until we reached Indaial. That is where I took leave of Mr. Boldt, with whom I had made the trip from the co-op in Witmarsum to the harbor in Itajaí many times.

The next morning my parents and I took the bus to Curitiba. We stayed with my sister Susanna and her three children. That was a very special time, even if short. My former friends who had moved there from the Krauel had planned a farewell party for Sunday evening. While I appreciated their kind gesture, I was inwardly torn, knowing that on this last evening I should stay with my parents and sister. On 6 June came my most difficult farewell at the train station in Curitiba to which I referred earlier.

My nearly twenty-hour train ride to São Paulo was uneventful, except for the fact that I traveled third class in a car with bare wooden benches and open windows. That did not distract me from enjoying the wildly gorgeous scenery. What did spoil my ride, however, was a fellow-passenger sitting across the aisle, who deprived me of my fountain pen, the only writing instrument in my possession. Another passenger had seen him take it out of my pocket while I was napping. Now the thief was arrogantly displaying my pen in his jacket pocket. I asked him to give it back, but he refused, got up and went to sit elsewhere. That incident spoiled my trip, because I valued that pen. I had saved for a long time to be able to buy such a treasured item, one which I would need in Bible school. To this day I am fascinated by fountain pens, even though they have become nearly obsolete as useful writing instruments.

Upon arriving in the big city I was met by Mimi Janzen and Agnes Fehdrau, friends from the Krauel, who were working as maids in São

Paulo. I stayed at the MCC headquarters, a center for Mennonites from different colonies, who were either seeking employment in the city or already working there. MCC provided an ideal place for church services and social gatherings. During my four days in São Paulo, I visited friends, changed some currency into Canadian funds, got my visa for Canada, and tried to secure a transit visa for the United States. There in the office of the American Consulate I had my first real culture shock; it taught me a lesson for life. It suddenly hit me that there are cultural differences between peoples and countries—not that I did not know it, but I was unprepared for it.

On 8 June, I made an appointment with the American Consulate for 3:00 p.m. the following day. Time consciousness was not a priority in my culture, especially not when dealing with officials. What I knew about Brazilian officials was that they always made people wait, thereby showing their superiority. Having to wait an hour or two for an appointment was more the rule than the exception. When it came to the concept of time, I had developed a dual standard. In the family, church and at work, I operated on Mennonite punctuality. But in the Brazilian culture, such adverbs as *mais tarde* (later) and *manhã* (tomorrow) had become trade words we could live by.

When I showed up thirty minutes late for my appointment at the consulate, the American official shouted at me: "Why were you not here at 3:00? Our office closes in half an hour and will be closed tomorrow. Don't expect to get your visa today." I was not only shocked, I also found his gruff manner highly offensive and thought to myself that the man lacked social graces. I needed my visa that day, lest I miss my flight in Rio. I swallowed my pride, apologized for being late, and humbly asked him to issue the needed transit visa for landing in New York, where I was scheduled to transfer to Canadian Pacific Airlines. I got my visa, thanked him politely and said, "*Adeus, senhor*"; but I withheld the normal, warm Brazilian handshake.

On Friday evening, 10 June, I boarded the train for Rio de Janeiro, the capital of Brazil at that time. Since I traveled at night, I had to miss out on the extraordinary beauty of the terrain between São Paulo and Rio. Frederico Arentz was at the train station to meet me and take me to his home. He and Mrs. Arentz were the most gracious hosts I could have wished for. Mr. Arentz was a Mennonite from Prussia transferred to Rio by his company. He had at various times been an effective diplomat for our people when they needed someone to represent them at the government level. He had also offered to assist me with final travel arrangements. Thankfully, I had all my papers in order. On Saturday, Mr. Arentz gave me a walking tour through parts of the city, including the commercial center, the buildings housing the federal government, and parks with magnificent historical monuments. The next day (12 June) we took an open streetcar into the mountains along the most scenic route of Rio. As the tram wound its way around mountains and hillsides, we saw a panoramic view from different angles of the city with its buildings, beaches, boulevards, and parks—an unforgettable experience.

That same Sunday evening at 10 o'clock, I was scheduled to fly with Pan American Airlines to New York. Mr. Arentz came with me to the airport to make sure that I would get to the right place in time to catch my flight. While I was checking in, I heard the familiar rumbling of a frightful tropical storm. Tons of water, a literal deluge, came down on Rio. As soon as the rain let up, all passengers were called by name and instructed to line up by number. Armed soldiers were standing ready to guide us to the gate for boarding. I said farewell to my kind host and moved forward with the flow.

My First Airplane Trip

That was still before the jet age. The airplane was propelled by four giant motors with huge rotating blades. We made three stopovers between Rio and New York. The first was in Belém, capital of Pará in Northeastern Brazil. There we had an early breakfast of polenta, black bean sauce, heavily peppered fried eggs that had barely touched the skillet, and a Brazilian *media*, half coffee and half milk with lots of sugar. The next two landings were in Port of Spain, Trinidad, and San Juan, Puerto Rico. In San Juan things did not go as smoothly as expected. Near the end of the runway before takeoff, facing the Atlantic Ocean toward the Bahamas, we felt a tremendous jolt and the airplane came to a complete halt. All four engines were either turned off or stalled. The pilot announced mechanical difficulties. He ordered all passengers to take their carry-on luggage, evacuate immediately, walk away from the runway onto a sandy beach and wait for further instructions. About forty-five to sixty minutes later two buses came to pick us up and take us back to the terminal. After waiting for over three hours, we had to transfer to a different airplane that was to take us to New York. The fear that I would miss my connecting flight to Toronto became reality.

My experience in that world metropolis called New York was not the best. For one thing, we arrived late in the evening, hours behind schedule. My flight to Toronto had left. Then too, going through immigration was an exceedingly slow process. This was not what I had expected, judging by my experience with the American Consulate in São Paulo who had taught me a lesson in punctuality. Here things seemed to be different; hours of flight delay and slow documentation control could hardly be called punctuality. Besides that, the building where our documents were being processed was unbearably hot. When I saw people drink Coca Cola to quench their thirst, I also decided to try it; but that did not do the trick. I felt sick to my stomach and have never developed a taste for that black carbonated syrup water and whatever additives it contains. Worst of all, I did not know the English language. For all practical purposes, I had become *incommunicado* within the last twenty-four hours. That gave me an uneasy feeling.

When I finally got to the hotel where PAN AM put me up for the night, I was given a room on the fifth floor with a bathroom at the end of the hallway. That led to another frustration. I got up early the next morning to take a bath. As I left my room, the door closed automatically behind me without any effort on my part. I admired such a clever invention, but not for long. When I came back from the bathroom I discovered that the door had not only closed, it was locked. Never in my life had I seen a door with a lock that snapped shut without a key. I had left my key in the room. It was locked in, I was locked out. Luckily, I had taken pants with me, but no shirt. I was frustrated.

Before long, I found myself at the check-in counter on the first floor, with pajama tops tucked into my pants. I was profoundly embarrassed and would have liked to disappear. What added to my dilemma was that the gentleman at the counter understood neither Portuguese nor German. He did not even catch on to my sign language. No matter how hard I tried, I could not bring it across to him that I was locked out and needed a key to get back into my room. Other guests became impatient. The line got longer and longer. Then I noticed the clerk speaking to a dark man in uniform, a porter, I assume. "He must be a Brazilian," I thought; "surely, he will understand me." I breathed a sigh of relief. But alas! I was again mistaken. Finally, I grabbed the porter by the arm. He got the hint and came with me to the fifth floor. When he saw me trying to turn the locked door handle he smiled, mumbled some words in an unknown tongue, left me there, and went to get a key. I need not say how relieved I was.

Through all that commotion I had missed breakfast, but not the taxi back to the airport. I also got my flight on Canadian Pacific Airlines to Toronto. I must admit that my experience in New York had caused some apprehension as to what I might expect in Toronto, a major city of the land where I was to go to Bible school. The friendliness and courtesy of the flight attendants, who served a very tasty noon meal, dispelled my apprehension somewhat. The items on the menu that impressed me more than any other were two slices of bread, white and fluffy as cotton and soft as cottage cheese. Never had I seen or tasted anything like it in my life. However, I have since then learned that the appeal of a food to the eye and the palate does not necessarily match its nutritional value.

Welcome After Farewell

Once I had passed visa clearance, received my Landing Permit—a document of inestimable value—and gone through customs, I proceeded to the waiting area in the hope that someone of my relatives would be there to meet me. I had written them about place and time of arrival, but no one seemed to be there. I went to the information desk. Again I failed to make myself understood. When I slowly and distinctly articulated the words: *deutsch, português; alemã, portugiesisch*, the person at the booth called over the loudspeaker for anyone who could speak German or Portuguese. Within minutes my uncle Peter Wiebe and his grandson Peter Penner welcomed me to Canada. That was a moment of great deliverance. They took me to their homes in the Beamsville and Vineland area. I stayed with the Wiebes, my aunt and uncle, for the first few days before I started work in the summer fruit harvest.

I began this chapter with the farewell words from my parents at the train station in Curitiba. It is time to add a few concluding thoughts about that scene. Time seemed to have come to a near standstill on that Monday morning. Not that I was anxious to embark on my first train ride since babyhood, nor was I eager to take leave of my parents and sister. Just the opposite was true. My lingering anxiety seemed to stretch every minute into hours before the actual moment of departure arrived. It was this inevitable moment which all four of us dreaded. The wait seemed long, but in reality was far too short. The last embraces and farewell kisses were emotionally charged. So were the moments when the train began to roll along its tracks in a northerly direction. We waved our goodbyes to each other—no mere motions of waving our hands in the air; those were genuine and final gestures of filial affection. Eight years went by before I again embraced my father and siblings, kin and cousin—but not my mother. That day is still to come when she and I will meet again.

More than fifty years have passed. Countless events and experiences have crossed my path since that memorable Monday morning of 6 June 1949. I can still visualize the scene at the old train station in Curitiba, taking leave of Father, Mother, and my oldest sister. That morning marked for me the *kairos*, that very eventful moment of time, when those profound and practical farewell words of my parents began to take hold of me. They became the reference point for my life and my mission.

The warm welcome I received from my relatives upon arriving in Canada and subsequent conversations with my aunt Katharina and uncle Peter Wiebe were to me an affirmation that I was on the right path.

At 13 months: My road ahead unsure, God's providence secure.

Part of my family before escape from Siberia, 1929. Back: Greta, Maria, Father; Front: Katja, Nikolai, and Mother with me on her lap.

A glimpse of present Alexandrovka, the village of my birth,
Photo by Peter Penner, 2000

The gate to Slavgorod today.   Photo by Donald Loewen, 1998

Facing uncertainties at the "Gates of Moscow," November 1929.

My family and other refugees on board the Alexey Rykov arriving in Swinemünde, 2 December 1929.

Source: Peter Klassen, *Die russlanddeutschen Mennoniten in Brasilien,* Vol. 1.

Our refugee quarters in Mölln 1929-1930. Standing on the parking lot 70 years later, 1999.

Crossing the Atlantic on the *Monte Olivia*, 16 January-6 February 1930.
Source: Hamburg Süd, Hamburg Germany. Used by permission.

River boat *Blumenau*, which took us from the ocean harbor to the city of Blumenau.
Source: Peter Klassen, *Die russlanddeutschen Mennoniten in Brasilien*, Vol. 1.

"Sommerkamp Barracks," temporary shelter upon arrival in the Krauel, February 1930.

Our group at the headquarters of the Hanseatic Land Association in Ibirama,

Building our first house in Brazil, February-March 1930.

Family in front of our home, May 1930. Kornelius (brother-in-law) and Susanna Funk, Heinrich, Father and I, Greta, Katja, and Mother (Maria and Nikolai not pitured).

Returning from first Harvest Thanksgiving in the Krauel, 1931.

Our one-room school in Waldheim with teacher Johann Penner. Center row, fourth from right, in second grade.

My brother Heinrich (center) and other men using oxen to harvest logs from jungle.

Father and others transporting logs to saw mill.

A giant pinheiro yields to the ax of father and son.

"Easter Swing": Three days of fun and entertainment each year.

My parents and siblings with their children. I am standing center row, left. 1937.

The day I was baptized, 25 May 1947.

With my parents before I left for Winkler Bible School, 1949.

Lonely months in Canada, 1949.

Winkler Bible School students and teachers bringing "Christmas cheer" to elderly and lonely. Far left, next to Mr. Seibel.

Serving on WBS student council, 1951.

Earning my keep as Bible school janitor, 1949-1953.

My WBS graduation, 1953, back row, third left. Teachers: John Goossen, B. B. Boldt, H. H. Redekop, G. D. Pries, John Boldt.

Frieda Reimer and I on our engagement, 5 July 1953.

Our wedding in Yarrow, BC, 20 September 1953.

Graduation from Mennonite Brethren Bible College, Winnipeg, MB, 1958.

Frieda with our daughter Dianne in East Chilliwack, BC.

Reimer family, 1956. Back row, from left: Nick Reimer with Madelyn, Bill Henry, Margaret Henry, Hilda Reimer, Hans Kasdorf, Mary Driedger, Jake Driedger with John. Front row, from left: Erna Reimer with Paul, Mrs. N. N. Reimer, Mr. N. N. Reimer, and Frieda Kasdorf with Dianne.

Church and parsonage in Blumenau.

Blumenau church youth group. Frieda and I at center behind 4-year-old Dianne in front row.

Meeting with evangelical pastors in Blumenau. Back row, fourth left.

On a preaching tour in Brazil, 1971: with Evelyn in front of my former home on the Krauel.

Our family in Fresno, 1972.

Two graduates: David from Hoover High School, and I from Fuller Theological Seminary, 1976.

Church Mission Institute at the Biblical Seminary in Fresno. Front right, with teachers Henry Schmidt and David Ewert (behind me); Elizabeth (front left) next to Tom (in wheelchair) Brewster with missionary candidates.

In my seminary office, planning and preparing lectures for the semester.

At my retirement from seminary in Fresno, honored with a Festschrift on Mission and Pluralism, presented by the academic dean, Howard Loewen.

With faculty and students at the Freie Theologische Akademie in Gießen, Germany, 1998.

Speaker at a Bible family conference at the Bibelheim am Klosterberg, Höningen, Germany, 2000.

Our family at our golden wedding anniversary, 2003. Back row: Dianne, Steven, and Maren LeVá; Natalia, Evelyn and Donald Loewen; Julia and David Loewen, David Loewen, Frieda Kasdorf and Amelia Kasdorf. Front row: Hans Kasdorf, David Loewen, Frieda Kasdorf and Amelia Kasdorf.

PART III

Learning the ABC of My Life's Mission (1949-1962)

Adjustment-Bible-Culture +Theory, Practice, and More

Christian fellowships should so participate in the living, dynamic presence of Christ that they interact with the world in exactly the same way Jesus did and as he continues to do today—with redeeming love. The community of faith is not an ark which is, when filled, taken out of the world as though the church exists for itself. It is a redemptive community which is in solidarity with all humankind, yet it judges the very world with which it expresses solidarity. It sees itself as part of the divine plan to bring all things into proper relationship with Jesus Christ.
–Donald R. Jacobs, *Pilgrimage in Mission: Mennonite Perspectives on the Christian Witness Worldwide* (1983)

26

First Months in Canada
(June-October 1949)

When things go wrong, as they sometimes will,
When the road you're trudging seems all uphill,
When the funds are low and the debts are high
And you want to smile, but you have to sigh,
When care is pressing you down a bit,
Rest! if you must—but never quit.
–In Wm. J. Bennett, *The Book of Virtues*

Geographically, I was now nearly half a world removed from my *Heimatland*. For many years I had shared that spot on our globe with my parents and siblings, my church and my people whose language I had spoken, whose way of life I had intimately known, and whose land had been my land. I had been enculturated into the very fabric of that socio-cultural milieu in the Krauel. Now everything was different. Everything. I was wondering how things would be once I got to Winkler.

My immediate challenge was to learn to live in another world. If I wanted to pursue my youthful aspirations and achieve my goal, I would have to make adjustments. I was aware of the challenge, but ill equipped to meet it. My unassertiveness and tendency to withdraw did not help. But the Lord did—and that for a specific purpose unknown to me at the time. The experiences during my first few months in Canada made me to view the world from different angles and prepared me for a ministry with students from other countries who came to study where I was teaching in later life. I can only marvel at the custom-made curriculum God must have designed just for me at that particular time of my life. It was sometimes entirely nonacademic, but never nonpedagogical. It was truly a matter of learning the ABC required for my mission in years to come.

I found myself in a part of the world where I knew neither place nor people, customs nor culture. My ill-fitting clothes were no match compared to the tailored suits worn by Canadian young men of that day. When I sat next to sharply dressed young men in church, I was so distracted that I could not even listen to the sermon. All I saw were my lanky wrists sticking out of sleeves that were three inches too short, my

First Months in Canada 189

ugly neck that was two sizes too thin for the shirt collar draped around it, and a shiny old tie that must have been a decade older than I—I had bought it in Brazil from Waldemar Kröker who had received it in a care package from relatives in Canada. I began to realize that I simply did not fit in, either with or without a tie. Others must have thought the same. Some good folks talked about me as being "backward." They meant no ill, I suppose. But I did not take such comments as a compliment and avoided their company.

I also had positive experiences. Never will I forget my first Sunday breakfast in Canada. I had been invited by Abe and Erna Friesen of Camden, not far from the Wiebes in Vineland where I was staying that first week. Erna was their granddaughter and thus a close relative of mine. I felt the presence of godliness in that home. What impressed me even more was the aesthetically and richly set breakfast table with a linen table cloth, beautiful cups of fine bone china, equally pretty side plates, glass tumblers for milk, serviettes, and a knife and spoon for each person. (At home we had one or two knives for the whole family.) Everything was tastefully done. Besides that, there were three boxes of cereal: one of corn flakes, one, I believe, of Rice Krispies, and the third one I don't remember. I had never heard of any of them. Then there was a small container with cream and a large pitcher with milk. Erna had baked sweet bread, *Tweeback,* and two kinds of *Plautz,* one topped with plums, the other with peaches. Those baked goods were as delicious as they looked. The expression "fit for a king" was apropos, at least by my standards. What puzzled me most was a dish with butter and other dishes containing two or three kinds of jam. Somehow that seemed extravagant and was contrary to my concept of food culture. Things just did not fit.

After Abe had read a passage of Scripture and thanked the Lord for the food, I was to see with my own eyes that everything did fit. To my utter amazement, my hosts spread butter and jam on *Tweeback.* I could come to only one conclusion: they must be very rich people. I soon found out that I was wrong. I had perceptions, but my interpretation of them was incorrect. They were actually humble people living in a modest house and extending hospitality to me. Abe worked at McKinnes Industries in St. Catharines, and Erna was a frugal homemaker, taking care of family and household.

That same Sunday afternoon I went to live with David and Mary Unrau in Jordan Station where I got a job picking fruit at the Scoll Farm; David worked there as foreman. He was great to work for. Mary was my first cousin. They took me in as their own. Despite all the kindness and accommodation of my relatives, I was painfully lonely. It was not the kind of loneliness that results from boredom or from a feeling of rejection or from a sense that no one cares. It was rather a type of loneliness that was socioculturally determined and can best be captured by the combined German noun of *Heim+Weh=Heimweh*. Such loneliness results from a feeling of displacement, a sense of social and cultural disconnectedness and isolation.

As soon as I learned where and how to take a bus (even if I had to walk five kilometers to the nearest bus stop) to Niagara-on-the-Lake, I went there on Sundays whenever I could, to spend time with the Johannes and Waldemar Krökers and two other recent immigrant families I knew from Brazil. All of them were working for the Boese fruit packing and canning enterprises. They also felt lonely and uprooted; we understood each other. We sang the songs we had sung in the Krauel. We talked and ate, played and prayed together. They were dealing in the new environment with the same emotions and perceptions I had, and I found it very reassuring to be with them. However, those visits lasted only for the first summer. As soon as they had earned enough money to pay for tickets, they packed their bags and moved back. I would have liked to do the same, but could not.

One of the things utterly shocking was that women in the orchard next to the Scoll Farm wore shorts and sleeveless tops for picking fruit. Not only that, the next Sunday I saw those same girls singing in the Vineland church choir where I attended services. I found that offensive and was profoundly shaken up. Only once in my early teens had I seen something remotely similar. One of our "progressive" and intellectual young men from the Krauel could not cope with the cultural and mental restrictions in our small world between the *serras* and had gone to find a job in Rio de Janeiro. (Some years later he moved to Canada and became professor of acoustical engineering at the University of British Columbia.) When he came home for Christmas one year, two young women wearing pants, lipstick and painted fingernails came with him to see a remote part of the world where the way of life was simple and strikingly different from that in the big city of Rio. Their appearance became the talk of the colony. I remember the conversation in our own home. My parents, at least Mother, must have been remarkably tolerant. She was willing to overlook the way these young ladies were dressed—after all, what could one expect of "heathen girls" from the city of "Sodom and Gomorrah?" They did not know better. They needed the Gospel, not harsh judgment. That incident came to my mind during my first weeks in Canada.

I could not help but wonder what my parents might have said about the apparel of the girls in the neighborhood of the Scoll Farm. They were not from "Sodom and Gomorrah"; they were from "Zion and Jerusalem." They obviously knew the Gospel. They were church members in Vineland. Would my parents have understood the situation better than I did? Perhaps. But how could I bring it all together? Well, I could not. I simply had no way of dealing with such "profound" issues I had never encountered

First Months in Canada

before. I had little perception of right and wrong beyond what I had brought with me from the Krauel based on subjective impressions defined in terms of black and white.

Eventually, something began to dawn on me which has occupied much of my thinking, my reading, my learning, and my teaching ever since, namely the perpetual tension between the Gospel and the prevailing culture. This is a subject the church has always had to deal with; but it has not always done so wisely and redemptively. Perhaps God gave me those early cross-cultural experiences to learn to live with creative tension in a redemptive way.

Then there was that awful peach fuzz to which I was allergic. One very hot and humid day the itch over my entire body became nearly unbearable. Every visible part was red and my face badly swollen. I would have liked to ask my mother for a home remedy; she usually had a solution for things like that. But I realized that Mother was not there. I was now on my own. Completely on my own. I had to assume responsibility for myself—peach fuzz or not. There were moments when I seriously debated whether to go back home or to Bible school. I believe I would have gone back to Brazil within the first few weeks, if only I had had the money. It was providential that I did not have it; for if I had, I would have acted like Jonah: I would have bought the ticket and run "away from the LORD and headed for Tarshish" instead of fulfilling my mission to which God had called me (Jonah 1:1-3). That would have been not only an act of disobedience, as in Jonah's case, but also one of bad stewardship. I was working to earn money for tuition in Bible school, not for a return ticket to Brazil. Being poor can sometimes be a blessing.

By the end of that first summer, I had come to an important realization. Not that I no longer felt alone or isolated. The kind of loneliness I referred to earlier is like sticky adhesive: it does not want to let go or disappear in haste, especially when a person is more reserved than assertive by nature. I struggled for more than a year in a labyrinth of loneliness with jarring jolts, or whatever one wants to call a time of transition and adjustment to a new culture. My body was in Canada, my mind in Brazil. I decided to bring the two together. A word from my parents came to mind. Whenever Father wanted to teach us boys to make a straight furrow with the plow, he said: *"Tjitjt nijh tridj, tjitjt bloos no feari."* He quoted Jesus, saying: "No one who puts his hand to the plow and looks back is fit to serve in the kingdom of God" (Luke 9:62). Mother quoted the same words when I was thinking of going to Bible school in Canada.

I must confess that I never liked to hear those words, especially not from Father when plowing the field. It was easy for him to say, because he had been able to make furrows like a horizontal plumb line stretched between two points across the flat steppe of Siberia. But that was impossible in the Krauel where I grew up. One could not make a furrow without a bend or curve on a steep hillside dotted with big stumps and their long roots. Yet I understood the spiritual principle Father intended to convey. Now the time had come for me to prove it. I could either look back and make a blemished furrow in my journey, or look ahead toward my goal.

As I became more rational about my purpose in coming to Canada, I renewed my determination not to lose sight of that goal. I made a twofold decision. First, despite all the bumps and stumps on the hilly fields of my host culture, which I could not remove, I would make adjustments and keep on plowing to serve in the kingdom of God. Then, too, I felt indebted to the Mennonite Brethren young people of Manitoba. They had paid $487 for my ticket from Rio to Toronto, so that I could attend Winkler Bible School. In those days it took a rich man's purse to pay that much for a one-way air fare. David Reimer of Morden and Abe Froese of Boissevain, provincial youth leaders, wrote, and later told me personally that I was in no way obligated to repay that money. But I could not have lived with myself, if I had gone back to Brazil without going to Bible school. I was so anxious to pay back what I felt I owed, that I even bought three lottery tickets at $1.00 each in the hope of winning a Studebaker car displayed in a showroom in St. Catharines. I prayed that God would let me win that car, which I would sell, repay my ticket and have money left over to buy myself a winter coat. I did not win the car, stayed without a winter coat or jacket, and could not repay the airfare in a lump sum. But I went to Bible school and not back to Brazil. Over the next four years I was able to pay back the $487 of which Mr. Reimer returned $100 as a gift.

As the time drew nearer to leave for Bible School in Winkler, David Unrau, my good host and boss, felt uneasy that I had neither coat nor jacket to keep me warm in the frigid Manitoba winter. The Unraus were genuinely concerned. I am quite sure that if David had had two coats, he would have given me the best one; he was that kind of a generous Christian. But all he could give me was well-intentioned advice, if not the wisest, as I was to discover later.

David told me that the prairie provinces could be frightfully cold. I never questioned his word. The stories he told about his experiences in a northern Saskatchewan logging camp were chilling enough to convince me that he was right. He urged that I should at least buy myself heavy long johns and long, thick woolen stockings to cover my knees. That, he said, should keep me warm. Again, he was right. They did keep me warm. I soon discovered, however, that although long johns and heavy woolen stockings are comfortable for outside activities, they are not meant to be worn in an overheated classroom. When I returned to Ontario the following summer, we had a hearty laugh and agreed that loggers' underwear is more suited for lumberjacks in ice and snow than for Bible students in a warm building.

27

Winkler Bible School
(1949-1953)

Your word, O LORD, is eternal; it stands firm in the heavens.
Your word is a lamp to my feet and a light for my path.
Your decrees are the theme of my song wherever I lodge.
Your faithfulness continues through all generations.
—Excerpts from *Psalm 119*

It was during my first summer in Canada that George Pries, Bible School teacher from Winkler, was visiting friends and former students in Ontario. The young people of the Vineland Mennonite Brethren Church had a picnic at the Queenston Heights Park at Niagara Falls in honor of Mr. Pries and his family. I was invited as a special guest. As I listened to Mr. Pries and to testimonies by several young people about the meaning of Bible school I resolved to pursue my goal, come what may. Father's farewell words to "stand firm as a good soldier of Jesus Christ" came to mind. I realized that the time to be an adult had come. No one else but I would be responsible for every decision I made and accountable to God for the consequences of those decisions. I began to thank God for my past in Brazil. Those had been good years, though not without shortcomings. Now was my chance to replace them by unknown opportunities that lay before me at the Winkler Bible School. I was now on the other side of the ominous *serras* surrounding the narrow Krauel Valley, where I had had visions of some day discovering things I did not know. That vision, those dreams, had become reality. I looked with anticipation to new discoveries—some charted, others uncharted.

Initially I had planned to go to Manitoba by train. Then I learned to know John Janzen from St. Catharines who was also going to Bible school in Winkler. He had his own car and offered me a ride. We left the first part of October 1949. Driving through the Canadian Shield with all its rocks and rivers, countless lakes and multifarious evergreens, their scrubby tips rising above white poplar and other deciduous trees and shrubs without number, all in brilliant fall colors, was a striking contrast from what I had seen in the Brazilian jungle.

While I have many pleasant memories of that trip, one is unpleasant. I believe it was the first night that we stayed in a "Room to Let" of a private house. As we drove on the next day, I noticed to my horror that I did not have my treasured ΩMEGA pocket watch which my parents had given me as a special keepsake before I left home. John telephoned to the place we had stayed, but was told that they had "found nothing" in the room. Neither he nor I was convinced that we were told the truth. I left my address but never heard from the place again.

We arrived in Winkler three days later, in the afternoon. On the main road leading into town were business signs with such familiar names as C. J. Funk, and J. A. Kroeker. I walked into the first door and introduced myself to a somewhat stocky, but very friendly gentleman by the name of Funk. He noticed my broken English and responded in German. When I asked for directions to the residence of H. H. Redekop, Mr. Funk kindly offered to take me there by car. In the open garage next to the house I met Mr. Redekop, principal of the Winkler Bible School, winterizing his car. He looked up, removed his gloves, greeted me with a handshake, and said in the form of a question: "*So, Du bist dann der Jüngling von Brasilien?*" (Well then, you are that young man from Brazil?) I was rather shy and had not much to say. He, too, seemed to be frugal with words. But I cannot say that about his gaze. He looked me over from head to toe. It would be unfair to speculate what he might have thought about that encounter with the first foreign student from Brazil. He invited me into the house, introduced me to Mrs. Redekop, and then took me to the boys' dormitory. He made sure that I got a room, and went home. In subsequent months I gained genuine respect and appreciation for him; our friendly relationship lasted beyond my time in Winkler.

Winkler Bible School offered much more than head knowledge. Theory and practice were interwoven in the entire curriculum. The school's priorities lay in character formation with a vision for discipleship and service in the kingdom of God. I did not learn much *about* the Bible in a critical sense; I learned the *Bible itself*—what it is and what it stands for. The Holy Scriptures as God's written Word were simply accepted as normative for belief and action. We had to know the books of the Bible, their essential contents, the author of each book in its historical setting as far as that was possible to determine, the key lesson of each chapter or section, and to memorize certain portions associated with given themes. To this very day I greatly treasure that foundational Bible knowledge.

I do not recall that students ever raised critical questions about authorship, historicity of certain books, hermeneutical approaches, methods, and the reliability of the Scriptures. The curriculum was not designed to answer every question about the Bible or about life in general; it was designed to view all of life from the perspective of the plain biblical texts as we had them before us. "The fundamental aim of Biblical instruction and exposition," writes Mr. Pries in *A Place Called Peniel*, "is to assist the student to grow spiritually through an intelligent understanding and personal appropriation of the Bible for faith and Christian living."

Discipleship and service were written large over every subject. Students were encouraged to be involved in local churches and in the community. During my four years at the school we had an average of thirty students teaching in some fifteen different Sunday schools in Winkler and surrounding villages. I was teaching in Schanzenfeld during my third and fourth years. This was an opening to the homes, especially during Christmas time. Each Christmas three or four students and a teacher visited the poor and elderly in the villages. We called this "Christmas Cheer." The school sought to live by a motto borrowed from an old sage, who said: "Those who are kind to the poor lend to the LORD." I was moved by the way people responded to the Christmas stories, Scripture readings, singing of carols and hymns, and some tangible gift appropriate for the season. It was delightful to serve as an envoy of "Christmas Cheer."

Music, too, played an important role in the school. The choir under the direction of John Boldt was superb. I have never claimed a special gift for singing, but I do claim a profound appreciation for good music that has stood the test of time. Mr. Boldt was as much a master in the selection of church hymns, anthems and chorales as he was in motivating students to put voice, heart and soul into music ministry. When I listen to tapes and records from those years, I am reminded of Bruce Metzger, who writes of the hymns recorded in Revelation (*Breaking the Code*) that "they make some of our modern ephemeral ditties appear incredibly trite." Mr. Boldt evidently thought it to be wiser to teach us the great music of the church than to waste time on "modern ephemeral ditties."

I enjoyed singing so much that I decided to take voice lessons. They helped to improve not only my singing, but also my voice modulation and speaking ability. Even some of the breathing and articulation techniques that I learned from John Boldt have stood me in good stead through the years. The song I sang for my evening recital was based on the conversation between the risen Lord and his disciple Peter recorded in John 21:15-17. The searching question that Jesus asked Peter provided the title: *Hast du mich lieb?* (Simon, son of John, do you love me?). I also took a class in conducting. That, too, has been helpful in leading singing groups and directing the church choir in Blumenau until we had someone else to do it. In addition, I sang in a male quartet and in the school choir. Visiting and singing in churches throughout Manitoba gave me an excellent opportunity to get to know many church people as well as local and conference leaders of the province.

During my first year in Bible School I had Johann G. Wiens as one of my teachers. He had been a missionary to India, sent out by the Mennonite Brethren Church in Russia, and later became one of the pioneer teachers at WBS. He taught an introductory course in homiletics, his favorite subject. He challenged us to listen critically and write down the text, the subject, and the outline of every sermon we heard. I took him up on that and learned to be an attentive listener. One year when Jakob G. Thiessen was speaking at a Bible conference on the theme, "The Kingdom of God on Earth," I crafted careful notes on every message he presented. I did the same when I listened to messages preached in church by Heinrich S. Voth, G. D. Pries, H. H. Redekop, and other speakers of that day. Mr. Voth had a long history with the M. B. Church and its mission in the United States and Canada. He was pastor in Winkler when I joined the church there. On numerous occasions he invited me to visit him in his home. Those visits were true learning experiences that deepened my understanding of the structure and mission of the Mennonite Brethren Church.

In my final year, I took a course in homiletics taught by Mr. Pries. In that course, more than in any other, I learned to concentrate on a given subject and to make an outline in logical sequence that would give cohesion to the topic under consideration. His class proved to be very helpful, not only to improve my notes on sermons I heard, but also to make my own outlines for sermons—even for research papers in college and graduate school. One of the requirements of the four-year Bible course was the delivery of a twenty-minute *Probepredigt* (test sermon) in the school auditorium, to which the public was invited. I spoke on Acts 16:16-29: the conversion of the Philippian jailer. The purpose of the sermon was to test the student's public speaking skills according to given homiletical principles. After the presentation, each sermon was critically evaluated by the teachers and graduating class in the presence of all students and guests who had come for the event. The experience was scary, especially for the more timid souls. After I had delivered my sermon and critics made their comments, Mr. Pries concluded with these words: "Brother Kasdorf was teaching as he preached, and was preaching as he taught." I was simultaneously humbled and encouraged.

Winkler Bible School sponsored different conferences especially designed for preachers, Sunday School teachers, music directors and other church workers. Quite early in its history the school had become a member of the Evangelical Teacher Training Association (ETTA). The regular curriculum of the first three years was designed to train qualified Sunday school teachers. Upon successful completion, students received the prized ETTA Certificate. In addition, the school conducted periodic seminars for teachers who wanted to improve their skills and methods and bring their resources up to date. What made these training sessions particularly attractive to students were the special speakers invited for the occasion.

During my third year, the Bible school had invited A. A. Kroeker and I. W. Redekopp to speak on such topics as "The influence of the environment [home, day school, neighborhood] on the child"; "The soul of the child" [perceptions, receptivity, etc.], and similar subjects pertaining to children as learners. I was immensely impressed by the insights of these men and determined to learn as much as possible about the Sunday school pupil and teacher. When I was at the Bible College in Winnipeg, Mr. I. W. Redekopp was my professor of Christian education. He was a very pragmatic person, always concerned that his students would translate classroom theory into practical teaching. These teacher training courses in Winkler and the studies in Christian education in Winnipeg gave me a solid foundation for my ministry in Brazil, which included equipping Sunday school teachers and leaders in the local churches.

Of equal importance were Bible and mission conferences. They were exceptionally inspirational and challenging. Such speakers as Annie E. Dyck from Colombia, William G. and Margaret Baerg from Africa, and Abram A. and Annie Unruh from India were among those who impacted me most because of their evident love and passion for the people in the lands where they served. Each time I heard a missionary speak, I was challenged to obey God's call in my own life and to broaden my horizon. More and more I began to see the world as a mission field. I had great admiration for men and women who had gone to different parts of our globe, sharing the gospel of the kingdom with people who had never heard the Good News.

My understanding of mission was enhanced through a course taught by Mr. John Boldt. He used *The Progress of World-Wide Missions* by Robert Hall Glover as a text. It became my favorite book. I still remember Glover's definition of mission as "the proclamation of the Gospel to the unconverted everywhere according to the command of Christ." Glover's focus was on people everywhere, not only in the non-Western world. Entirely new to me was his explanation of the term *mission* as sentness, which implies a sender, a sent one, and one to whom sent. The supreme Sender is God Himself, for He sent His Son, Jesus the Messiah, into a needy and redeemworthy world. Furthermore, mission, according to Glover, includes the physical, material, intellectual, and spiritual dimensions. These concepts became the basis of my missionary practice in later years. With some modifications, they also have been influential in the formulation of my own philosophy of world mission. I still treat this book as a classic among several hundred missiological books in my private library. These books deal with a variety of historical, theological, ethnological and a host of contemporary issues in world mission, issues to which I have devoted most of my life and labor since my days in Winkler. One of the central questions for me has always been how to interpret and apply the Gospel in a given cultural context without compromising biblical principals and without denigrating cultural values.

Another emphasis at Winkler was prayer as the school's greatest source of strength. The year I graduated, I wrote in the *Yearbook*: "Prayer is the source of joy and strength for the teachers and students of Peniel. For this reason we are nurturing a vital fellowship in prayer. . . . These are the times when prayer is made for missionaries, for the sick, for those who are in trying times, for the unsaved, for one another, and for ourselves."

Years later when I read Myron Augsburger's book, *Called to Maturity: God's Provision for Spiritual Growth*, I was reminded of the stress placed on prayer during my time in Winkler. Augsburger summarizes how prayer affects a person's life at various levels, saying:

> Prayer [gives] God's Spirit permission to do his work in and through us.
> Prayer makes life God-centered rather than self-centered.
> Prayer brings us a true knowledge of ourselves and our needs.
> Prayer gives us an inner power to be victorious in temptation.
> Prayer will give us wisdom to understand the Word of God. . . .
> Prayer will help us govern our actions, reactions, and our tongues.

I was blessed by these lines and challenged to deepen and nurture a vital life of prayer along my way from childhood through Bible school and beyond, all the way to journey's end.

28

Beyond the Prescribed Curriculum

Be happy, young man, while you are young.
Let your heart give you joy in the days of your youth.
Follow the desires of your heart. But know this:
For everything you do, you have to give an account to God.
–Adapted from *Ecclesiastes 11*

I had learned a smattering of English during my first summer in Ontario, but in Winkler I immersed myself in the language. With the exception of two or three subjects, including German grammar, all instruction was in English. When I heard that I could take free evening classes in English as a second language, I enrolled immediately. My first instructor was Mrs. Isaac from Ireland, an excellent teacher. Her husband was an attorney in Winkler. One evening she invited us to have tea and biscuits at her house in lieu of a class. However, there was a condition: each participant had to tell a short story from personal experience. George Sawatzky, a photographer by trade and an actor (not to say clown) by talent, told about his forced separation from his young wife in the Soviet Union. The story was very sad, but the way he told it, combining his heavy Russian accent with an Irish brogue, nearly brought the roof down.

In my night classes I was in good company: refugees from the Soviet Union were as anxious as I was to learn the "Queen's English." To my delight I discovered that those of us who spoke Low German had a distinct advantage over those who did not, because this older German tongue of the flat European Northland has much more in common with Old English or Anglo Saxon than with the younger and more sophisticated High German of the mountainous Southland. I truly enjoyed the adventure of learning a new language and something about its history, even if I had to struggle with it day and night. It was not so much the English grammar, but the pronunciation of words like *word*, *world*, *strength*, *things*, *through*, *clothes* that gave me great grief. I spent hours before going to bed, trying to pronounce those words in a way that would not betray me as a foreigner. My roommates, Dave Reimer and Jake Suderman, were remarkably tolerant of my gibberish; but there were times when they had heard enough and told me to continue that hodgepodge in my dreams. I obliged.

Actually, I became so absorbed in my effort of learning English that I had dreams and nightmares about it. They gave me no relief. Dreams can be stealthy and deceptive. Instead of rehearsing my English lesson, as I thought I did, I verbalized my dreams in Portuguese. I even prayed in Portuguese, so my roommates told me. At first, they thought it was funny. But before long they found my nightly monologues in a strange tongue as uninteresting and disturbing as my English phonetic lessons and pronunciation drills in the evenings.

What I found very helpful in the process of learning English was the memorization and repetition of such Bible passages as John 1:1-10, Luke 2:4-7, and Philippians 4:10-13, which in the old KJV contain those jaw-breaking and tongue-twisting words that caused me such strain and stress. I also concentrated hard when I listened to others, especially my teachers, and tried to reproduce each phoneme—vowel or consonant, diphthong or digraph or any combination of letters—exactly as I heard it.

There were challenges other than learning English. The gap between an unfinished third grade in Brazil and the ninth grade in a public high school in Canada was fairly wide. As I tried to leap across to the other side, I was pleasantly surprised by what I found. The old building of the Winkler Collegiate Institute stood across the street from *Peniel*. Bible School instruction usually ended toward the end of March or in early April. The high school program ran three months longer, during which time the entire curricular material of the year was being reviewed in preparation for final exams, of which some were administered by the Department of Education in Winnipeg. Both institutions, the Winkler Bible School and the Winkler Collegiate, supported this arrangement. Principal Peter Brown wrote that the Collegiate appreciates "the spirit of friendship and good will it enjoys with the Bible School, and welcomes the chance to help students who wish to take academic work."

I decided to do just that. During my second, third and fourth years of Bible School, I took grades nine, ten and eleven of high school in the remaining three months of the Manitoba school year. Several of my immigrant friends from the Soviet Union did the same. What the regular high school students did in nine months, we had to do in three. It was intensive work, to say the least, yet I enjoyed every minute of it and always passed my tests with better grades than expected. Since I took first year high school after the second year Bible School, I was able to complete only grades nine through eleven. Grade twelve had to wait until I was in Winnipeg. There I took three subjects from the Department of Education, and the rest of grade twelve I completed in Brazil by correspondence from The Academy for Adults in Chicago.

At the Winkler Collegiate I learned to know teachers and students in a more secular environment, quite different from that in Bible School. It gave me some idea how the Canadian public school system operated at that time, and how discipline problems were handled—or not handled. We older students were at times simply aghast at the creative bent certain ones of our much younger classmates had for mischief. Some of it was outright malicious. I wondered why they were in school. Instead of being grateful for the opportunity to learn, they appeared to take pleasure in creating an atmosphere that made learning extremely difficult for everyone—except in Mr. Peter Brown's classes. He kept order from start to finish. He was truly a great teacher, a true pedagogue, especially in chemistry and mathematics. Not only that, he was also a remarkable disciplinarian and effective administrator who commanded high respect both in the school and in the community at large. It was a real loss to Winkler when he accepted a call to teach at the University of Manitoba in Winnipeg. I met him only once more after those years, when he had already retired. At the Bible School's Fiftieth Jubilee in April of 1975, I saw Mr. Brown sitting toward the front in the audience. As soon as I had delivered my jubilee address, he came up to me and said: "I came from Winnipeg especially to hear you speak and am not disappointed." He added a gracious compliment, shook my hand and said, "God be with you." Those were for me encouraging words from a man with the stature of an academic statesman.

Before coming to Winkler I had agreed to be janitor at the Bible School. Mr. Redekop gave me a tour of the place before it opened for classes. He took me to every room, including the basement where the coal bin and the big furnace were located. The last place he showed me was the library on the second floor. The room was large enough for a table and ten chairs in the center and bookcases on the side walls with five or six shelves in each. A third bookcase covered only about two thirds of the eastern wall, leaving space for the door to the hallway. On the opposite end was a large window, facing the street and the Winkler Collegiate on the other side.

There I stood surrounded by what could have been as many as a thousand books, all within my reach. I was overwhelmed. Never had I seen so many books in one place. I was thrilled by the thought of having all those books at my disposal. Was this a dream come true from the time I was still in the Krauel Valley hemmed in by granite *serras* too steep and high to see what might be on the other side? It dawned on me that I now was on that "other side." Even if I was only semiliterate at best, now was my chance to improve my reading skills. While Mr. Redekop was still standing there in the library, I surveyed those shelves with a gleeful glance. Except for several Bibles and songbooks, I could not differentiate one from the other. Books were as foreign to me as my ignorance of them was profound. But now the moment had arrived to make my acquaintance with books. Since then they have become intimate friends and indispensable work tools.

Being both greedy and gullible, I grabbed for a multivolume set with a blue linen cover and the title imprinted in gold. It read: Jean-Jacques Rousseau, *Schriften*, translated from French into German with a different subtitle for each volume. They were old books, but looked like new. As I studied the titles, I decided to start with the tome called *Zurück zur Natur* (Back to Nature). I understood only enough to be disappointed. I gave up without finishing a single volume. Years later in graduate school I read Rousseau again and understood a bit more; I actually enjoyed him.

My second choice was Ruth Paxson's *Life on the Highest Plane*. This book holds a view of human nature opposite to Rousseau's. While Rousseau treats human nature in its natural state as entirely blissful and happy, free and unencumbered by sin, Paxson sees it as totally depraved, yet redeemworthy and redeemable. Once redeemed by God's grace through faith in Jesus Christ, Paxson argues, the Christian must leave the natural and sinful way of life, strive to overcome the carnal, and reach for the spiritual level, which she calls "the highest plane." Her focus on sanctification and holy living is, indeed, a compelling call. But since I knew next to nothing about theology, I may have misinterpreted Paxson's thesis. I became consumed by fear that the Holy God would strike me down and I would be lost, unless I could reach the highest plane.

I was so taken up with that book that I saw **SIN** written in bold and big letters in every thought I had, every deed I did, and nearly every item I possessed. That drove me to an "obsessive piety," as one might call it. It had little to do with true godliness, but had everything to do with the belief that I could achieve perfection by self-effort. One Saturday morning while cleaning my room, I took my diary, a book of Grimm's fairytales which I had received as a bonus for ordering *Knaurs Lexikon A-Z* (which I still have), and my treasured notebook with a collection of about 200 handwritten German, Low German and Portuguese poems, lyrics, Christmas carols and folk songs. Many of them I knew by heart and often recited or sang to myself.

In my sincere quest for piety and holiness that morning, I went to John Heier, a fellow student in charge of the dormitory furnace in the basement. I asked him to come with me and open the door to the huge "coal eater," as we called those old fire boxes. When he did so, I threw those items in my hand onto a pile of glowing coals and saw "my sacrifice for holiness" go up in flames. It soon hit me that I had burned some irretrievable and irreplaceable mementos. I waited, yet made no progress in my reach for the "highest plane." In fact, I felt I had regressed by my irrational act.

During that time I corresponded with Katharine Nickel (my mother's first cousin of Reedley, California) about my spiritual dilemma. She sensed the direction I was headed and wrote that going to Bible school was no reason to become a fanatic in matters of the Christian faith. On the contrary, she explained, anyone studying the Bible should also read good secular books and keep a balanced approach to life. In support of her argument she mentioned such preachers as J. B. Toews, pastor in Reedley at the time, P.R. Lange, whom she highly respected, and a "young man by the name of Dan Friesen." All of them, she wrote, were educated men; all of them were reading both religious and secular books. I could not argue with her.

I had my first exposure to secular literature at the Winkler Collegiate after completing second year Bible school. I read several Shakespearean plays, Jack London's *Call of the Wild,* Charles Dickens' *Oliver Twist,* and the poetry by Emily Dickinson and Henry W. Longfellow. A master at weaving together intellectual tapestries from the old and the new world, Longfellow is still one of my favorite poets of an older generation. I began to understand what Aunt Katharine meant and have followed her wise counsel without losing my vision for "life on the highest plane."

Living a genuine, honest spiritual life, explains Henri Nouwen in *Making All Things New*, does not mean that we must give up our jobs or withdraw from social life or lose interest in literature and art. What it does mean is that "we live in the world without being of the world"; it means "that we have moved from the many things to the kingdom of God." That is, I believe, what my mother had tried to impress upon me when I left home. She quoted Matthew 6:33 and said that I should "first seek the kingdom of God." But I had never understood it in the terms of Nouwen's explanation. Society at large lives by the standards of culture which are "of the world"; followers of Jesus Christ live in the same world, but by standards based on biblical principles. That means much more than our trying to follow the teachings of Jesus, as C. S. Lewis reminds us in *Mere Christianity;* it means surrender and humility to follow Jesus Christ as Savior and Lord.

During all four years in Bible school I lived in the boys' dormitory. That in itself was a stretching experience. I left some undesirable edges at that place. Living together with other boys helped to make my relational and social skills somewhat smoother. That was a gratifying experience for many of the boys. Some, however, had a hard time of it. A few remained (or became) stubbornly resistant to any adaptations, and that to their own detriment in later life. I shall refrain from detailed examples, except to say that some disciplinary measures were quite hilarious, whereas others, such as cold showers in mid winter (administered only once in those four years, and that to a deserving student) may have been a bit too icy.

Personally, I found dormitory life quite enjoyable, except that Christmas was at times a trifle quiet. Yet I was never alone. My first year in Winkler, if I remember correctly, John Janzen and I were the only students who had no place to go for Christmas. John was quite outgoing, had a cheerful disposition and a delightful sense of humor without being frivolous or artificial. I appreciated that immensely. He had relatives in Winkler, yet chose to stay in the dorm most of the time. He even helped me keep the school furnace hot and clean.

Since we had time to spare, we decided that my roommates would appreciate having clean beds when they returned after the new year. We experimented with Jake Suderman's bedding, from pillowcase to heavy flannel sheets. We washed them, soaked each item in heavy starch and put them out on the line to dry. Everything froze stiff and crisp. When we took the laundry in the next day, we could set the flannel sheet against the wall like a piece of cardboard. It would neither fold nor bend. While we were pleased with the outcome, there was one slight problem: we had to treat every piece with tender care, lest it would crack while making the bed. Jake never thanked us for our efforts. Instead, as soon as his head hit the pillow, he jumped out of bed and uttered a set of words seldom heard within those walls. I was glad John was there to witness the spectacle. If our friendship with Jake was ruptured at all, the break was only of short duration.

The Scoll brothers for whom I had worked the previous summer had offered me a job in their fruit orchards the following year. Thus I decided to go back with John Janzen to Ontario. The weather had been nice for graduation, but indications for change were on the horizon. John's uncle and aunt, the John Konrads, and H. H. Redekop suggested that we wait a day or two. But the daring spirit of youth does not always heed the seasoned wisdom of age. John assured them that he had weathered snowstorms before and was bent on going. That was the first mistake. More followed. Shortly after lunch on 12 April 1950 we left Winkler for Ontario. That was the second error. Barely had we reached the border crossing from Manitoba into the United States when the snow began to fall. We continued, hoping for change in the weather. That was mistake number three.

Within a short time we were in a heavy snow storm with visibility close to zero and the night upon us. Following a snowplow was helpful, but not for long. Besides, it slowed us down considerably. When John got tired, he let me drive. That was probably the fourth act of foolishness. I had little driving experience and had never driven in snow. By now we would have liked to stop at some place for the night, but there was no visible sign of either light or life, except for our car lights piercing the snow only a few meters ahead. We talked about stopping at the side of the road, but without either blankets or candles to provide warmth we were afraid of freezing to death. As we drove on there was a sudden bang with a jolt and a jerk, and the car stopped short against a telephone or hydro post. By the time I became aware of the invisible "T" in the road, it was too late to turn either to the left or to the right on that icy road covered with snow.

By now it was past midnight. There we sat in a snowstorm with a damaged car, not far from Fargo, North Dakota. We put on every garment we had and waited for the morning. By daybreak the storm had let up. We could see a faint light and discovered a country store only a few meters away. The owner was firing the stove for the day. We knocked on the door and the kind man let us in. When he learned about our problem, he asked why we had not come sooner. While we explained, he offered us coffee and some kind of pastry. His warm welcome was heaven-sent after that frightful, freezing night. The good man was also helpful in getting us in touch with a Ford garage just a few blocks down the road.

The damage to the car was so serious that part of the front axle had to be replaced. Our dilemma was that neither of us had enough money to pay for parts and labor. The manager of the shop must have had a soft spot for these stranded strangers. Rather than simply saying, "Sorry, I can't help you," he invited us into his office on the second floor. There he asked who we were, what we were doing, where we had come from, and where we were going. We responded by saying that John was from Ontario and I from Brazil, that we were Bible school students in Winkler, Manitoba, now on our way to Ontario where we had summer jobs waiting to earn money, and that we would go back to Bible school in the fall. If he would be so kind and repair the car, we assured him, we would send payment as soon as we got to Ontario. John Janzen remembers him saying in response, "If I cannot trust Bible school students, whom can I trust?" The word of a Bible school student seemed to carry much weight in those days. The man trusted us, repaired our car, and by mid-afternoon we were again on our way. As soon as we got home to Ontario we paid our debt to the kind man.

That summer I had two jobs. First, I worked again at the Scoll Farm, picking strawberries and trimming fruit trees. After that I got a job at the golf course in St. Catharines where Peter Penner, a relative of mine, was working. Peter and his wife Justina lived with her parents, the Henry Janzens, in a big farmhouse and offered me room and board at moderate rates. When they left for Bible college later that summer, I moved to Henry and Greta Rempel, who had previously invited me to stay with them. I appreciated their gracious hospitality.

This was also the summer when I met Jake Braun, a recent refugee from the Soviet Union. He had neither parents nor siblings and lived with relatives in Canada. Jake and I became friends and spent many Sunday afternoons together. Though we are now geographically separated, our friendship has not been severed.

Then there was Peter Banman from Winkler, who spent the summer in Ontario. He had bought a used car and was looking for passengers to ride with him to Manitoba. John Janzen, two young ladies and I—all Bible school students—agreed to share the cost and go with him. It turned out to be an eventful trip. The car frequently stalled along the way and caused Peter much frustration, especially when driving through Chicago where the traffic was thick and fast. Some hours later, in an area where the highway curved through forested mountains, we met a group of hunters strategizing their next move. Peter failed to see the warning signs to slow down, and before he knew it he rolled over one of their choicest hunting dogs, causing fatal injuries. The ensuing scene was not pretty. Not far beyond that point, Peter prudently chose to take his car to a repair shop and the rest of us took a bus to Winkler.

In the summer of 1951, I was working for Mr. McGee, painting grain elevators along the CPR line from Manitoba all the way to Medicine Hat, Alberta. John R. Dyck, who graduated from Bible school that year, told me about the job. We both applied and were accepted. He started work right after Bible school, and I joined the crew after high school. It was not the safest job and the atmosphere not always pleasant. It was a rough gang and a tough way of living "on the road," so to speak. We ate under a makeshift tent and slept in the back of the truck or in a grain elevator, always fully exposed to mosquitoes without number. We were a crew of six and painted with brush and bucket in hand one elevator with all adjacent buildings in a day. The pay was adequate, and so was the food. Leo, a Frenchman from La Salle, was an excellent cook. John and I bowed our heads and said a silent prayer before each meal. There were occasions when we also discussed our faith in Christ with the men. They could not understand, but respected our way of life. John quit early in September to get ready for medical school at the University of Manitoba.

After finishing the painting job, I took the bus to Carruthers, Saskatchewan, and visited Peter and Mary Kasdorf, my first cousins. I was thrilled to meet them and their youngest two children, Sara and Willie. From there I went to the Johann Arndts in Glenbush. I knew their sons, Peter and Henry, from Bible school. As it turned out, they needed help to bring in the rest of their wheat harvest. Loading the stooks of wheat with a pitchfork onto a wagon, and from the wagon into the threshing machine did not make me an expert harvester, but I was glad to lend a helping hand.

29

Two Are Better Than One
(1953)

Two are better than one, [said the preacher of old],
because they have a good return for their work:
If one falls down, his friend can help him up.
But pity the man who falls and has no one to help him up.
—From *Ecclesiastes* 4

On the way back to Winkler from my summer job in 1951, I had to change buses in Winnipeg. There I met the Reimer sisters, Frieda and Mary. They had been in Bible school the year before and were now returning. I was thrilled to see them, changed my ticket, and traveled on the same bus from Winnipeg to Winkler. The bus was overfilled, leaving only standing room in the center aisle. I had talked with the Reimer girls before, but had never noticed the interesting manner in which they spoke of their family, church, and life in Yarrow, where they had grown up.

In the course of that conversation with Frieda, something happened. I cannot explain how the human psyche, or mind, or the innermost being, the very soul, reacts so totally differently in one situation from the way it has always reacted in similar settings. To paraphrase an ancient proverb, it seemed as though "she spoke with wisdom and could laugh at the days to come" (Prov. 31:25). I found Frieda not only pleasantly conversational, but also attractive in her total demeanor. I thought she was charming and beautiful. But I kept that exhilarating thought to myself.

Some people may take this casual meeting in Winnipeg and the bus ride to Winkler as mere coincidence. I see it as providence. In fact, as I was to discover later, this providential encounter was the beginning of the fulfillment of a year-old "prophecy" made by Frieda's father.

When in the previous year the two sisters had left home for Bible school in Manitoba, their father, noticing Frieda's apprehension, jokingly said: "Well, Frieda, you are now going to Winkler. There you will meet that boy from Brazil whose picture we saw in the yearbook. Chances are that you will fall in love, marry him, and then move even farther from home—all the way to Brazil." At that moment Frieda vehemently rejected even the remotest thought that such unthinkable thing could ever happen.

She recalls saying: "Him? He is the last guy I would ever marry!" But the "prophet" had spoken. And, as providence would have it, she fulfilled Father Reimer's prediction by marrying "that boy from Brazil." Indeed, he was not only "the last guy," but also the first she ever married. And, happily, she is still married to him.

In those days Winkler Bible School was a place where young people were not supposed to fall in love. Yet contrary to all rules, they did anyway. Institutional ordinances may be strong enough to bar private meetings between opposite genders, but they cannot prevent the glance of the eye from meeting another glance under the same roof. That is precisely what happened between Frieda and me when I was in my third and she in her last year of Bible school. Even if the object strikes only obliquely at first, eyes have the remarkable capacity to adjust and focus more clearly.

Before too long into the school year, Frieda and I discovered that the look of two pairs of eyes was as strong as a magnet and as communicative as spoken words, yet as secret as coded messages. Not even my closest friends knew the secret and power of love in my heart for Frieda. Only after she had graduated and was no longer bound by school rules did they find out. I also thought that Mr. Redekop, the school principal, should know. Although I was somewhat apprehensive about what he might say, I decided to tell him. He looked at me in his unique manner, half smiling and half serious, and said in a tone of affirming relief: *"So, die Frieda ist es? Ich dachte immer du hattest dein Auge auf jemand anders."* (So, it is Frieda? I always thought you had your eye on someone else.)

In the summer of 1952, a number of students from different Mennonite schools, the Reimer sisters among them, volunteered to serve in an MCC-sponsored program at the provincial institution for the mentally handicapped in Portage La Prairie. Most of them started work immediately after Bible school. I joined the group three months later after finishing the tenth grade in high school.

That summer, Frieda and I had an ideal opportunity to get to know each other; we often got together to visit, talk, pray, and make plans about our future. It was also during this time that Frieda's parents came to visit their daughters and friends in Manitoba. That, too, was providential. Not only did it give me an opportunity to meet her father—the "prophet" who had made that remarkable prediction which was now visibly becoming reality—but also her mother, as a kind and compassionate woman. That occasion became my moment for the boldest step of my life. Though timid and shy at first, I had full confidence in the outcome. And thus I ventured to ask them for the hand of their daughter Frieda. I do not know what they said beyond giving their consent, but I know that I felt some undefined weight slip off my mind and a surge of joy take its place in my heart. It was an experience of a lifetime. I sensed an immediate mutual bonding between my future in-laws and myself, a filial love that never faded. My life has been blessed by wonderful parents-in-law and by my becoming an integral part of the larger Reimer family.

At the end of that summer, Frieda went home with her parents to British Columbia and continued her education. That meant that our courtship would henceforth be carried on by letter only. I have not kept count, but I am quite certain that it was the year in which I broke my own record of punctuality in letter writing.

Meanwhile, I continued working at the institution until Bible school began again in October. The wage we got as MCC volunteers was adequate to cover expenses, but not much more. Thus I took a second job in Portage La Prairie: filling 100-pound bags with peas at the local elevator. Since I got paid by the piece, and since I had energy and ambition to match that of any healthy youth, I earned enough money to buy a set of rings for my upcoming engagement and wedding, to pay the Manitoba Youth Organization the remaining balance on my airfare from Brazil, and have some left over for tuition and incidentals.

While spending Christmas holidays with the Driedger family in Moore Park (Justice), I had to have an emergency appendectomy. One day Mr. Henry Loewen, deacon in the Justice Mennonite Brethren Church, came to visit me at the hospital in Brandon. After a brief conversation and prayer, he said in his gentle, caring manner: "Brother Kasdorf, the church in Justice wants me to tell you not to worry about hospital costs. We will pay for the surgery and other expenses. I have already talked with Dr. Purdy and the accountant." Such acts of kindness and love are humbling, and in my case undeserved. Some thirty-five years later, shortly before he went to be with the Lord, I visited Mr. Loewen at his daughter's place in Brandon to thank him once more for his caring ministry.

After graduating from Bible school in April 1953, I took grade eleven high school. As soon as I had completed my exams, I got a ride with Jake Driedger who, together with his mother and sister, was driving to British Columbia. Since I could not get a visa to travel through the United States, the Driedgers decided to cross the Canadian Rockies via Crows Nest Pass, a treacherous road at that time. But we eventually made it to Yarrow, where we planned to be engaged, Jake to Mary Reimer and I to Frieda.

On Saturday 4 July 1953, we had a preengagement celebration with family and close relatives in the home of Frieda's parents. Johann Peters, Frieda's uncle, blessed us with a brief meditation based on Psalm 27. He pointed out the importance of looking to the Lord as our salvation, stronghold, and shelter. The next day Herman Lenzmann, pastor of the Yarrow Mennonite Brethren Church where Frieda was a member, made a public statement in the morning service, saying: "I have been asked to announce the engagement of Frieda Reimer and Hans Kasper [a bad slip of the tongue!] as bride and groom. We wish them the Lord's blessing." In the afternoon the entire Reimer family went to Harrison Hot Springs for a picnic as a continuation of our engagement celebration.

On Monday I went to Vancouver to look for a job. As I had no money for streetcar or bus fare, I walked for several days from morning until evening, praying to God and asking for work at every unemployment office I could get to in one day. On Thursday of that week, I got a job with Dominion Construction, digging ditches and making forms to pour concrete. Work was steady and the pay good. I lived together with three or four other boys, including Bible school students, in an upstairs rented apartment. On weekends I often went to spend time with Frieda at her family home in Yarrow. Those were times that bring to mind delightful memories.

We were married on 20 September of that year. Mr. Lenzmann officiated at the ceremony and presented a challenging meditation on the testimony of John the Baptist about Jesus: "He [Jesus] must increase, but I must decrease" (John 3:30). Mr. C. D. Toews preached a message on 1 Corinthians 13:13: "And now these three remain: Faith, hope and love. But the greatest of these is love." Both meditations set the tone for the overall theme of service to the Lord. We had decided to have a simple wedding without bridesmaids and best men, but not without rich music that would glorify God and edify the wedding guests. Judging from compliments we received, our wishes were fulfilled. The well-known Neufeld brothers, Menno and Walter, honored our request by playing the piano and the violin. Their instrumental rendition of *Jesus, Savior, Pilot Me*, filled the halls when we walked up to take our place at the altar in front of the church. The melodious tune of the solemn prayer, *Savior, Like a Shepherd Lead Us*, played by the Neufeld brothers, accompanied us as we walked out.

During the ceremony the church choir, directed by Mr. George Reimer, sang several songs, and Frieda's Sunday School class of girls dedicated a special number to her by singing the lovely hymn, *Footprints of Jesus*. Frank Funk, a friend from Winkler Bible School, blessed us and all the wedding guests with his mellow baritone voice, singing, *O Lord, Most Holy*. Personally, I thought that the entire celebration of our marriage was nearly perfect. If I could have wished for one more thing, it would have been the presence of my family, at least my parents, from Brazil. But that was not possible.

After the service in the sanctuary of the Yarrow Mennonite Brethren Church, all the guests were invited to a reception in the basement dining hall. Both the main auditorium and the dining hall were beautifully decorated with hundreds of roses which Frieda's father had cut in his nursery, and a variety of wild branches in the glowing colors of early fall which Frieda and I had gathered in nearby woods.

Having observed the life of our parents, both Frieda's and mine, I always knew that the preacher was right when he said, "Two are better than one." At our golden anniversary I told our children, "After having been married to your mother for fifty years, I have come to know the full meaning of those words. Sharing my life with her has been a wonderful journey and an enriching experience."

30

Winnipeg and Chilliwack
(1953-1957)

Everything in the Scriptures is God's Word.
All of it is useful for teaching and for helping people
and for correcting them and showing them how to live.
The Scriptures train God's servants to do all kinds of good deeds.
–The Apostle Paul in 2 *Timothy* 3 (Contemporary English Version)

When I started Winkler Bible School in 1949, I thought that in four years I would have reached the height of wisdom and knowledge. That is also the impression I had of fourth-year students. I recall an incident from my first year. One day Jake Dyck from the fourth class came to where I was standing by the window and asked how I was getting along and how I liked Canada. I was flattered that this "educated" student would talk to me. As soon as I got back to the dormitory I told my roommates, Jake Suderman and Dave Reimer, that Jake Dyck had talked to me. They looked at each other, wondering why I was so excited. Obviously, their view of being "educated" was different than mine and saw nothing special in a conversation between a fourth-year and a first-year student.

By the end of my first year I already realized that there was much more to learn than what four years in Winkler would have to offer. I began to prepare myself, at least mentally, for a longer haul and started to think about studies at the Mennonite Brethren Bible College (MBBC) in Winnipeg. But how would my parents respond to that idea? And what would the church in Brazil say? Not that I received any material support from there, but there was a mutual nonverbalized understanding that, after finishing Bible school, I would return to Brazil and serve the church.

In the course of time I wrote to my parents about further studies. While they were supportive, C. C. Peters, a Bible teacher from Canada, who was teaching in lower South America at the time, was not. "Don't let him stay longer," he urged my father, and wanted me to come back immediately after graduation. "The church needs you now," he wrote. "I can give you all the education you need as we work together in the Bible school here [in Brazil]. Besides, think of your sick mother. She has only one wish and that is to see her youngest son once more before she dies." His emotionally charged appeal was compelling. My father, however, questioned whether either Mr. Peters or I would have any time for the kind of education he (Mr. Peters) was talking about. I sought further counsel from my teachers in Winkler, from Frieda's parents, and from the Bible College President H. H. Janzen. They encouraged me to transfer to the college in Winnipeg. Frieda agreed.

After we returned from our honeymoon in the interior of British Columbia, Frieda and I packed our earthly goods and boarded the train for Winnipeg. Friends from Bible school surprised us with a wonderful reception—an after-wedding celebration. One never forgets such gestures of kindness. Nor does one forget friends of long ago. Even time and distance do not destroy those memories that are not measured in degrees, but in kind and quality. "There is nothing so precious as a faithful friend," Ben Sira once wrote, "and no scale can measure his excellence" (Sirach 6:15).

During my first year of college studies we lived in a very tiny room on the second floor in the old part of the Mennonite Brethren Collegiate Institute (MBCI) at 173 Talbot Avenue, adjacent to the Bible College at 77 Kelvin Street, now Henderson Highway. The small room, however, was big compared to our kitchen, which was three by three feet, facing a window at the end of the hallway. If there was a measure of discomfort with our living quarters, it could not be blamed on oversize. We got this unfurnished suite as partial payment for janitorial work at the school.

The second year we moved next door into a suite in Ebenezer Hall on the college campus. A number of married couples with or without children and some unmarried female students lived in that same famous EE Hall. No one ever complained about too much space there either. Frieda and I were grateful to have room for a bed, a table with two chairs and a small cooking stove. Those were still the days when little was much and frugality a virtue. The expression, "living on a shoestring budget" was a meaningful idiom. Since I had worked four years as janitor of the Winkler Bible School and one year at MBCI, I continued to do the same at MBBC. By the time I graduated from college I had become quite skilled in handling the coal shovel along with broom and brush and bucket—and whatever else a janitor needs—to keep the halls of learning cosy and clean. It was all part of earning my keep. It was a job Frieda and I could do together.

During the first year Frieda worked as secretary in a downtown office. It was neither a well-paying job nor a pleasant atmosphere, but she persevered until our first child was born. Each Wednesday afternoon I worked at Rudolph Furriers. My job was to vacuum the carpet, keep the linoleum floor shiny and the washrooms clean. One day Mrs. Rudolph, wife of one of the owners, observed me more closely than before. At the end of the day she complimented me on the work I did and asked if I would come and clean her house every Saturday. I did: washing dishes, floors, and windows, and vacuuming rugs and carpets. During the summers I worked in construction. Frieda and I together earned enough to pay for my education and for things we could not do without.

Despite a rather full schedule of studies and work, we had time for entertainment and relaxation. On weekends, for instance, we watched the Religious Section of the *Winnipeg Free Press* for special speakers, Christian films or missionary reports in city churches. Occasionally, we spent time with friends in the Assiniboine Park. Those were always highlights, except the Sunday when Frieda's wallet with our last $3.00 was stolen. Whenever we reminisce about those years we can only marvel at God's goodness in the way He supplied our basic needs. When I graduated from Bible College in 1956, we owned little, but owed nothing.

While I had great pleasure in reading and studying, I was not the brightest student in those hallowed college halls. My problem was not laziness or lack of motivation; my problem was slow reading. I actually felt handicapped. My potential of being a good reader was still dormant. For some time I blamed my poor reading ability on the fact that I had been deprived of reading material from the time I was in grade three until I got my first book at eighteen. In college I felt that deficiency more than ever.

Another problem was my tendency to be a perfectionist, a trait that affected my study habits. When I wrote a paper, for example, or when I drew maps and charts, I spent an excessive number of hours to do a perfect job at the expense of other assignments. Even the course on *How to Study* did not prove to be helpful in overcoming my problem. It was a rather mechanical course, dealing with the height and size of a desk, the kind of chair to sit on, the amount of light one should have, how one should hold the book for reading, and many more such technical items. That was not what I needed. Some years later I took a course in speed reading, and in graduate school I learned how to study.

Nonetheless, I profited greatly from my studies at the Bible College. I have always considered it a distinct privilege to "sit at the feet" of great teachers, as the Apostle Paul says about his studies under Gamaliel (Acts 22:3). Among the "Gamaliels" during my time at MBBC were seasoned men like A. H. Unruh and H. H. Janzen who teamed up with such younger professors as David Ewert, J. A. Toews, Jake Quiring, and others. Everyone was committed to serve the Lord and His church. Such courses as homiletics and expository preaching, the Life of Christ, the prophetic sayings of Jesus, Pastoral Epistles, Acts of the Apostles, principles of missionary practice, medieval history of mission based on V. R. Edman's book *Light in Dark Ages*, and church history were an integral part of the ABCs that shaped my life and labor for the years that lay before me.

If I were asked to describe with one phrase the essential mark of my teachers at MBBC, I would say that they were *disciples and servants of the Master Teacher in the kingdom of God*. I am neither idolizing them as persons nor idealizing their teaching; I am merely reflecting the impression they left on my life. I do not recall that they ever talked about "servant leadership"; they modeled it. In preparation for a series of lectures in Germany, I read Oswald Sander's book *Spiritual Leadership* in which he writes: "If we forget the priority of service the entire idea of leadership training becomes dangerous." My Bible college teachers were guided by that same operational principle by which they sought to shape another generation of leaders as servants in God's kingdom.

I have never aspired to hold a public *"Amt"* or "office" in any of our church institutions. I had a hard time dealing with conflicts. There have been times, however, when I had leadership responsibilities in schools and churches. During my college years I became heavily involved as a student leader in organizing a variety of service groups on and off campus. Among them were prayer groups, mission conferences, and ministries in cooperation with existing churches and such service agencies as the Winnipeg City Mission on Main Street. The late Gerhard Jantz, who subsequently served as missionary in Austria, was my principal partner. The people who frequented the City Mission were primarily homeless, often alcoholics or drug addicts. We provided refreshments, assisted them to find a bed for the night, when needed, or a place for rehabilitation; we always shared with them God's love of forgiveness and healing. Only the Lord knows the outcome. I valued the opportunity to work togther with Gerhard, a true servant with the gift of contagious compassion.

Frieda and I experienced more blessings during our Winnipeg years than we could count. One very special blessing was the birth of our oldest daughter, Dianna Ruth on 23 January 1955. She was a healthy, strong girl who has through many years brought much joy to our life.

Meanwhile, graduation was coming closer and we were beginning to plan our move to Brazil. For me it meant going back home, though not to the Krauel; for Frieda it meant leaving home and homeland, family and friends, and everything associated with them.

I had been corresponding sporadically with my former home church which had moved from the Krauel to Colônia Nova. While there was no formal commitment that I would work in this particular congregation, there was a nonverbal understanding that I would serve the church in Brazil. In a letter of July 18, 1956, Gerhard Schartner, the leading minister in Colônia Nova, wrote that the church and he personally were "anxiously waiting" for my coming. The Board of General Welfare and Public Relations (BGW/PR), a Mennonite Brethren service agency with offices in Hillsboro and Winnipeg also approached me about ministry in South America.

The history of this board goes back to 1924 when it was established as a parallel agency to the Mennonite Central Committee (MCC) on the one hand and that of the Board of Foreign Missions (BFM) on the other. Its field of operation was defined within the parameters of existing Mennonite Brethren Churches with German-speaking membership of European background, existing in Brazil, Paraguay, and Uruguay. As J. A. Toews explains in *A History of the Mennonite Brethren Church*, one of the board's functions was to provide "spiritual and material assistance to the Mennonite Brethren churches in South America."

The assistance to which Dr. Toews refers included two kinds. First, monetary subsidy for local preachers and teachers, who had some income from their own land or small business; second, the board also sent and fully supported additional personnel from Anglo America, provided they were citizens of either Canada or the United States, and were able to speak German. By the mid 1950s, Mr. and Mrs. C. C. Peters and several other couples from Canada were serving in South American churches and schools under the auspices of the BGW/PR. Since I was originally from Brazil and not a citizen of either Canada or the United States, I did not fit any category of Board policy and was not eligible to receive full support. However, according to the *General Conference Yearbook* of 1954 I could be classified among "the ministering brethren from amidst the churches in Paraguay, Brazil, and Uruguay and also the teachers in the Bible school" to receive some remuneration for my services. Mr. Peters negotiated with the BGW/PR and requested that I teach together with him in a traveling Bible school, rotating every four months between Brazil, Paraguay, and Uruguay. It was probably providential that his plan did not materialize.

As we began working with our visas, the Brazilian consulate pointed out that I was stateless and could face serious roadblocks. Time went by and our move had to be postponed indefinitely. That is when the East Chilliwack Bible School asked me to join its faculty for at least one school year. We accepted the invitation as a gift from the Lord in a special time of need. The area churches even built a small house for us next to the school ground. In the meantime we lived with Frieda's parents in Yarrow. I was working for my father-in-law, budding roses, ornamental shrubs, and fruit trees in his nursery. It was a back-breaking but delightful job. I loved every day of it, knowing that the end result would be beautiful flowers and delicious fruits.

On weekends I had frequent preaching engagements in the Fraser Valley churches. These made the purchase of a car necessary. So we bought our first automobile for $175. It was a used lemon-yellow British Hillman, which turned out to be true to its color: a real "lemon." Whenever we came to a hilly area, the *man*-part of the name sometimes left the *Hill*-part insurmountable, and thereby left us in the lurch. Some hills were simply too steep for the Hillman. That was not its only weakness. One Sunday morning I had to speak at the 43rd Street Mennonite Brethren Church in Vancouver. It was raining when we left Chilliwack, but pouring by the time we came to Langley. The windshield wipers rarely worked. This Sunday they came to a complete stop. Fortunately, clever engineers must have foreseen the potential problem: each wiper had a separate switch connected by a rod to a large knob fastened on the inside dashboard and could be operated manually. While I had to concentrate on my driving, Frieda labored hard to keep the windshield wipers turning.

In early October 1956, we moved into a brand new house next to the East Chilliwack Mennonite Brethren Church, where the Bible school classes were held. George Thielmann was principal of the school, pastor of the church and a farmer on the side to support his family. Jake Friesen and I were full-time teachers. That was a very good year for us in more ways than one. Not only did I enjoy teaching together with those devout men of God, I also learned to know most of the Mennonite church leaders and pastors in British Columbia. I was able to observe from close up some of the tensions within local congregations caused by two major historical shifts: from German to English in worship services, and from ministry as unpaid service to ministry as a paid position.

We were members of the church in Yarrow, the largest Mennonite Brethren congregation in the province at that time. I was asked to serve on the *Vorberat* (church council). That, too, was a valuable learning experience. The church had more than twenty ordained ministers who took turns in preaching. Some had more to offer than others, and others preached more frequently than some. But none was paid for his services, not even Mr. Lenzmann, the church leader.

Those experiences and observations in the B. C. churches left several impressions which I took with me to Brazil the following year. First, the tensions caused by those shifts and changes of language and leadership were not always constructive. Second, I often wondered about motivation and method in the process of language change. The way things were done made sense only to a bilingual insider. Strangers or those who could speak only one language found themselves on the periphery, if not completely excluded. Finally, some of the younger men of my generation seemed quick to gravitate toward position-consciousness in exchange for service-consciousness. I resolved to learn from the wisdom of the older generation, work with the younger, and together seek to build up the body of Christ.

When we left for Brazil in 1957, the dealer in Chilliwack from whom we had bought our Hillman, was kind enough to take the car on consignment, eventually sold it for $80, sent the money to us in Blumenau, and we bought a bicycle for exactly that amount.

31

Long Road to Blumenau
(1957)

The right word aptly spoken
is like apples of gold in settings of silver.
Listening to good advice is worth much more
than an earring of fine gold.
–From *Proverbs 25*

In a book entitled *Blumenau: A Loira Cidade no Sul*, historians refer to the city as "a dream come true." What they describe is the progressive university city with its modern industry, mixed with quaint Continental architecture and a rich tradition of European culture in the subtropics of Southern Brazil. That is how the adventuresome young German by the name of Hermann Bruno Otto Blumenau had envisioned it when he and his exploration party canoed along the Itajaí River some eighty years before the Mennonite refugees navigated on the same waters to the same spot. Both parties had to stop in front of the same waterfalls that blocked further navigation. But there was one major difference: when Dr. Blumenau arrived there in 1850, he stayed to build a city along the river bank; when our people arrived there in 1930, they found lodging for one short night — and then had to move on, deep into the interior. When Frieda and I arrived there in 1957, Blumenau already had gained the reputation of being "the beautiful city of the south."

The contact between the Lutheran citizens of Blumenau and the Mennonite settlers of the Krauel Colony can be traced back to that first encounter in 1930. Meanwhile, the relationship between business people and church leaders had grown to one of mutual respect and interdependence, particularly in the commercial sector. For at least two decades Blumenau had been a major market for our agricultural products and we, in turn, reliable customers of the city's manufactured goods. In the early pioneering years, many of our young people found employment in the textile and leather industries of Blumenau. Entire families moved there to stay. Occasionally, preachers exchanged pulpits. Little could I have known then that less than thirty years later I would be living in Blumenau with my family, teaching and preaching the Word of God. Again, it was neither by choice nor chance, it was God's providence—even if the road to Blumenau was much longer than it might have been. I must explain briefly.

For one thing, there were the legal obstacles. I have explained earlier that in 1929 we had been forced to surrender our valuable documents to the Soviet authorities in Moscow and were subsequently processed as people without a country. I was one of them. Even as a child I was registered as a nonperson without either origin or destination. In 1930 Brazil had accepted us as "stateless aliens" with no claim to citizenship, land or country, and without the possibility of naturalization. That is a precarious classification which immigration officials do not know how to handle, as I again discovered in 1956.

In my *Carteira de Identidade para Estrangeiros,* the official identity document issued to me in Florianopolis on 22 September 1947, I am classified as *sem nacionalidade* (without nationality). That was also the status entered in my temporary passport on the basis of which I received my "Non-Immigrant Visa for the Purpose of Studying Religion" in Canada. When I arrived at the Malton Airport in Ontario, I was given a landing permit as a "Temporary Entry Record," dated 14 June 1949. In compliance with Canadian immigration laws, I took my documents, went personally every year to the closest immigration office and applied for an extension. I prayed before I walked in and thanked God when I walked out with the official stamp on a piece of paper that began to look increasingly worn and crowded. Eventually, another sheet had to be added. I accepted that in good faith, confident that immigration officials knew what they were doing. Evidently they did not.

Prior to graduation from MBBC in 1956, I wrote to the Brazilian Consulate in Toronto and also went to the Canadian Immigration headquarters in Winnipeg to inquire about a visa and other documentation Frieda and I would need for Brazil. Neither of them cleared the way for me. When we came to the West Coast, I immediately went to the Canadian Immigration in Huntingdon, B.C. to get necessary documents. The officer scrutinized my papers, looked sternly at me and said: "Don't you know that you are in this country illegally?" I was shocked and pointed to the extension permits which every year had been stamped on the "Temporary Entry Record," dated and signed by an immigration officer. The gentleman shook his head in disbelief, saying: "Somebody made a big mistake. You should not be here. If you are born in Russia, as your papers indicate, then Russia is the only place where we can send you." He sounded serious. Frieda protested, explaining that she was born in Canada, that we were married and that we had one child, also born in Canada. Many more interviews followed, making the paper trail of red tape long and tedious.

To make the story short, this is what happened. First, the officer gave Frieda a form to fill out as though I were still in Brazil. It was in essence an application by which she made a formal request that I be granted permission to enter Canada as an immigrant. Second, the officer gave me the name and address of an immigration doctor in Vancouver to get medical clearance. When I came there for my appointment, the doctor asked me two questions in one sentence: "Do you have two hands with five fingers on each and two feet with five toes on each?" Upon my affirmative response he issued me a health certificate. Third, I had to go back to Huntingdon for a signature. Upon affixing stamp and signature on both papers, the officer evidently wanted me to know that he had treated my case with extraordinary consideration, explaining: "It is Canadian Immigration policy to admit people so that they stay in Canada. But in your case we are admitting you so that you can leave the country." Fourth, I sent my papers to Ottawa with an application for a special passport issued to noncitizens. Finally, this special passport satisfied the Brazilian Consulate in Toronto to grant me a visa for Brazil, but again only as a stateless alien. We had no problems securing needed documents for Frieda and our daughter Dianne.

Another issue on our long road to Blumenau had to do with the definition of my future service assignment. While I was teaching at the East Chilliwack Bible School and working with my visa, we were also in conversation with the Board of General Welfare and Public Relations about the place and nature of our ministry in Brazil.

As I said in the previous chapter, C. C. Peters was anxious that I become his assistant to make his vision of a "traveling Bible school" a reality; at the same time the church in Colônia Nova wanted me to serve its congregation as Bible teacher. I must confess that initially I lacked the commitment required to move with wife and a small child three times a year from one country to another in order to teach in a mobile Bible school, as Mr. Peters requested. But once we had resolved that question and were prepared to serve wherever most needed, God opened a totally unforeseen door to a church of non-Mennonite background. A call had come from Wilhelm Koettker, the leader of a small congregation in Blumenau, geographically distanced from all Mennonite churches in Brazil.

Instead of supporting the idea of a traveling Bible school, the South American churches expressed the need for more permanent Bible training centers in each of the three countries. The BGW/PR responded favorably to that idea. Thus the most compelling need for a full-time worker seemed to be in Blumenau. Although the church was small at the time, the large unchurched population in the city and in surrounding towns and villages was inviting. Besides, this congregation was at that time the only church in Santa Catarina, my former home state, affiliated with the Mennonite Brethren.

The Board of General Welfare informed us that it would pay our one-way air fare to Brazil and subsidize our work financially with an unspecified amount each month. The major portion of support was to come from personal income (e.g., farm or business, which we did not have) and the local church. We were not included in the negotiations. That was good. I knew, however, that I did not qualify for a salary as other WGW/PR workers did, because I was neither a Canadian nor a United States citizen. That Frieda was born in Canada was inconsequential at that time.

Our support from the Board was determined by the policy governing the subsidy of local church workers who had some income from land or business "so as to allow them time and strength for evangelistic work and for shepherding their flocks," as the 1951 *General Conference Yearbook* puts it. We soon discovered that the total amount of our income with the subsidy was $38 a month. We agreed to the arrangement and accepted the assignment of "evangelistic work [and] shepherding the flock." We took a step of faith, were at peace about the decision, and looked forward to our ministry in Blumenau—though not without fear and trepidation.

Several months before we actually moved, I requested by letter to be allowed to visit my father and my former home church prior to starting work in Blumenau, about one thousand kilometers away. I had been gone for eight years. My mother had passed away in the meantime. My aging father was as anxious to see me as I was to see him. I also wanted Frieda to meet my family and considered my request fair and legitimate. The chairman of the board evidently did not agree. He responded rather curtly with the words of Jesus to a would-be disciple as recorded in Luke 9:60: "Let the dead bury their dead: but go thou and preach the kingdom of God." If my request was not unspiritual, my reaction to the chairman's response certainly was. I was hurt, even angry. I should have said so, but I was silent. I will say more about that later.

The time to say farewell had come. This was especially hard for Frieda. I was in a sense going home, at least to my former homeland; but Frieda was leaving home, parents and siblings, relatives and friends—even the place and land of her birth. We took the train to Manitoba where I had a number of speaking engagements in churches. From there, Frieda's sister Mary and her husband Jake Driedger took us by car to Chicago. On 4 October1957, we flew with Aérea Real from O'Hare International Airport to Rio de Janeiro.

We have flown many times since then, but never have we encountered a storm so fierce and furious as we did on that flight. As we flew over the Antilles, nearing the Caribbean Sea, that old four-engine machine was tossed to and fro, up and down, from side to side like a toy kite in strong wind. Passengers were frightened, expecting the end to be imminent. It seemed then as though we were not only covered by the wings of the

Almighty, as the Psalmist might suggest. I believe that our machine together with pilots, personnel, and passengers was literally borne on those wings, which Moses once likened to "the everlasting arms" of Almighty God. After several stopovers, including one in Caracas and one in Belém, we finally landed in Rio, the same airport from which I had left for Canada eight years earlier.

Our stopover in Belém was not conducive to seeing the brighter side of Brazil. Frieda still remembers the breakfast we had there at the airport restaurant—at least the half-raw, runny fried eggs are still in her mind. Neither ambience nor menu had changed from eight years ago when I was on my way to Canada and had breakfast in that same restaurant. Such were the first impressions Frieda got of Brazil, the land where we would live and serve for an undetermined number of years. As we look back on that experience, we do not dispute that first impressions may be lasting, but they are not always indicative of reality, as we have experienced it many times over.

When we made our travel arrangements in Canada, we discovered that tickets to Colônia Nova were no more expensive than to the airport nearest to Blumenau. The day we arrived in Rio, we were able to make connections to Pôrto Alegre. We got there late and had to stay in a hotel overnight. The next day we flew from Pôrto Alegre to Bagé, about forty kilometers (twenty-five miles) from Colônia Nova. My brother-in-law Gerhard Giesbrecht met us at the airport and took us to the city office of the colony co-op where he was the manager. Late in the afternoon we got a ride on a freight truck to the colony. The reunion with Father and siblings was a joyous occasion. We were warmly welcomed by the entire Kasdorf clan, which numerically had more than doubled in eight years. Despite heavy rains and nearly impassable roads, the church had arranged for nightly meetings. The meetinghouse was always full, with adults and children present. That meant double duty: a children's feature and a sermon.

The week went by fast. Rains increased and road conditions deteriorated. We went by tractor from the colony to the main road, and from there by truck back to the city of Bagé, where we stayed the first night on our way to Blumenau. The next day we took the bus to Pôrto Alegre. That trip was like an adventure of a lifetime. There were flooded roads and roadless floods. Some major bridges had been washed out. Flood waters deluged long stretches of roadway. It was obvious that the bus drivers knew not only the road to travel under normal conditions, they also knew the entire lay of the land. They took their turns in the driver's seat and had to meander their way around flooded areas on the open pampas. Minutes later they had to tread on water where there was no road.

For many kilometers we saw no human beings, with the exception now and then of a *gaúcho* riding between large herds of grazing sheep and cattle, flocks of flamingos with pink and scarlet plumage standing tall on their long legs, and an occasional ostrich pair guarding their young. What we found most amazing was that all the while passengers remained jolly, visiting and singing, joking and laughing as though they had known each other for years. They seemed totally unconcerned about the flooded roads. If anyone got motion sickness, as our daughter did, or had urgent needs of a different nature, the driver stopped, waited until everybody was back in the bus, and then continued the jolly journey. At one point, however, our drivers lost their direction. Yet a Brazilian always maintains that there is a *jeito,* a knack of doing things with intuitive ease. It also seemed to work this time. Eventually they found their way back to the road where the flood had not yet come. It was dark by the time we reached Pôrto Alegre; we took a hotel and stayed overnight.

Early the next morning we took a different bus to Florianopolis. Road conditions were no better, only different than they had been the previous day. We were no longer traveling in an easterly direction on the flat, endless and flooded pampas with or without roads; we were now between and on top of rugged mountains pushing northward along the Atlantic Coast. Wherever the road was closed, our drivers improvised their own detours, heading toward the ocean. Sometimes they drove along mere oxcart trails through small hamlets and fishing villages, and then headed north again, driving on the freshly washed sandy beach with the *serras* to the left and the ocean to the right. I suppose that was one way of staying on the northward course. Two fellow passengers were not so sure. They were Mormon missionaries from the United States. Not knowing Portuguese and not being able to find any markers that had the slightest resemblance to what they were looking for on their map, they felt totally lost. I was reminded of my experience in New York eight years earlier. I could empathize with them and offered to help find accommodations in Florianopolis where we also stayed for the night. They were greatly relieved and expressed their gratitude. We were no longer sure if that trip was an adventure; it seemed more like a nightmare. At least to us.

The final part of our trip from Florianopolis to Blumenau could have been uneventful if the bus had not sunk into shifting rock debris so that the chassis rested flat on the sand. But that episode, too, passed within about two hours. In the end we could only say: "Thank you, Lord God, for granting journeying mercies on this very long road to Blumenau, *A Loira Cidade no Sul."*

32

Back to Serve My *Heimatland*
(1957-1962)

God, make my life a little staff,
Whereon the weak may rest,
That so what health and strength I have
May serve my neighbors best
—In Bennett, *The Book of Virtues*

The church in Blumenau had made arrangements for us to move temporarily in with an elderly couple, Karl and Adelina Haak. They lived in a plain house, built on high posts on the side of a steep hill. We had a room in the upper part of the house but ate our meals downstairs with the Haaks. They had electricity, but no running water or plumbing. Karl worked as a night watchman in a tannery. Adelina took care of the household and a granddaughter Lilli, who was living with them. They were humble and godly people, willing to share everything they had.

We soon learned that these dear people experienced great hardships with their two children. Their daughter Leni (Lilli's mother) was married and lived in Blumenau with her dysfunctional family. Their son Willi was unmarried—they had not heard from him for years and had no idea where he was. Both caused their aging parents untold grief. Each day they poured out their hearts with tears and supplication to God, fervently praying for their children and grandchildren. One day there was a response.

I will never forget the scene by the cement steps leading down from the road to the open well in front of the door that led into the kitchen. Willi had apparently come home during the night and was waiting for daybreak. Just as I came out of the house to draw water from the well, Karl was coming back from work. And there the two met, father and son, at the bottom of the cement steps by the open well. Willi was a tailor by profession; yet here he stood in clothes tattered and torn and shoes so badly worn that the toes were sticking out. I heard no exchange of words, but witnessed a long embrace with many tears. If ever there was an object lesson about Jesus' parable of the lost son as recorded in Luke 15, I had one that morning. The experience of that morning symbolized the kind of work we could be facing as we continued our ministry in Blumenau.

As our work progressed, I felt relatively comfortable with the level of biblical training I had received in Winkler and Winnipeg, but I was ill-prepared to deal with the cultural demands, the unforeseen social problems, and spiritistic challenges with which I was constantly confronted. Alcoholism, fragmented families, the teachings of Spiritism and esoteric practices were rampant. The forces of the occult were evident everywhere, from the medical profession in the city to the practitioners of black magic in the interior. Spiritual battles were raging at every level of society. Even Christian families were not immune to these influences, especially in times of illness and death.

The church in Blumenau was unique. Its membership was made up of people from various religious and denominational backgrounds. The primary language was High German. Leadership lay in the hands of two elderly men: Wilhelm Koettker, the preacher, and August Rutter, the deacon. On 9 April 1950, both had been ordained by the Mennonite Brethren Church in the Krauel. The two congregations continued their fraternal relationship even after the mother church moved from its original location in Santa Catarina to Colônia Nova in Rio Grande do Sul. The geographical distance between the two congregations, however, was not conducive for a meaningful partnership. By the time we came to Blumenau, the church had already become affiliated with the Mennonite Brethren in Boqueirão that was geographically much closer than Colônia Nova.

Mr. Koettker had been an officer in the German army during World War I, had emigrated to Brazil where he worked as business executive, and was now retired. Rutter also had a European background. He was a tanner by vocation, like Simon of Joppa (Acts 10). These two men were so different in nature and temperament that they seldom complemented one another, or gave a compliment to each other. Rutter was still fully employed. Although he was always willing to work in the church, he had limited time and lacked family support in his ambitions. Koettker was a man of order and integrity, known and respected in business circles throughout the city. He was my primary mentor, always open to discuss issues pertaining to church life, evangelistic outreach and personal concerns. The rest of the membership was made up of predominantly factory workers, although some had small businesses. While several families had fairly comfortable homes, none were wealthy or lived in luxury.

On 24 December 1957, we moved from our quarters at the Haaks into a rented house not far from the church. It was one of the simplest houses in the area, brand new with electricity and a water tap in the veranda where Frieda did the laundry. The cooking stove, made of brick and clay, was inside. A bake oven of the same material was outside. That oven caused more frustration than the baked goods were worth. I felt sorry for Frieda but could be of little help. Rent for the unfurnished place was

$28 a month, leaving us $10 for other living expenses. We were happy to live by ourselves and enjoyed our little house next to a wooded area that separated our dwelling from a small river. On the open side lived two single women whom Frieda befriended, especially Modesta, a dear soul, but involved with the occult. Eventually, her broken life became whole when she turned it over to the Lord Jesus Christ.

Toward the end of March the following year, C. A. and Elizabeth DeFehr of Winnipeg paid us an unexpected visit. It was near midnight when they arrived by taxi from Curitiba, about two hundred kilometers (125 miles) north of Blumenau. It was too late to borrow bedding from neighbors, so we gave them what we had. By all indications, they had slept more comfortably in our bed than Frieda and I on the bare floor in the next room. Mr. DeFehr was a member of the BGW/PR. Mennonites in Canada may remember him as a prominent businessman; I also came to know his pastoral side. That became evident by the questions he asked and the conversation he had with my colleague, Wilhelm Koettker.

While the two men discovered their immediate common interest in business, they quickly turned their attention to the church in Blumenau and beyond. It was delightful to hear two businessmen talk with concern about the mission of the church. Mrs. DeFehr was an astute observer. She noticed, for instance, our unfurnished rooms, bare floors, and the plain house with cracks wide enough to let the sun peek through. Frieda and I appreciated the brief visit by the DeFehrs. We too kept our conversation with them mainly on the church and its opportunity for evangelistic outreach and growth. Not long after their visit, our remuneration increased to $80 a month.

Four or five months later we had another gift from God, infinitely greater than the monetary increase we received from the Board of General Welfare and Public Relations. "To us a child was given, a [healthy] son was born." That is how we could declare the event. We called him David Mark. *David* is, indeed, our *beloved* son.

Mr. Wiese, the only owner of a car on our street, made us promise that we would ask him—by day or night—to take Frieda to the *Maternidade Evangélica* when the time came for the baby to be born. As a good neighbor and trustworthy taxi driver, he deserved that priority. Before dawn on 22 August 1958, I knocked hard on Wiese's door and told him that this was the moment we had been waiting for. Despite sleepy eyes, he was excited, jumped into his car and—nothing happened. The battery was stone dead. Poor Mr. Wiese was so embarrassed that he could hardly find words to apologize. I actually felt sorry for him, yet neither he nor I could change the situation. I hurried to the closest telephone by the Wippel textile factory at the end of our road, called a taxi from downtown by the bus depot, and rushed home. Frieda was by now wondering where I had stayed. The taxi came in short order and took us to the Evangelical Lutheran Maternity Hospital.

Two hours later Frieda held our son in her arms. As the wife of a pastor, she received royal treatment. Her room was spacious with a door leading to a patio with beautiful geranium planters overlooking the city. That is not what we had asked for or expected, but that is what we were given. Dr. Hafner and the Lutheran deaconesses (nurses) could not have been more generous and kind. They gave her and the baby the finest care and kept her there for eight days—and all that for $32. We never complained that they had overcharged us!

Soon after we came to Blumenau, the church was planning my ordination, which was to be a historical event. The members talked about it with animation and looked forward to it with anticipation, especially the young people. As I have already said, our congregation had become affiliated with the Mennonite Brethren Church in Boqueirão near Curitiba. That is where Peter Hamm was the veteran leader and preacher. The two congregations, Blumenau and Boqueirão, had a fine relationship. It seemed only natural, therefore, that we should invite Mr. Hamm to officiate at the ordination, with the local leaders, Koettker and Rutter, assisting him. I was fully in support of that plan, not suspecting that other leaders in the Curitiba area would object. But they did, and that for reasons not worthy of an explanation. Somewhat disappointed, our church had to look for help elsewhere.

Mr. Koettker then wrote to Elder Gerhard Rosenfeld, who was now serving the church in São Paulo. Rosenfeld had officiated in the Waldheim church when Koettker and Rutter had been ordained there eight or nine years earlier. Elder Rosenfeld was also well known in Christian circles of non-Mennonite background and highly valued as a visiting speaker in Blumenau churches. Besides that, Mr. and Mrs. Rosenfeld had been close friends of my parents during the years in the Krauel, where he had been one of my mentors. With that background and with no involvement in the Curitiba conflict, we all agreed that he should serve at my ordination. Unfortunately, he became ill and was unable to come.

The people of our church were greatly disappointed on both counts and were in the process of finding a third alternative. But that, too, was taken out of our hands in an unexpected way. One learns to live with both pleasant and unpleasant surprises. At the personal level, however, we felt very sorry for our church. Yet in all of those disappointments, our people conducted themselves in an admirable Christian manner. What follows is my translation of the event as recorded by Mr. Koettker in the official church ledger, 19 October 1958:

The [ordination] celebration for our dear brother and sister Hans and Frieda Kasdorf had already been planned twice, but could not be carried out either time because on 25 May there were disagreements among the brethren of our mother church [in Boqueirão], and on 28 September our brother G. H. Rosenfeld, who was to officiate at the ordination, was unable to come because of illness.

On Friday, 17 October, Brother Wilhelm Janzen, leader of the MB church in Bagé [Colônia Nova], arrived here in order to take part in the ordination service which was supposed to take place the following Sunday. Unfortunately, we had received no information either by letter or by cable which arrived the week thereafter. Instead, a busload of dear visitors from Curitiba arrived unannounced on Saturday, at 7 o'clock in the evening. Among them were Gerhard Balzer, chairman, and Heinrich Friesen, secretary of the South American MB Conference, both from Filadelfia, Paraguay. These brethren officiated at the ordination service with the proclamation of the Word and by dedicating our brother and sister. Brother Wilhelm Janzen also took part in the dedication ceremony with prayer and laying on of hands. Thanks to the ministry of these brethren the ceremony turned out to be festive. Everyone was blessed.

In addition to these brothers, several others had come from the Mennonite Brethren church of Boqueirão together with their [new] leader, Peter Friesen. The church choir of Vila Guaíra under the direction of Abram Klassen, and several brothers and sisters from that congregation had also come. The director [Erwin Thiessen] of the orphanage in Curitiba was there as well.

On Sunday morning the order of service was changed. Brother Thiessen brought a message on mission; Brother Wilhelm Janzen and Brother Heinrich Friesen served with the Word.

The ordination service began at 2 o'clock in the afternoon. Despite the short time [between services], the young people had beautifully decorated the church with flowers. At the beginning of the festive occasion the congregation sang the hymn, "The work is Thine, O Christ, our Lord." After the introduction and prayer by Wilhelm Koettker, Brother Balzer assumed leadership for the service, assisted by Heinrich Friesen and Wilhelm Janzen.

The course of the celebration proceeded in a dignified manner, as I already indicated. All were blessed, especially by the presentation of a testimony by Brother Kasdorf. It afforded us some insight into his life. Everyone was deeply impressed and moved.

After that we celebrated the Lord's Supper in which Brother Balzer officiated. The festivities were concluded with prayer and a song.

While I have never doubted my call to discipleship and Christian service in the kingdom of God, I was not unequivocal in my convictions about ordination until George Thielmann, my colleague at the East Chilliwack Bible School, approached me about it. He and other church leaders, Thielmann said, saw that God had given me the gift of preaching and teaching the Word. "If you were a member of our [East Chilliwack] church, we would have liked to ordain you before you leave for ministry in Brazil." Ordination by the church, he went on to explain, is a "corporate confirmation of God's call in a person's life." We were members of the Yarrow MB Church that year and the time for departure was fast approaching, and thus too short for the ordination to take place.

When the church in Blumenau raised the same question, I was humbled and inwardly ready for that "corporate confirmation of God's call" in my life. Yet when the day actually came, I went through a terrible struggle. Saturday evening, the day before the ordination, I was conducting Bible studies in Pommerode and came home past midnight. Frieda greeted me and said: "Today is our ordination. A whole bus load of people from Curitiba has come for the event. Among them are conference leaders from Paraguay." After taking a deep breath, I said emphatically, "No! I will not be ordained. Not this time." With those words I gave vent to my utter surprise at the news that shocked my deepest senses and unleashed an inward battle such as I had not experienced before. It was not the idea of the ordination itself, but the manner in which it was thrust upon me and the church.

The rest of the night I wrestled with God (and with myself?) until daybreak. Thielmann's words, *corporate confirmation of God's call*, must have raced through my mind a thousand times. I finally said, "Yes" to God, explaining to myself, what He already knew, that neither our church in Blumenau nor I had any part in the internal conflicts of the Curitiba churches. Therefore, I had neither a legitimate right nor a valid reason to add to the strife by refusing to be ordained and thereby draw our entire congregation into something it did not deserve. The rest is history.

That same year the church began building a parsonage, with added space for Sunday school and youth meetings. Mr. and Mrs. Seibel had given the substantial sum of $500 toward the project, provided we would buy the lumber from a small sawmill in Ribeirão do Salto, quite far in the interior. We gladly obliged. I knew the owner and personally went there to purchase the lumber. Brother Harry Gauche, one of our church members, owned a transport truck and hauled the material free of charge. Frieda's parents and aunts in Canada also made significant monetary contributions. Koettker's experience in business was in our favor. He knew every major business in the city, and every manager knew and respected him. Despite severe heart problems, he handled the finances and made all major purchases. I served as his assistant. That gave me an excellent opportunity to become acquainted not only with the business world in Blumenau, but also with key people in the city. Our own church members demonstrated a high level of motivation and willingness to support the project. They donated much of their time and helped financially as they were able. We all worked hard. Everyone was anxious to see the parsonage completed in less than a year. The Lord honored that commitment. Just days before Christmas we made another move, this time from a rented house to the one built by the church. On 14 January 1959, the parsonage was officially dedicated.

Our parsonage was built behind the church away from the street. A cement stairway with sixteen steps led onto an elevated porch and the front entrance. The house was simple, but practical. It had a living room, two bedrooms, a bathroom with cold running water, a kitchen and even a tiny study room. I built kitchen cabinets with shelves, sink and countertop. No need to ask what they looked like; but they served their purpose, and Frieda was happy for them. I also made frames to fit each window and stretched a piece of cheesecloth across to keep the mosquitoes and flies out. That was a double blessing. The stove we had is a different story. Before we purchased it, Mr. Koettker asked Frieda if she wanted a wood stove or a gas stove. Knowing that not many of our church members had the luxury of a gas stove with oven, she opted for a wood stove. It was of such poor quality that she always had to bake the bread first on one side, then take it out, turn the loaf over and bake the other side. She managed remarkably well, never regretted the choice, and none of the other women ever had reason to wish for a stove like hers.

Since our back yard was adjacent to a wooded area, we got frequent company from the woods. I do not mean only birds and butterflies. The most frequent visitors, not to say intruders, were snakes, *Lagartos* (giant lizards) outside and *lagartixas* (wall lizards) in the house, ants by the thousands, some bugs and the occasional frog. They respected neither border nor boundary. I had grown up with these creatures and still remembered them well. Frieda had to make adjustments, but never got used to snakes and lizards. Snakes have never been man's best friend since time immemorial. When I encountered a deadly coral snake on the church steps one Sunday morning and a *jararaca* just as deadly in the sandpile where our children played, I confess that I was less tolerant of snakes than Mother Eve apparently was in the Garden of Eden. She conversed with the subtle intruder; I did not. I struck twice before the beasts had a chance to do so once.

All in all, we truly enjoyed our parsonage in Blumenau, where we entertained many guests from far and near. Besides that, we no longer needed to pay rent, and our living conditions were much improved.

One of our treasured guests was my father, who lived in Colônia Nova, where three of my sisters and one brother with their families were also living. Father came at least once a year to spend five to six weeks with us. It was quite an undertaking for him at age eighty, not knowing the language, to travel by bus more than a thousand kilometers each way. I usually wrote a note, explained the situation to the bus driver and his assistant that my father did not speak Portuguese, and requested their kindness and consideration. They were always courteous and helpful. We appreciated having Father at our place, even if only for a limited time each year. He was just as pleasant to be with now as I remembered him. It was a pleasure to see how he loved Frieda and the children, especially after the first visit. Father also enjoyed the services, prayer meetings and Bible studies at our church, and the church people treated him with respect.

Three highlights stand out about Father's visits. Ever since age sixty-two, Father suffered from severe *trigeminal neuralgia,* a sharp pain on one side of the face, emanating from one or more of the three branches of the fifth geminal or cranial nerve. On one of his visits I took him to see Dr. Franz at the Evangelical Lutheran Hospital in Blumenau. Since there was no effective medication at that time, Dr. Franz suggested surgery. Not knowing the high risks of permanent damage, Father agreed. Thankfully, the surgery was successful and left no trace of facial paralysis. Once the wound had healed, Father lived without those agonizing pains during the last years of his life.

On another occasion I took Father to the old river harbor in Itoupava Secca (Altenau) where in 1930 our water voyage had come to an end. I rediscovered this place soon after we came to Blumenau in 1957. Whenever I went with my bicycle to visit people in their homes or stopped to say a quick hello at their work place, I deliberately chose to cross the Itajaí on that old bridge by the old harbor in Itoupava Secca. Not that there were no other bridges to cross; there was another one close by. But I was particularly attracted to this one next to the old harbor. For one thing, I found this long, narrow, well-worn covered bridge fascinating. I also was aware of the historical significance this place had for my family and people. When I came to that point, I often paused for a few minutes at what now looked more like an abandoned warehouse than a river harbor, where once people were coming and going between the interior wilderness and the hustle and bustle of city life.

To stand there on that bridge and to think that I had been there as a small child thirty years earlier was for me always an emotional moment. Now I stood there together with Father. He was totally silent, obviously engrossed deep in thought. He stared at the swift water current rolling across the rapids on one side of the bridge and then at the muddy waters on the other. I noticed his emotional involvement in an all-absorbing contemplation. I too was deeply moved. Even though I would have liked to have a verbal exchange about his thoughts and feelings, I was unable to initiate the conversation. Out of respect for Father's profound experience I decided not to interrupt these moments of sacred serenity and silence. It was evident that Father was dealing with memories and sentiments from thirty years ago, too deep to be articulated in mere words. There are times when silence speaks louder than words. And so I let it be.

A third highlight for Father was a musical performance by the Chamber Orchestra (rated "the best in Brazil," 1988) sponsored by the Blumenau Philharmonic Society. This was the first time in his eighty years that he ever attended a concert of classical music. And how he enjoyed it! For one thing, Father was impressed by the interior structure and comfortable seats of the *Teatro Carlos Gomez*, designed and built by the senior Mr. Brunner, a German building engineer living in Blumenau with his family. Furthermore, the acoustics in the auditorium were nearly perfect, allowing the sound waves to flow evenly throughout the building. Being hard of hearing, Father was simply amazed how well he could hear the music even without a hearing aid. Then, too, we sat in the middle row toward the front, so that he could see the individual players, including the violinist, Horst Brunner, a member of our church and grandson of the original builder of this fine edifice. We were Horst's guests of honor, which made the event doubly special. Father never forgot that evening.

In late November of 1959, Frieda's parents from British Columbia came to visit us in the new home to which they and other family members had contributed financially. We enjoyed their visit immensely. It was also a special treat for our children to celebrate Christmas with their *Oma* and *Opa* from Canada. Dianne was nearly five and David a little over one year old. It was a real blessing to have my parents-in-law in our home for about five weeks. They, too, enjoyed their stay at our place. They also became fond of the people in the church. It was a delight to see them blend in so beautifully.

One of our church couples, Harry and Amanda Gauche, owned an apartment at the beach in Camboriú and offered it to us for a week when they would be there too. I could not take time off, but Frieda with the children and her parents went. They had a wonderful time, enjoying the *praya* with its clean, white sand and the tranquility of shallow waters of the Atlantic Ocean. It was the first time Frieda had gotten away from the daily routine, and that together with her parents.

Father Reimer and I also took a bus trip to Rio with a stopover in São Paulo, where we stayed at the MCC headquarters. The Abram Dycks from Kitchener, Ontario, were the directors at that time. No sooner had they met than Father Reimer and Mr. Dyck engaged in a lively conversation, as though they had known each other for years. That was amusing and delightful to observe. We also visited the Rosenfelds in São Paulo. Here, too, was an immediate bond. Mr. Rosenfeld and my father-in-law knew each other from Russia, and I knew the Rosenfelds from the Krauel. We had a meaningful visit, reminiscing, conversing, and praying together. This happened to be the last time I saw my esteemed mentor, preacher and teacher of my youth.

From the many other attractions, we selected to see the world famous *Instituto Butantan* where over one thousand varieties of snakes and vipers are housed. Here one can see how highly trained scientists and medical experts extract venom from live snakes to prepare serum for treating humans and animals who have been bitten by a poisonous viper. This, together with a large insectarium with displays and research laboratories on the same general premises, was an educational and most interesting visit.

A nurseryman by profession and a lover of flowers and trees by nature, Father Reimer became completely absorbed in the multifarious varieties of the tropical flora along the bus route from São Paulo to Rio. In Rio itself he enjoyed the Portuguese service (I translated for him) at the large and famous *São Carlos* Plymouth Brethren congregation, where the Lord's Supper is celebrated every Sunday. One of the members was Hermes Lemos, a prominent baker in great demand at government and other prestigious social functions in Rio. I knew him as a friend of our church in Blumenau. As soon as he saw us, he embraced each with a genuine Brazilian *abraço* and the shoulder taps that go with it. After the service we were invited to have dinner at the home of a medical doctor and his wife. She served chicken with rice and a fruit salad, a typical Brazilian dish of the upper-middle class. After the meal we took the city bus and went sightseeing. Father Reimer enjoyed every part of it, but nothing as much as the famous *Jardim Botânico* (botanical garden) of Rio.

Those parental visits were a special bonus in our ministry. They also made us mindful of the overwhelming blessing we enjoy in wholesome family relationships between parents, children, and grandchildren.

33

Rewarding Missional Service

Since through God's mercy we have this ministry,
we do not lose heart. . . .
But we have this treasure in jars of clay to show that
this all-surpassing power is from God and not from us..
—The Apostle Paul in 2 *Corinthians* 4

Sometimes I think of our mission in Blumenau as the practical phase of an extended apprenticeship for which my studies in Bible school and college were the theoretical phase. The two phases combined can be likened to what the great masters of German literature of the eighteenth and nineteenth centuries described as *Lehrjahre* and *Wanderjahre* In other words, the two phases together lead to an open future of potential *Meisterjahre.* In my case, however, the analogy is not entirely applicable, because my teachers of the theoretical phase were absent during my practical phase..

Having said that, I am in no way minimizing the input I received from my esteemed senior colleague, Wilhelm Koettker. On the contrary, I was fortunate and grateful to work together with him. We did not always see eye to eye on how to deal with sensitive family problems, but we never became personally disagreeable. He was unwavering in his convictions, but constant in his support. Whenever we faced what seemed to be an insurmountable problem, he would say in an almost commanding fashion: *"Bruder Hans, jetzt müssen wir danken."* (Brother Hans, now we must give thanks.) At first I was somewhat bewildered, thinking that I might have misunderstood. Before I could respond he was already on his knees. I joined him and was impressed by his expression of gratitude not for the problem, but for the people to whom God now had a chance to speak.

If I were to characterize the most fruitful aspect of our mission, I would do so with one key word: *visitations.* That is the key to unlock hard hearts and darkened minds. Mr. Koettker and I made many visitations to families, singles, and workers in their shops and places of employment wherever that was feasible. As health of my senior colleague declined, I continued on my own. Sometimes I took a bus to distant villages and cities, but as a rule I went by bicycle. When people accepted Christ, we started home Bible studies and invited others to join, often on Saturday nights. No other part of our ministry was as fruitful as consistent personal contacts, especially in the homes and at the work place. I had seen my father do it years ago and discovered that it was still the most effective way of reaching out to people in need. The reward was to see the Lord transform people's lives in a most remarkable way—some Christians, some non-Christians.

I have witnessed many conversions to Jesus Christ. While none are exactly alike, each is a unique event that unleashes rejoicing in the heavenly realms. Jesus compares each incident with the joyful emotions expressed by a shepherd who retrieves his lost sheep, or a woman who recovers her lost money, or a father who embraces his son who has gone astray and returns home. Some conversions we saw in Brazil were nothing short of sudden, cataclysmic experiences, whereas others were more gradual and less dramatic. I will mention only two examples.

Fred Brunner had godly in-laws, Fritz and Anni Schäfer, whose only daughter was named after her mother. While visiting the Schäfers I got to know Fred and Anni Brunner and their four children. Mr. Brunner had served in the German army during World War II and was one of three survivors in his entire battalion that was decimated in the siege of Leningrad. Now living in Blumenau, the Brunners owned a small grocery store in *Rua Alameida*, one of Blumenau's somewhat exclusive neighborhoods. I made it a point to stop by once a week to buy an item or two, depending on what Frieda needed for the table. They never had many customers, but enough to make a living. Among their most profitable sale items were liquor and tobacco.

During a week of special meetings in our church with G. W. Peters as guest speaker, the whole family attended our services, including the aging parents of Mrs. Brunner. On the final night the oldest two children, Edeltraud and Horst, sat in front ready to receive Jesus Christ as Savior and Lord. When the mother saw that, she joined them, saying: "If my children need Jesus, I need Him even more." They threw their arms around each other and wept tears of repentance mixed with outbursts of joy. Fred was outside, pacing back and forth wringing his hands. I walked over to him, put my hand on his shoulder and asked if he would like to join his family inside. In response he not only walked, he ran and sat down next to them. That night I witnessed four miraculous conversions to Christ. Later that year, Mrs. Brunner and Horst were baptized and received into the church upon their confession of faith. Mr. Brunner and Edeltraud together with six other new converts took that same step of obedience on 12 November1961.

Within a relatively short time after their conversion to Christ, the Brunners discontinued selling and serving liquor in their store, filling the shelves with other products instead. I had never urged them to do so, but the Holy Spirit had. Shortly thereafter, Brother Brunner called my attention to his popular corner shelf by the door, where he used to stack cigarettes, cigars and other products to feed the nicotine habits of his customers. Now he had removed these articles and replaced them with Bibles and Christian books. It was most encouraging to see these young Christians grow in grace and knowledge of Jesus Christ. They became spiritual pillars in the church. The family was quite musical. Horst Brunner went to Bible school in Curitiba where he met his future wife, Leni Penner. He also studied music at the university, gave violin lessons, and established a successful music academy. The Lord has also used him and his family for many years as an effective evangelistic team in Brazil and Germany.

Oskar Withöfft was raised in an environment that was as rough and tough as the one that provided him with a job. He had a truck route, delivering beverages to the *bodegas* and taverns in his part of the city. Spirited beverages were a lucrative business in Blumenau. Since I knew his route, I often stopped my bicycle next to his truck where he was unloading his cargo, greeted him, exchanged some friendly words, and left him to do his job. He appreciated my short and casual visits and began to call me *Bruder* (brother) *Kasdorf*. He did not mean that in a Christian sense, but as a gesture of friendship. I also visited him and his wife in their home. Mrs. Withöfft was a godly woman. Each week at our Bible study she asked the church to pray for Oskar that he would get saved. His buddies had no scruples, inciting him to participate in their carousals. Oskar had insufficient stamina to resist temptation. He had become addicted to alcohol. Two spirits were clearly in combat for his soul: the Spirit of God and the spirit of brandy. As time went on, his struggles became evident. One day he said to me: "*Bruder Kasdorf*, next Sunday I want to get saved." He was sincere. He was there the next Sunday and made a commitment to Jesus Christ. Not long thereafter he was baptized and joined the church. His growth in Christ was slow and not without conflicts. But he prevailed. I continued to visit him regularly on his service route. Eventually, he gave up his job and opened a small laundry business. That was a step in the right direction. Much like the Brunners, the Withöffts have proven themselves as a couple "full of faith and of the Holy Spirit" by serving as faithful deacons in the church.

The more I visited people in their social and cultural environment, the more I learned about their worldview. I soon discovered two things that were part of their culture and tradition for which I had little understanding. For one thing, many of the people I visited, especially in outlying villages, were steeped in religious superstitions and in the practice of soothsaying, incantation, and other forms of spiritism or occultism. Then there were those who considered our church to be a sect, if not a cult. I was surprised how widespread that rumor really was. In Bible school I had learned about sects and cults, but that applied only to *others,* never to *us.* Now I found myself among the *others,* suspect of being a cultist. I did not know how to deal with that, except that we had to clarify our doctrinal position on the basis of the Scriptures and trust the Holy Spirit to help people see that we were not a cult. One way of doing so would be through radio ministry. That way we could reach a large audience. I felt that God was leading in that direction.

When I shared this idea with Brother Koettker, he was delighted. But which of the two radio stations in the city would give us time to broadcast *15 Minuten Sonntagssegen* (15 Minutes Sunday Blessing), with a biblical message? And how could we finance the program? I had no answer. Those questions required a step of faith. The director of the Catholic station was willing to give us time at midnight. That was not a time when people listened to radio. The receptionist of the secular station would not even consider my request for an appointment with the director. I was disappointed. As I was about to leave, the director came in and politely asked if he could be of help. I briefly explained my mission. His response was that their Sunday schedule was completely filled and he could not give us any time at all. I thanked him for hearing me and took leave. Deep within me, however, I felt that the conversation with the director had been arranged by the Lord, and that it would turn out in our favor.

Saturday evening that same week several members from the church met for prayer at the Brunners' store. We asked God very specifically for two things: One, fifteen minutes radio time, early Sunday evenings before people went to bed and, two, finances to pay for it. The following Monday, the director was at our door and wanted to speak with me. Without a long introduction he offered me prime time to broadcast a Bible message with Christian singing each Sunday evening from 8:00 to 8:15. I knew that it was God's doing. The first lines of a German hymn flashed through my mind, and I sang them to myself:

> The work is Yours, O Christ, our Lord,
> The cause for which we stand;
> And being Yours, 'twill overcome
> Its foes on every hand.

Clearly, the Lord had opened the door for radio time at the stronger of the two transmitters in the city. We were confident that He would also provide the finances to pay for it. He did.

That same week Mr. Koettker and I went to visit Harry and Amanda Gauche, members of our church. They had just bought the only dry-cleaning business in all of Blumenau. No sooner had we told them about the available radio time, they declared themselves willing to underwrite the broadcast, provided we would reserve one minute of commercial time for their *Lavanderia Luxor*. When the program was extended to thirty minutes, we received additional support from Frieda's parents and aunts in Canada who had a real heart for mission. This entire episode was a tremendous encouragement to our church, bringing about a renewal in prayer. Years later Fred Brunner wrote in a letter how he still remembered that unusual prayer meeting in his family store where we prayed about the radio program: "There is great power in prayer and intercession whenever we permit the Holy Spirit to lead. That is our experience now as it was then. God answers prayer."

On 15 October 1961 we aired our first program, live, directly from the studio. Our young people were elated to have a major part in this ministry. God had blessed our congregation with gifted people, among them good singers and excellent musicians, who were willing to serve. The broadcast was well received and favorably rated. Before long we were able to offer a correspondence Bible course in Portuguese and German, which we subscribed from *Palavra da Vida* (Word of Life) in São Paulo. Within a relatively short time we had close to one hundred students enrolled. That was about all we could manage without neglecting needs in the local church.

It seemed that the time was ripe. Many people accepted Christ. Others wrote how glad they were to get our program in addition to the broadcasts of HCJB and TWR. Bible study groups emerged in Pommerode, Massaranduba, Encano do Norte and other towns. Several of them eventually developed into churches. Even though growth was slow, it helped to change our public image from sect or cult to that of a legitimate denominational confession with the right to exist and operate side by side with Catholic and Lutheran churches in the city.

Every year we had one or two weeks of evangelistic services. They were well attended and fruitful. Franz Heinrichs, my blind friend from Ribeirão do Salto, was an effective evangelist. Sometimes Peter and Elvira Penner from Witmarsum came to help us with music. Peter was a gifted soloist and sang the message of the saving Gospel into the hearts of many people. One year we hosted a Bible and evangelism conference with John Wall from Uruguay as speaker. I went to the chief of police to get a permit to hold such meetings in German. After issuing the document, the gentleman removed his hat, shook my hand and wished us God's blessing. That was an unusual gesture of goodwill on the part of city officials. When the H. K. Warkentins from Dinuba, California, came to Blumenau to show their films, we rented such prestigious places as *Teatro Carlos Gomez* and the facilities of a social service club (comparable to Rotarians) which attracted professional and business people. The Lord blessed these efforts beyond what we could have asked.

When I look back over the years I have been involved in church related work, I cannot help but marvel at the vision and energy God gave us during our time in Brazil. Each Sunday I went with a group of young people, frequently accompanied by older church members, to a senior citizens home. We served with singing, music, shared the Word of God, and visited with the people. The appreciation these older citizens expressed was simply overwhelming. A number of them came to know Christ and openly professed Him as their Lord and Savior. They could never say enough how these weekly visits impacted their life. I should also mention a monthly meeting we had in the public park in front of the old city hall. It was a time when people were hungry for the Word of God. I have participated in similar public meetings in Canada and in Switzerland, but never have I experienced such encouraging response as in Brazil. The listeners, both young and old, rich and poor, were always attentive and respectful, eager to listen and to accept a tract or other Christian literature.

In addition to our ministry in Blumenau and surrounding areas, I was often asked to speak at youth rallies, deeper life services, evangelistic meetings, Sunday school teacher conferences, and other church functions in Paraná, Rio Grande do Sul, even in Uruguay and Paraguay. That was the beginning of my extended ministries away from home, leaving Frieda and the children alone. Since then I have spent many months on the road. Yet Frieda has always been supportive, carrying much of the household and family responsibilities by herself. I may have fallen short of giving Frieda "the reward she has earned," but God knows that I have thanked Him many times for giving her to me as a tireless partner in His service.

When the Bible school in Curitiba was short of teachers, I was compelled to help out for one semester. Since I had not yet learned to say NO, it turned out to be a year when the burden of ministry became especially heavy for the church and the family, to say nothing about how it affected me personally. Early each Monday morning I took the bus from Blumenau to Curitiba, arrived there late that afternoon, taught a heavy load during the week, then I again took the bus to Blumenau on Friday afternoon, and returned home at 10 o'clock in the evening. Saturday and Sunday I spent with the family and the church, including preaching. Since in those days I knew nothing about the malady of "burnout"—be that artificial or real—I never did burn out. I believe, however, that such a heavy schedule was not the wisest choice on my part, but I simply accepted the assignment as an integral aspect of our mission.

One of the contributions that I consider to have historical significance was my involvement in conference work. In 1948, the Mennonite Brethren churches in Brazil and Paraguay came together to form the South American District Conference. That same year, G. H. Rosenfeld from Brazil and Kornelius Voth from Paraguay attended the General Conference of the Mennonite Brethren Church in North America as representatives of this new South American venture. When I came to Blumenau in the late 1950s and visited the various congregations, it became apparent that each local church was an island unto itself. There was neither a common vision nor a platform to share mutual concerns pertaining specifically to the respective country. It was also evident that, while the churches in Paraguay and the churches in Brazil were sharing a common faith, their opportunities and needs to put that faith into action were unique to their historical and sociocultural circumstances. This realization surfaced for the first time at the ninth District Conference held in Guarituba (near Curitiba) in 1960 when the issue of two separate conferences was raised, but tabled. The question, however, was ripe for action. The churches in both countries worked toward that goal without any intent of dissolving the existing District Conference, which by now also included the Mennonite Brethren congregations in Uruguay.

Upon consulting with church leaders, I drafted a working document as a basis for moving the organization to fruition. On 24 April 1960 our church in Blumenau hosted nine delegates and several visitors, representing the local churches of Boqueirão, Colônia Nova, Guarituba, Vila Guaíra, Witmarsum, Xaxim, and our own congregation. Already during our prayer time it became clear that the meeting was of the Lord. There were fervent expressions of anticipation that God would do something among us. Not only was there evident desire that we as individual churches would be drawn closer to each other, but also that God would give us a common vision for mission and unite us for a common purpose to realize that vision. Since I was asked to chair the meeting, I presented the issues as I envisioned them, distributed a paper that was accepted as the founding document, and proceeded with the agenda.

By way of summary, the organization of the conference was based on the following principles: (1) Uniformity of biblical and theological teaching; (2) practice of spiritual fellowship and mutual edification; (3) educational seminars and conferences for Sunday school teachers and church workers; and (4) strengthening of a common missionary vision to match existing mission challenges in the land. The delegates stood as one man to form the Conference of the Mennonite Brethren Church of Brazil. In conclusion we committed our cause to the Lord by singing the song, "The work is Yours, O Christ, Our Lord." Thus began a new chapter in the history of the Mennonite Brethren Church in Brazil. I declined to serve as chairman, but agreed to serve in other ways until I would move back to Canada in 1962.

34

Mission Interrupted
(1962)

God, make my life to be a little light,
That it in darkness of the road may glow;
A tiny flame that's always burning bright
Wherever I may be or go. Amen!
–Adapted from a children's prayer.

It is unthinkable that any journey through life could be without either detours or crossroads. They are bound to come. Some are predictable, others not; some can be outright bewildering, others cause little concern. When we had to interrupt our mission in Blumenau, we were facing a road ahead with unclear markers. I have sometimes referred to this time as a fourteen-year-long detour. Not that I ever doubted my calling to serve in the kingdom of God. That goal remained unaltered, but how to stay on course was a different matter. There were segments in my detour with signs pointing in different directions. There were times when they seemed to disappear in the fog. Those were times when a childlike prayer was all I had: to be "a little light . . . a tiny flame" that would not only brighten my own way, but also shine for others walking on similar trails.

For some time I had felt an annoying sensation on the upper part of my nose near the left eye. There was a visible lesion, though small and inconspicuous at first. When I had it checked by a dermatologist at the cancer clinic in Curitiba, he urged that it should be burned out. But because of its proximity to the eye, and because I had no way of letting Frieda know that I might have to stay in the clinic for a few days, I declined the treatment at that time. Besides, we had no health insurance. As the discomfort increased, however, I decided to go back to the clinic in Curitiba and have it checked once more. The doctor whom I had seen previously was on vacation and his colleague showed little interest in the case. The following day I took the bus and went home without taking care of the problem. Yet it was as though a voice told me that this was no ordinary skin cancer and should not be ignored.

Frieda and I decided to talk with Brother Koettker about it. While he showed understanding, he gave me a look of utter helplessness, saying:

"Hans, was sollen wir dann tun?" (Hans, what then are we to do?) He felt very strongly, as we did, that our time in Blumenau was not yet over. The Lord had blessed our ministry in the church and vicinity in so many ways and we had no reason to believe that He would not continue to do so. We loved the people and they loved us. We assured them that we would not leave, unless they found a replacement. Yet that nagging problem by my left eye caused growing concern. We all agreed to pray about it. Since there now was a functioning conference structure, the Mennonite Brethren congregations in Curitiba shared our concerns for the ministry in Blumenau. Before long, we made contact with Abraham and Helene Dueck. I had grown up with Abraham and knew him well from the Krauel. In the meantime, he had studied at the Lutheran Theological Seminary in São Leopoldo and was now teaching at the Mennonite school in Witmarsum. When our church extended a call to the Duecks, they were open to make the transition and serve the Lord in Blumenau.

Meanwhile, Frieda's parents wrote from Canada: "Don't trifle with cancer. You can have it treated in Vancouver where we have good doctors and insurance." I also asked Waldo Hiebert, member of the BGW/PR, when he and B. J. Braun were in Brazil for the South American District Conference, what I should do. He became our "advocate" at the board level and soon informed us that the BGW/PR was prepared to pay one third of the cost of our fare to Canada. That was generous and helpful so that we could begin to work with our papers. The most cost effective way to travel was with the Japanese freighter Argentina Marú from Santos, São Paulo, to San Francisco, California. The *R.Woehrle Ltda. Agência de Viagens* made the travel arrangements and assisted with documents. I faced the same visa problems as I had faced before, a subject I need not describe in detail.

Saying farewell to our church people and other friends in Blumenau was painful. The only consoling factor was that the Duecks would move in as soon as we had vacated the parsonage. The Brazilian Mennonite Brethren Conference requested that I be the speaker at its second annual convention scheduled to be held at the church in Colônia Nova near the city of Bagé, not far from the Uruguayan border. That was a meaningful experience on two counts. For one thing, it was gratifying to see the conference well established and the leadership motivated to pursue the goals which the founders had agreed on when we met in Blumenau nearly two years earlier. Then, too, it gave us as family a chance to visit my father and siblings in Colônia Nova before leaving for Canada.

After the conference we took the bus for São Paulo where we stayed two days at the MCC guest house. In the morning of 28 January1962 we left for Santos. That same day in the afternoon we boarded the Argentina Marú and were on our way, heading north along the Atlantic Coast of

Brazil. Our ship docked at several ports en route to load and unload freight and to pick up passengers. In one of the ports, so we were informed, three hundred Japanese farmers boarded the ship to move back to Japan. We traveled economy class, but had a private stateroom for a family of four. Dianne was seven and David three-and-one-half years old. During the entire twenty-three-day voyage we had ample opportunity to participate in entertainment and be the recipients of courteous service and treatment Japanese style.

On the fifth or sixth day of our journey, a Japanese Brazilian family of five from São Paulo was struck by tragedy. The time was a few minutes past noon. We had just begun to eat when the sudden sound of sirens hit with such alarming force that everybody jumped up and ran out onto the open deck. The twenty-six-year-old daughter had jumped overboard. We could hear and feel how the gears were being activated to slow down the big ocean liner. Within minutes it had made a perfect circle, while emitting a massive ring of a white, foam-like substance floating on the water to indicate the whereabouts of the missing person. In less than twenty minutes the rescue squad had recovered the victim and a medical team was working hard to keep her alive. According to a missionary couple, the young lady had taken an overdose of pills. She died six hours later. The next day we witnessed a Buddhist burial ceremony which ended by lowering the coffin wrapped in a Japanese flag and sunk into the depths of the ocean. To make sure that the spirit of the deceased would not starve, the sailors and others hurled large quantities of food after the coffin into the sea. Neither the parents nor the two younger brothers showed the slightest visible emotions throughout the ordeal. Their stoicism might have made Zeno proud, but Jesus would have wept with compassion.

Going through the Panama Canal from the Atlantic into the Pacific was a once-in-a-lifetime experience. The Canal runs south and southeast from Limón Bay at Colón on the Atlantic to the Bay of Panama at Balboa on the Pacific, a distance of sixty-four kilometers across the narrow Central American Isthmus. This sounds plain and utterly simple. Yet the canal in itself is an extraordinary achievement of human ingenuity and engineering. Only after passing through it can one visualize what D. G. Payne means when he describes history and construction of the canal as *The Impossible Dream*. The eight-hour-long maneuvering of the Argentina Marú through three sets of giant locks and the monumental Guaillard Cut to cross the Continental Divide was the most mesmerizing segment of our entire voyage from Santos to San Francisco.

Included in our tickets were two stopovers on the Pacific side of the journey where passengers were allowed to leave the ship. The first one was at Cristóbal, the American residential suburb of Colón, and the second was a day in Los Angeles where the scheduled sightseeing tours were drowned out by heavy rains. We left Los Angeles harbor that same evening. With daybreak the next morning the sun was shining and the atmosphere clear. But the mighty Pacific was everything else but passive and peaceful. It was restless, with high waves and foaming breakers all around us. Thus far God had protected us as family from motion sickness beyond minor discomfort. But on this last day of our voyage the Argentina Marú rocked and swayed back and forth so much that many passengers preferred to stay in their cabins instead of eating their noon meal in the dining room. I wish I had done the same. Motion sickness is not unto death, but it can make one feel like dying.

Entering the Bay of San Francisco with the Golden Gate Bridge in full view is nothing short of spectacular. We passed the small island with the once (in)famous Alcatraz Penitentiary and arrived at the harbor of San Francisco early in the afternoon on 20 February 1962. Bill Henry, who is married to Frieda's oldest sister, was there to meet us. We stayed three days with the Henry family in Watsonville and then took the bus to Portland, Oregon, where Frieda's brother Nick from Yarrow, British Columbia, was waiting for us at the bus depot. He took us home by car. I recall the lively conversation we had about developments in the Canadian church scene. Much of it was new to us and we were wondering how it might affect us and if we would fit in.

Time went by fast. Shortly past midnight we were at the Sumas/Huntingdon border crossing into Canada. Frieda and the children were readily admitted, but my old "stateless status" which had caused endless problems all my life immediately raised a red flag. Fortunately, I had a letter from the Canadian Consulate in São Paulo stating that, in accordance with the immigration papers which I had secured in 1956, I was legally eligible to enter Canada as an immigrant. But the officer in charge that night was of a different opinion. Not only was he rather discourteous toward me, he even suggested that the Canadian officials at the Consulate in Brazil did not know what they were doing. His demeanor of superiority reminded me of my experience at that same Huntingdon immigration office where six years earlier one of the officials had told me that the only place he could send me was to the Soviet Union where I was born. Now this gentleman threatened to detain me right there, while Frieda and the children could go with my brother-in-law to Yarrow. After much talking, the officer relaxed—even relented a bit. He wrote up a statement, made Nick Reimer sign it, and let me go on the promise that Nick would bring me back to the office early the next morning. When we showed up at the appointed time, the head officer was polite and apologetic for what had happened, gave me the needed papers, and wished me well as a new immigrant in Canada.

After applying for citizenship I was summoned on 27 May the following year to appear before the judge in Chilliwack to become a naturalized Canadian citizen. Not only did he give me the official Certificate of Naturalization, but also a Bible as a book to live by. I was impressed. It was truly a day of jubilation. I was no longer a "stateless alien" in this world, but a citizen of Canada.

We had a happy reunion with Father and Mother Reimer and those of the family living in Yarrow. Frieda's parents had bought a small farm with an older house on Dyke Road and offered it to us as a place to live. We could not have wished for anything better. I immediately started to work at Reimer's Nursery, cutting off young hawthorn trees about four or five inches above the ground so that the cultivated bud would get the full benefit of growing into a beautiful, healthy tree. That type of work requires a sturdy back and a strong hand. Normally, I had both. But since I had not done much physical work for several years I was totally out of shape. Besides, I had just come from the tropical summer heat in Brazil to the cold winter in Canada. By the end of the first week I was physically at the point of collapse. Frieda urged me to work only half days to give my whole system time to adjust to climatic conditions and to the type of work I was doing, but I was too proud for that. Then the Lord intervened. He sent a strong wind with a rich supply of snow and ice that made manual labor on the field impossible. Nick Reimer let his entire crew go home in the middle of the day. Seldom have I thanked God for pleasant weather as sincerely as I thanked Him that day for bad weather which gave me a break before a breakdown. In about a week or ten days the weather had much improved and I was ready to go back to work. I truly enjoyed working at the nursery with shrubs, trees, and flowers. I could have spent a lifetime doing so if that had been my calling.

In the spring of that year I went to St. Paul's Hospital in Vancouver to see an oncologist about the tumor that had troubled me for some time. About a week after the diagnostic tests, Dr. David Cowan called back and told me to come in again. The test results showed that I had an aggressive type of cancer that needed immediate attention. In the meantime he had consulted with another specialist who confirmed his prognosis. Surgery was scheduled for early July. During the delicate procedure very close to the left eye the surgeon discovered that the roots of the tumor had spread to the bone structure and thus required partial removal of the upper nasal bone. It had also affected the tear duct which took about a year to get back to normal. After nine days in the hospital I was released and able to recover at home.

On 15 October that same year we experienced the joy of the birth of our third child, Evelyn Rose. True to her name, she was a strong, healthy baby, full of vitality and vigor, and beautiful as a true rose. Like Dianne and David before her, Evelyn has brought much joy and blessing to our family.

The Board of General Welfare and Public Relations asked me to visit the Mennonite Brethren churches in the western provinces and report on our work in Brazil. We discussed that in the family, prayed about it and agreed that I should accept the assignment. That took me away from home, leaving Frieda and the children alone for six weeks. The schedule had been drawn up by the office in Hillsboro in conjunction with the respective leaders of the provincial conferences. Beginning in Edmonton, Alberta, and concluding in Winkler, Manitoba, I was in a different church every day of the week—usually in two churches on Sundays. The following spring I also visited the churches in British Columbia, but only upon invitation by the local pastors. While I had been in all of the churches in Manitoba during my Bible school and college years, those in Alberta and Saskatchewan were new to me. As I look back on that particular phase of ministry, I can only marvel at the graciousness with which my reports and messages were received by the churches. Numerous people, including church leaders, expressed genuine appreciation for clarifying the nature of the work done by the BGW/PR and how it was different from that of the Board of Foreign Missions at that time. I was humbled by that response from the churches.

From the time we returned from Blumenau to Yarrow until the time we left for Tabor College the following year, I was involved in radio work. The church in Blumenau asked for taped messages to continue the program we had been instrumental in starting there; the Yarrow Mennonite Brethren Church also requested that I preach on the *Frühe Morgenstunde,* a German radio program that was aired from Chilliwack every Sunday morning.

Although our mission had to be interrupted, the Lord provided a wonderful bridge through continued radio ministry to keep in touch with the people we had left behind in Brazil and opened a door to serve the churches in the Fraser Valley—a meaningful experience of ministry in transition.

PART IV

Detour in Academia (1962-1976 [1978])

Signposts and Crossroads and Reorientation

Don't let anyone look down on you because you are young, but set an example for the believers in speech, in life, in love, in faith and in purity. ...devote yourself to the public reading of Scripture, to preaching and to teaching. Do not neglect your gift, which was given you through a prophetic message when the body of elders laid their hands on you. Be diligent in these matters; give yourself wholly to them, so that everyone may see your progress. Watch your life and doctrine closely. Persevere in them, because if you do, you will save both yourself and your hearers.
—1 Timothy 4:12-16

35

Summer School and Tabor College
(1962-1964)

*I devoted myself to study and to explore
by wisdom all that is done under heaven. . . ,
but I learned that this, too, is a chasing after the wind.
For with much wisdom comes much sorrow;
the more knowledge, the more grief.*
–Excerpt from *Ecclesiastes 1*

What I have chosen to call "A Detour in Academia" is, in effect, a quest for guidance; I mean divine guidance to fulfill my life's mission. When my journey in mission was interrupted, I chose to take a detour through halls of learning, confident that I would eventually get back onto the main road as a pilgrim in mission. My goal was clear, the road hazy. I had no illusions that the route on which I could "devote myself to study and to explore wisdom," as the Preacher put it, would be without hurdles. I envisioned it to be a rather plain service road with stop signs and loading zones, even dead end streets. What I did not envision, however, were occasional forks and crossroads, signaling potential loss of orientation. It happened at the University of Oregon where I immersed myself in graduate studies that opened up vocational options I had never considered before. Some were alluring, to say the least. I thank God for guiding me back on track.

Things were different now than they had been fourteen years earlier when I came to Winkler Bible School, where I began to learn the ABCs of my life in mission. Then, I was alone. Now, I had a supportive companion who shared my aspirations. Then, I prayed by myself for God's guidance. Now, Frieda and I prayed together for His leading. As things fell into place we believed that it was within His will to pursue academic studies for a more effective mission ministry. However, I also had to bear in mind my responsibility to support the family. I knew that our children—ages eight, four-and-a-half, and nine months—would have fewer things and less conveniences than some other children their age. That in itself was not a serious deterrent. But two things gave me concern: They should have a home in which to experience love, feel secure, and learn Christian values; and they should have an environment in which they could develop and unfold socially, culturally, and spiritually through wholesome friendships, educational opportunities, and a healthy church life. These were personal concerns with implications for our future.

Furthermore, there were major changes in Mennonite Brethren mission I could not ignore as I looked for direction in preparation for further service. Some of the changes had already taken place, whereas others were in process during the time of my studies, while still others evolved later. But such is always the nature of change, requiring constant vigilance, perceptive discernment, and wise decisions on the part of those caught in such processes.

Ever since the historic General Conference which convened in Yarrow, British Columbia in 1957, the Board of Foreign Missions had been undergoing radical restructuring in terms of administrative lines of responsibility and field policy. Such missiological concepts as "indigenization" and "partnership in obedience" were becoming an integral part of the administrators' vocabulary. The "New Plan" initiated at that conference was in keeping with the postwar reappraisal of the worldwide Christian mission that resulted in the radical repatriation of western missionaries and a significant reduction of the number of those being sent out. The Mennonite Brethren found themselves in the midst of this missional transition without being sure of the outcome.

At the 1960 Centennial Convention in Reedley, California, a proposal was submitted that the Board of General Welfare and Public Relations was to merge with the Board of Foreign Missions, a process that was finalized six years later at the 1966 General Conference in Corn, Oklahoma. The new name for the joint boards was Board of Missions and Services (BOMAS). This organizational restructuring impacted the work force of the German-speaking Mennonite Brethren churches in Brazil, Paraguay, and Uruguay in more ways than one. At the personal level, these changes made a return to Brazil in the foreseeable future unlikely and called for a reorientation for future ministry.

Another factor that prompted my detour in academia were other options for ministry. Upon returning from Brazil I received a challenging invitation to assume the administrative responsibility for a conference institution in Ontario and calls from churches for pastoral ministry. While I believed to have the gift of service at different levels of church work, I have always been reticent to accept leadership positions including major administrative roles, either in the context of conference institutions or of a local church. Therefore, I could only thank the respective committees for their confidence in me and decline the invitations. That led me to explore other possibilities of service in the area of mission within the Mennonite Brethren conference.

I considered my biblical and religious education received in Winkler and Winnipeg combined with one year of Bible school teaching in Chilliwack and the years of practical mission experience in Brazil as the indispensable foundation for further missional service. I realized, however, that the foundation alone was not enough. The "New Plan" approved at the conference in Yarrow in 1957 and the merger of the two boards proposed at the convention in Reedley in 1960 were harbingers of new mission thinking and new mission structures for the Mennonite Brethren. If I wanted to serve in that context I would need to immerse myself in missiological studies to be more effective in further mission work wherever the Lord would lead us.

Since I had some background in Portuguese and German, subjects I found fascinating and challenging on their own merits, Frieda and I agreed that I should enter language studies, acquire the needed credentials and tools to teach at the college level so that we would have a source of income to support the family. I could then devote all my "spare time" to studying such basic missiological ingredients as theology, church history, world religions, and cultural anthropology. But first I needed to complete my undergraduate studies. And thus the detour took on concrete dimensions without our knowing either the road or the destination. I went by a precept which had come to me in the form of a rhyme during Bible school days in Winkler before I was fluent in English: *Gehe deinen Weg, so weit er offen steht, dann wird der Herr dir zeigen, wie er weiter geht.* (Walk on your road as far as it's open before you; then the Lord will show the rest of the way to you.) That is precisely how we embarked on our detour.

Soon after we returned from Brazil I enrolled at the University of Wisconsin to take courses by correspondence in Portuguese grammar and Brazilian culture. During the time I recovered from cancer surgery I took advantage of summer school offered by Western Washington State College in Bellingham, where I studied geology, American history, and German literature. I also wrote to Tabor College and inquired about the requirements and costs to earn a B.A. degree in humanities. Mr. John L. Ewert, registrar and officer of admissions, responded immediately saying that high school graduates with a degree from MBBC "generally spend from one to one and a half years on campus to complete their degrees," and that "tuition will be $550 next school year." That was good news. Due to medical, legal, and financial difficulties we thought it prudent to wait one year before going to Tabor. Meanwhile I received letters from Drs. Lando Hiebert, Vernon Wiebe, and Jake Loewen as well as from Mr. John F. Wiebe, director of student financial services, offering assistance to make the transition as easy as possible. We were overwhelmed by the kindness of the faculty and staff.

Toward the end of August 1963, we packed our belongings into a small, ultra-light trailer, hitched it to our Volkswagen and, together with our three children, were on our way to Hillsboro, Kansas. We took the Canadian route east to Manitoba where I helped my brother-in-law, Jake Driedger, with a late grain harvest. From there we headed south to Kansas. Once we got to Hillsboro, we stayed in a motel the first night. The next day we rented an old house from a certain Mr. Epp who had a number of similar dwellings throughout the town of Hillsboro and was eager to rent them to students. We found our abode on 205 C Street, across from Mr. and Mrs. H. R. Wiens, newly appointed General Secretary of the Board of Foreign Missions, only two or three blocks from Tabor College. That same day I met with the registrar who had all my transcripts and other school records on file. If I took a heavy load (including physical science, biological science, literature, and history) during the year and one language course the following summer, and if I passed all examinations, he emphasized, then I could meet the requirements for a B.A. degree in humanities in one year. I was more than pleased. We also had to enroll our children in their respective schools: Dianne in grade three and David in kindergarten.

My studies at Tabor went much better than I anticipated. What helped me a great deal right at the beginning was a course in speed reading. I learned how to be a more efficient reader and remember the essential issues an author was dealing with. In two or three courses under Wesley Prieb I studied great American literature, English literature, and grammar. I found these studies delightful, particularly English grammar. I was also fascinated with courses in sociology and cultural anthropology taught by Roy Just and Jake Loewen respectively. By the time I completed my courses of the academic year, plus one subject by directed studies, Mr. Ewert informed me that I had passed all exams with good grades, paid all fees, including rent, and thus was eligible to receive the degree. I was delighted and ready to move on to graduate school.

A special bonus of my year at Tabor College was the privilege of getting to know the mission leaders working in the Hillsboro office as well as a number of churches and their pastors in Kansas and Nebraska where I was asked to preach. One of the people I met was J. B. Toews, who was in transition from his post as general secretary of the BFM to the presidency of the Mennonite Brethren Biblical Seminary in Fresno. I had met him on several occasions in Brazil and Paraguay when he, Waldo Hiebert, and B. J. Braun came there in the interest of foreign mission, the work of the Board of General Welfare and Public Relations, and Christian higher education. All three had at one time or another encouraged me to pursue further studies. Shortly before J. B. Toews left for Fresno, he extended a personal invitation to study at the seminary there.

I found the interaction and visits with H. R. Wiens, the newly appointed general secretary of the BFM, and A. E. Janzen, a veteran missionary statesman of the conference, especially meaningful. From them I learned much about the internal concerns and conflicts brought on by the transition in mission with which they were constantly confronted and how they sought to resolve pressing issues through intense prayer and mutual counseling. On several occasions I also visited with Mrs. Hiebert, the widow of P. C. Hiebert with whom I had corresponded in 1956 and 1957 before leaving for Blumenau. Then there were those very special times of visiting and sharing with M. A. Kroeker, secretary of the BGW/PR. Just as he had always appeared in his letters while we were in Brazil, so he was during times of personal conversation: caring and encouraging. He was a man with a pastoral heart and an understanding mind.

Prior to our move to Hillsboro, I corresponded with Lando Hiebert, professor of Bible at Tabor College, about the possibility of getting part-time work. He was most helpful in suggesting that I write to the headquarters of the Evangelical United Brethren Church in Salina, Kansas (in the process of merging with the Methodists), and inquire about an opening in one of the churches in the area. Unfortunately, on 6 July that same year (1962), Professor Hiebert was killed in an automobile accident while attending the Canadian Conference in Abbotsford, British Columbia. When I got to Hillsboro the following year, the Lord opened the door for me to become a circuit preacher—even if not a traditional "circuit rider"—for the churches in Lincolnville, Lost Springs, and Tampa. This was something I had read about but never thought that I would one day step into that kind of ministry. Every Sunday we made a round trip of about seventy miles (112 kilometers). Filling up the tank of our small Volkswagen at seventeen cents per gallon never gave us cause to complain about travel expenses.

Each congregation had several gifted and active members, particularly among the women. They planned the entire weekly program, including Sunday services. My responsibility was to preach on Sundays and conduct special meetings on request. Our first service was in Tampa, starting at 9 a.m. It was the oldest and most beautiful of the three buildings, especially the woodwork inside. The second service was in Lincolnville, the largest of the congregations in our circuit. We started at 10:15. After this service Dianne and David, our oldest two children, stayed for Sunday school, while Frieda and I with Evelyn were on our way to Lost Springs, where the service was scheduled for 11:30. On the way back we picked up our children and went home. We never missed a Sunday, nor do I recall ever being late for a service. The children were remarkably cooperative, always sitting through two services and attending an hour of Sunday school. In the afternoons, sometimes also during the week, we visited the sick and families with needs.

In a recent family gathering our children talked about those "circuit rides" in Kansas. I was surprised by the details they still remembered. In a brief tribute at our golden anniversary, David even reminded the family that he had heard my "lukewarm sermons" which I had preached in those churches. I am sure, he is right about that; and I complimented him not only on his sharp memory (he was four and a half at the time), but also on his clever play on words to describe a message about the lukewarm church in Laodicea (Rev 3:14-22) as a "lukewarm sermon." Frieda and I were pleased that after some forty years our children can speak with humor about those times that were not always easy for them.

Several young people—on one occasion three in one family—and two or three adults accepted Christ as Savior during that year. One of them was Mr. Smith, father of a large family from Lincolnville. He had spent most of his adult life working in the oil fields. While he was suffering from lung cancer, I visited him regularly and spoke to him freely about the Lord in the presence of his wife and daughters, who were fine Christians. During a visit in the hospital he expressed the desire to be saved. We prayed together and Mr. Smith turned his life over to Christ. That was a great victory. The following week he went to be with the Lord.

The members of all three churches were most appreciative and hospitable. They sometimes invited us for Sunday dinner and occasionally shared with us some of "the fat of their land" which usually consisted of a package or two of frozen meat. After I spoke at a high school graduation during the week, one family with several teenage boys from the Lost Springs congregation expressed special appreciation for the graduation address and asked us to have dinner with them the following Sunday. When we were about to leave, the mother said to one of her sons: "Get two from the deep freeze." When he returned with two packages, the father revealed the secret of the contents: "The jack rabbits were so plentiful this year," he declared with a great smile, "and so we have stocked our freezer with meat to spare."

With that explanation the boy handed the rabbits to Frieda. I was grateful and looked forward to an old-fashioned rabbit roast as I remembered it from my days in the Brazilian jungle, where I was in charge of the rabbits we raised for meat. But Frieda had very different memories about rabbits. Suffice it to say that she had developed a rather strong aversion to this rodent species, as she referred to them, and found the mere thought of cooking them utterly repugnant. When I volunteered to do the cooking, she had only one response: "Not in my pots!" That settled the matter about my rabbit roast. Well, not quite—at least not after years down the road.

Some twenty-five years later during one of my preaching and teaching assignments in Europe, we also spent time with Johannes and Cornelia

Reimer visiting churches in Romania. People lived in dire poverty. We stayed with a Christian family who raised a few rabbits for meat. Between church services that Sunday they gave of their best: rabbit roast for dinner. I would have enjoyed that dinner immeasurably more, if only I had not felt so sorry for Frieda. It was as though I could feel how every muscle in the passage to her stomach was getting tighter with each bite that went down without chewing. Surely, that was no treat for a selective digestive system. Yet she ate it in total silence without revealing her dilemma to our gracious hosts. Both of us were grateful that in days ahead she recovered from that "rarebit" of rabbit roast.

— 36 —
University of Oregon
(1964-1967)

*But as your first duty keep on looking
for His standard of doing right and for His will,
and then all these things will be yours besides.
So never worry about tomorrow,
for tomorrow will have worries of its own.*
—Jesus in Matthew 6 (Williams)

While studying at Tabor College, I wrote to several universities for information about their language departments. Professor Jake Loewen at Tabor recommended the University of Washington in Seattle where he had earned his Ph.D. degree in cultural anthropology and linguistics. He assured me that I would like the language program there. The location appealed to us because of its proximity to the Fraser Valley in British Columbia where Frieda's parents, several siblings, and friends were living at the time. However, once I had information from different universities, was able to compare their language programs and learn about the schools for our children, we decided on the University of Oregon in Eugene, a decision we have never regretted.

As we had made the trip in our Volkswagon from British Columbia to Kansas a year earlier, so we traveled again in June 1964 from Kansas to Oregon. The monumental Continental Divide at the Berthoud Pass on Highway 40 west of Denver with an elevation of over 11,300 feet was a spectacular highlight in the true sense of that word. Ever since childhood in Brazil I have been captivated with natural beauty and the created wonders of God's fingers. Here we stood at the apex of them all displayed in streams and forests, rocks and mountains.

Farther northwest we stopped in Salt Lake City. The golden angel on the pinnacle of the tower of the Mormon Temple was another visual highlight. Even though it is not the handiwork of God, it is, nonetheless, a magnificent piece of human craftsmanship worth seeing. Besides, the temple had another appeal to us that went back to my college days in Winnipeg. Every Sunday afternoon a local radio station aired a guessing game. The question asked by the program host was this: "Where would you like to hide?" Frieda sent in her answer: "I would like to hide behind the organ in the Mormon Temple in Utah." The panel failed to guess, and she was awarded the prize of twenty-five dollars, an amount that fattened our lean grocery budget for several weeks. The sight of the temple—even without seeing the organ—brought back memories from our years in Winnipeg when we listened to that entertaining radio program.

We arrived in Eugene on a Sunday evening. Darkness had already set in and we were tired. We took a motel, got something to eat, and settled down for the night. Not knowing a soul in the city and being unfamiliar with the area, I must admit that I was somewhat apprehensive. On the recommendation of Clarence Hiebert of Tabor College, I had written to the Chamber of Commerce. The information I received might have interested tourists, but was of little help to us. After all, we had not come to see attractions in the Willamette Valley or the Oregon Coast; my objective was to study at the University. Our primary questions had to do with family housing, schools for our children, and churches where we could become involved. These concerns were, understandably, not on the agenda of the Chamber of Commerce. All we could do that first evening was to place these matters into God's hand and go to sleep.

With daybreak the next morning things looked much brighter. We began to learn how the Lord guided us step by step to take care of each of our concerns. As I walked to the car on the parking lot I saw the entrance gate to the University campus across the boulevard from our motel. That made our orientation to the city quick and easy. After breakfast we checked the real estate section in the local paper for housing. What we found was less than encouraging. Rentals for families with children were scarce and the cost was prohibitive for our budget. My first errand that morning was to the University Housing Office. There I was told that due to a major renovation project of the older, inexpensive apartments, the University was facing a critical housing shortage. Unless I had a reservation, there was no vacancy. The only chance for an apartment would be a cancellation or someone moving out. Neither was likely.

In the meantime, I went to register for a full quarter (eleven weeks) of summer school, taking courses in Spanish language, German grammar, and literature. Since Tabor College was at that time not accredited outside the State of Kansas, I was admitted on probation. Fortunately, out-of-state tuition did not apply to foreign students enrolled for summer studies. That was more than I had expected. But even more was to come.

When I returned to the Housing Office, I was given the good news that a couple from the Westmoreland Apartments on West 18th Street had moved out; the apartment on the second floor was being cleaned and would be ready for occupancy by 4 p. m.—but only until the end of the summer. I literally ran to tell Frieda and the children, praising God all the way to the motel. The Lord had provided living quarters for us. That evening we ate our first meal in our rented apartment close to an elementary school and only three miles from the university. Before the summer had ended, the Housing Office called to let us know that another furnished apartment in a ground-level duplex on 2175 W. 18th Street would become available for the fall quarter and that we were first on the list. The cost was $75 a month. It goes without saying that we gratefully accepted the offer, moved in at the designated time, and lived there for three full years. And they were good years. But before I talk about my academic pursuits at the university, I want to give a testimony about the providence of God in the way we managed our family affairs during my years in graduate school.

I have talked about providence before without attempting to explain its meaning. My reason is simple: I do not know how to explain even the naked word, let alone the weighty substance it is made to convey. Nonetheless, I feel compelled to say that by providence I do not mean that God was there to satisfy all my wishes and fulfill all my hopes, great or small. Nor do I mean to say that every decision I made and every step I took was foreordained by God. To make such claim would be utterly arrogant. My experiences in connection with graduate studies at the University of Oregon are for me a confirmation that God's providence is above and beyond my intellectual grasp. I simply do not understand how things happened as they did, unless I accept them as providential. Symbolically speaking I mean—if I may paraphrase a sentence from C. S. Lewis's *The Problem of Pain*—"that a master's hand" is holding mine as I trace the letters to write about my university experience and that my script "need only be a `copy,' not an original." The Lord was guiding; I was seeking to discern His direction.

God's direction was evident in all areas of basic needs. One was in relation to church participation and ministry, and the other in the realm of financial income to cover ongoing costs of living. We had borrowed $500 for moving from Hillsboro to Eugene, had enough savings for about one month rent and groceries, and were confident that we would find work to earn our keep beyond that time. I got a part-time job in the hospital washing dishes at $1.29 an hour. On Saturdays I did yard and garden work and on Sundays I often preached in different churches. Frieda soon became known as a professional typist and typed term papers, theses, dissertations and manuscripts for professors and students. We got by with what we earned.

On our first Sunday in Eugene we attended a Mennonite Brethren church service held in the chapel at Northwest Christian College, a school sponsored by the Christian Church/Disciples of Christ. The college was situated adjacent to the university. Harold Schroeder and his wife Susan were just then beginning a Mennonite Brethren work in the city. The college allowed them to meet in its facilities until they had their own building. Here we learned to know not only the Mennonite Brethren families in Eugene, but made other contacts and acquaintances that proved significant for years to come. Those experiences confirmed for me once again that the providence of God can be neither planned nor predicted; it is far above and beyond human comprehension.

My interest in Christian higher education led me to visit with the academic dean (whose name I cannot recall) of Northwest Christian College. He told me of the Institute of Church Growth, founded there by Donald A. McGavran and his colleague, Alan R. Tippett, missionary from Australia to the Fijian Islands. Mr. Tippett was just then completing his Ph.D. in anthropology under the eminent Professor Homer G. Barnett of the University of Oregon, known for his theory of *Innovation: The Basis of Culture Change*. Dr. McGavran's books, especially *How Churches Grow*, made headlines throughout the Anglophone world, and Tippett's writings were not far behind. I was interested in taking courses at the Institute, yet before I was able to do so, the entire faculty with library and students was moved to Pasadena, California, to become the School of World Mission and Institute of Church Growth at Fuller Theological Seminary. That meant that I would have to postpone missiological studies for another time. In retrospect, that was the best thing that could have happened. In the course of my conversation with the dean of NCC, he asked if I would be available for substitute preaching in congregations of the Christian Church denomination in the Willamette Valley during the summer months. That turned out to be an interesting ministry.

Our first Sunday in Eugene we also met Orval and Bertha Johnson, who happened to attend the morning service of the newly started Mennonite Brethren Church in the city. Mr. Johnson had been a chaplain in the U.S. army during World War II and was now a semiretired pastor. Mrs. Johnson was a high school teacher in Springfield, about thirteen miles east of Eugene. The Johnsons were godly people and we became close friends. The day we met them, they invited us to their home for hamburgers and potato chips. During our conversation at the dinner table they shared with us some episodes from their varied church experiences and expressed interest in starting an entirely new work near their home in Springfield under the auspices of the United Brethren in Christ (UBC, Old Constitution) denomination. But they needed help.

At the beginning of the fall quarter we volunteered our time and energy to join the Johnsons in their church-planting venture. At first we met in a high school, then in the Springfield Grange Hall. As more and more people accepted Christ and joined the growing congregation, the need for a church building became crucial. The group was highly motivated and within a relatively short time bought property and built its own house of prayer.

Though modest, it was functional and adequate. This became our church family and family church for the next two years. Both Frieda and I were teaching Sunday school. We were spiritually nurtured and experienced a meaningful time together with our children. It was through this church that I became acquainted with Huntington College, a UBC school in Indiana. But more about that later. Once the church was established and the Johnsons had qualified Sunday school teachers, including university personnel, we went back to the Mennonite Brethren and spent our final year in Eugene with our own denomination.

Since I had received high grades during the summer quarter, I was officially admitted as a graduate student for the fall quarter on two conditions. First, I would have to demonstrate the ability to meet the criteria for quality graduate work specified by the division. Second, I would have to pay out of state tuition which was three hundred dollars above regular fees. Yet there was nothing I could do, except work hard and pay what was required if I wanted to stay in the program. I thoroughly enjoyed my studies. The readings in literature and history of Indo-European languages and philology opened up a new world to me. With more than a million books in its catalog, the University Library had excellent resources and study facilities, especially in the humanities division, the oldest part of the huge complex. The approach to the building was impressive. Two magnificent portals, one leading in and the other one out, gave the library a classic look. Above each door between two massive columns were engraved the words of Jesus recorded in John 8:32:

> YOU SHALL KNOW THE TRUTH [entrance]
> THE TRUTH SHALL MAKE YOU FREE [exit]

It was an arresting inscription even for the casual passerby to behold and an exhilarating experience for the serious student to walk through those imposing doors into an atmosphere of stored wisdom and knowledge accumulated from many generations.

By the end of the first quarter I knew all nine professors in the department of German and most of those in the Spanish, French, and Portuguese sections. All of them had their offices in Friendly Hall, where also a number of classes were being taught. When I got my grades between Christmas and New Year, I had reason to be more than elated; I was jubilant and gave thanks to God. Our children had also had a good experience in their schools. As a family we had a comfortable apartment, wonderful friends and fine neighbors. I still had my dishwashing job at the hospital, and Frieda was typing for students and teachers so that we had sufficient income for a tight budget. We even managed to buy an old piano so that the children could take lessons from a church pianist who lived in the area. Everything seemed to go much better than we could have imagined.

To my great delight, my probationary status was removed from the record after my first regular quarter. At the same time I received a congratulatory letter from Dr. Kenneth Ghent of the Office of Student Affairs, saying that I was placed on the International Student Honor Roll. By God's grace I was able to maintain that distinction throughout my years of graduate studies in Eugene. That entitled me to a refund of the three hundred dollars out-of-state fee I had paid at the beginning of my first fall quarter. All in all, things went much better in my academic pursuit and for us as family than we could have asked for.

During the Christmas holidays I received a telephone call from Professor Wolfgang Leppmann, chairman of the department. Without much of an introduction, he told me that he had observed me as a student, reviewed my record, and would like to see me in his office. Within a split second I had already formed my conclusion why he wanted to see me. I feared that I would have to terminate my graduate studies because I had an undergraduate degree from a nonaccredited institution. Those thoughts were unsettling, but false. Professor Leppmann had a very different agenda. "Mr. Kasdorf," he said, "our enrollment for the second quarter is higher than expected. I have a class of thirty-two students in first-year German for whom I have no teacher. Would you be willing to teach that class? If so, I would like you to come to my office to talk about details."

As I sat in his office, Dr. Leppmann told me how pleased he was with my progress and that he would like me to teach the freshman class for the winter and spring quarters with the possibility of extending the assistantship through the summer and beyond. I would be paid for teaching, receive free tuition, could share an office in Friendly Hall with two doctoral candidates, and have such other advantages as secretarial assistance related to teaching. I thanked him for his confidence in me and assured him that I would do my best, so that the students would not be disadvantaged for not having one of the professors or doctoral candidates teach their class. When I came home from the University that day and shared with Frieda my conversation with Dr. Leppmann, we could only praise God for His marvelous leading. From that time on I taught a class of first- or second-year German every quarter and advanced grammar during intensive summer sessions.

I enjoyed my teaching immensely. Judging by the cards, letters, and notes I have on file, I had only students who enjoyed studying German. From more than thirty notes, here are a few random samples of what students wrote about the classes I was teaching: "Of the five instructors I have had in German the past two years, you are by far the most conscientious." In another card a student writes: "I would like to say that I have gained the most from this course. Your approach, your desire to have your students learn, and your devotion to German language in all respects makes you a most pleasant and interesting professor. ...Your knowledge of idioms helped me a great deal.... Danke sehr." Among those who commented also on aspects besides language, one wrote: "This was the first class I took, which was taught by a missionary of a faith other than my own (Catholic), and I am glad that you shared some of your experiences and personal views with us. Thank you for a very profitable year."

Upon completing the Master's degree, I was promoted to being an instructor with the additional assignment of teaching introduction to literature and a course in third-year German grammar. I found both delightful, especially grammar. The exercise of reflecting on such simple aspects as the structure of the case system, the order of verb conjugation, the declension of nouns in each gender, the laws of strong and weak vowel changes is like retreating into a gallery of esthetic beauty. By doing so one can meditate on the Creator's grand imperative: "Let there be light." Language is God's gift to humankind and grammar a central component which gives it form and structure as well as order and beauty. In the process of language learning, it is grammar that sets the mind free and enlightens the pathway for words, phrases and sentences to communicate in an orderly fashion with God and fellow humans. That is one reason why grammar deserves respectful treatment, particularly by teachers and preachers.

37

Facing an Alluring Crossroad

*No temptation has taken hold of you
but what is common to human nature.
And God is to be trusted not to let you
be tempted beyond your strength,
but when temptation comes,
to make a way out of it,
so that you can bear up under it.*
–The Apostle Paul in *1 Corinthians 10*

While teaching German at the university students often talked to me about their experience in the classroom. Their faith was sometimes sorely tested, particularly in the social and human sciences. They may have been right. I got to know several fine Christian professors in other disciplines, yet I knew none in the Division of Modern Languages, except Stanley Rose, professor of Portuguese. Natural religion played a significant role in lectures and class discussions whereas faith in the transcendent God revealed in Jesus Christ was seldom mentioned. It was this subtle aspect rather than outright denial of God or open expressions of ridicule that troubled some Christian students. In all fairness, however, I must point out that there were professors who made no claim to faith, yet respected those who did.

Nonetheless, the academic atmosphere in a secular university is just that: secular, this-worldly, human-centered. It tends to maximize the values of the human-secular and to minimize the values of the Christian-spiritual. The very nature of the secular worldview is to regard the well-being of humankind as self-sufficient and without the need of a faith commitment to the transcendent God of the Bible. Not so for the Christian who believes in the God who has created humankind for a purpose. That is why in personal conversations with students I found it important to point out the difference between the secular and the spiritual in the academic context. I do not mean just any kind of the spiritual, but that which is anchored in the revelation of the Judeo-Christian Scriptures. In the course of my studies the words which Jesus spoke to the disciples in Gethsemane took on special meaning not only in my conversation with students, but at the personal level as well. "You must all keep watching and praying," Jesus said, "that you may not be exposed to temptation. Man's spirit is willing, but human nature is weak" (Matt. 26:41).

In my first year of graduate school, Frieda and I had immersed ourselves so heavily in extracurricular activities to earn our keep that we took little time for family recreation. I was paying more attention to my studies and things we needed than to the kingdom of God. One day George Mowry, a doctoral candidate in the School of Music, pointed that out to me. The Mowrys had become our friends and were concerned about our physical and spiritual well-being. "Take our tent and go to Crater Lake for at least one weekend," George said emphatically. "You need to get out with the family, and Crater Lake is a gorgeous spot, not too far away." No sooner had I mentioned it at home than we began to plan our first camping trip.

We were all excited but ill equipped for this new venture, which turned out to be a disaster. Murphy's Law went into action. Everything that could go wrong, did. Upon arriving at the campsite we left the key in the locked car and had to call the park ranger for help; setting up the tent proved to be more difficult than expected, especially in evening darkness under big trees; it was late by the time we finally settled down to eat supper; our borrowed plastic mattresses let out the air nearly as fast as our lungs could collect a new supply to refill them; our blankets were woefully inadequate, leaving us shivering all night; around midnight a roaming bear grumbling and growling near our tent added fear to frost and frustration. When we drove home the next day and ended up with car trouble just as we entered Eugene, we had enough sense to thank God for protection along the way, even if not for our camping experience. In the end, however, this event gave us the incentive to save money for a tent and the basic furnishings needed for family camping. It was a worthwhile investment for inexpensive family traveling and recreation. Whenever we talk about our camping experiences over much of the North American continent, they bring back many pleasant memories of joyful family times.

My graduate studies in the secular sector coincided with the "turbulent decade of the 1960s." I had already become aware of the profound changes taking place in world mission; now I saw another area of change that would affect every level of society and culture in the years ahead. The years of 1965 to1967 were a time when the atmosphere at the university was heavy and tense. One of the reasons was that the student leaders invited Timothy Leary to give a series of lectures on campus. Not only was he a controversial figure at that time, but also an outspoken advocate of the hallucinogenic drug LSD. In keeping with the spirit of the sixties, Dr. Leary spoke on the topics "Tune in," "Turn On," "Drop Out."

Simultaneous with his lectures came buses from all directions, bringing students from other universities to Eugene.

The Hippies had arrived. They literally invaded the university campus and parts of the city. I remember one morning walking from the parking lot to my office in Friendly Hall and seeing crowds of rather unconventionally dressed young men and women walking across campus in the direction of the Student Union. Referred to as "flower children," they formed an integral part of an emerging generation that descended on university campuses throughout the land. Many of them were self-invited guests who occupied Eugene's finest city park for about one week, leaving behind unsightly amounts of rubbish and debris when they moved on. Being an eyewitness of some of the things that transpired at the university in those years helped me understand, at least to a degree, the subsequent conflicts between various movements of the counterculture and the existing status quo. Both secular and religious institutions were confronted with cultural and philosophical trends inherent in movements and organizations with roots in the tumultuous 1960s. Postmodernity was emerging. Our society has not been the same since.

Though unrelated to the social and cultural turmoil on campus, I was confronted with a temptation that blurred my original goal of graduate studies and nearly caused me to lose my orientation.

Upon completing course requirements for an M.A. in German language and literature with a minor in Spanish, I wrote a thesis entitled "Die Bibeldramen Klopstocks." Not only did I find the three biblical dramas (*Der Tod Adams* [1757], *Salomo* [1764], and *David* [1777]). fascinating, but also challenging, because no one had ever made a study of them. The author, Friedrich Gottlieb Klopstock, a great intellectual and master of the German language, was known throughout Europe for his religious fervor. He became famous for his contributions to philology and spiritual writings, including the great epic, *Der Messias*. He was sought out by eminent masters of his day. Even Samuel Coleridge and William Wordsworth came to visit him and to probe his mind.

The more I read of this particular literary genre, the more captivated I became. In fact, I believed I had discovered a branch on my detour that seemed as smooth and attractive as any road could be. It appeared to be much wider than the service road on which I had started out and on which I expected to end up. I had the impression that my detour was becoming better and brighter with each quarter. At that point I came to an alluring crossroad with arrows pointing in several directions. One of them was particularly attractive, offering the option of a Ph.D. degree. One of my professors objected, saying that I was too old and that I should take a job while the market was good. But with the approval of Dr. Leppmann and the encouragement of other professors I decided to continue the doctoral program with a major in seventeenth and eighteenth century German literature and a minor in Brazilian literature.

I must say, however, that I was not entirely at peace about the whole idea. Was I facing a new direction in God's leading or was I merely tempted to do what I had come to enjoy doing? Was I about to exchange my missional focus for selfish ambitions? Could I not take a shortcut as an appealing way out of what otherwise would still be a long road ahead? Why should I not work toward academic credentials and teach in a secular university and forego years of seminary studies toward my goal in mission? Could I not be a Christian witness in the secular context just as well as in a church setting? Why not shorten my detour for the benefit of the family? So I rationalized and argued within myself. Theoretically, it would have been possible to complete the doctoral program—including a dissertation—within two or three years and then begin full-time teaching without having to spend another seven to ten years teaching in a college while simultaneously studying missiology in preparation for effective mission ministry. The idea was tempting.

During my final year I studied philology and medieval literature under Heinrich Nordmeyer, a visiting professor from the University of Hamburg, Germany. Henry Kratz, professor of linguistics and history of Indo-Germanic languages, offered to be my major adviser. He was a great scholar, but always congenial and accommodating. Since I shared some of his interests, he gave me specific assignments with an open-ended reading list, including such pre-Reformation and early German Christian mystics as Meister Eckhart, Johann Tauler, Johann Arndt and Jakob Boehme all of whom left indelible marks not only on their contemporaries, but also on certain elements of Protestant Pietism and other facets of German religious thought and literary genres for generations to come. It was in this historical context and tradition that Klopstock played a major role.

Inspired by his spiritual legacy as well as by the writings of John Milton, the sentimentally intellectual Klopstock was a central figure in the preclassical literary era and a pioneer in the transition from Latin to German in academic circles. His contributions to philology in general, especially in his later years, and to the German language in particular were unprecedented achievements. I was mesmerized by these developments in the history of the German language, which contributed to the unification of Germany as a nation. But I was equally fascinated by Portuguese and decided to include it as part of my studies, with special emphasis on language and literature in the Brazilian context. Professor Rose fully supported the idea and was glad to be my adviser. I read extensively and found great pleasure in writing and presenting seminar papers. That is when I realized more than ever the value of the homiletical studies I had taken in Bible school and Bible college. The distinct advantage I had was the ability to analyze literary texts and to organize my thoughts in a logical sequence around a major theme. That added to the pleasure of research, writing, and seminar presentations.

Things went so well that I could see the end of the detour. But in the meantime I had become so preoccupied with my progress that I was in danger of losing sight of my original goal in mission. Now was the time to take stock. I needed to reevaluate my journey and refocus my vision. Was I in danger of betraying my calling to serve the Lord in world mission? Could I with a good conscience pursue a teaching career in a secular university? Not that these institutions were not in need of Christian teachers, nor that Christians did not or do not have an important role in such places. That was never in question. My question was rather whether this was for me a legitimate shift in my journey or merely a test of my faithfulness to my calling. What consequences could such a change of direction have for the family? Was I prepared to leave the Mennonite Brethren Church where both Frieda and I had been spiritually nurtured during our most formative years? These questions demanded a definitive answer.

It was around that time that Waldo Hiebert and Elmo Warkentin were on an itinerant ministry for the Pacific District Conference, promoting the vision known as "Decade of Enlargement." They surprised us with a brief visit to see how we were doing, what my goals were for the future, and if I was still interested in seminary studies. In that moment I was reminded of a letter (14 July 1962) which I received while recovering from cancer surgery. In it Mr. Hiebert wrote words of encouragement and also expressed deep grief over "the home-going of my [his] very dear twin brother, Lando" who had died in a car accident while attending the Canadian Conference in Abbotsford. In a postscript was this note: "I still hope we shall see you in the seminary some day."

As Frieda and I sat there in our living room listening to the brothers share their burden for the growth of our denomination and prayed for God's leading in my personal life, I was torn between a university career and service in world mission. Little did they realize that their visit was already an answer to that prayer and that the words of that handwritten P.S. were going through my mind: "I still hope we shall see you in the seminary some day." Beyond that there was nothing dramatic that happened on that day. But the visit itself was to me another sign of divine providence pointing toward my original goal, not only academic achievements.

Yet there was also an accumulation of signs which could be interpreted as pointing in another direction. My last quarter of teaching and studying put several enticing baits right on my path. I had barely completed resident requirements for a Ph.D. in foreign languages when I got another complimentary letter from Dr. Ghent stating that I had "received all `A' grades" and was on the international student honor roll. I was humbled and pleased by that report. But I was also tempted to prepare for my comprehensives and go from there to writing a dissertation on the language transition of the eighteenth century when the use of classical Latin in the university setting was gradually replaced by modern High German. Potentially, that research could have been a good preparation for making university teaching my career. Then there were expressions of appreciation from students about my teaching. They, too, pointed in the same direction. Another inviting sign was when I was asked to supervise student teachers of high school German in the Lane County School District. My assignment involved going from school to school for observation in the classroom, holding conferences with student teachers on a personal level, and writing a performance evaluation on each. Dr. Edward Diller, professor of language teaching methodology, headed the program for the university. I had studied under him, learned much from him, and was now responsible to him.

As we considered the options at the crossroad, we concluded that I should pursue my original goal, even if that meant giving up a Ph.D. degree in languages and literature. At the same time I had found the opportunity to combine full-time studies with part-time teaching and training upcoming language teachers enjoyable and meaningful. When I shifted back to pursue my original goal, I thanked God for those rich experiences of secular studies in graduate school. The years at the University of Oregon prepared me for eleven great years of full-time language teaching and provided a good background for missiological studies.

38

College Teaching and Seminary Studies
(1967-1978)

Take my yoke upon you and learn from me,
for I am gentle and humble in heart,
and you will find rest for your souls.
For my yoke is easy and my burden is light.
—Jesus in *Matthew 11*

Before terminating my studies at the University of Oregon I had two offers to teach modern languages, one from Pacific College in California and the other from McPherson College in Kansas. Because Pacific College (now Fresno Pacific University) was a Mennonite Brethren school with a biblical seminary nearby, I made that my first choice. The interview on campus with Academic Dean Elias Wiebe, Division Chairman Dalton Reimer, and President Arthur Wiebe went well. I had no reason to think otherwise. However, the position was contingent on a government grant that in the end was not forthcoming. Admittedly, I was disappointed. Upon returning from Fresno to Eugene President DeWitt Baker of Huntington College was visiting the United Brethren in Christ churches on the West Coast, including the new congregation that Frieda and I had helped to start in Springfield. We met with Dr. Baker at the home of our friends, Orval and Bertha Johnson, for an interview. He conferred by telephone with the Dean, Gerald Swaim, and a day or two later called me to confirm a position to teach German and Spanish, beginning in the fall of 1967. Again, we could only accept this offer as God's leading.

We arrived in Huntington on a Saturday evening toward the end of August 1967. Charlie Wagner, superintendent of grounds and buildings, came to greet us, gave us the key to a house owned by the college at 608 Hime Street, and helped us unload the boxes and whatever we had in our little trailer. We had never met Charlie before, yet there was an instant bonding. He was one of those genuine, down-to-earth Christians who can walk on golden streets with the rich and famous and on dusty roads with the poor and simple, never feeling out of place. Before leaving for home that night, he said: "And where will you go to a meetinghouse tomorrow morning?" Before either of us could reply, he invited us to his home church. "Since you don't know where it is," he continued, "I will come here and meet you, and you follow me to the church. After the service you come to our place for dinner." And that is what we did. At the church we met Charlie's wife Mildred, the Pastor Dick Frederick, and other church members. We were most warmly received and made that our church home during our time in Huntington.

The alluring fork I had faced at the academic crossroad while in graduate school lay behind me. I was about to embark on a new phase with new challenges on my detour. No longer was I studying first, and teaching second, as I had been doing at the University of Oregon. The order was now reversed. I was now investing my primary energy and time in teaching, which I found quite satisfying. I had a full teaching schedule with large classes in both German and Spanish. Unfortunately, the college required only two years of language study, which provided little challenge for work beyond the elementary level. Since the seminary on the same campus offered classes on weekends, I took a course in world religions from Professor Pfister and one in practical theology from Professor Burkholder, involving all day on Saturdays. That left my evenings free to be with the family and for reading and writing.

One of the highlights for our family in Huntington was Bible memorization. Mildred Wagner was the representative of the Bible Memory Association in our church. She invited us to enroll as a family, but at different levels. We recited our Bible verses and passages to each other and at the end were tested by Mrs. Wagner. Our David liked nothing more than to test me on my memorization skills. He was particularly delighted when I floundered or did not know what he called "the address" (reference) of my verses. He was a hard master, keeping me on guard. We shared a great deal of pleasure learning the Scriptures together.

We had barely moved in and settled down when Dalton Reimer of Pacific College called and asked if I would consider coming to teach there the following year. He emphasized that the college was interested in expanding the language department and assured me that this time the appointment was not contingent on a grant.

We were in no hurry to make a decision and waited until January 1968, before giving a response. Besides, there were other issues I had to weigh before making a conclusive commitment. Academic Dean David Ewert of the Mennonite Brethren Bible College in Winnipeg had written earlier, asking if I would consider joining the faculty there "some time in the future (sooner or later), for the purpose of training men and women for Christian service." Then there was that standing invitation from the churches in Brazil to serve in a double role as evangelist and Bible teacher. In a personal letter, Professor J. A. Toews wrote about the need for workers and highlighted that call, saying:

> During my recent visit and ministry to South America I found also some distinct "footprints" of the work and witness of Brother and Sister Kasdorf. Many leading brethren in Brazil, and I could add, South America, hope and pray that Br. Kasdorf will some day return to the "land of unlimited possibilities." . . . I would appreciate an opportunity for sharing my concerns about the work of our Brotherhood in the South— but where and when? . . . We must find the time for a "heart to heart" talk.

Regrettably, the opportunity for such "heart to heart talk" did not present itself until years later when J. A. Toews spent time in Fresno, writing *A History of the Mennonite Brethren Church*.

At the time I received those letters from Ewert and Toews, I was theologically ill-equipped to teach at MBBC in Winnipeg or at a growing Bible institute in Brazil. I knew the churches there, was familiar with the people and culture, and was deeply aware of the need to train national leaders and missionaries within the land. I had the passion to do so, but not adequate tools. I was still on my detour in academia and had not yet reached the place where I was able to pursue the type of education needed for those tasks. Therefore, I had to decide whether to continue teaching languages where I was or accept the invitation from Pacific College and move to Fresno, where the prospects to pursue theological and missiological education appeared to be brighter than in Huntington. The longer we stayed in Indiana, however, the more attached we became to the college and the friendly, hospitable people of "Hoosier Country."

The thought of terminating after only one year of teaching was hard; it even seemed unfair. Yet if I wanted to serve within our denomination and simultaneously pursue missiological studies, it seemed most prudent to make the move while the children were still young and the door to teaching and studying in California was open. We prayed about it and decided to accept the call to Pacific College. Melvin Loewen, the new academic dean, sent me the contract which I signed on 30 January 1968, with plans to make our move that coming summer.

We arrived in Fresno on 5 July. The summer heat was intense, reminiscent of the temperature in Brazil. We rented a dormitory apartment at the college until we found a more permanent place to live. John and Esther Berg, local realtors, were most helpful in finding a house that was affordable and suitable for our family needs. On 27 July we moved into our own home on 4646 North Third Street, situated near Franklin Thomas Elementary School, Tioga Junior High School, and Hoover High School, where our three children enrolled that fall. The financial arrangements were in our favor. That was the first home we owned. It was truly a place where we felt at home. There our children grew up; there we entertained many guests from near and far; there we lived until one year past my retirement from teaching at the Mennonite Brethren Biblical Seminary (MBBS).

From 15 to 26 July Pacific College and MBBS cosponsored the "Institute on Evangelism," an intensive course for pastors, church leaders, and missionaries. Seminary students could take it for credit. Already in April, when I was still at Huntington College, I received a letter from J. B. Toews inviting me to "join this group for intensive study." Among the teachers were such eminent guest lecturers as Myron Augsburger, Donald Jacobs, and J. J. Toews. I was tremendously impressed with their depth of insight, scope of knowledge, and the eloquence with which these men presented their lectures. These seminars were for me an affirmation that I had come to the right place where I could become seriously involved in the mission of the church. Even if my primary assignment was teaching languages, which I thoroughly enjoyed, I also envisioned teaching mission courses, an opportunity that came sooner than expected. A few years down the road I was asked to design a special curriculum and head a summer school for missionary training.

Our first few months in Fresno were quite eventful. Before school started in the fall, Pacific College had its annual faculty retreat at Hume Lake Bible Camp to which the spouses and children of faculty members were invited. The drive from Fresno into California's magnificent Sierra and scenic forests all the way to the campground was in itself a serene experience. The first afternoon was given to sports and recreation before tackling the more serious agenda items. Frieda and the children were somewhat surprised to see me sign up for baseball, a game I had never played before. They found a nice spot to sit under a shade tree and proudly watched the game, saying to each other: "Just watch dad run the wrong way." That shows at what level their confidence in my potential performance really was. But that's not all.

When my turn came to bat the ball, I hit it like a pro, making my family exceedingly proud—but only for a second or two. Pleased by the fact that I had hit the ball so hard that it flew through the air to the other side of the field, I gave it all I had to make a home run. On the way I met my colleague, Don Braun, who was coming in the opposite direction. I had no idea why until I saw him wave his hands and heard him shout: "Hey, Hans, you are running the wrong way!" That not only disqualified me for the game in progress; it also ended my exceedingly short baseball career for good. But it did not end the utter amusement, fun and laughter which these brief moments brought to those who watched my actual performance, especially my children. They and their mother have not forgotten that episode, even after more than thirty years.

During my first two or three years at Pacific College I concentrated on teaching German and Spanish and a small class in Portuguese. The majority, however, took German. With the approval of the academic dean, I was able to purchase an excellent language program developed by Hermann Kessler and Associates in Germany. It was at that time a new method of language learning by total immersion. The program was called *Deutsch für Ausländer* (German for foreigners) and consisted of three levels. Each level was built on the other with a clearly defined focus on listening (the key to language learning), conversation, reading, and writing. Grammar, history, and culture were pedagogically integrated and supplemented by maps, cards, charts and other practical tools which made learning enjoyable and teaching effective.

The students were as pleased with the program as I was. But that does not mean that every student in my class was successful in learning German. In fact, I have had two or three students who may have been brilliant in other disciplines but could not learn a foreign language. One such student went on to graduate school, got a Ph.D. degree in psychology, served as counselor and later became a Mennonite Brethren pastor. When I was invited to speak at a mission conference in his church, he introduced me to the congregation as a most effective teacher in every subject, except one. "In German," he said, "Mr. Kasdorf did not teach me anything." When my turn came to speak, I thanked him for his gracious introduction and added by saying to the congregation: "Your pastor is right. In fourteen years of language teaching I have had a few students who did not even learn the difference between German and Spanish, let alone the language itself. He was one of them." That broke the ice, but not our friendship.

In the spring of 1971 I completed my third year of language teaching at Fresno Pacific College. They had been good years in terms of both classroom experience and relationship with faculty and students. Edmund Janzen in the Bible Department and Wilfred Martens in the Department of English were especially supportive of my endeavors. We shared many common interests in the ongoing life of the College. Wilfred's office was next to mine which made it easy to discuss and exchange ideas about language and literature. I found his knowledge and use of the English language always stimulating and inspiring.

As I had done at the University of Oregon and Huntington College, so I continued my involvement with students on a personal level regarding their academic progress as well as their spiritual welfare. That opened opportunities to assist several of them to establish or deepen a vital relationship with Jesus Christ as Savior and Lord. Another thing I found very encouraging was the openness of the administration to suggestions from individual faculty members. From the president and the academic dean to the departmental chairpersons there was an apparent eagerness to listen to innovative ideas as long as they contributed to the overall benefit and goal of the school. That gave me boldness to introduce several new courses, among them Latin American Cultures and Issues in World Mission. That proved to be a good move.

In the meantime the college hired a Spanish teacher which reduced my load in the language department and allowed me to teach one or two courses a semester in other disciplines. I even teamed up with my new colleague, Samuel Resendez, and took students to Mexico City for crosscultural exposure and learning experience. My purpose for doing so was to assist the students in developing a vision for world mission through crosscultural studies, to learn as much as possible about Mexican history and culture, to enrich my own teaching in those areas, and to deepen my personal insight for missiological studies. It was also on that first trip that three students in my Spanish class expressed a desire to become saved. Two of them knocked on my door at 5 o'clock in the morning, and I was able to help them find their way to the Lord Jesus. In retrospect I can only hope that my ten years of teaching foreign languages and other subjects at Fresno Pacific College have made a modest contribution to its expanding vision of shaping and training men and women to be disciples and servants of Jesus Christ in this postmodern world of the twenty-first century.

Before accepting the teaching assignment at Pacific College, I had expressed my intent to take courses at the seminary in the area of theology and mission. The administration gave its endorsement, and I enrolled at the Mennonite Brethren Biblical Seminary adjacent to the college and began studies toward an M.R.E. degree with a focus on evangelism and mission. The courses I found especially helpful in this particular program were cultural anthropology with Paul Hiebert, principles and practice of mission with J. B. Toews and Melvin Loewen (guest lecturer), Christian education in the local church with George Konrad, the Synoptic Gospels with Orlando Wiebe, and Asian church history with Henry Krahn.

In addition, I immersed myself in reading and directed studies to cover areas of personal interest and course requirements. I wanted to know and understand the *why*, *how*, and *what for* of the demands for the rapid changes of quasi-revolutionary proportions that had ushered in a new era in the worldwide mission of the church. Concurrent with these mission studies I was also working on an M.A. program in historical theology for which my final year at the University of Oregon had provided a good foundation, especially the reading of primary sources covering the period from the twelfth through the fifteenth centuries. The greatest challenge in both programs was to stay focused on the centrality of the message of God's kingdom in relation to the kingdoms of this world. What I was really studying was in essence the tension between Gospel and culture.

Furthermore, my studies coincided with what was known as *Evangelismo a Fundo* (Evangelism-in-Depth), a Latin American movement conceived by R. Kenneth Strachan, general director of the Latin America Mission.

From its very beginning I had taken a vital interest in this exceptional undertaking. God was visibly honoring the vision and efforts, method and means of this movement. Men and women were involved in mobilizing the entire church in one country at a time to take the revitalizing message of God's kingdom to village after village and city after city, bringing the campaign to a climax in the national capital. The entire operation of the movement was based on a rather simple principle formulated by Dr. Strachan in these words: "The expansion of any movement is in direct proportion to its success in mobilizing its total membership in continuous propagation of its beliefs." What I found most intriguing about this *Strachan Theorem* was not its theological basis, but its almost simplistic sociological premise with profound implications for fruitful mission.

As I read Strachan's book, *The Inescapable Calling,* plus countless articles and reports in English and Spanish journals and church papers, I decided to write a missiological project on "A Decade of Evangelism-in-Depth in Latin America." Again, my superiors at Pacific College supported the idea, and my committee at the seminary with Paul Hiebert as chairman, accepted my proposal without reservation. Frieda and the children shared in the sacrifice that allowed me to do field research in different Latin American countries. By putting in extra hours of teaching during the month of November, it was possible to finish my classes a week ahead of schedule. That gave me time for research from the second week of December 1970 through January 1971. That meant being away from my family during Christmas.

Careful planning allowed me to meet with church leaders, teachers, professors and some missionaries in Mexico, Guatemala, Costa Rica, Panama, Colombia, Equador, and Brazil. Although I was a complete stranger to most of the people I met (except in Brazil), I was always cordially received and graciously hosted. Whenever possible, I went to the city where EID had its headquarters, usually the capital. In most countries the EID campaign had already run its course, but the results were still evident. Only in Mexico did I witness EID in action. What impressed me more than anything else about the movement as I saw it in Mexico City was the focus on and commitment to prayer. That was also the first thing Juan Isais, the director of the campaign, pointed out to me when I visited with him. He spoke with enthusiasm and fervor about the things that were beginning to happen because people across the land were rallying to pray for revival. "Wherever you go," he said, "you will find people praying for EID." He was right. In shops, restaurants, stores, and hotels were posters on walls, windows and doors saying, *Aqui Rogamos Para Evangelismo a Fundo* (Here we pray for Evangelism-in-Depth).

The highlight of my trip was at the Latin American Theological Seminary in San José, Costa Rica. Not only did I find there most of the resources

I needed for my project but also an ideal place to interact with such key Latin leaders and educators as Justo González, Rubén Lores, Victor Monterroso, and Dayton Roberts. Their vision and faith was the driving force that made EID an authentically indigenous movement to meet spiritual, social, and material needs at the grassroots level. They interpreted evangelism to include literacy programs, health services, and a variety of developmental projects locally designed to improve the quality of life for the people. In a personal conversation over Sunday dinner in the home of Dr. and Mrs. Roberts, they characterized the ongoing movement in Spanish and Portuguese America as nothing short of a revolution—not a political one, but "a spiritual revolution in evangelism."

Due to surgery, hospitalization, and extended recovery time, I was unable to complete my thesis that spring quarter. Gratefully, however, the Lord gave sufficient strength to finish my teaching responsibilities at Pacific for the year. In late spring of 1972 I submitted a 290-page research project to the seminary faculty. Meanwhile, I was also studying historical theology with a major in Anabaptism within the larger context of the Reformation. With the approval of my advisers, A. J. Klassen and J. B. Toews, I wrote a thesis on "The Church Concept of the Mennonite Brethren in Anabaptist Perspective" which I submitted in October of the same year. These studies were an incentive to teach a course at the college on the Anabaptist movement. My special emphasis was on the Anabaptists' understanding of the church and their contribution to missionary thinking and action at a time when few of the mainline Reformers gave any thought to the evangelization of the world.

39

Lengthening the Service Cords
(1968-1970s)

Enlarge the place of your tent;
let the curtains of your habitations stretch out.
Lengthen your cords and strengthen your stakes.
—Excerpt from *Isaiah 54.*

The Mennonite Brethren Churches of the Pacific District envisioned the 1960s to be their "Decade of Enlargement." In denominational terms that meant intensifying evangelistic efforts, multiplying local congregations, and deepening the spiritual life of church members. By way of analogy, the 1970s were for me a decade of enlargement in terms of theological education, missiological thinking, and church ministry within and beyond my own denomination.

When the Institute of Evangelism, jointly sponsored by Pacific College and the Biblical Seminary during the 1960s, was phased out, the decade of the 1970s was rife with ideas and efforts to fill the gap. One of these was what we tentatively called a Community Lay Training Program (CLTP) envisioned and designed by the college. The purpose was to offer pastors and lay leaders in churches and Christian service agencies the opportunity to improve their education through evening classes, summer school, and other modules to fit their needs and schedules.

In the summer of 1969 I had the assignment to visit pastors and religious leaders in Fresno and surrounding areas to introduce and discuss with them the proposed program. My notes reflect that many expressed keen interest. Over seventy pastors signed up for more information. They also gave me additional names of potential participants, who were followed up with a letter and appropriate literature. While I do not know the actual number of those who enrolled in these courses, the administration was pleased with the outcome.

These contacts gave me a picture of the religious mosaic of Fresno and a vision for the inner city with its glare and glamour as well as its woes and wants. These experiences enhanced my own teaching effectiveness and opened the door for the college to increase its involvement in inner city ministry programs. My colleague Edmund Janzen, chairman of the

Bible Department, was my strong supporter and became the leader in this area of service. Through all of this I was inspired to learn more about the nature and dynamics of urbanology for a more fruitful ministry—even while I was teaching foreign languages.

The early years at Pacific also paved the way to conference involvement. I was familiar with the Canadian Mennonite Brethren Churches and their conference structures, but less so with those in the United States. In April 1971 William Neufeld, Pacific District Minister, asked me to be the speaker at the annual conference at the Convention Center Theater in Fresno. The theme was "The Biblical Basis for Evangelism." Some months after the convention I received an invitation from the Commission of Evangelism and Christian Education to speak at a convocation on evangelism to convene in Denver, 20-22 March 1973. Loyal Martin, secretary of the Commission, wrote, "We [have] in mind something in the nature of the messages you presented at the Pacific District Conference last fall. . . . We hope to bring together 250 Mennonite Brethren from across the United States for these sessions."

Even if the overall theme was the same, I did not want to repeat what I had said at the conference in Fresno. Guided by the apostle Paul's challenge in Colossians, I asked God for appropriate Bible passages, insight and wisdom to grasp (and be grasped by) the redemptive content, and the ability to proclaim the mystery of Christ in a manner that would motivate the participating brothers and sisters to act wisely and to make the most of every evangelistic opportunity in conversations and relations with outsiders. I worked long hours in preparation for the convocation, only to discover the true nature of "the jar of clay" in which I carry the treasure of ministry, including lectures and sermons. On the flight to Denver I wanted to reread the biblical texts and review my notes as I usually did on my way to a speaking engagement. But this time that was not to be. Instead, I had the shock of my life: neither Bible nor notes were in my briefcase. I had left them on the shelf in the entry hall of our house. Fortunately, the Gideons had been in the hotel where the convocation was held and placed a Bible in each room. That's where I made another discovery, namely that "the all-surpassing power for [ministry] is from God and not from us," as Paul puts it. I have often had great liberty, though not without fear and trembling, in delivering lectures and sermons. My experience in Denver stands out as a case in point.

The decade of the seventies presented more opportunities to speak in local churches and at mission conferences than I was able to fulfill. The reason, I believe, lay in the nature of the changing times in the wake of World War II. During the 1950s and 1960s independent nation states had emerged in large numbers; the so-called "daughter churches" had become "sister churches" in partnership; the unprecedented resurgence of world religions was rapidly becoming a competitor of Christianity. Our own congregations of the third and fourth-generation Mennonite Brethren had gone through a variety of changes as well. The older people still remembered the "golden age" of mission when missionaries went out for a lifetime of service. They were anxious to hear what God had done through these men and women in other lands and cultures. The younger generation, particularly those of high school and college age, did not think so much of a long term commitment; yet they, too, showed a vital interest in world mission and came to find out where they would fit in to serve the Lord. People whom I missed most often at mission festivals and conferences were families with teen-age and younger children. That gave me no minor concern for the future of Mennonite Brethren mission.

This was also the time when the reverberations of Evangelism-in-Depth (EID) from the northern and western Latin American countries reached the Mennonite churches in Brazil. That seems to have given the impulse for launching a more modest campaign of their own designated as "Thrust Evangelism." This independent effort was initially aimed at reaching pockets of German-speaking people in rural areas and small towns who were neither an integral part of the Mennonite colonies nor of the Portuguese-speaking population of Southern Brazil. As such, they would most likely have been overlooked by the regular EID program if and when that would ever come to that part of the country. Unfortunately, it never did. That increased the incentive of the Mennonite Brethren to expand and reenforce their plans for intensive evangelism beyond the ethnic German communities.

Upon the request of our churches in Brazil, the Board of Missions and Services asked me to serve as a consultant in drawing up a preliminary draft with a tentative timetable, geographic perimeters, service teams, goals, and financial implications for Thrust Evangelism. I had been away from Brazil since 1962. Much had happened since then. What I found particularly gratifying upon my return in 1970 was the unity of the German conference which was organized during my time in Blumenau; there were also signs of a healthy development of a Portuguese counterpart. My hope and prayer from the beginning was for the two to merge into one strong conference of Mennonite Brethren churches for greater missional impact.

Despite the brevity of my visit I had the opportunity to preach in most of the German-speaking congregations during parts of December 1970 and January 1971, and to assist our brethren in explaining to our churches the plans and operative principles envisioned by the Thrust Evangelism committee. An extra bonus for me was that I could visit with family, friends and relatives between services and meetings. However, I missed my father, who had gone to be with the Lord two years earlier.

Before I left for home in early January 1971, representatives of the South American Conference (SAC) invited me to come back for a longer period of time to serve as evangelist and speaker at deeper life meetings which the churches within various colonies were planning for the winter months from June to September of that year. The request was that I serve at least five weeks in Paraguay, five in Brazil, and one week in Uruguay. That was also to be the time to finalize plans for Thrust Evangelism. The task seemed overwhelming. I went home without making a commitment, except to say that I would pray about the matter. As we parted, the brethren pledged to do the same.

When I came home I shared these requests with my family and discussed the question with the college administration. Things worked out faster than expected. Meanwhile, I enjoyed my teaching at the college. The time I spent preparing messages to preach at sixty-five to seventy meetings scheduled for the months of June through August was inspiring, yet not without some anguish.

As soon as the school year ended, we went to British Columbia. Frieda and the children stayed with her parents, while I drove back to Fresno and left for my first assignment in Paraguay. After five weeks of intensive preaching and counseling, I flew to São Paulo where I was to meet Frieda and Evelyn. They arrived on schedule at the international airport in Campinas and traveled with me for the remaining six or seven weeks of ministry. Dianne and David, our oldest two children, stayed with their grandparents until we returned from Brazil. This turned out to be a beneficial time in their lives, getting to know their *Oma* and *Opa* Reimer as well as their great-aunts, uncles, aunts, and cousins more intimately than they had ever known them before. Besides that, they also had a chance to earn some money. David worked at Reimer's Nursery and Dianne in the raspberry fields. Evelyn traveled with us and met for the first time in her life my side of the family, including some thirty of her first cousins. All three of our children have pleasant memories of that eventful summer of 1971.

The itinerary in Brazil included the younger churches in Santa Catarina. Brother Hansi Görtz, pastor of the Xaxim church in Curitiba and moderator of the Mennonite Brethren Conference, took us in his small Volkswagen to different churches in Santa Catarina. Some of these congregations were the fruit of our earlier labors when we served in Blumenau; others were the result of concentrated mission efforts on the part of our conference.

One of the personal highlights on this trip was when brother Görtz stopped at my old family homestead in the Krauel. To stand together with my wife and daughter in front of the house my parental family had built more than thirty years ago, the place I had at one time with deep affection called *Home*, ignited my mind with a thousand memories. This was the very place from which many prayers had ascended to our Father in heaven. It was also the place where I had personally experienced the saving grace of God and turned my life over to the Lord Jesus. Then, too, this was the place where the call of the Lord had become clear to me that *some day* I should make known to others the same "amazing grace" that He had made known to me. That *some day* had become *now*. I was moved as I saw the evidence of God's transforming grace in the lives of people I had known during the years when I lived at the Krauel.

One Sunday after the evening service in a rural church, we were invited by the Heinrich Grasmücks for hot chocolate. As they were telling their conversion story, Heinrich turned to me and said in his Swabian dialect (which I will translate): "You know what a rascal I was when you worked as clerk in the co-op store. But the Gospel has changed me and my entire family. If it had not been for you Mennonites, I would not have come to Jesus." Such moments animated my faith in the power of the Gospel which I was now privileged to proclaim with boldness and joy.

Throughout the entire time in Paraguay and Brazil attendance at the meetings was encouraging and the Spirit of the Lord visibly at work among men, women, and children. Even years later I have met people who told me that they were among those who accepted the Lord when I preached in their church. I was also much encouraged when I met with the leaders of the German-speaking *Associação* in Curitiba and the Portuguese-speaking *Convenção* in São Paulo to finalize plans for the Thrust Evangelism program. The unanimous decision was to invite J. J. Toews from Canada as evangelist accompanied by local teams of men and women to serve as organizers, singers, musicians, and counselors.

That brings me to the final days of my itinerary. While preaching in Colônia Nova, my siblings offered to take us to Uruguay in a Volkswagen Combi and my nephew, Hans Esau, volunteered to drive. We traveled from east to west along the northern rim across the entire country. The population was exceedingly sparse with few trees and shrubs in sight. The road was good, but there were next to no services along the way. Due to political unrest and economic depression, Uruguay had fallen on hard times. That was evident everywhere, even in the churches. People seemed to be discouraged. We witnessed some of that in Montevideo when we stayed a day or two with Henry and Helen Dueck, friends from college days in Winnipeg.

We got home in time for the new school year and were glad to be together once again as one family. The children were in school, Frieda was busy taking care of the household and typing for university students and professors, I was back in the classroom, and life was back to normal.

Several weeks after returning home, Vernon Wiebe, General Secretary of the Board of Missions and Services, sent me a copy of a letter from Jacob

G. Penner. As secretary of the South American Mennonite Brethren Conference, Mr. Penner writes in behalf of the M.B. churches of Brazil, Paraguay and Uruguay to express their gratitude to the Board of Missions for "the richly beneficial ministry of Brother Hans Kasdorf in our midst. . . . The Lord has been pleased to use him and has confirmed his ministry."

In view of the rapidly changing scene of world mission, demands for intensive training of missionary candidates became more imperative than ever. In fact, many veteran missionaries who had been forced to come home in the 1950s and the turbulent decade of the 1960s, were being reassigned and asked for updated training for their new assignments. An increasing number of short-term missionaries designated as Christian Service and Good News Corps workers also needed training in special skills for their tasks. That led to the creation of a summer school for prefield missionary education which became known as "Church Mission Institute" (CMI). I was asked to head this program and remained deeply involved in it from its inception in 1973 until 1985, when my colleague Henry Schmidt became its new director.

My first task was to draft a curriculum proposal on "Prefield Missionary Training for the Sending Church." The idea of prefield education with a focus on cross-cultural witness was for me like a vision come true. Since I had never had that kind of training I knew from experience how important it was for serving in cross-cultural settings. That made my assignment even more exhilarating and challenging. In consultation with the seminary and college faculties and administrators of the Board of Missions and Services, I envisioned a rather intensive training program for eleven weeks from June through August. While the curriculum was specifically designed to meet the requirements for Mennonite Brethren long- and short-term missionaries, we also attracted participants from Missionary Aviation Fellowship, Wycliffe Bible Translators, Inter-Varsity (Christian) Fellowship, and even from the *Liebenzeller Mission* in Germany.

After each summer session I wrote a comprehensive review, including positive and negative feedback from participants. I soon realized that format and length of the program was unrealistic for a variety of reasons, especially for families with children. So we reduced it to seven, and eventually to four weeks. The shorter program no longer allowed us to take students for a week or two to Mexico, as I had done before. But it did not diminish the quality of training under competent men and women I had learned to know in different contexts and was able to recruit as teachers. Most of them had field experience and were skilled in training missionaries to serve and live among people of other cultures and worldviews.

While I found the administrative aspect of the program least enjoyable, the pleasure of teaching and interacting with highly motivated participants made up for much of the drudgery. Throughout those twelve years, I tried to project myself into the situation of the candidates, visualize the context of the field where they would subsequently serve, and then designed personalized courses that would help them serve effectively in their cross-cultural settings. The most frequent compliments I received from CMI "graduates" were on such subjects as Field and Area Studies, Language Learning Skills, and Bible Study Methods.

When I did my research on Evangelism-in-Depth in Latin America, I also scheduled a visit with Dr. Ross Kinsler at the Presbyterian Theological Seminary in Guatemala, the center for Theological Education by Extension (TEE). This concept gained wide appeal in a relatively short time, particularly in the younger churches. I was intrigued with the program and shared with the seminary faculty in Fresno some of my insights based on the fundamental principles of operation. While the idea of TEE was in its earliest phase of germination, the level of interest was high. Under the leadership of the Academic Dean A. J. Klassen and in cooperation with the Board of Missions and Services, the seminary launched a pioneer project at the *Instituto Biblico Asunción* (IBA) in Paraguay. The IBA requested teachers from Anglo America who could offer advanced courses specifically designed for church leaders, preachers, and missionaries working among their own people in the Paraguayan context.

From July to November 1976, I was invited to teach in one of these extension programs. I had been in Paraguay numerous times before, but for Frieda this was the first time. Our youngest daughter Evelyn was also with us, whereas the oldest two children stayed in Fresno to work and continue their education. We lived in a modest house close to the school where I was teaching. Evelyn enrolled in the International School at the opposite end of the city and had to spend several hours in a school van each day. Frieda participated in women's meetings and made some wonderful friends. At the end of the Paraguayan school year, we took the bus to Brazil where I had additional speaking engagements. Along the way the bus stopped at the Iguaçú Falls that rank high on the list of the magnificent wonders of nature. We have fond memories of those months.

From 1975 to 1987 I was privileged to serve on the Board of Missions and Services. During my year at Tabor College I learned to know the mission administrators and staff in the Hillsboro office and became somewhat familiar with the dynamics of our mission operation. I also read the mission reports in conference yearbooks and church papers. All this served as a valuable background to make a knowledgeable decision when I was nominated and elected to become a member of the Board. Up until then I had never generated much affection for board or committee work. I simply did not see that to be the best investment of my time and energy and declined to serve on conference boards. But this time I could not do so with a good conscience. I accepted the challenge and believe that I was able to make a positive contribution to advance the cause of world mission, even without being the most vocal member of the board.

What I found particularly energizing was the opportunity to assist our Board in its demanding task of informing local churches about the global shifts and changes in mission, particularly since World War II. My concern was to dispel myths and misconceptions and help churches understand the current conditions in the light of historical, religious, and sociopolitical developments. Without negating weaknesses and failures of the past, my focus was more on the positive outcome anchored in the abiding biblical principles that are an integral part of the gospel of the kingdom entrusted by the Lord of mission to His church in the world.

40

Deepening Missiological Stakes

*The good news for man and his world is
that God is working to bring about total harmony
in the whole creation through Jesus Christ. . . .
Here is the basis for the world's mission.*
–Yamada Takashi in D. Jacobs, *Pilgrimage in Mission*

While teaching at Pacific College I received unanticipated invitations for speaking in churches and at conferences within as well as outside my denominational boundaries. This confirmed my conviction that the kingdom of God is much bigger than any group of churches in its embrace, be they Catholic, Protestant or Anabaptist in confessional orientation. As these invitations increased, the nature of my ministry became academically and spiritually more demanding.

A vision for personal growth in public ministry is not without exposure to hazards along the way. It requires an appropriate foundation to endure the test of time and carefully defined criteria of accountability to assess and measure the results. As a tree with shallow roots grows emaciated branches and produces lean fruit, so the historical records bear witness to the fact that Christians can easily fail and falter without a reliable foundation. Menno Simons, one of the founding fathers of the free church movement, was guided by that same principle and placed the following epigraph at the head of his fruitful ministry: "For no one can lay any foundation other than the one already laid, which is Jesus Christ" (1 Cor. 3:11). My desire was to have that kind of foundation for my present ministry as well as for a possible future cross-cultural assignment. That would mean spending another three or four years in missiological education to anchor the stakes of the ever-lengthening service cords in a solid foundation. While this was not a new insight, the idea became more urgent within the college context where I saw the potential for developing a missionary training program.

I felt comfortable with the foundation I had gained for teaching foreign languages at the college level, but I could not say the same for missiology. To train those who would serve cross-culturally meant being a missionary to missionaries, a task far bigger than I was able to assume at the time.

For one thing, we had come upon an era in the history of world mission with unprecedented sociopolitical and ethnoreligious upheavals. The missionary movement often found itself overwhelmed and floundering in its own weakness. Furthermore, mission as a task and missions as agencies for that task had become objects of criticism, especially in some academic circles. Moreover, the mounting volume of books and articles written on the subject and the increasing number of national and international councils, conferences, and consultations organized to discuss historical and emerging mission issues gave evidence of growing tensions that were often less creative than destructive.

Under these new circumstances I had come to a deep conviction gleaned from an old prophetic metaphor which I could not ignore. Slightly paraphrased it reads as follows: "Whenever the cords of service become longer, the stakes to hold them must be put deeper" (Isa. 54:2f.). The message for me was clear. If I wanted to serve my generation in the area of mission in a rapidly changing world, I would have to become serious about missiological studies.

Through courses taken at the seminary in Fresno, extensive readings in missional literature, and teaching a course on "Issues in World Mission" at Pacific College, I began to understand missiology as a discipline different from any other; I began to see and recognize it as a multifaceted field of study in its own right. By its very design, missiology crosses curricular frontiers and boundaries while at the same time embracing academic disciplines within the social and human sciences as well as the classics. Its purpose is to clarify and aid the dissemination of the transcending message of the kingdom of God, anchored in the teachings of the Scriptures. While the human sciences provide a useful framework and structure at the horizontal level, biblical studies form the core of the theological content which gives missiology a distinctive vertical dimension reaching out to the transcending God in Christ. Without that biblical core, missiology is no more than an intellectual exercise that may generate compassion for physical needs; but seldom will it develop a vision and compassion for the lostness of the human soul. Christian missiology calls for a comprehensive approach to every aspect of the human predicament in this world and for keeping the Gospel central in its task.

That was a valuable discovery. To reach my goal at the end of the detour, I needed to apply myself to in-depth studies of the demanding discipline which the Germans wrote about under the rubric of *Missionswissenschaft* (science of mission) and the Dutch had talked and written about *Zendingswetenschap* (science of sentness) centuries before the term *missiology* was ever used in the English language. That awareness led me to reconnect with the Institute of Church Growth (ICG) and its founding fathers, McGavran and Tippett, with whose work I had become acquainted during graduate studies in Eugene, Oregon. In the meantime, this modest ICG had moved to Pasadena, California, and become the prestigious School of World Mission (SWM) of Fuller Theological Seminary with Arthur F. Glasser as the new academic dean.

After four years of teaching at Pacific College, I was granted one semester of study leave. In the fall of 1972 I attended a two-day orientation seminar in Pasadena during which the professors of the SWM introduced themselves and the courses they would teach that semester. Students from many countries participated in these sessions and told of things God was doing in their lands. I was impressed by the spirit of prayer and intercession evident among faculty and students, and by the positive manner in which people spoke about world mission. That was refreshing.

Once my application had been processed and I was accepted into the doctoral program of missiological studies, I was fortunate to find a modest room for rent in the attic of a huge house across the street from the seminary in Pasadena. It was a quiet corner that served me well as a "prophet's chamber" for that fall quarter. There I could meditate and study early and late when the library was closed; there I was also undisturbed to cook and eat my meals or rest and sleep as needed. It was about as ideal as I could have had it to concentrate on missiology. Every Friday afternoon I took the bus for a five to six-hour ride to Fresno, spent the weekend with the family and then returned to Pasadena on Monday evening to be at the seminary for classes on Tuesday.

During the winter and spring quarters of 1974, I was able to make similar arrangements to complete residence requirements for a doctorate. By "similar arrangements" I mean that I was again commuting every week between Fresno and Pasadena, the only difference being that I was simultaneously teaching a full load at Pacific College. Thanks to the gracious accommodation of the administration, the considerate cooperation of the students, and an extra amount of energy supplied by God, I was able to teach my weekly courses between 8:00 a.m. and 5:00 p.m. every Monday. During the summers of 1973, 1974, and 1975 I read as much as possible and wrote numerous papers to complete course requirements and prepare for qualifying examinations.

I found the time spent at the SWM of Fuller Theological Seminary very enriching. There was something about that place that was not only intellectually challenging, it was also spiritually invigorating. The professors came from a variety of church backgrounds and diverse academic training. Among them were engineers and sociologists, theologians and historians, anthropologists and linguists—all working toward one common goal: the growth of the church. This was based on the premise that God wants the church to be planted, nurtured, and to grow within every race and people group around the globe. These men and women were not mere theoreticians. Every one had years of missionary experience, was proficient in several languages, and well equipped to transmit from their wealth of knowledge to the students those interdisciplinary and transcultural elements that were in keeping with the discipline and character of missiology.

What impressed me most deeply about my professors was their unequivocal commitment to the authority of the Scriptures and to the great mandate of the risen Christ: "Make disciples of all peoples." I interpreted the emphasis on disciple-making as a prerequisite for discipleship, a central theological and ethical issue of evangelical Anabaptism. In several shorter class presentations and in a major seminar paper, I sought to incorporate the Anabaptist understanding of the church and mission as well as their concept of discipleship. In each case I was as pleased with the response from my professors and fellow students as I felt gratified for treating a subject in mission which heretofore had obviously been less known than it deserved to be, especially in a place as the SWM. Even if I was not convinced of the prevailing principles of pragmatism promoted by some of my teachers, I was profoundly impressed with the theological depth evidenced by others, particularly Arthur F. Glasser, J. Edwin Orr and Alan R. Tippett. It was an undeserved privilege to sit under their teaching, read their writings with an open and critical mind, and interact with them on a personal level.

Under the deanship of Dr. Glasser, the School of World Mission attracted church leaders and intellectual Christians from all over the world. Many of those enrolled in the doctoral program were urged to write a dissertation in their mother tongue. The purpose was to make the result of their research available to the churches of their homeland. In my case, even though I was not a native of Germany, Professor Glasser asked me to write my dissertation in the German language. His interest was in Gustav Warneck (1834-1910), the founding father of protestant missiology and first professor ever to occupy a legitimate chair of mission studies at the University of Halle. Glasser suggested that I explore and analyze Warneck's comprehensive mission theory in historical context, keeping in mind the church growth philosophy. But where could I find the sources? Only God knew.

In books by his son Johannes, missionary educator among the Batak of Indonesia, I had read *about* Gustav Warneck, but little *by* him. Neither my colleagues at Pacific College nor the teachers at MBBS could offer any help. My search in Fresno's libraries turned up two items: *Abriß einer Geschichte der Missionen von der Reformation bis auf die Gegenwart* and an article on "Missions to the Heathen B: Protestant Missions" in *The New Schaff-Herzog Encyclopedia of Religious Knowledge*. That was barely a drop in the bucket about the missiological thinking of a man who had penned more than four hundred books and articles on the subject, carried on a voluminous correspondence with missionaries and mission thinkers around the globe, taught missiology at the university, and for twenty-five years edited the first scientific missiological journal which he founded in 1874.

Efforts of the Hiebert Library staff as well as my own research in the Theological Union Library in San Francisco brought meager results. But then the unforeseen happened: In March of 1973, I was invited by the *Liebenzeller Mission* in Germany to give a series of lectures at its annual missionary consultation on biblical principles of church growth. Men like Ernst Vatter and *Pfarrer* Lienhard Pflaum of Liebenzell were just as eager to expose European missionaries to the church growth movement as Dr. Glasser of the School of World Mission was to introduce the subject to the German church context. I felt inadequate for the task and accepted the assignment with fear and trembling. This was my first trip to Europe and I did not know what to expect. Yet the people accepted me as a "brother in Christ." They were also most gracious in their response to my fourteen lectures which the *Verlag der Liebenzeller Mission* subsequently published in a book entitled *Gemeindewachstum als missionarisches Ziel*.

The meetings were held at a retreat center in Wildberg, a serene spot deep in the Black Forest. While heavy layers of snow still covered much of the forest, the presence of crows and sparrows, larks and finches plus a variety of other birds gave evidence that spring was approaching. Among the mission executives, missionaries, and pastors who attended the consultation were several pioneers of the prestigious *Neuendettelsau Missionary Society* where both Warnecks, father and son, had been household names in their time. When I mentioned my interest in G. Warneck's writings, two retired veterans came up to me after the session and said that they had some of the books in which I might be interested.

I was back in Fresno barely a week when I received a letter from one of the older brothers, saying:

> Heart-felt thanks, dear brother in the Lord, for your blessed ministry! I am returning back to my work with new inspiration. For thirty years—from 1936-1966—I was missionary in New Guinea . . . and during the course of my activity was privileged to lead thousands of Papuas through holy baptism into the Church of Jesus Christ. . . . God be with you and bless you! Yours in Christ, Hans Wagner.

A separate note in the same envelope reads: "Missionary Berghäuser sends warmest greetings. The five volumes of Professor Dr. Warneck's *Evangelische Missionslehre* are available to you and will be mailed to your address in America at once." That was clearly the Lord's response to my need.

Not long thereafter, Dr. Glasser went to Europe where he met Dr. Arno Lehmann from the University of Halle (Martin-Luther-Universität) in the German Democratic Republic. Professor Lehmann was at that time occupying the chair of missiology established by Warneck some eighty years earlier. I wrote to Dr. Lehmann, and in October 1974 received a letter from him expressing delight that a student at the SWM in America might be willing to write a dissertation in German on the founder of *Missionswissenschaft*. At the same time he offered to be my *Doktor-Vater* and guide me through my doctoral program by proxy. The SWM gave its approval, appointed Professor Glasser as my principal adviser, and gave me the liberty to recommend an outside reader whom I found in J. B. Toews, my former teacher at MBBS in Fresno.

I could not have wished for a more qualified committee. Each of the men was known for his scholarly competence in the academic arena as well as for his outstanding work as missionary and/or mission administrator within his respective denominational tradition. It was a unique international and interconfessional triad, representing the best of Evangelical/Lutheran, Conciliar/Reformed, and Anabaptist/Mennonite theology of mission. I treasure their counsel, which helped me become a *hybrid missiologist* anchored in the biblical theology of trinitarian mission with the gospel of the kingdom of God in its very center of the message. When my dissertation was published I dedicated it as a tribute of gratitude to these three men.

None of the advisers knew my particular field of research as well as Professor Lehmann. He put me in contact with Warneck students in Europe. Within weeks I was corresponding with missiologists from Finland to the Netherlands. Although I was a complete stranger, they treated me as a colleague, directed me to libraries where I might find primary and secondary sources, and sent me bibliographical listings and copies of articles to facilitate my research. The archivist of the Day Mission Library of Yale University and Divinity School in New Haven, Connecticut, was also helpful. One thing led to another and before long I had compiled a fifty-page bibliography. Even with a limited budget I was able to acquire over six hundred items of primary, secondary, and tertiary sources for my dissertation, entitled "Gustav Warnecks missiologisches Erbe," which was subsequently published by *Brunnen Verlag* in Giessen and Basel.

By the time I had completed my course work and written comprehensive examinations, I was eager to work on the dissertation. I did some in my office on college campus, but most of it at home when the children were doing their homework and after they had gone to bed. My "office" in our house consisted of one half of a coat closet (twenty-four inches deep and thirty inches wide) in the entry hall to the living room. A piece of plywood served as desktop and three boards as shelves for books and papers. It was perhaps the tiniest office in Fresno with just enough space to put the folding chair under the desk to close the door when not in use. That left the appearance that everything was tidy and neat.

As soon as I had done my research and written a chapter by hand, Frieda took over and typed the scribbled manuscript. That was no easy task. But once she had put it through the typewriter it was legible and easy to revise. I mailed chapter by chapter to Professor Lehmann in Halle, showed a copy to J. B. Toews in Fresno, and discussed the major issues with Dr. Glasser, my committee chairman, in Pasadena. With every chapter I wrote I had one or two to correct or revise.

The closer I came to the deadline, the shorter the nights seemed to get. On 16 May 1976, Frieda finished typing the final revision. At 9 o'clock that evening we went to Pacific College where I had been given permission to use a duplicating machine to make three copies. Since it was no speed-copier, we worked through the night without a break. By 5 o'clock the next morning we were finished, paused to thank God for sustaining energy, and prayed for strength and safety on the road to Fuller Theological Seminary in Pasadena. That Monday, 17 May at 9:45 a. m., fifteen minutes before the final deadline, I submitted my dissertation of over five hundred pages to the person responsible to check for technical inconsistencies.

The spring semester of 1976 was for us as family an exceptional time of graduation celebrations. Evelyn graduated from primary school, David from high school, Dianne was at Pacific College, I completed my doctoral studies at Fuller, and Frieda was instrumental in helping each of us separately and all of us corporately through our academic pursuits. She deserves to be saluted for "graduating" together with us. Another factor that enhanced our celebrative mood was the award of a plaque from the School of World Mission for the "best dissertation" in a foreign language that year.

In the spring of 1977, Dr. Glasser called me for help. "Campus Crusade for Christ is sponsoring a group of over sixty European pastors and church leaders, most of them from Germany. They have come to tour selected churches and Christian schools in the United States." He continued by saying that their itinerary included one day at the Fuller Seminary, and that they requested at least one lecture—if possible in German—on the nature of theological education and the church in America. "And that is where we need your help," he added. "Can you come and speak to the group?" It may have been naive on my part to accept the challenge, but how could I say no to my esteemed professor and friend, who had done so much for me, and whom I had observed giving up rest and comfort, even sleep, to the last ounce of his energy whenever someone needed help?

Two or three days prior to my assignment, I called my trusted friend Robert Seibel, whom I had known since 1947, and asked if he would be interested in accompanying me. I knew that a man as inquisitive as he, and one who had for many years taken a vital interest in my spiritual and intellectual development, would never say no to an opportunity like this.

On the way to Pasadena we discussed the main issues of my talk. I appreciated his constructive words of wisdom. "Speak boldly," he advised. "You have nothing to fear. The Lord is with you."

A lively discussion followed my presentation. The main questions revolved around the difference between the lighthearted, almost superficial approach to theological issues in America and the serious, almost somber manner in which the German mind deals with the "queen of the sciences," the ultimate of all knowledge, as some Europeans like to think of the sacred discipline of theology.

As soon as we concluded our session, several men wanted to know if I would be open to come to Germany for a speaking tour. They offered to reimburse Pacific College for my salary, pay travel costs for me and Frieda, and take care of all the logistics and schedules of my itinerary. Since I was eligible for a study/service leave in the spring quarter the following year, I indicated tentative willingness to accept their invitation. Günther Hopp, director of *Brüderhaus Tabor,* a theological school in Marburg, offered to make all the arrangements from his office for our visit.

Having always been frugal with money, regardless of who pays my expenses, we discovered that Icelandic Airlines from Chicago over Reykjavik, Iceland, to Luxembourg, the capital of Luxembourg, would be the most economical way to get to Germany. So we flew with Icelandic. Wolfgang Baake, a student at the *Brüderhaus,* met us at the airport in Luxembourg and took us by car to Marburg, where we were cordially welcomed by Mr. Hopp and his staff. They also provided temporary lodging and meals until we could move into a basement suite on Rollwiesenweg No. 10, located between the *Brüderhaus* and the city center. That became our home base where Frieda and Evelyn spent much time while I was on my speaking itinerary. Our son David and his friend Mark Manoogian, another bicyclist from Fresno, also stayed there whenever they needed a rest from their cycling tours.

My itinerary from15 March through 15 June 1978, was rather full. According to the date book prepared by Mr. Hopp's secretary, I was scheduled to preach and lecture 145 times. That number increased as the weeks went by. The nature of the assignments included short-term teaching in Bible schools and seminaries, speaking at ministers' seminars, at Christian workers' retreats, and preaching in churches and at two deeper-life conferences, one in Marburg and the other in Gunzenhausen. The itinerary covered seven denominations within free churches and state churches in Germany, Switzerland, and Austria. It was a rather demanding schedule for a mortal being like me. The reality struck me one day when one good brother called to inform me that I should be at the retreat center in good time. I traveled all night by train in coach class and complied with his request. Little did I know that I was expected to speak three times that first day and seven times the second day. Despite my own injudiciousness in the matter, God sustained my physical, mental, and spiritual fortitude for the task. While I have seldom, if ever, declined serving under demanding circumstances, this particular event became the occasion to learn an important lesson for the future, namely this: saying NO to an unreasonable request is a reasonable response.

During my second major assignment in a state church at Herschweiler-Pettersheim, *Pfarrer* Johannes Günther Moll surprised me with a set of keys for a Mercedes Benz car, which one of his church members made available at no cost to us during our stay in Europe. When I traveled by myself it was more economical to go by train. But whenever Frieda and Evelyn went with me, we always took the car.

The three months went by remarkably fast. Even if the workload was a bit heavy, the gracious reception and treatment I received made my ministry spiritually and educationally rewarding. It was an ideal opportunity to meet many pastors, Bible teachers, Christian leaders, students, and entire families from church traditions different than my own. It also resulted in invitations for ministry in years ahead and in many contacts with students interested in studying at Pacific College and the seminary in Fresno. Then, too, we formed friendships with individuals and families which we treasure to this day. Upon completion of my itinerary we took a week of vacation in Italy—a bonus for personal historical and cultural enrichment *par excellence.*

As I look back at ten years of teaching at Fresno Pacific College, from 1968 to1978, and review various aspects of ministry in which I was privileged to be involved during that time, I am moved to bow my knees before God and thank Him for the many opportunities I had to preach and teach the Word, especially as it relates to the mission of the church; for a wonderful and understanding family who supported me with prayer and love — even when I was away from home; and for the college administration and the institution as a supportive base from which my ministry was made possible. Upon completing my tenure as instructor of foreign languages at Pacific College and before beginning my assignment as professor of missiology at MBBS, the academic dean of the college blessed me with a letter in which he wrote:

> Dear Hans: I wish yet to express in writing my appreciation and thanks for your service as a faculty member of the College during the past number of years. You have served faithfully and well, not only in the classroom, but also in your public ministry beyond the College. Your diligence and

the quality of your work has not gone unnoticed. . . . I am pleased that you have chosen not to move far, so the opportunity will exist for our students to enroll concurrently in your courses at the Seminary and for you to participate on occasion on a part-time basis in our program. I wish for you God's best in your new assignment! Sincerely [signed], Dalton Reimer, Dean of the College.

PART V

On the Missiological Service Road (1973-2003)

Missionary to Missionaries and Churches

Missiology is the study of mission with multidisciplinary components anchored in the Bible to facilitate the church's witness in a fallen world. Its greatest challenge lies in its pilgrim-like nature, always on the move along the paths on which the missioners are moving. Sometimes it must forge ahead as a pioneer breaking new ground; sometimes it must rest on paralyzed knees before closed doors entreating the Triune LORD of Mission to open the portals or show another way to move on. Missiology cannot afford prolonged armchair comfort in an atmosphere of theories, lest it forfeit the ability to walk the rough service road. Neither can it afford extended seasons of action without concentrated study and reflection, lest it lose the capability to dig for treasures that are indispensable for useful service. Missiology must be informed about the past, both its gains and its losses; it must stay abreast with the present, both its changes and its constants; it must give direction to the church and its mission, both in terms of abiding responsibility to maintain a healthy base and to nurture a clear vision of global opportunities for sharing the Good News. Biblical missiology is always missiologia viatorum, a discipline en route, holding onto the risen Lord and reaching out to the fallen world. It has not arrived; it is on the open road to an open future with a blessed hope.

41

Full-Time Seminary Teaching
(1978-1993)

Continue cultivating these matters;
devote yourself wholly to them,
so that everybody may see your progress.
Make it your habit to pay close attention
to your life and to your teaching.
—Excerpt from 1 *Timothy* 4

The closer I come to the present in the design of my journey, the more difficult it becomes to write about it. It is as though I have to shift from the more natural to a quasi preternatural mode if I want to tell my story of the last two decades or so. To talk about teaching at the seminary, for example, I am forced to retell events and experiences that happened as recently as yesterday—events that have no history. One can be forgiven for repeating stories of thirty or forty years ago. But people are less tolerant when one repeats the things that are still fresh in their own memories. And why talk about things everybody knows? Most of my contemporaries "are still living, though some have fallen asleep," to borrow a Pauline phrase from a different context (1Cor. 15:6). My colleagues and former students, friends and family near and far know how things were and how they are. That makes it difficult to recount them.

What makes it even more tedious are all the boxes stuffed with folder upon folder filled with correspondence and reports, position papers and statements of all sorts; drawers and shelves loaded with binders full of unpublished manuscripts, lecture notes and sermons; envelopes and slipcases with fragments and poems and chips from a mental block, crafted mostly for myself in my more serene, contemplative moments. Then there are the gracious student compliments and critiques plus those generous tributes, both factual and fictitious, penned by my esteemed colleagues. Despite some inhibitions to write about these recent times, I am under compulsion to make some observations about the years I served as missionary to missionaries and churches.

During the fall semester of 1976, I was involved in a pilot project of leadership training at the *Instituto Biblico Asunción* in Paraguay. Known as

"Theological Workers Course," the program was designed for local church leaders and jointly sponsored by the Biblical Seminary and the Board of Missions and Services. While there, I received an invitation from Acting President George Konrad to join the seminary faculty on a full-time basis, beginning in July 1977. The letter explicitly stated that I was to teach in the area of missiology. As I explained earlier, I deliberately chose a detour in academia to become more adequately trained for full-time missionary service. I wanted to be flexible and open to whatever direction God would lead to serve the church in world mission, either at home or abroad. Now the time seemed to have come with the door ajar before me.

In principle, I was not averse to making the shift from Pacific College to MBBS. But I needed at least one year for the transition. If I was to teach at the most prestigious educational institution of the Mennonite Brethren Conference, then I needed to know more about the school's history as well as its long-range vision than what the mission statement in the catalog was saying. Conversely, the seminary administration and faculty needed to know more about me than what they remembered from my student days and from teaching a few evening courses.

I had no intention of revolutionizing the curriculum or of starting a new mission program. After all, the seminary had a twenty-five-year history, and thus a foundation on which to build. But to do so, I had to know what there had been, what there was, and what would be needed to train missionaries most effectively for the twenty-first century. My purpose simply was to submit to the faculty for review and discussion a comprehensive statement of my findings, together with a modest proposal as to how I visualized my task for the mission department. I wanted to be understood and corrected before making a commitment.

In September 1977, I handed a preliminary draft to Professor A. J. Klassen, academic dean of the seminary. He gave me valuable feedback and asked that I be prepared to give what he called "an inaugural address" to the entire faculty, scheduled for 1 October. I was delighted to do so and made available a paper of over fifty pages. In a condensed oral presentation I focused on what I perceived to be the central issues for missionary training at the seminary. In the months following I worked through a series of missiological questions. In that process I spent much time in personal prayer and reflection on the nature of the assignment that loomed ever larger with each passing day. I sought counsel from colleagues and friends. It was during that decision-making process that I experienced the leading of the Lord in two unusual incidents. One was a conversation with J. Edwin Orr, the other a luncheon with Elmer A. Martens.

While studying at Fuller Theological Seminary, I took a course in apologetics from Professor Orr. The man impressed me greatly, not because he had legitimately earned five doctorates, but because he was a man with a brilliant mind, a burning passion for mission, and a humble spirit with a compassion for people. Upon my recommendation, Pacific College invited him for a lectureship on Christian apologetics. Since he had been my professor, I had the privilege of hosting him. In the course of conversation I discussed with him the prospect of teaching at MBBS and mentioned that I was thinking of taking additional studies in Third World theologies, which I felt were needed for teaching missiology. His response was quick and affirming. "I have just the right school for you," he said: "the University of South Africa." I pursued his advice.

During that same academic year I also got to know Elmer Martens, professor of Old Testament and newly appointed president of our seminary. I had met him before, but do not recall ever having had a heart-to-heart talk about world mission and what he envisioned the seminary's role to be in that area. Nor do I remember ever spending a time of prayer together as we did when he asked me to have lunch with him at Sal's Mexican Restaurant on East Kings Canyon Road. That is when I discovered—perhaps we both did—that he and I shared a mutual passion for mission. While no details were spelled out, I sensed the nonverbalized presence of a common vision how the seminary might deepen and expand its missional ethos on campus and equip men and women to cross frontiers to serve the Lord among the peoples of the world.

Both the conversation with Professor Orr and that luncheon meeting with Dr. Martens became for me academically and spiritually the decisive milestone for crossing the threshold from teaching languages at Pacific College to teaching missiology at the seminary. My decision was confirmed when some months later, while speaking at a leadership seminar in Austria, I received a letter from Martens in which he wrote:

> I want to express my great satisfaction and delight that you will be part of our team, beginning this summer and especially this next fall. . . . This morning our passage for exegesis in the Prophets course is from Isaiah 61:1ff. I was impressed once more with the theology of ministry represented there and its end product which is to be planting for the Lord. We shall need to think more towards a perspective which calls for our pastors to produce leaders. The first verses are balanced with the last verses and picture the paradise-type of conditions. I greet you with that passage and pray that God will give you strength, blessing and favor plus joy in your assignment. Cordially, Elmer A. Martens President.

In August of 1978, just prior to my new assignment at the seminary, I took part in the conference of the International Association for Mission Studies (IAMS) in Maryknoll, New York. Here I witnessed the intensity and seriousness with which the foremost missiologists of the world were dealing with abstract ideas shrouded by such topics as "Para-Missiological" and "A-Missiological" thinking that had replaced biblical missiological teaching in seminaries and universities.

As I listened to the papers given in the plenary sessions and participated in the discussions in seminars and workshops, it soon became evident that many professors of mission were deeply troubled by such pseudo-missiological jargon. One of them was Professor Bede McGregor from St. Patrick's College in Ireland. At the concluding plenary session, McGregor presented an eloquent summary statement of the conference highlights. He expressed disappointment that the workshops had focused unduly on "the paralysis of mission" without offering a solution. Upon articulating with great clarity the fundamentals of a biblical missiology, he concluded by saying that the solution to the paralysis of mission begins "with the paralysis of the knees." With those few words McGregor extended a compelling call to prayer, reminiscent of what Andrew Murray of South Africa had expressed nearly a century earlier, when he wrote that "our only hope [in mission] is to apply ourselves to prayer." It was also at that conference where I read Roberta Winter's book, *Once More Around Jericho*, in which she describes the miraculous beginning of the US Center for World Mission in Pasadena as God's response to prayer.

During my first semester of teaching at the seminary, I had to face an unscheduled "interlude under the knife," as I could call it. Ever since my teenage years in Brazil I had undergone numerous surgical procedures, some less serious than others. But I had never faced a coronary artery bypass until now. On 11 November 1978, as I was walking from my office to the administration building I felt limpness in my right arm and a tightening sensation in the chest. These symptoms became frequent and more intense as the days went by. A week later I was preaching at the annual Thanksgiving/Mission Festival of the Mennonite Brethren Church in Garden City, Kansas. By Sunday afternoon Garden City looked more like a snowfield than a garden. My flight was canceled, and I had to take the bus to Denver, traveling on icy roads through the night. At the airport I discovered that Flight UA 249 to Fresno had also been canceled and that I was in for a long delay. I got home the following day and needed medical help.

Since our daughter Dianne was working in a laboratory for cardiologists, I received immediate attention. After a series of tests Dr. William Owen, a heart specialist, told me that I had severe arterial blockage. Upon consulting with his colleagues, including Dr. Sathaporn Vathayanon, a renowned cardiovascular surgeon, he advised me that the only known remedy would be a triple bypass graft. Surgery was scheduled for 27 December. In the meantime I was to take it easy and rest. We had invited foreign students for Christmas dinner at our home, were encouraged by their presence and prayers, and rejoiced that we could together with them celebrate the birth of Jesus Christ, Savior of the world.

The operation took place as scheduled. The after-effects were neither pleasant nor painless, leaving my chest as well as my teaching and preaching schedule for the 1979 winter quarter somewhat scarred—and that is no figure of speech. After eleven days in the hospital and seven weeks of recuperation at home, I had sufficiently recovered to resume teaching and other activities.

In March and April I was able to take part in the Mission Board meetings in Hillsboro, serve as speaker at a mission conference in Oklahoma, and prepare messages for a Bible conference in British Columbia later in April. On my way home I thought about what had actually transpired at the events in Kansas and Oklahoma. My reflections "sent me on a contemplative pilgrimage," as I have recorded in my notes. On that reflective journey in airports and in flights I reviewed questions and issues that were highlighted in those meetings. It was both sobering and inspiring to take stock of my denomination's investment in world mission. Our mission administrators under the leadership of Dr. Vernon Wiebe, together with the board, had worked hard to deal vicariously with lingering problems from the sixties, were prudently engaged in making the most of the opportunities of the prosperous seventies, and were forging ahead to an open future. That was encouraging. However, based on my observations in the constituency, I was not convinced that the mission board and the local churches were operating within the same field of vision. The eyes of the former seemed to be directed toward the world "out there," whereas the chief concern in our churches appeared to be more focused on their own welfare "in here." Clearly, the need to find an integrated balance between our conference institutions and the local churches was real.

What implications, I was led to ask, might that have for the seminary in general and for the Department of World Mission in particular? If my perceptions were correct that our mission leaders and seminary had a sharper vision for mission in the world than their constituent congregations, then the challenge in training men and women as pastors and missionaries was much greater than I had initially perceived it to be. I was compelled to respond to my own questions by drafting a paper on "Facing the Eighties Responsibly." I delineated my vision for the immediate decade before us. To help our denomination keep alive (or renew) its vision for the world, our students who will be future pastors and missionaries—so I wrote—must come to grips with a missiology of boots (practice) as much as a philosophy of roots (theory); they must move from the whence of our past to the whither of our future; they must have a goal with a large vision and clear direction on how to get there; and they must be committed to obedience of faith to serve the present generation in church and world.

In my contemplative state of mind, I was further reminded of the words of my former college professor, J. A. Toews, who once said with great passion and conviction: "The church that ceases to evangelize, dies." I took the liberty to paraphrase those words this way: "The church that does not missionize, ceases to be the church." That statement is based on the assumption that the church is "(co)missioned" and that evangelism is an integral part of the mission of the church. The Bible and church history were on my side of the argument. As there is no holistic Christian mission without evangelism, so there is no substitute for biblical teaching and preaching to motivate the church to cross frontiers in order to be Christ's missional witnesses on the other side of those frontiers. That led me to the conclusion that, while there may be a plurality of missions in terms of agencies and organizations as historical reality, there is only one mission of the church: its sentness with the gospel of the kingdom for holistic witness in a broken world. This, in a nutshell, was my passion for teaching at the seminary and for preaching in the constituency.

In the meantime, Hugo Janz and I were asked at the spring mission board sessions in Hillsboro to serve in the interest of leadership training in Europe from 11May through 13 June 1979. Our assignment was to meet with Mennonite Brethren leaders, missionaries, and educators. The question was whether a program of Theological Education by Extension (TEE) similar to that in Paraguay could also be feasible for Europe. As we met with key leaders in Bible schools and churches, we listened to their concerns, responded to questions, and together tried to find ways how we might best meet existing needs of training leaders for the church in mission. Other agencies and institutions were wrestling with similar issues; some achieved fruitful results.

While my call to teach missiology clearly came from the Mennonite Brethren Biblical Seminary, I perceived it also as a mandate from the Mennonite Brethren Conference with global missional dimensions. I interpreted that dual mandate to the best of my ability from a missiological perspective within the context of history. From the very beginning I tried to help our students understand and appreciate more fully that the missionary vision of the Mennonite Brethren in general and that of the Biblical Seminary in particular was not an invention of my generation, but was historically and theologically anchored in the Anabaptist/Mennonite tradition. Much like that of the early Christians, the original Anabaptist vision for the world was one of passion for the lost and compassion for the needy. That vision was not based on ethnic or racial homogeneity, but on their biblical understanding of the church as a community of believers sent into the world by the risen Christ to flesh out in the power of the

Spirit what they perceived to be their sentness, their true mission to the world.

Another concern was that my students should neither glory in the Anabaptist legacy of the past as an end in itself, nor should they denigrate it as an obsolete or outmoded tradition. I had seen incidents of both. Whenever that happens, as experience and history have taught me, the missional dynamic of the church as well as that of an educational institution is bound to suffer. My aim was to correct errors of the moment and to recapture whatever had been lost. At no time, however, did I perceive myself called to downgrade what was still in place and begin something new. I saw my assignment to build on the foundation that was already there. All I needed to do was to fill the vacant spaces with creative ideas put into action. I operated on what I call the principle of continuity with innovation, which brings a wholesome dimension to the dynamic of inevitable change.

Furthermore, I wanted our students to recognize and be able to identify various crosscurrents that have in the course of history either helped or hindered our missionary commitment. Such currents are many and come in different forms. Sometimes I wearied the students by challenging them not to rely only on books *about* mission; they had to read, interpret, and digest primary missiological sources until they began to "taste sweet as honey," to use a figure of speech from the prophet Ezekiel (3:1-3). In the twentieth century alone the missionary movement produced more statements in the form of reports, decrees, declarations, and manifestoes on the church's missionary activity than in all previous centuries combined. Granted, reading such documents may be intellectually demanding, as it should be. But it is much more than an academic exercise. In fact, it can bring us to our knees with wonder and amazement as to what our Triune God has done, is doing, and will yet do through His people in the world between Christ's first and second coming. It was my contention that no student of world mission should ever graduate from our seminary without working through at least a dozen major documents that are historically informative, theologically reflective, and intellectually challenging and motivating to missional action.

As important as those powerful documents may be, I tried to impress upon my students that there is one document that excels them all in quality and longevity, namely the Judeo-Christian Scriptures. It has always been my unequivocal conviction that the Bible is the first and supreme primary document on mission. Therefore, we should read and study it with respect and dignity as *the* missionary book *par excellence*. For it is here that we encounter the God of mission and learn to know the mission of God. If that does not motivate us, little else will.

I have said elsewhere that missiology is a multifaceted discipline. It can neither be captured by nor contained in an academic box of theories and fixed propositions. It must remain flexible and practical without forfeiting principles and standards of scientific inquiry. Missiology will always be *missiologia viatorum,* a servant science designed to help the missionary movement become more efficient in reaching people for Christ. Its abiding challenge lies on two fronts—one academic, the other practical.

One of my goals in teaching was to assist students on how to use the missiological method in a functional manner. For one thing, missiology must describe in no uncertain terms for the present and future generations how the church in mission has come to the point where it is at present. It must also guide the church as to where and how it must go from here if it wants to sharpen its vision to cross frontiers from its comfort zone to the world in need. In other words, missiology has a descriptive function.

Then, too, missiology has a normative task. It must use the norms of the Scriptures and reflect critically and theologically on issues that the church faces in our postmodern culture and society. It must call the church to its abiding missionary mandate to cross frontiers to the world in order to witness in a holistic manner on the other side of those frontiers. Missiology understands the verb "witness" as a comprehensive term, touching every phase of human need with the gospel of the kingdom as the very center. Not priority, but the centrality of the Gospel undergirded by prayer and obedience is the key to the abiding missiological task.

Finally, missiology has an integrative role. It must become attractive by both presence and penetration. In other words, by its very character missiology should humbly and unapologetically seek to influence all facets of its closest academic allies, such as biblical, theological, and historical studies. Unless these disciplines become intentionally missional in their relationship to the world outside, they run the risk of becoming trapped in their own world of academic inertia. That is why I have for years, in the Americas as in Europe, advocated the need for a mission of theology in our seminary education. Without recognition of its missional dimension, theology loses its vitality and purpose for existence, a subject which deserves more attention than it has received from evangelical Bible scholars, theologians, and missiologists.

42
More Studies While Teaching
(1978-1986)

I like to think
That all my life was laid
In Thy great plan of love, my Lord;
And that according to Thy Word
Its changes have been made
From link to link.
—*Direction*, Spring, 1994

About a year before he went to be with the Lord in January of 1995, my esteemed colleague and friend, D. Edmond Hiebert, quoted the above lines in an article on "God's Creative Masterpiece," which he wrote as a contribution to my *Festschrift*, published in the journal *Direction* in Spring 1994. Dr. Hiebert's quotation is a fitting epigraph for this chapter. For what I am writing here are fragments and links within the longer chain of events to fill in "from link to link" some gaps in the chronicle of my journey from the late 1970s to the late 1980s.

One of the pieces consisted of theological studies at the University of South Africa (UNISA). I sent in my first application while still teaching at FPC but was denied acceptance on the grounds that I already had a doctorate in missiology from Fuller Theological Seminary. In my response I explained my reason for further studies with a special emphasis in non-Western theologies which were at that time rapidly emerging in the younger churches of Africa, Asia, and Latin America. The Division of Missiology, Church History, and Science of Religion, with over eighty full-time professors headed by the internationally renowned Professor David Jacobus Bosch, was at that time rated among the best schools in that field. When I wrote Dr. Bosch personally with accompanying letters of recommendation from my former professors, Arthur F. Glasser and J. Edwin Orr of Fuller Theological Seminary, I was accepted into the program.

I went to work immediately, read scores of books in missiology, Third World theologies, systematic theology, world religions, and church history, and wrote and submitted position statements, research and seminar papers, and exams. In one of the papers on "Missiology as a Discipline"

I attempted to develop a "Believers' Church Missiological Model" with subjects built around what I considered to be an indispensable missiological core. With a premium grade and compliments from Dr. Bosch and others, I adapted this model, in principle, for teaching at the seminary. While every assignment was challenging, the ones in systematic theology were especially demanding, stretching my intellectual capacity to the limits. But that was precisely the discipline I needed. Overall, I was pleased with the way my professors were assessing my work. In fact, they expressed confidence that, if I would continue at the present level of performance, I would qualify for the rigorous examinations which I had to take on the UNISA campus in Pretoria two or three years down the road.

By 1983 I had completed all course work for a doctorate in theology. The orals exams were scheduled for April and May. There was much at stake: what would my colleagues and friends in Fresno say if I should fail those tests? Then, too, there was the question of finances. I wanted Frieda to accompany me, but travel costs were prohibitive. Frieda accepted an extra amount of typing for students and professors, and the children helped with the housework. God blessed our joint efforts to earn needed funds for the long and truly adventuresome trip to Africa.

We left Fresno on 11 April and arrived in Johannesburg two days later. Professor and Mrs. Bosch were at the airport to meet us. They took us to Pretoria, about thirty kilometers away. They had already talked to their married daughter Annelise about living quarters for us. Annelise was a teacher and her husband, Leon Coetzee, worked for Youth With a Mission. Both were much involved in the Hatfield Baptist Church and in social ministries. They were also managing a kind of half-way house for troubled students in Pretoria, about five kilometers from the University. Not that they classified us as troubled students, but we fit in well with several other couples and singles who lived in the same big, old mansion, known as "The White House." We shared the cost of living, ate our evening meals together as far as that was possible under different work schedules, and once a week met for a time of prayer and fellowship. It was a great experience to live with mostly younger South Africans during the week and worship in different churches on Sundays.

For Monday, 18 April, Dr. Bosch had arranged a meeting with the examination committee to discuss the time and nature of my upcoming orals. After eight sessions over a period of several weeks with individual professors, I had a final three-and-a-half hour oral test by the entire male quartet of erudition. While these men were evaluating my performance, I spent about twenty anxious minutes waiting in the spacious hallway on the tenth floor of the magnificent Administration Building. Finally, Professor Bosch came out of Room 11, shook my hand and said: "Congratulations! You passed with honors." As I followed him back to his office, I whispered, "Thank you, Lord, thank you!" I also expressed my appreciation and gratitude to my examination committee, said farewell, and took the elevator to the ground floor. Frieda and I had agreed to meet in the city and celebrate over a typical South African scone with raspberry jam and a cup of tea. It was a great day which the Lord had made. We rejoiced and were glad in it.

Now came the time to finalize the question of a dissertation topic. I needed to submit at least two proposals. Since my church history professor, Dr. Abraham Viljoen, was a specialist in Reformed Pietism, and Dr. Brian Gaybba, my major professor in theology, was always speaking about "God-talk," including the newly emerging Liberation Theology and non-Western theological currents, I was contemplating on writing a dissertation in one of these areas. To be on the safe side, I also suggested a study of the philosophy and practice of mission within my own denomination. To my surprise, this was the subject my thesis committee approved.

To prevent duplication with what others had written, I limited my focus to a Mennonite Brethren philosophy of mission that I considered to be the driving force behind the *why, where, how,* and *what for* of our mission. Professor Bosch made clear from the outset that the work should be historically and theologically thorough and as comprehensive as possible, regardless of its length. He cautioned, however, that the merits would be assessed on the quality of the content, not on volume. The academic administration of the Department of Missiology, Church History and Science of Religion at UNISA appointed Professor Bosch to be my promoter and recruited Professor Paul Hiebert, a Mennonite Brethren missiologist teaching at the School of World Mission in Pasadena, to be my outside reader.

Once the exams were over, the Bosch family asked if we would be interested in an excursion to the famous Kruger National Park, one of the world's largest wildlife sanctuaries. On that trip we got to know David and Annemarie Bosch not as academicians, but as loving parents who could laugh and sing and tell down-to-earth stories in the company of family and friends. The countryside was gorgeous, vegetation and topography were magnificent, and the roads good. When we got into the park we stayed in the vehicle except in special guarded and safe places. Wherever we drove along its nearly two thousand-kilometer road system, we observed the wonder of the animal world at close range. I had seen many varieties of smaller animals, reptiles, birds, and insects in the jungles of Brazil, but never such giant species as elephants, giraffes, zebras, crocodiles, and hippopotamuses in great numbers, roaming on open fields or swimming in the waters. It was an extraordinary visual experience to behold parts of God's creation Frieda and I had never seen before.

More Studies While Teaching

Another memorable event was our trip to visit Irwin and Lydia Friesen, missionaries at Selebi-Pikwe in Botswana. Dr. and Mrs Bosch offered us their little Datsun to drive to Botswana on our own rather than take the bus or train which, we were told, would be an arduous journey. Despite the fact that I had to learn to drive on the left side of the road, shift gears with the left hand, and sit behind the steering wheel on the right side of the vehicle, the roughly 1,200-kilometer round trip through the countryside was interesting and enjoyable. We were spared any direct and hazardous contact with cattle, donkeys, and goats on the road. Not all travelers were that fortunate and not all animals got away unharmed. We witnessed one scene where the family was still standing by their damaged Mercedes Benz while the inhabitants of the village were already skinning the steer that had collided with the vehicle.

We spent three interesting days with the Friesens, who were serving with Africa Inter-Mennonite Mission within the Africa Independent [Indigenous] Churches. On Sunday I was asked to preach (with the help of a Tswana translator) in one of the churches. Surely, that was not the most dramatic sermon they had ever seen and heard. Their singing, however, especially that of the choir, was quite demonstrative and magnificent, and may have compensated for what was lacking in my message. The elders were dressed in white robes, standing on each side of the preacher behind a pulpit, and holding on to a long staff to symbolize their position as shepherds of the flock. The service lasted from morning until evening. As a token of courtesy toward us they inserted a recess at noon and indicated that we could now take leave.

One of the homes to which the Friesens took us was that of Nightingale Kgakge. As the Minister of Education and niece to the President of Botswana, this elegant lady spoke a refined English. Her mother, who had long exceeded the biblical age of eighty, lived in the same house with the extended family living in thatched round houses on the same property. During our conversation the older lady held her eyes fixed on Frieda. Now and then she also gave me a glance that penetrated every layer of my skin. She spoke Bantu and Tswana, but no English. It was evident that something much more profound than the language barrier was troubling her. Finally, she told her daughter to ask us if we were traveling together. Our positive response puzzled her. "Are they married?" she enquired. "Yes, I believe so," her daughter replied. By now the gracious elderly lady was perplexed. After a brief verbal exchange between the two women, the daughter went into the house and returned with a pure-white woolen shawl that she draped around Frieda's shoulders. With a delightful smile and a nod of approval, she conveyed a nonverbal message to us: "Now you are married. Now you can travel together." The cultural implications of this encounter have a much deeper meaning than can be expressed in this brief vignette.

Two or three days before we were scheduled to leave for Zaïre, Mrs. Bosch made arrangements to have tea with Rev. and Mrs. John B. K. Tsebe, the bishop in Atteridgeville, a township near Pretoria. The Tsebes had invited several teachers from local schools. We sensed at once that we were in the company of fine Christians and highly informed people. Their hospitality toward us was genuine and the atmosphere warm. The purpose of our visit was not mere tourism; we had come to see how the people in segregated townships lived and to hear from them personally what life in the system of Apartheid was like. The houses we saw were well-built brick structures, but close together and far too small for families with ten or more children. Our hosts and the teachers spoke freely and openly about the sociopolitical conditions in their land. While they themselves expressed appreciation for many of the privileges they had, they also talked about the restrictive conditions with lack of freedom to move and live and work where they would like to. An oppressive atmosphere is bound to explode into violence. And that is what we experienced on our way home from Atteridgeville.

As we approached Pretoria, Mrs. Bosch saw what we did not yet see. "Not again," she sighed. But it had happened. Major streets were cordoned off. Guards were directing traffic. Ambulances, fire squads, military and police were everywhere. Two car bombs had exploded in front of the government buildings just minutes after 4 p.m. as people were going home from work. Many were dead and many more injured. We were profoundly shaken by the tragedy around us. We had actually planned to be in that part of the city at that time to have our tickets confirmed and our visas for Zaïre checked, but because Bishop Tsebe and the teachers in Atteridgeville could meet with us only in the afternoon, we had changed our appointment with the travel agent and took care of our needs in the forenoon.

Due to flight cancellations by Air Zaïre, the travel agent in Pretoria went far beyond her call of duty so that we were still able to get to Kinshasa. When we got there we discovered that our missionary friends, Betty Funk and Louise Oppel, had also gone the second and third mile, either by sending someone or coming themselves for several days in succession to see if they could by chance meet us at the airport. Letters and telegram about flight change and arrival time reached them several days after we did. Nonetheless, they were there when we arrived. They had told an officer about our coming, who in turn told other officials that we were missionaries and should be cordially treated. The checkpoints to obtain visa and customs clearance seemed to be without number. Yet we finally got every rubber stamp with the respective official's added signature to each and were admitted as visitors to Zaïre.

Louise and Betty had come with their little truck to take us to their home where we stayed during the next week. For years I had wished to witness African missionary life in action and to see the fruit of their labors. That moment had come. We were in the very country of Africa, even if not at the same location, where Aaron and Ernestina Janzen had pioneered in sowing the seed of the Gospel in remote Bololo as early as 1912. Many faithful men and women followed their example sowing, cultivating, and nurturing for growth and harvest. The fruit was evident. I was impressed by what we saw and heard, where expatriates and nationals joined their efforts in reaping a crop for eternal life, rejoicing in the process (see John 4:36-38).

From Kinshasa we flew to Belgium and from there to Rome. Because of time constraints we were able to spend only five days in that ancient city. Yet with every step one takes and with every move one makes, one touches components of the Christian story from the time of the apostles to the present. In Rome we boarded the train for Zürich, visited our friends, Eberhard and Ingrid Herring, and went on to Starnberger See, where I was scheduled to speak at a missionary retreat held at an old castle owned by Word of Life in Germany.

A final highlight of that rather lengthy itinerary in Africa and Europe were eleven days we spent in Berlin. I spoke at two Bible conferences associated with the Marburger Fellowship within the larger Protestant wing of the State Church. Thanks to our friend Wolfgang Baake, founder and director of the School of Christian Journalism in Wetzlar, and to Eide and Helga Schwing, a young couple with a vision for evangelistic ministry in the German church structure, we saw and experienced much of the natural and spiritual heartbeat of divided Berlin at that time. It always was a joy to interact with missionaries and local people in their homes and churches and to encourage them to contend for the faith committed to the believers.

On 24 June we took our flight from Frankfurt via London and San Francisco home to Fresno. Now that I had written all exams and passed my arduous oral examinations, I was faced with writing the dissertation in my "spare time." From the summer of 1983 through the spring semester of 1986 I spent countless hours in reading, archival research, and writing. I wrote everything by hand and Frieda typed every rough draft, every revision, and every revision of revisions. Finally, after working through stacks of major documents, mission board minutes, field reports, correspondence, conference yearbooks, and other pertinent sources, I was able to submit to my doctoral promoters at UNISA "the fruit of my labors" in a seven hundred-page thesis entitled "A Century of Mennonite Brethren

Mission Thinking, 1885-1984." Upon making the corrections and changes to the satisfaction of my advisers, I was promoted to receive the D.Th. degree and graduated in absentia.

— 43 —

The Seminary Decade of Mission
(1980s)

> Many, O LORD my God,
> are the wonders you have done.
> The things you planned for us no one can recount to you;
> were I to speak and tell of them,
> they would be too many to declare.
> –Psalm 40:5

"Very deliberately and resolutely the Seminary Board of Directors and the Seminary faculty have designated the decade of the 80s as the decade of mission." So wrote President Elmer Martens in the Preface to "A Vision Statement from the Mennonite Brethren Biblical Seminary." The words "a decade of mission" appeared in faculty minutes, reports, and letters where the mission curriculum was mentioned as a vital part of the seminary program. While I liked that description, I was not its originator. It was God's design, however, that much of my missiological teaching coincided with that invigorating decade. Not only that; I was simultaneously privileged to serve on the Board of Missions and Services (BOMAS) that was also moving forward with a special vision for world mission in the 1980s.

In the fall of 1979 BOMAS appointed a task force with the mandate to give direction for the decade ahead. Keeping in mind the vision expressed in the current seminary curriculum, I was asked to prepare a working paper on the theological foundation of our mission. Each of the other members, Peter Hamm, Paul Hiebert, F. C. Peters, and Vernon Wiebe, was also preparing a statement on a specific topic. When we met in Denver to discuss what we had drafted, totally independent of each other, we discovered how our thinking had been guided in a unified way. Moved by that realization we spent much time in prayer and reflection, asking God for direction how we as a denomination might best capture the opportunities of our time and meet the challenges of mission in the world.

The opening paragraph of the vision statement for Mennonite Brethren Mission in the 1980s reads: "The Mennonite Brethren Church faces an uncertain time with the unchanging Gospel of Jesus Christ, and the still uncompleted commission to preach the Good News to all peoples. What shape should its mission take in the 1980s and beyond?" Much of this document reflects remarkable unity in which the Biblical Seminary and Missions/Services were working together in the training of missionaries and church leaders to meet the demands of the day. That was an encouraging sign for both institutions. The charge to bring that vision for training to fruition lay largely with the seminary.

In the fall semester of that same year Henry Schmidt and I initiated a revision of the curriculum for the Department of World Mission with the proposal to offer an M.A. degree in mission studies. While Henry's particular strengths were in the area of the home front with an ever-growing trend on urbanization, my major emphasis was on the church crossing frontiers on a global scale. Thus we complemented each other and were able to build and maintain a balanced program of studies which attracted a relatively high number of students majoring in world mission.

In February of 1981, Howard Loewen, John E. Toews and I participated in a symposium on Theological Education in Missional Perspective sponsored by the Council of Mennonite Seminaries and the Missionary Study Fellowship in Elkhart, Indiana. In my paper on "The Call to Theological Education in Mission Perspective" I emphasized the integrative principle of missiology with an appeal to every discipline within a seminary curriculum to highlight the need for missional awareness in the educational process of each student. My contention was then as it is now that a missionary vision derived from the Bible leads to missional vitality of the church in the world. It was interesting that Professor David Bosch, guest speaker from the University of South Africa, presented a paper on a similar topic. His was a pedagogical masterpiece on theological education from the viewpoint of mission. He confirmed and deepened my conviction that we need to focus intentionally on the mission of theology in our schools. Those present at that conference were as impressed as I was by Dr. Bosch's brilliant presentation.

The dynamics of the missionary vision on our campus continued to expand with increasing momentum. Among the major items was a proposal to establish a Center for Training in Mission, to host a mission consultation on campus in February 1983, and to publish a vision statement—all in support of the decade of mission. The president, the academic dean, and other faculty members stood behind these ideas and gave me the assignment to write the statement which I entitled *It's Sunrise in World Mission: A Vision Statement from the Mennonite Brethren Biblical Seminary*. Henry Dueck, assistant to President Martens, was instrumental in having it published and in disseminating it to leaders in the constituency.

The 1980s were not only a decade of mission for the seminary, but also for me personally. Increasing opportunities and demands for missional services in Europe and the Americas far exceeded the time and energy I was able to devote to them. Since my first responsibility was teaching, I frequently declined invitations that involved weekdays. Then, too, my first open heart surgery had made me aware of physical limitations, a factor I had theretofore never taken seriously.

What in the 1970s had been a mere pilot project in Theological Education by Extension (TEE) had by the 1980s become a scheduled seminary program. A. J. Klassen, academic dean at the seminary, was the key person behind this program with support from the Board of Missions and Services. Since I had served in Paraguay on several occasions during the 1970s, I was now asked to be "on loan," to BOMAS. That meant, instead of teaching at the Seminary in Fresno, I was to teach at the *Instituto Bíblico Asunción* (IBA) in Paraguay from early July through 6 November 1981. The courses included mission of the early church according to Acts, principles and practice of mission, history of world mission, church history, and selected topics on mission for women from the community.

Our children were by now independent, had jobs and stayed home on their own. Frieda and I lived in married student housing on campus. Our suite was none too big, but adequate. At the end of the academic year in Paraguay we participated in the commencement exercises at the IBA and on 7 November moved on to Brazil and Uruguay to visit missionaries, preach in churches, and speak at conferences. While those six months were physically no vacation and mentally no retreat, they were culturally, socially, and spiritually rewarding. It also gave us an opportunity to touch base with my side of the family and to travel together with my widowed sister Katja who came to visit us in Fresno. We got home just in time to celebrate a joyful Christmas with our children.

Whenever I had a study/service leave in Europe or Latin America, I made a special effort to meet with potential students and discuss with them the possibility of studying at our seminary in Fresno. It was my unequivocal opinion that we offered one of the finest missionary training and theological programs within the Anabaptist/Mennonite educational institutions. That appealed to many young men and women abroad, including some from within the state church tradition. On one occasion I handed a list with forty names (including thirteen spouses) of potential students to the Office of Admission, of whom twenty-four men and three or four of their wives came to study at the seminary, some also at Fresno Pacific College.

Having been a foreign student myself, and having served in different cultural contexts, I had a warm spot for students from other lands; I could empathize with them during their times of transition and adjustment.

Perhaps that is why the seminary administration asked me to assume the role as Foreign (International) Student Adviser. I tried to stay abreast through current literature and special conferences with the bane and blessing experienced by those undergoing cultural transition in academic, social, and church settings. Not only the students needed attention, but entire families. We had many in our home for a meal. In the mid-1980s we had a foreign student community of some forty people, not counting Canadians. It was a delight to reach out to them across such lines as customs and culture, language and loneliness. Even greater was the joy of observing their progress as they became multilingual and multicultural to the point where they no longer noticed particular barriers between *us* and *them*. At least once each month we ate our sack lunch (an American custom) together and talked about our conquests and concerns in our process of acculturation. Each semester we put on an international dinner which always included domestic and foreign dishes, making the event truly an international highlight.

While the 1980s were for me personally, as well as for my calling and ministry, primarily a decade of mission, they were for us as a family also a decade of weddings. Blessed are the parents who can celebrate the marriages of their children in a Christian manner. We experienced that when our three children were married within three years. Dianne's wedding with Steve LeVá on 30 July 1983, took place at the home in Gonzales, California, where Steve had grown up. Upon their request I gave a brief meditation on 1 Corinthians 13:13, lifting out faith, hope, and love as three indispensable pillars for a Christian home. Evelyn was married to Don Loewen on 17 August 1985, at the Butler Avenue Mennonite Brethren Church in Fresno. Since they wanted me to speak on a text of my choice for them, I was guided to present a meditation based on Colossians 3:12-17 where the Apostle Paul lists pertinent ingredients for Christian living in the family setting. Then on 27 July the following year, David and Julia Spicher celebrated their wedding at the Laurelville Mennonite Church Center near Scottdale, Pennsylvania. They too requested that I have a brief message, for which they chose words of Jesus in the Sermon on the Mount as recorded in Luke 12:22-31. Each wedding was an occasion of thanksgiving to God. It provided the foundation for three new families and increased our family of five to eight people in three years.

For the spring semester through the summer of 1987 I was granted another study/service leave for preaching, teaching, learning, research, and writing in Europe. But first I had to finish my teaching assignment for the January interterm at the seminary. In the middle of that month Frieda left for Abbotsford, British Columbia to meet her sister Mary from Manitoba. They spent time with their aging parents and visited siblings and friends. That had become an annual pilgrimage for the two sisters, one which they truly treasured. From there Frieda went to Salinas, California, to stay with Dianne and Steve, who expected the birth of their first child. After that she was scheduled to join me in Europe. On 4 February, Frieda called to tell me that I had become the grandfather of a healthy baby girl named Maren Stephanie. That was good news and we rejoiced in God's wonderful gift of life to the family. But that was not the whole report, as I was to learn later.

Meanwhile I completed my four weeks of teaching at the *Jüngerschule* in Switzerland and late in the evening of 27 February took the train to Belgium to meet Frieda at the airport in Brussels the next morning. I had to change trains several times along the way. Whether I was half asleep or simply careless, I do not know. But I do know that I was jolted to an unpleasant reality when I discovered that my third train was headed for Ghent, not for the airport in Brussels, and that I had no Belgian currency for another ticket. I will refrain from telling the rest of the story, except to say that I made it on time for Frieda's arrival. As we sat there in the airport, not altogether free from weariness due to busy schedules, night travel, and waiting in vain for lost luggage, we shared some of our experiences with highlights and low points. Despite much joy and gladness, Frieda had something to tell me I did not yet know: Steve, our son-in-law and father of our first grandchild, had been diagnosed with cancer. Seventeen years later and two major surgeries plus other treatments, Steve's cancer is in remission, and he is working full time. Meanwhile, little baby Maren has become a fine Christian teenager, who gives her parents and grandparents much cause for gratitude and pride.

During the month of March I was teaching missiology at the *Bibelschule Kirchberg an der Jagst*, not far from Nürnberg. One weekend we drove to Korntal near Stuttgart and visited with Mr. and Mrs. G. W. Peters. Dr. Peters was at that time teaching at the *Freie Hochschule für Mission*. It was refreshing to share with a veteran Anabaptist/Mennonite scholar a common vision for the role missiology plays within the German church context.

Toward the end of March and the first part of April, I served as guest lecturer at the *Freie Theologische Akademie* in Giessen. The director of the school, Dr. Helge Stadelmann, raised the question whether we would consider moving to Germany to teach full time in the area of missiology —even if after retirement in Fresno, which was still six years away. We left the question open for several years, but took it with us in our hearts.

Our next major stop was Neuendettelsau, one of the few remaining Lutheran centers of classical mission. The director, Dr. Johannes Triebel, had invited several evangelical scholars to present papers at their annual *Block Seminar* on current theological issues in missiology. The topic assigned to me was "Christian Conversion and Church Growth." The audience consisted primarily of theology students and professors from the *Augustana Theologische Hochschule*. The discussion following my presentation had to do with the question whether Christian conversion was still relevant. One young theologian in particular seemed to be upset and suggested that concepts like repentance and conversion were obsolete and should be "demythologized" or eliminated from our vocabulary. The response of one of the professors was something like this: "If we as Lutherans cannot speak of these core concepts in the Gospels, then neither Jesus nor Luther has anything to say to us and we have nothing to say to the world. That is precisely why we have invited evangelical theologians to call us back to such central biblical truths as repentance, conversion, regeneration, etc." His comments resonated well with the audience. I was pleased to see a number of students stand firmly on his side.

From early April through early June we spent eight educational weeks at the University of Aberdeen, Scotland, founded in 1494 where the Dee River empties its icy waters into the North Sea. As Visiting Research Fellow in "The Centre for the Study of Christianity in the Non-Western World," I was given faculty privileges. The "Centre" was headed by Professor Andrew Walls. The major benefits for me personally were access to a fine collection of missiological resources and interaction with international scholars who met weekly for seminars and symposiums dealing with hard issues pertaining to the Christian church in various religious and cultural contexts. With the exception of reporting on the progress of my research and presenting a paper at the graduate seminar, I had neither preaching nor teaching assignments. That in itself was relaxing and invigorating. Our lives were also blessed by great preaching from the pulpit and magnificent singing by the choirs and organ music in the (Free) Church of Scotland.

A special highlight for us was when our children Evelyn and Don came to visit us. They had a rented car, and since my schedule was not restricted by classes and lectures, I took several days off to see historical places of special interest. One of them was the small Island of Iona separated by a short waterway from the southwestern tip of the Island of Mull in the northern portion of the Inner Hebrides. It is reported that St. Columba, a Scot from Ireland, landed there in 563, and made Iona the headquarters of his missionary labors until his death in 597. Others carried on his work of the evangelization of Scotland and eventually also of England.

On our way back to Germany we made a three-day stopover in Edinburgh. What attracted us to this place more than anything else were two things connected with the University of Edinburgh and its role in the missionary movement. Professor Walls from Aberdeen met us here and gave us a special tour of both places. First he took us through the hallowed halls of learning of the University's New College. He pointed out the place where Alexander Duff, the first overseas missionary of the Church of

Scotland, had in 1867 established the first chair of evangelistic theology, and thereby laid the foundation for the scientific study of mission in the British Isles. Then he took us to the Assembly Hall of the United Free Church of Scotland where the Missionary Conference of 1910 had taken place. As we stood there on the platform of this imposing auditorium, our host again pointed out the historical significance of New College in general and the Assembly Hall in particular for the worldwide mission of the church.

Back in Germany, I had several speaking engagements in churches and one special project to complete, namely the *Festschrift* that Klaus W. Müller and I were preparing for publication in honor of G. W. Peters' eightieth birthday. We were able to give it the final editorial touches and with Frieda's help revise the index before submitting this rather impressive bilingual tome to the publisher.

Upon completing our work in Germany we left for Austria, where I was scheduled to preach in Wels, Linz, Steyr, and Vienna. From there we went together with Johannes and Cornelia Reimer to visit churches in Romania. That was another extraordinary experience in more ways than I am prepared to recount here. Alone the ordeal of clearing customs and crossing the border into Romania made us wonder what we might encounter on the other side. Marks of oppression and exploitation by the excessive cruelty of the Ceausescu regime were evident everywhere.

Johannes and Cornelia had received money from German churches to buy basic necessities for some needy Romanian families. While the stores for the ordinary citizens were completely empty, we as foreigners could go to government-operated markets and buy everything we wanted—but only with hard foreign currency, which any native was forbidden to have. That made it impossible for the average Romanian to buy such ordinary commodities as soap, fabrics, or toys. Flour, bread, sugar, meats and other food items were strictly rationed. We used up our foreign money, purchased whatever we could, and delivered the goods to those who, according to the pastor, were in greatest need of food.

Johannes Reimer and I were invited to preach in numerous churches. I was particularly impressed by the fearless witness of the Romanian Christians. On our way back to Austria, we made a brief stopover to visit some Christian leaders in the city of Oradea. One of the church leaders in that city was facing a serious court hearing the following day. He worked as an engineer and his wife was a physician. While we were in their house for tea, outside were three men in plain clothes watching every move we made. "They are not there because of you," our host said in a calm voice. "They are there because of me. But don't you worry about that. We are used to their presence and will deal with it when you are gone."

One of the Brothers asked me if I would go with him and speak to a group of university students who would be gathering for prayer that night. I was glad to go along. On the way to the designated place of prayer, this Brother turned off the headlights and drove into a completely dark alley where a person with a container of gasoline was waiting for him. I noticed no exchange of words, only the motions necessary to transfer the contents of the container to the gas tank of the car. And we drove on to the house of prayer. After my brief message on 1 Timothy 2:1-6, the entire group of some eighty or ninety students broke out in fervent prayer, imploring God to bring those in authority to a saving knowledge of the one and only Mediator, Jesus Christ, and to give enduring strength to the persecuted believers not to deny their Lord. I felt as though the entire room was filled with the presence and power of the almighty God. As history has demonstrated, the prayers of these students and countless other saints in the country of Romania have been answered, at least to a degree: the regime of the Ceausescu dynasty collapsed in 1989 and a notable revival movement has continued throughout the land, resulting in more than a thousand new churches with a measure of freedom to worship the living God.

44

Committed to Servanthood in Mission
(1988-1993)

After all, what is Apollos? And what is Paul?
Only ministering servants.
So then, men ought to think of us as servants of Christ,
who have been charged with handling God's revealed truth.
—The Apostle Paul in *1 Cor. 3 and 4* (my paraphrase).

During the decade of mission at the Seminary, Mennonite Brethren Missions/Services was very much involved in disseminating that same spirit of mission to the Mennonite Brethren churches throughout the world. The single major event toward the realization of that goal was "Curitiba 1988." This international conference became the climax of all other mission conferences held in many local churches of our denomination during that decade. Much prayer and planning preceded this event. The mission staff in Hillsboro and Winnipeg, under the direction of General Secretary Victor Adrian, spent countless hours in making it all happen. Delegates from churches in Africa, Asia, Europe, and the Americas gathered for five days (February 17-21) in Boqueirão, a suburb of Curitiba, to hear and learn what God had been doing through Mennonite Brethren efforts during the past one hundred years. It was inspiring and encouraging to hear representatives from our churches in those continents tell of the salvific acts of the Lord among the peoples in their lands. I was privileged to be an active participant in this dynamic event and to present a paper on the topic, "Clarifying Our Mission." All the papers given at that conference were subsequently published in a book entitled, *Committed to World Mission: A Focus on International Strategy,* edited by Victor Adrian and Donald Loewen.

My assignment continued for several weeks after the conference by speaking in our churches in São Paulo, Curitiba, Colônia Nova, Witmarsum, and Blumenau. As I moved from congregation to congregation in the southern states the Lord gave grace and liberty to highlight the cause of world mission for those who could not be at the assembly in Curitiba. I felt particularly moved to use what I called the *quadruple approach* in missiological communication.

First, I read or recited an appropriate Scripture passage and made some expositional observations as a means of *inspiration* to draw the hearts and minds of the audience to listen what the Bible says about mission. Second, it was also my deep concern to share with my listeners selected items of pertinent historical and demographic *information* that might otherwise not be accessible to the people at the grassroots level. Third, profoundly aware of the fact that, unless local churches could be motivated to be involved in world mission within their immediate surroundings, my preaching was in vain. Thus I asked God to bring about an urgent sense of *motivation* for missional action. Finally, when believers see and experience what God is doing through men and women engaged in mission they will rejoice in a grateful spirit of *celebration,* giving glory and honor to the Lord of mission.

I experienced Curitiba 1988, combined with the preaching itinerary in the churches, as a watershed of the decade of mission. I returned to Fresno encouraged, motivated, and challenged to pursue with renewed commitment what I perceived to be a God-given vision for a mission of theology that needed to penetrate every aspect of our educational endeavors at the seminary and in our local churches. I had the impression that my colleagues who were at the conference, including our new Seminary President Larry Martens, shared that conviction. Yet there was something I had observed in conversations about day-to-day life in the churches that left me inwardly restless.

Before leaving for Fresno, church leaders expressed concern about unwholesome undercurrents in their congregations. They asked me to come back and address some of the problems from a biblical perspective. My initial response was that I could perhaps come for a few weeks of biblical teaching and evangelistic emphasis, but I would leave internal problems for them to solve. Thus I left for home with an unfinished agenda that weighed heavily on my mind and heart. Why, I asked myself, was I reluctant to address some of the problems from a biblical perspective? After much prayer and in consultation with my colleagues at the seminary, I wrote back that I was willing to accept their invitation, but not before the summer (their winter) of 1991.

For the fall of 1988 I had promised to speak at the commencement exercises of the *Jüngerschule* in Walzenhausen and its sister school in Kirchberg. Each was a three-day event designated as *Absolvierungskonferenz* to which the public was invited. The graduates requested that I deliver four messages at each conference based on the specific theme they had chosen as their motto for life and service. They advised me to bear in mind that many of the guests in these large audiences would be unbelievers seldom exposed to the preaching of the Word of God. That made me aware of my twofold mandate: to declare God's boundless salvation grace, inviting unbelievers to faith in Jesus Christ; to proclaim God's rich supply of service grace, challenging the graduates to a life of servanthood.

Sandwiched between the two graduation conferences I had the opportunity to meet with about twenty MBBS alumni. We met at the *Freie Hochschule für Mission* in Korntal. It was good to hear our former students talk about the value of their seminary training to deal with experiences in real life; they also mentioned gaps that had not been covered in the curriculum. I treasured these meetings and gained new insights to enhance my own teaching and preaching ministry in cross-cultural settings. Another layer in that sandwich was a visit together with two of our Fresno alumni to the campus of the *Evangelische Theologische Faculteit* (ETF) in Leuven (Heverlee), Belgium. Founded in 1925 by the Belgian Gospel Mission, that school has grown to become an autonomous evangelical training center on the Continent with university status licensed to offer a legitimate doctorate in theology.

The year 1989 was less demanding in terms of overseas ministry assignments than some other years had been. I would have preferred to stay home altogether, yet could not do so with a good conscience. Already two years earlier I had promised to speak at a missionary retreat in *Friedegg* and preach at evangelistic meetings nearby. Both events were sponsored by the *Vereinigung Freier Missionsgemeinden*. This relatively young and dynamic church movement in Switzerland has an unusually high number of skilled members, including theology professors and government officials, artisans and farmers, bankers and engineers with a vision and commitment to evangelize secularized Europe. It was a highlight to serve among them and witness their response to the teaching and preaching of the Word

On rather short notice I received an invitation from the German Mennonite Historical Society to present a paper at a special symposium during September in Bielefeld. The purpose was twofold: to commemorate the bicentennial sojourn of Mennonites in Russia, 1789-1989; and to enhance our understanding of Mennonite history together with the tens of thousands who in recent decades had emigrated from the Soviet Union to Germany. Historians from Western Europe, Russia, and Anglo America read papers on a variety of topics. Volkswagen of Germany funded the entire event. The topic of my paper was *"Mennonitische Mission: Entstehung, Formen und Verständnis in Russland"* (Mennonite Mission: Origin, Shape, and Understanding in Russia). Upon the request of several historians at the symposium, I agreed to expand my paper into a book which I entitled, *Flammen unauslöschlich: Mission der Mennoniten unter Zaren und Sowjets 1789-1989*. The book was published by Logos and has been well received by Mennonite readers in Europe and Latin America.

In the fall semester of 1990, I had my final study/service leave before my projected retirement from full-time seminary teaching, effective in three years. We left Fresno for Düsseldorf on 17 September and returned on 14 November. The day after arriving in Germany, we picked up a car in Bielefeld and drove to Korntal, where I did research in the archives and library of the *Freie Hochschule für Mission* (FHM). While there we spent some time with Mennonite Brethren missionaries John and Mary Klassen as well as with missionary educators Klaus W. Müller and *Pfarrer* Lienhard Pflaum to discuss nature and demands of missionary training for the new century. Beyond that my schedule was again filled with lecturing in schools and preaching in churches, concluding with a week of ministry at the European Mennonite Bible School *Bienenberg* and the Mennonite church in Schänzli, near Basel. I have greatly enjoyed serving and interacting with church leaders at the *Bienenberg;* it was always a highlight to be there together with Frieda. This time was no different.

Earlier in this chapter I mentioned that I had made a commitment to church leaders in Brazil for a Bible teaching ministry in the summer of 1991. The question was about the role of the Holy Spirit in the life of the church. I must confess that I find it easier to speak on issues that enhance the mission of the church than to deal with divisive elements that prevent the church from engaging in fruitful mission. Yet I was grateful for the opportunity to teach a balanced view of the Holy Spirit to be God's dynamic gift to the church according to the Scriptures. That was one way in which I was able to place my shoulder under the shoulders of my friends and brothers in leadership, and to encourage them to be faithful in their task of shepherding the flock and feeding the sheep.

The highlight of this six-week intensive itinerary was a Bible conference at the *Centro Nova Vida* near Indaial in the State of Santa Catarina. This was the state in Southern Brazil where I grew up during the 1930s and 1940s, and where Frieda and I served in evangelism and church planting during the late 1950s and early 1960s. Nearly all the attendants at the conference were people of non-Anabaptist background. I still remembered and knew many of them from my teenage years in the Krauel, and others from the time we were serving in Blumenau. I had vivid memories of some of the men my age and older who in those by-gone years were enslaved by alcohol, living a lifestyle that brought honor to none and hardship to many, including their families. The majority had grown up in the same jungle land where I also had lived and grown up. Now they traveled long distances to hear the Word of God preached by one "of their own." They accepted me as one of them. By God's grace we now had much in common, singing hymns of faith and thanksgiving. Together we gave glory and honor to the living God who had transformed their lives through faith in Jesus Christ. I was deeply moved by that experience.

As I prepared my course syllabi for the spring semester of 1992 and looked at my date book from January through August, I realized that there was no time left for relaxation, let alone for a week of vacation together with Frieda. Even the interterm for January and part of February was completely booked with teaching and preaching assignments in Germany and Canada. One of the delightful tasks in those weeks was to speak and officiate at the wedding of our seminary alumni Peter Penner and Katharina Braun in Lage.

The spring semester, the summer months, and the fall of 1992 were as busy as the previous months and years had been, but they were also valuable times of prayer at home, alone in my office, and together with colleagues and students. Such times were most profitable for relaxation and recreation. They were spiritually and mentally edifying and refreshing, confirming the words of the Lord to the prophet Isaiah: "They who wait upon the Lord shall renew their strength." I cannot overestimate the weekly prayer times with several seminary colleagues during the lunch hour.

Our Christmas break at the seminary had barely begun, when on 19 December we received word that Frieda's father, Nickolai N. Reimer of Abbotsford, had passed away just in time to celebrate his ninety-ninth birthday with the Lord. He was a wonderful man: godly, witty, intelligent, compassionate. I treasured every occasion when I could spend time with Father and Mother Reimer. Since Mother's death in August of 1987, Father spent his last years as widower. Now the time had come when he, too, was called into his eternal mansion prepared for him by Christ. On 27 December 1992, his family, relatives, and friends gathered for a memorial service in the Clearbrook Mennonite Brethren Church, and after that we committed Father's body to rest in the Lord.

On our way home, Frieda and I encountered such an abundance of snow and ice on the highway, that forced us to take a long detour. But there, too, strong winds and flooded roads made driving hazardous. When we got to Fresno on New Year's day, the sky was clear and the sun shining brightly.

On 3 January 1993, I flew to Winnipeg to teach a one-week course at Concord College on theology of non-Christian religions. From there I flew to northern Germany where a workload for teaching, preaching and leadership training was waiting for me, leaving little space for either leisure or boredom. Upon returning to Fresno on 1 February, I began my last semester of teaching at the seminary. That marked the end of one service road along my journey and the beginning of another. I was now in transition.

Throughout my years at the Seminary, I found classroom teaching and interaction with students on a personal level most meaningful. In a number of cases I was moved to express sentiments similar to those of John the Baptist when he pointed to Jesus and declared to his disciples: "He must increase, but I must decrease." It is particularly gratifying to see among my former students those who have not only experienced saving grace (Eph 2:4-9), but have also learned the meaning of service grace (Eph 3:2-9; 2:10). By virtue of the pedagogical nature of the grace of God, they have become fruitful teachers, preachers, and leaders, who "make the teaching about God our Savior attractive" (Titus 2:9-15), while remaining humble and diligent learners. I endeavored to transmit to them a simple philosophy of ministry as demonstrated by our Lord: no master is too great to be a servant; no Christian teacher should ever be too proud to be a learner.

45

The Rite of Passage Called Retirement
(1993)

Not a brief glance I beg, a passing word,
But as Thou dwell'st with Thy disciples, Lord,
Familiar, condescending, patient, free,
Come, not to sojourn, but abide with me.
—Quoted by William Barclay in *The Letters to the Galatians and Ephesians*

In 1991 I was given the opportunity to take early retirement. But after considering the options and with support of the faculty, I thought it more prudent to continue teaching full-time until age sixty-five. That proved to be a wise decision. But those two years seemed to pass as quickly as a fresh breeze at sunrise in the heat of summer. And before long my colleague Ron Penner, dean of students, informed me that the seminary community was planning an event to celebrate my time of teaching and my retirement in a special chapel service scheduled for 30 April 1993. He outlined more details in a written memorandum and asked that I present a farewell message, reflecting on retirement, "or something of that nature."

That may sound simple, especially for a seminary professor who has lectured a thousand times on subjects more profound than this one. But such thinking is deceptive, to say the least. Retirement is a difficult topic to talk about. While I honored my colleague's request, I worded my subject in a way that allowed me to include some substance of my life's calling and entitled my address: "In the Passage of Time: Reflections of a Missiologist in Transit." Events like that leave neither the intellect nor the emotions unaffected. That day was no exception. So many items had to be compressed into one short hour that the program appeared to be a plethoric occasion with no second to spare. Initially, I had entertained the erroneous impression that I would give my speech and that would be it. But not so. The architects of the chapel service had other ideas, involving both the faculty and students. And that was good.

Several students from my last church history class had been asked by the chapel committee to write in three or four lines what they had appreciated about that class. Two samples must suffice. "When Hans comes to class," one student wrote, "you know that he is genuinely excited about his topic. This comes through in the way [he] makes his presentation and in the way he prepares. It seems as though he has every date and every name memorized." Another student commented, "[I appreciate] his profound love of history and depth of knowledge. This makes me as a student grow fascinated with history as well. His enthusiasm is contagious! I also appreciate how he draws from history to help us understand the implications . . . for the current church."

The entire farewell event after enjoyable years of teaching was for me both humbling and encouraging. Both students and colleagues spoke kind words of tribute; some sounded somewhat allegorical as though they were meant for someone else. One such piece was "An Appreciation Statement" from former president Elmer Martens. Since he had to be at mission board sessions in Wichita, Kansas, he sent the letter to the seminary and asked one of the teachers to read it in his absence. The statement was penned in a superlative tone. Among other things Elmer wrote:

> Hans, I am always impressed by your physical posture. You stand erect like an exclamation mark. . . . You are the kind of person who can read Scripture, with that deliberate, expressive manner, that brings a lump to my throat. You are the person, whom I seek out for prayer fellowship. Strong in my memory will be the times when over the lunch hour we have met in your office or in mine and have called on the name of the Lord. . . . Were I to cast what I want to say in biblical terms, it would be a paraphrase from 2 Thess. 1:2: We as an institution, and many of us in this room, and many more around the globe are bound to thank God always for you Hans, as it is fitting, because of your dedicated scholarship, your inspirational instruction, your personal modeling, and your spiritual stature. In all of these you stand tall, like a giant exclamation mark!

As editor of *Direction,* Elmer announced in the same statement that "the issue a year hence, Spring 1994, featuring global mission, will be dedicated in your honor!" After much was said and done, it was my turn to speak. I opened my talk by reciting excerpts from *Ecclesiastes 3:*

> There is a time for everything,
> and a season for everything under heaven
> [mused the preacher of ancient days]:
> A time to be born and a time to die,
> A time to plant and a time to uproot,. . .
> A time to weep and a time to laugh,
> A time to mourn and a time to dance,. . .
> A time to be silent and a time to speak.

The Rite of Passage Called Retirement

As I glanced at the clock on the chapel wall, I realized that the time designated for my presentation was nearly over before I had started. That called for fast thinking about how I could shrink my seventeen-page script to a mere two or three pages without losing the most essential parts I intended to say. Admittedly, that could not be done and caused some fleeting moments of mental strain and emotional discomfort, not to say agony. The only way was to change my presentation format from reading a carefully crafted farewell address to a short impromptu speech. My "time to speak" consisted of the following:

> After listening silently and intently for some forty-five minutes to all those gracious words of affirmation in terms of fact and fiction, my time to speak has come. It is the last time that I am privileged to address the seminary community as a teacher of this institution. This is the place where I have had my time to plant and time to reap; now is the time to uproot. For Frieda and me that means transition. We are in transit, a befitting state for a missiologist of the road to be in.

Beyond those introductory crumbs, I briefly summarized my reflections on retirement as a personal rite of passage, on the changing shape of global mission in the world, and on the seminary's abiding challenge of its missional task. If there was one single missing ingredient in that otherwise uplifting chapel service, it was the fact that no missiologist was on the immediate horizon to take my place in the Department of World Mission. In conclusion, I shared with the audience our plans for volunteering our time and energy to teach at a seminary and preach in churches in Europe.

That farewell chapel service of the 1993 spring semester was for me like a road crossing, marked by the rite of passage from active employment to active retirement On the one hand it concluded a very important season of my life; on the other, it set me free to enter another season with an open door and an open road full of challenges and opportunities for voluntary service. Granted, neither Frieda nor I had ever traveled that road before. Yet we had prayed about it, had the support of our children, and were looking forward to a new experience of life together. At the same time we were also aware of the transition between the seasons, a transition that involved much more than a simple shift from teaching at the Mennonite Brethren Biblical Seminary in Fresno to teaching at the *Freie Theologische Akademie* (FTA) in Giessen. While we had carefully planned how to deal with the foreseeable factors, there were some unforeseeable aspects we could only anticipate with a degree of uncertainty; still others remained totally hidden and demanded steps of simple faith.

From the middle of October to the first week of November 1993, I was in Europe by myself, fulfilling an earlier commitment to speak at a Bible week in Heuchelheim, lecture again at the *Freie Theologische Akademie* in Giessen, and serve for another week at a leadership conference in Friedegg, Switzerland. During the time in Giessen, I met with the administration to continue conversations about the possibility of establishing a mission department at the school. The idea was not new.

When I lectured there in 1987, Frieda and I were staying with Helge and Dorli Stadelmann that entire week. During that week, Dr. Stadelmann asked if we would ever consider moving to Giessen after my retirement in Fresno. His vision was that I should establish a department of world mission at the FTA. That should include laying the groundwork for a structured and integrated curriculum, building up a mission library, teaching missiology, engaging in research and writing, and preaching in churches. That was no minor agenda and we mutually agreed to pray about the matter.

What struck us in the intervening years between 1987 and 1993 were the letters and telephone calls from students, friends, and church leaders, encouraging (even urging) me to consider seriously to serve the Lord in Germany. On one occasion, only a day or two apart, a German *Pfarrer* and a student from opposite ends of the country expressed the identical words saying, *Hans, wir brauchen Dich in Deutschland.* (Hans, we need you in Germany.) We took these affirmations as a sign that the invitation to teach at the *Akademie* was of the Lord and made a tentative commitment to move in that direction. Meanwhile, Mr. Karl-Heinz Kuzcewski, business manager of the school, had rented an apartment not too far from the FTA and only about one kilometer from the nearest bus stop. It turned out to be a satisfactory arrangement.

Initially, we were planning to move to Germany early enough to be there for the new semester which started in March. We bought tickets and booked our flight for 7 March 1994. But that was not to be. Instead of going to Germany for teaching missiology, I had to go to the hospital for a second open heart surgery. Nearly fifteen years had passed since my first bypass operation. They had been good years. I feel safe to say that not a single day went by in which I did not thank God every morning for His goodness and mercies which I experienced throughout those years. But then some time before retirement, recurring symptoms of angina pectoris and fatigue became more frequent and intense. I was reminded of the wise counsel the preacher of ancient times gave to his son saying, "My son, pay attention to what I say; listen closely to my words. . .keep them within your heart. . . . Above all else, guard your heart, for it is the wellspring of life" (Prov. 4:20-23). It soon became evident that the "wellspring of life" was no longer well.

Medical examinations confirmed my fear: I would have to submit once again to the surgeon's scalpel, this time for a quadruple bypass. Dr. William Owen, my cardiologist, was less optimistic than the surgeon, Dr. Sathaporn Vathayanon, about the outcome. But neither of them was able to suggest a viable alternative. Needless to say, Frieda and I had our own reservations. We shared our concerns with four other couples from our Sunday School class and spent an evening of prayer together with them at our house. After that I had a measure of peace about the matter and decided to have the surgery.

On 28 March 1994, the same team of doctors who had performed the first operation in 1978 also did the second one. Unfortunately, the procedure took ten instead of the projected six hours. Not long after surgery I discovered that, in the physical sense of the word, something had gone awry with my "wellspring of life." Something was not right. My angina pectoris was increasing and my energy decreasing. That was disappointing. Yet in His enduring mercies, God has extended my life. Even ten years later I can only thank Him with all my heart and serve Him with all my strength.

In the meantime, we put our house on 4646 North Third Street up for sale and bought a small lot at a proposed gated retirement village. Personal health problems combined with trying to sell our house at a time when the market was flooded, to have a new place built, and to move from one residence to another turned out to be a heavy undertaking with the major burden resting on Frieda's shoulders. Then there was the sense of duty to fulfill my commitment of teaching at the seminary in Giessen. Not that the school put on any pressure; on the contrary. The administration was most understanding, urging us to take all the time needed for recuperation and assuring us by letter and telephone of prayer support.

With the consent of my doctors, we flew to Frankfurt on 7 June where friends met us and took us to Giessen, about seventy kilometers north of the airport. That turned out to be a good move. For one thing, I was mentally strong and motivated to go by faith, trusting God to energize my whole being. And He did. He provided sufficient strength, so that I was able to teach a concentrated course in missiology, a subject the seniors needed to graduate in October. I had over sixty students waiting to take that class and was impressed by their participation and performance. It gave me a foretaste of what to expect in subsequent years.

Then, too, these weeks in Giessen were beneficial for us personally. We were able to distance ourselves from problems connected with the building project in Fresno. Wesley and Beverly Gunther, who were also building at the same time, always kept their eyes on our place as well, and kept us informed of the progress. Alvin Pauls, another friend and retired building inspector for the State of California, was kind enough to check periodically during our absence that the construction would proceed according to blueprint and contract. He did so in a most professional manner. Moreover, those weeks also afforded us an opportunity to make a preliminary transition to Giessen. We became acquainted with the infrastructure, geographical layout, societal and religious makeup, and cultural dynamics of that old University City. At the end of the semester in July, we went back to Fresno to look after a variety of unfinished business items.

In retrospect we have sometimes said that 1994 was for us a notoriously difficult year. But we also have to say that it was a year in which we experienced God's miraculous provision of help and healing. The timing in all of our decisions was simply amazing. No sooner had the realtor sold our house on North Third Street and cleared all business transactions than the city building inspector gave approval to move into our new house on Morningstar Lane. We moved the next day, and three days later we locked the doors with most of our belongings still in boxes and moved to Germany just in time for the new academic year which started after graduation in early October.

I have gradually learned to live with severe physical limitations due to congestive heart failure. On the one hand, that means pacing myself according to the rationed portions of energy which the Lord provides for each day. On the other hand, however, neither my mental capacity nor my joy of life and service have notably diminished. With Job's friend Elihu I rejoice in "the Breath of the Almighty [who] has given me life," that extraordinary quality called "living soul" (Job 33:4; Gen. 2:7). In one of his poetic meditations Henry Longfellow has penned these meaningful lines:

> Life is real! Life is earnest!
> And the grave is not its goal;
> Dust thou art, to dust returnest
> Was not spoken of the soul.

Knowing that my time is in my Maker's hand, as the psalmist put it millennia ago (Ps. 31:15), I no longer take life for granted. I treasure each day as a gift supplied from the storehouse of God, Creator of heaven and earth. Strength and energy are a special bonus from Him, my Helper and my Healer.

I must add a concluding word about the love and support we received from family and friends. Our daughter Dianne, the only one of our children living in California, has helped in more ways than I could even begin to enumerate. The same is true of Wesley and Beverly Gunther, our neighbors across the street. They have through the years given countless hours building bookshelves and looking after our place while we served in Germany. They put into action the proverbial saying of an ancient sage in a literal way: "Better a neighbor nearby than a brother far away" (Prov 27:10b).

46

Giessen and Frankenthal
(1994-2003)

Let us, then, be up and doing,
With a heart for any fate;
Still achieving, still pursuing,
Learn to labor and to wait.
— Longfellow in *A Psalm of Life*

As I began my assignment at the *Freie Theologische Akademie,* I found it interesting that there were some similarities between this school and my beginning of full-time teaching at the seminary in Fresno. There were, for example, twelve or thirteen faculty members, several adjunct and visiting professors, and about 110 students. Then, too, my primary task in each school was to teach in the area of missiology and expand or build up the Department of World Mission.

There were also striking differences. In Giessen the language of instruction was German rather than English; missiology was compulsory for all students, rather than only for mission majors. Also, besides proficiency in English as a second language, every student, including mission majors, had to take biblical languages and pass rigorous exams in Hebrew and Greek. All exams were based on standards set for theology students at public universities. No student at the *Akademie* was permitted to graduate without writing and passing scheduled mid-term and prescribed final examinations of three hours in each subject. Furthermore, I was impressed by the conscious efforts made by the faculty, staff and students to keep maintenance and overhead cost to a minimum. Lights, for instance, were turned off when a room was not in use; two secretaries and one business manager took care of all paper work (e.g., typing for faculty, correspondence, mailings, student registration) and financial transactions.

At the beginning of the year the administration informed me of the practice that a new faculty member was expected to present an *Antrittsvorlesung* (inaugural address) from within his or her discipline. I chose the topic, *Die Aufgabe der Missiologie in der theologischen Ausbildung* (The Role of Missiology in Theological Education). I had great liberty and joy to give my address within the scheduled time on 8 December 1994. The lecture was subsequently published in *Evangelikale Missiologie* as well as in booklet form for distribution by the school.

From the very beginning of my teaching in Giessen, I was greatly pleased with the dynamic mission ethos on campus and the pursuit of academic excellence. I found that combination encouraging. One cannot take for granted to find a passion for mission in a highly competitive scholarly climate as I experienced it in Giessen. However, I also discovered that the missional center of gravity was perceived to be much more in the mission societies than in the church. That is a tension the modern missionary movement has had to contend with ever since the Protestant Reformation. While I always attempted to highlight the responsibility of the church in world mission as I understand it from the Scriptures, I am also aware of the historical reality that is hard to overcome, particularly in the European church context. Nonetheless, it was gratifying to find favorable response from students to the New Testament view of the church in mission, supported by some historical examples, especially that of the Anabaptist movement.

One of the ways I sought to ascertain the missional vision outside of the classroom was to meet personally with each teacher and talk about his perceived role in mission from the perspective of his discipline. I did this with the approval of the administration and with the objective of producing a book about the school's collective position on world mission. Due to prior commitments, not every faculty member was at the time able to write a chapter for the book, yet in principle each gave full support to the project. I was overwhelmed. Then, too, I was more than delighted that my teaching assistant, Friedemann Walldorf, could be persuaded not only to write a chapter, but to work with me as co-editor. I saw in him a future teacher of missiology—perhaps even as my successor. It was a pleasure working together with him. It reduced my workload considerably and gave him exposure to the wider constituency. We entitled the book *Werdet meine Zeugen* and submitted the manuscript to Hänssler Verlag in Stuttgart for publication. We were pleased with content and format of the book as well as with the positive feedback from reviewers and the evangelical press.

Books are indispensable tools for learning and teaching, yet the mission section in the library was exceedingly lean. I could give lectures in class, but I could not give appropriate reading assignments to the students because of inadequate library resources. The school was in desperate need of at least one thousand selected books to add to its current holdings on the subject of mission. But how and where could we get money to buy them? Frieda and I shared this need with our Discovery Sunday School Class at the Bethany Mennonite Brethren Church in Fresno and with Frieda's sister and brother-in-law, Mary and Jake Driedger, in Brandon, Manitoba. The response was beyond what we anticipated. During the short four years of teaching at the FTA, we were in the position to add more than twice the number of books to the mission library than we had initially envisioned. Frieda volunteered to help catalogue and shelve these and other books, a gesture which the administration appreciated.

During the spring semester of the first academic year in Giessen I was also asked to teach a course at the *Bibelseminar Bonn*. But I soon discovered that I had made an unwise decision. Driving that distance, lecturing for three hours and then driving back to Giessen was more than I could handle under prevailing conditions. I was glad that I had the physical strength to finish my commitment for the semester.

Since the FTA had a two-month break for mid-term exams for which I did not need to be present, we considered it prudent to go to Fresno for those weeks. That was also the time of year when I was able to honor the request of MBBS in Fresno to teach Anabaptist/Mennonite Brethren Studies during the January/February interterm. I treasured that ongoing contact with the seminary where I had spent much time and energy, both as student and as teacher. Besides, it also afforded us an opportunity to take care of some things that needed to be done in our new home.

Long before I retired from teaching at the FTA, President Helge Stadelmann and the Dean Stephan Holthaus, looked for a replacement. Other faculty members did the same. God answered. He provided not only one, but two full-time teachers to take my place. One was Dr. Klaus Müller, a veteran missionary from the Pacific Islands and seasoned missiologist from the mission school in Korntal near Stuttgart, where he was teaching together with the renowned G. W. Peters from Fresno, cofounder of that school. The other man was my assistant, Friedemann Walldorf, former missionary in Spain and a talented teacher who was working on his doctorate in missiology. He has since completed his studies with a dissertation on the re-evangelization of Europe. It was the Lord's doing that the relatively young Department of World Mission at the *Freie Theologische Akademie* was put into good hands, compassionate hearts, and brilliant heads committed to equip men and women for service in the unfinished, worldwide mission of the church.

As the time to terminate my assignment came closer, I was again faced with preparation and delivery of a farewell address. Inevitably, my mind turned to the future of the school and its strategic role in central Europe to train a new generation for service in the kingdom of God in the twenty-first century. That moved me to entitle my presentation *Mein Desiderium für die Freie Theologische Akademie*. The farewell was held on 10 July 1998. The school had invited friends and representatives from churches and institutions far and near to take part in the event of my *zweite Pensionierung* (second retirement), as Stephan Holthaus referred to it.

No sooner had I given my speech and sat down than Dr. Holthaus, our dean, called me back to the platform and asked Dr. Müller to read a laudatory statement on behalf of the school. The dean brought the session to a climax with the presentation of a *Festschrift* entitled *Die Mission der Theologie*, published by the *Verlag für Theologie und Wissenschaft* in Bonn. It was a tribute for my seventieth birthday. The content of the book is bilingual, consisting of essays written by missiologists, Bible scholars, theologians and church historians from Canada, Germany, Malawi, Paraguay, Scotland, and the United States. Not only was I jolted by total surprise, I was simply speechless and deeply humbled by such undeserved laudation.

The faculty and staff had done everything possible to create a truly festive atmosphere in a meaningful chapel service and to give leisure time to visit with friends and guests over coffee and cake which our gracious hosts had esthetically and tastefully prepared. Our daughter Dianne and granddaughter Maren had come from California to spend several days with us as an exceptional gesture of filial love. When the day was over, I was moved to express the words of the psalmist saying, "Not to us, O LORD, not to us but to your name be the glory, because of your love and faithfulness" (Ps. 115:1). I was fully aware that only through the faithfulness of God and utter kindness of my colleagues, friends and family was this day made possible.

But "there is a time for everything, and a season for every activity under heaven" as the sage of old once said. And thus the year 1998 marked the end of my teaching in Giessen, while I continued to lecture as adjunct professor at the Seminary in Fresno and to preach and teach in churches in Germany.

We also had the joy of visiting with our children and grandchildren and of hosting relatives and friends during our years of ministry in Germany. Our daughter Dianne and granddaughter Maren were the first to come and see us in May of 1996; in July of 1997, Steve came with them; the following year Dianne and Maren came once more in order to participate in the occasion of our farewell from Giessen. Evelyn and Don, who served at the Mennonite Center in Moscow from 1997 to 2000, together with their children Natalia and David spend Christmas and New Year 1997/98 with us. Evelyn and the children came for another visit in May. We were also delighted that David and Julia were able to visit us on their trip to Southeast Asia in June and July, 1998.

Ever since my first assignment with German mission organizations in Bad Liebenzell in 1973, I have had open doors to preach, teach and lecture in sundry contexts within German-speaking Europe. Demands and opportunities increased during the years I was teaching in Giessen. I will mention only two. From January through 5 February 1995 I was speaking at "Rogate," a Christian conference center near Curitiba, and in various churches in Brazil. Missionaries serving with the *Deutsche Indianer Pionier Mission* and the *Marburger [Brasilien] Mission* met at Rogate in separate groups for a retreat. I spoke on the "Role of Gospel and Culture in Mission." Most of the missionaries were working with tribal peoples in Brazil and Paraguay, including the *Kaingáng*, a people group related the *Xokleng* or *Botokudos* who lived in the Krauel before we settled there in 1930. During those early years we found arrowheads on our land, skeletons in caves, and sections of an old, overgrown road along the river.

Another specific request to continue our ministry in Germany was from the *Frankenthal Mennoniten Brüdergemeinde* (FMBG). Members of this rather dynamic local church meet simultaneously in two fairly large buildings in the city and in five or six smaller places as congregations emerge in surrounding towns and villages.

After preaching in Frankenthal one Sunday, we were invited to the home of Gerhard and Hilda Wölk for dinner. As the leading elder at that time, Brother Wölk told us about a new development undertaken by the church to expand its ministry. He called it *Bibelheim am Klosterberg* in Höningen. "That is where we would like you to serve as a resource person for Bible teaching and preaching." He continued to tell the story how the FMBG had purchased an older social institution with a fairly large lot. By investing ingenious architectural and engineering skills plus much donated labor and money by church members, they have completely renovated, rebuilt, and significantly enlarged the existing facilities. It has become an attractive and functional Bible conference center.

In 1999 and 2000 we lived in the *Bibelheim* in Höningen for several months each year. Höningen is a small, quaint old village, dating back almost a thousand years, when the Roman Catholic Church built a monastery and other institutions in an attempt to Christianize the peoples of that region. Silent ruins on the one hand, and ringing church bells on the other, bear witness to prosperous times of the past. The village is nestled on hills and in hollows within the beautiful *Pfälzer Wald* in the Palatinate. A number of the local residents from later generations have garnered some of the yellowish-grey stones from old ruins and put them to good use as they built their more modern family dwellings. As one walks through the village, one can clearly see here and there parts of the house bearing distinct marks of bygone centuries in an apparent attempt to immortalize at least some fragments of medieval culture and religion.

The FMBG gave us a comfortable apartment on the third floor of the *Bibelheim* from where we had a perfect view of the village. Its dwellings with some 180 residents are surrounded by trees and shrubs and flowers adjacent to old shops. That's where the blacksmith's hammer and anvil, the shoemaker's owl and waxed thread, the spinning wheel draped with wool and fiber, the carpenter's workbench with saw and plane are still on display as symbols of trades and crafts that once flourished in Höningen. Alas, they are no more. But there are remnants of yards and barns where roosters still crow and hens still cackle. Every day we were uplifted by the twitter of nesting swallows that joined a host of other chirping birds and singing larks to compose a melodious song as an ode to a common Maker: theirs and ours. Whenever we heard the dogs bark and the cats meow across the street, or when we saw the farmer and the shepherd lead their herds from the barn along the road to water fountains and lush pastures a short distance away, we could feel the serene, crisp and clean atmosphere around us, and we knew that we were in a world far removed in time and space from the hustle and bustle of city life in Fresno.

During our first year there, groups of seniors, young people, and families from various churches had signed up in advance and usually spent the week from Monday through Friday noon at the *Bibelheim am Klosterberg*. For some it was simply a week of leisurely repose, while others came there for serious study and reflection. Still others were there for spiritual edification and mutual sharing between families and friends. My assignments depended on the request of a given group or on a specific topic chosen by a church sponsoring a certain group of its members. Depending on age and composition of the attendants for the week, I usually had two or three hours of Bible studies focusing on a specific chapter, or on an entire book of the New Testament. Most of the afternoons I spent in preparation for the next day. In the evenings Frieda and I took part in activities planned by the guests. On weekends I was generally invited to preach in different churches. One of the practical benefits we had was a car made available to us by the churches for the time of our ministry there. That enabled us to go wherever and whenever we needed to go and allowed us to see much of Germany's scenic countryside and many fascinating historical sights. Even the drive from Höningen to the Autobahn and back was serene and peaceful as the road wound its way through forests, vineyards, vales, and villages. The fall colors were especially spectacular.

My assignments of the second year were similar to those of the first, except that we spent more time away from Höningen. I was preaching and teaching more often in the churches, rather than having the church groups come to the *Bibelheim*. This arrangement was advantageous for the churches in that the entire congregation—not only a relatively small group—could take part in the services. For me, however, it was much more demanding.

At a special farewell service on 29 October 2000 in the Frankenthal Mennonite Brethren Church, Gerhard Wölk extended an invitation on behalf of this large congregation that we should come back the following year. Among other things he said: "We will ask God for a miracle that your health will improve and you can return." In October 2003 the Lord granted us one more visit to Germany. For one week we lived again in the apartment at the *Bibelheim.* Each evening I spoke on the Book of Jonah in Frankenthal. Adults, young people, and about 150 children sitting in the front pews, filled the large building in every meeting. In addition, I was able to speak in other churches, we visited many friends, and spent a wonderful day at the *Freie Theologische Akademie* in Giessen.

Over the years of ministry in Europe our lives have been enriched by getting to know people from different walks of life and diverse confessional backgrounds. Some we met in churches and at conferences, others in educational institutions and professional settings. The friendships that developed are of lasting value. The words penned by Ben Sira millennia ago say it best: "There is nothing so precious as a faithful friend and no scales can measure his excellence" (Sirach 6:16).

Gunter and Ulla Mandler of Heuchelheim picked us up at the Frankfurt International Airport and took us to our apartment in Giessen more often than we have kept count. On shorter visits we stayed in their home and used one of their cars free of charge. Our neighbors Hans and Ingrid Wittke with their daughter Jennifer adopted us as part of their family. On our last visit they surprised us for our fiftieth wedding anniversary with a trip to Cuxhaven, where I had gone through in 1930 en route from the Soviet Union to Brazil. In France we frequently stayed with Günther and Rosemarie Moll, whom we got to know in 1978 when they served as *Pfarrer* in Germany. These and many other kind people have extended their hospitality in their homes and taken us to scenic, cultural and historical places we would never have gone to see on our own. Indeed, no scale can measure the excellence of friendship.

47

Concluding Reflections

I am pressing on to see if I can capture it,
the ideal for which I was captured by Christ Jesus.
... I do not think that I have captured it yet,
but here is my one aspiration... :
reaching out for what is ahead of me.
—The Apostle Paul in *Philippians 3* (Williams, excerpts)

If I were to identify in a few paragraphs one or two essential aspects that can be traced like a thread woven through my entire adult life, I would have to make some observations about my church experience and related areas of ministry emanating from it.

The first impulses that drew me to the church came from conversations in my parental home. I recall my parents telling us how their lives had been altered when in 1920 both had decided to be baptized and become members of the local church in their village of Alexandrovka in Siberia. Even though they did not elaborate beyond one or two things what exactly had changed, I knew that the church had become a vital part in their lives. Father also told of a meeting they had hosted on 25 May 1930, in our primitive jungle dwelling in the Krauel, where the first Mennonite Brethren Church in Brazil was founded.

My parents always spoke with deference and respect about the church, which they likened to a garden that needed to be cultivated or to a flock in constant need of care and guardianship. They also expressed concern, especially regarding the need for leadership. They were saddened when several preachers and teachers moved away from the Krauel, hoping to find a better way of life in Curitiba. One day when Father was reading Matthew 9, where Jesus likens the crowds of his day to "sheep without a shepherd," Mother made the comment, "We are like those crowds Jesus talks about: 'sheep without a shepherd.'" Only in my later teens did I begin to understand what that meant.

Ever since my conversion to the Lord Jesus and subsequent believers' baptism in 1947, I have been an active member of the Mennonite Brethren within the larger Anabaptist/Mennonite community of faith. It was here that I learned the rudiments of Christian discipleship; it was also here where my initial call to serve the Lord was spiritually nurtured and confirmed. Years later, it was again from within my own denomination that I received another call with purpose and direction: to move and serve also in other confessional contexts with the Word of God. Underlying that decision was a growing understanding of the fallen world on the one hand, and a deepening conviction of the saving power of the gospel of the kingdom of God on the other. I became convinced that the Gospel must be declared by word and deed to peoples who are *not yet* Christians as well as to those who are *no longer* Christian. I was committed to evangelism and service for which I had a wide open door, even if not without opposition.

During some fifty years of intra-cultural as well as cross-cultural ministry, I have come to see how important it is to understand a minimum of two things: the essence of the various facets of culture *within* which fallen and sinful humanity lives and operates; the power of saving grace inherent in the Gospel *by* which people can be saved to become disciples of the Lord Jesus. The Gospel also spells out the ethical norms for a Christian lifestyle. Jesus speaks of His followers in terms of being *in the world*, but not *of the world*. That same principle applies to the church today. Members of the believers' church cannot live outside of culture, nor without culture; the church cannot reject culture altogether, but neither can it be dominated by culture without losing its Christian witness to the world. The church is the only alternative followers of Christ have to live a purposeful life for time and eternity; it cannot afford compromise and accommodation. The more the church accommodates to the cultural trends of the times, the less it has to offer to the world, and thereby loses its purpose for existence.

Over a period of over five decades I have been privileged to be in touch with the reality of church life in different confessional and cultural contexts. That has enhanced my understanding of the worldwide church and deepened my appreciation for the church of my own generation. I have experienced countless blessings and some disappointments. I have witnessed changes and transitions: some wholesome, others hollow; some were prompted by serious studies of the Scriptures, others driven by pervasive trends and fads. On the one hand, I am grateful for every change that increases our awareness of the holiness of God, deepens our understanding of the Scriptures, and leads to a Christian way of life worthy of its name. On the other hand, I am deeply grieved and saddened by the changes that belittle the greatness of a holy God, inadvertently promote shallowness of thinking, lead to biblical illiteracy, and result in a secular lifestyle that disregards and cheapens the cost of Christian discipleship.

God has granted me a fulfilled life of service that has made my journey rewarding and, for the most part, enjoyable from one decade to the next. The mid-1940s were for me years of searching—at times without a purpose—until I found meaning in Christ. The 1950s turned into a decade of basic biblical and secular schooling combined with evangelistic mission. This combination of theory and practice became the foundational ingredients for personal growth and development. This was also the decade for marriage and the beginning of a family. During the 1960s I spent a large part of the decade on a detour in academia. It was not a smooth but still wholesome detour without losing the *Way*. The 1970s, particularly the latter half, were clearly a decade of lengthening the cords and deepening the stakes both in theory and practice; those were years of intensive teaching and learning combined with a variety of multicultural and international ministries with a focus on the church and its mission. The 1980s became a "decade of world mission" at the Mennonite Brethren Biblical Seminary as well as for me personally. I was motivated to carry out that mission by investing my energy in such areas as teaching, preaching, and publishing. In doing so, I was aiming at recruiting and training international leaders with a vision and a passion to cross frontiers as servants of the Lord to make disciple of all peoples.

To my own disadvantage, I have never invested sufficient time and energy to become proficient in biblical languages. Instead of bemoaning what I have missed, I have sought to compensate for that loss—at least to a degree—by devoting myself to serious study of the Bible, using different languages and translations as well as dictionaries and lexicons. In that exercise I have found J. A. Bengel's "golden rule" very helpful; he spelled it out in 1742 when he wrote his much celebrated exegesis of the New Testament entitled *Gnomon Novi Testamenti*. Himself an eminent Bible scholar with profound knowledge of the classical languages, Bengel formulated a sound pedagogical principle: *"Te totum applica ad textum: rem totam applica ad te,"* which in translation says this: "Apply yourself wholly to the text; the text apply wholly to yourself." It is important to get a good grasp of the text, but even more important to be grasped by it. I have used Bengel's rule for many years and still find it useful in personal Bible study, meditation, and reflection as well as in preparation for preaching and teaching about the "faith once for all entrusted to the saints."

Since my retirement from seminary teaching I have focused intensely on the character and mission of the Lord Jesus as revealed in the theology of the Fourth Gospel. I have also spent precious hours with Paul's letter to the Ephesians as the charter document of the Christian church. Through this document I have not only gained a deeper understanding of *saving* grace, but also learned the meaning of *service* grace. Saving grace leads to service grace which in turn enables the church to be useful and fruitful in its mission to the world. In addition, I devoted myself to a follow-up study of the Book of Acts as the primary source book for the history of the church in world mission.

From the Pastoral Epistles I have gleaned an overwhelming sense of awe of God's blueprint for church leadership and sound teaching. While the risen Christ gave to His followers the commission to make disciples of all peoples and the mandate to teach them all the things which He had instructed them to teach, the apostles define the content of that nonnegotiable curriculum for the church. While teaching an adult Sunday school class on John's "Revelation of Jesus Christ," I have been captured as never before by its compelling message to the church throughout the ages with special emphasis on the end times. It is a message about faithful living and serving in a chaotic world until Christ's second coming when He will establish His eternal Kingdom as King of kings and Lord of lords.

That moves me to conclude—not my journey itself, only these written fragments—with a personal reflection on

My Unended Journey

Your plan for me goes on, O LORD:
    Triune God of pow'r and might.
You are the Holy One, the Righteous:
    God of justice, truth and light.
You made order out of chaos,
    Gave creation time and space.
You called peoples into being,
    Sent Your Son to save each race.

You are the "ALPHA and OMEGA":
    Ever present "THE I AM."
You're the Creator, the Redeemer:
    God, the Savior, through the Lamb.
You're my Helper, are my Healer:
    Caring Shepherd, Leader, Guide.
You're my Refuge, my Protector:
    Walking with me at my side.

You know my whence; You know my whither;
    You also know my where.
You know the center, know the margins
    where I sit, lie down or stand.
You know my journey, know my story
    from beginning to the end.
You know that all I've done is to recount—
    reflect on what has been.
I've told what was and is and leave to You
    the things that are to come.

Concluding Reflections

A tale I've told—a story of my wand'rings
  through valleys and through vales:
  some too deep for words to tell.
A tale I've told—a story of my journeying
  on lofty hills and mountain tops:
  some too high for pen to spell.
A tale I've told—a simple pilgrim's story
  of spacious fields and jungle's depths:
  what paradox on which to dwell!
A tale I've told—an unpretentious chronic
  of transient life held in Your mighty hand:
  graced and guided, good and well.

I've walked through villages and hamlets:
  some filled with laughter, some with tears.
I've been in shanties and in mansions:
  some rich on wealth, some wrought by fears.
I've strolled with giants of Your choosing:
  some arrogant, some bright as stars.
I've trod with dwarfs on lowly pathways:
  some brilliant minds; some simply wise.
I've sat in schools with erudites and learn'd,
  observed the wisdom of this age.
Some raised sophisticated questions,
  searched for answers page by page.
Some were sorely disappointed;
  others humbly read Your Word.
Some laid claim to little knowledge,
  save of Christ, the Crucified.
Some hailed the power of Him risen,
  hailed Him Lord above all lords.

I've walked the dusty roads of servants
  who have shown me how to serve.
I've walked with saints in simple sandals
  and washed the feet of other saints.
I've served the church in divers manners,
  have been a shepherd, cared for flocks.
I've lifted high salvation's banners;
  have wept for hearts as hard as rocks.
I've taken detours on life's journey,
  beck'ning with alluring signs.
I've faced road forks, stood at crossroads—
  misleading arrows, crooked lines.

I've fumbled here and stumbled there,
    made blunders, hurtful to repair.
I've walked with heavy-footed trav'lers
    whose feet seemed weightier than clay.
I've run the race with rugged runners,
    and was as rough and gruff as they.

And then one day Your Holy Spirit
showed me cleats of brass on my own feet:
"Forgive me, Lord," I humbly prayed,
"That from Your upright path I've strayed:
Wash my heart from arrogance and pride.
Let charity and patience with humility abide.
Sustain my faith to trust alone in grace
and guide each step I take through time and space.
Forever let my hope be firmly fixed on You;
teach me to will alone Your will to do."

My story is unended, unfinished will be my report.
My heart is getting tired, my eyes are turning blurred.
My pen is nearly out of ink, my paper soon used up.
Here is my script: at best a fragment, quite undone.
Please, take it, LORD, and write a proper ending,
just as You once wrote my genesis into a book.
Then shall I see with clarified and unblurred vision:
This journey is not mine: by providence it's Your design.

Selected Bibliography

Only books, articles, and unpublished sources containing pertinent historical and cultural information relevant to my story are listed.

Adrian, Victor and Don Loewen, eds. *Committed to World Mission: A Focus on International Strategy.* Winnipeg: Kindred Press, 1988.
Bach, Adolf. *Geschichte der deutschen Sprache.* 7th ed., rev. and enlarged. Heidelberg: Quelle und Meyer, 1961.
Bender, Harold S. "Brazil." *The Mennonite Encyclopedia I* (1982): 408-410.
_____. "Krauel." *The Mennonite Encyclopedia III* (1982): 233-234.
Boockmann, Hartmut and others, eds. *Deutsche Geschichte im Osten Europas.* Vol. 10: *Rußland,* edited by Gerd Stricker. Berlin: Siedler Verlag [1998].
Coelho dos Santos, Silvio. *Os Índios Xokleng: Memoria Visual.* Pôrto Alegre: Movimento Editora da UFSC [1997].
Conquest, Robert. *The Harvest of Sorrow: Soviet Collectivization and the Terror Famine.* New York: Oxford University Press, 1986.
Ens, H. "Das mennonitische Schulwesen in Brasilien." In *Mennonitisches Jahrbuch für Südamerika 1968-1969.* Curitiba: Tipografia Santa Cruz (n.d.):68-73.
Epp, Frank H. *Mennonite Exodus: The Rescue and Resettlement of the Russian Mennonites Since the Communist Revolution.* Altona, MB: D. W. Friesen & Sons Ltd., 1962.
Epp, G., Ar. Rempel, Herm. Klassen, K. Neufeld, eds. *Vor den Toren Moskaus: Gottes gnaedige Durchhilfe in einer schweren Zeit.* Yarrow, BC: Columbia Press, 1980.
Epp, Reuben. "Plautdietsch: Origins, Development and State of the Mennonite Low German Language." *Journal of Mennonite Studies* 5 (1987): 61-72.
_____. *The Story of Low German and Plautdietsch: Tracing the Language Across the Globe.* Hillsboro, KS: The Reader's Press, 1999.
Ewert, David. *Honour Such People.* Winnipeg: Centre for Mennonite Brethren Studies, 1997.
_____. *A Journey of Faith: An Autobiography.* Winnipeg: Centre for Mennonite Brethren Studies, 1993.
_____. *Proclaim Salvation: Preaching the Church Year.* Scottdale, PA and Waterloo, ON, 1992.

Fast, Gerhard. *In den Steppen Sibiriens.* Rosthern, SK: Verlag von J. Heese [1957].

Fast, Karl. *Gebt der Wahrheit die Ehre! Ein Schicksalsbericht.* 2nd ed. Winnipeg: Canzona Publishing,1989.

Flögel, Alfred. *Mölln: Eine Rückblende.* Wildshire, England: Midway Clark Printing, 1998.

Friesen, Peter. "Unsere Flucht aus meiner Heimat, der Orenburger Ansiedlung Nr. 10, über Deutschland nach Brasilien." Unpublished manuscript [1990]. Private library collection.

Gerlach, Horst. *Die Rußlandmennoniten: Ein Volk unterwegs.* Kirchheimbolanden (Pfalz): Selbstverlag, 1992.

Giesinger, Adam. *From Catherine to Krushchev: The Story of Russia's Germans.* Lincoln, NB: American Historical Society of Germans from Russia, 1981.

Hamm, Susanna. "Lebenserinnerungen." Unpublished manuscript with old documents. Xeroxed, n. d. Private library collection.

Hiebert, P. C. *Mitteilungen von der Reise nach Süd-Amerika* [1937]. Hillsboro, KS: Mennonite Brethren Publishing House, n.d.

Hildebrand, J. J. *Sibirien. Erster Teil: Allgemeine Übersicht über Sibirien und der Gründung der Mennoniten-Siedlungen in Sibirien.* Winnipeg: By the author, 1952.

Janz, Willy and Gerhard Ratzlaff, eds. *Gemeinde unter dem Kreuz des Suedens: Die Mennonitischen Bruedergemeinden in Brasilien, Paraguay und Uruguay 1930-1980.* Curitiba, PR: Imprimax, 1980.

Kasdorf, Hans. "Becoming an Anabaptist Missiologist: Reflections from the Road." *Mission Focus. Annual Review* 10 (2002):135-151.

Klassen, Peter. P. *Die Rußlanddeutschen Mennoniten in Brasilien.* Vol. 1: *Rio Alto Krauel und Stolzplateau.* Weierhof: Mennonitischer Geschichtsverein, 1995.

Klaube, Manfred. *Die deutschen Dörfer in der westsibirischen Kulunda-Steppe: Entwicklung—Strukturen—Probleme.* Marburg: N. G. Elwert Verlag, 1991.

Krahn, Cornelius. "Russia." In *The Mennonite Encyclopedia,* IV (1959): 381-393.

_____. "Siberia." In *The Mennonite Encyclopedia,* IV (1959):517-521.

_____. "Slavgorod." In *The Mennonite Encyclopedia,* IV (1959):537-543.

Kroeker, Jakob. "Das Geheimnis vor Moskau." *Mennonitische Rundschau,* 105 (July 28, 1982): 9-21.

Loewen, Abram J. *Vor vielen wie ein Wunder: Fuehrungen durch 85 Jahre meines Lebens.* Abbotsford, BC: By the author, 1983. Private library collection.

_____. "Warum verließen wir Rußland?" Handwritten document, January 30, 1930. Kirchenarchiv Mölln, Carton 13. Xeroxed with permission, 1999. Private library collection.

Loewen, Heinrich H., Sr. "Mennoniten in Brasilien." In *Jahrbuch der Mennoniten in Südamerika 1961*: 73-75. Curitiba: Tipografia Santa Cruz.

Loewen, Jacob. A. "Toward a Phonemic Alphabet of Plautdietsch." *Journal of Mennonite Studies* 16 (1998): 128-146.

Lopau [City Archivist, Mölln]. "Das Flüchtlingslager für die Rußlanddeutschen in Mölln (1929-1933)." Complimentary copy from the writer, August 5, 1999. Private library collection.

Martins, Heinrich. "Erinnerungen an Moskau 1929." In *Vor den Toren Moskaus: Gottes gnaedige Durchhilfe in einer schweren Zeit*, edited by G. Epp and others. Yarrow, BC: Columbia Press, 1980. 51-60.

Mehnert, Klaus. "Deutsche—vom Sturme verweht." *Der Bote*, September 5, 12, 19 and 26, 1956.

Pauls, Peter, Jr., ed. *Brasilien: Heimat für Heimatlose*. Witmarsum—Palmeira, Paraná: Cidade Clima [2002].

_____, ed. *Krauel—Stolzplateau: Pioniere erzählen, wie es früher einmal war*. Witmarsum—Palmeira, Paraná: Cidade Clima [1999].

_____, ed. *Mennoniten in Brasilien: Imigração Menonita no Brasil 1930-1980*. Curitiba, PR: Imprimax Ltda, n.d.

_____, ed. *Urwaldpioniere: Erlebnisse mennonitischer Siedler aus den ersten Jahren am Krauel und auf Stolzplateau*. Curitiba, PR: Imprimax Ltda, 1980.

Penner, Peter. "Documents Relevant to the Wiebe Family Reunion (1998)." Complimentary copy from the writer. Private library collection.

_____. "Let My People Go! A Catastrophic Episode in German/Russian Emigration." *Journal of the American Historical Society of Germans from Russia* (Fall, 1995):40-45.

Pries, George David. *A Place Called Peniel: Winkler Bible Institute 1925-1975*. Altona, MB: D. W. Friesen & Sons Ltd., 1975.

Quiring, Walter, ed. *Im Schweisse deines Angesichts: Ein mennonitisches Bilderbuch*. Steinbach, MB: Derksen Printers, Ltd., 1953.

_____. "Mennoniten vor Moskau." In *Mennonitisches Jahrbuch 1956*, 10-19. Edited by Cornelius Krahn. Newton, KS: Mennonite Publishing Office, 1956.

Radzinsky, Edvard. *Stalin: The First In-Depth Biography Based on Explosive New Documents from Russia's Secret Archives*. Translated by H. T. Willetts. New York: Doubleday, 1996.

Rahn, Peter. *Mennoniten in der Umgebung von Omsk*. Winnipeg: Christian Press, 1975.

Salisbury, Harrison E., ed. *Anatomy of the Soviet Union*. London: Thomas Nelson, 1967.

Sawatsky, Walter. *Soviet Evangelicals Since World War II*. Kitchener, ON: Herald Press, 1981.

Schartner, David. "Wie es früher einmal war." *Bibel und Pflug*. [Twenty installments] April 1986-November 1987.

Schroeder, William and Helmut T. Huebert, eds. *Mennonite Historical Atlas.* 2nd ed., rev. and expanded. Winnipeg: Springfield Publishers, 1996.

Service, Robert. *A History of Twentieth-Century Russia.* Cambridge: Harvard University Press, 1998.

Solzhenitsyn, Aleksandr I. *The Gulag Archipelago 1918-1956: An Experiment in Literary Investigation I-IV.* Translated from the Russian by Thomas P. Whitney. New York: Harper and Row, 1974/75.

Strachan, R. Kenneth. *The Inescapable Calling: The Missionary Task of the Church of Christ in the Light of Contemporary Challenge and Opportunity.* Grand Rapids: William B. Eerdmans, 1968.

Stricker, Gerd, ed. *Rußland.* Berlin: Siedler Verlag [1998].

Thiesen, John. *Mennonite and Nazi? Attitude Among Mennonite Colonists in Latin America 1933-1945.* Kitchener, ON: Pandora, 1999.

Toews, John B. *Czars, Soviets and Mennonites.* Newton, KS: Faith and Life Press, 1982.

Unruh, Anna. "Aufzeichnungen aus der Vergangenheit." A handwritten manuscript by Anna (Löwen) Unruh about the life and death of her husband [my foster brother] Peter Unruh. Private library collection.

Unruh, B. H. "Die Massenflucht mennonitischer Bauern aus Russland und ihre politische und religiöse Hintergründe." Copy of a typewritten essay, n.d. Kirchenarchiv Mölln, Carton 13. Xeroxed with permission, 1999. Private library collection.

Unruh, H. "Die Mennonitischen Ansiedlungen in Westsibirien." In *Bundesbote Kalender für 1913* (1913):26-27.

Volkogonov, Dmitri. *Stalin: Triumph and Tragedy.* Edited and translated from the Russian by Harold Shukman. Reprinted from the 1991 Grove Weidenfeld edition. Rocklin, CA: Prima Publishing, 1996

Wiebe, Peter J. "Einiges aus meinem Leben und über russische Verhältnisse." Typewritten document with cover letter addressed to Pastor Paul Bruns, Mölln. February 13, 1930. Kirchenarchiv Mölln, Carton 13. Xeroxed with permission, August 1999. Private library collection.

Glossary

A glossary of selected German (G), Low German (LG), Portuguese (P), and Russian (R) names and expressions frequently used by Mennonites in Brazil and/or in Russia as part of their vocabulary—even if many of the terms were borrowed or adapted from outside sources.

aipim or mandioca—(P) a starchy tuber as staple source of food for humans and animals plus a host of other uses.

Altenau—original German name for a suburb of Blumenau, renamed Itoupava Secca.

Alto Rio Krauel—upper end of the Krauel River. See Krauel.

Anú — tributary of the Krauel settled by German Lutherans, Catholics, and Mennonites, forming part of the village Witmarsum.

Anwohner—(G) landless class in Russia living on land of landowners; there were Mennonites of both classes.

Bobbat—(LG) A Russian-Mennonite yeast dough baked in a flat pan with pieces of smoked sausage and/or ham, served hot.

Bulktjhe —LG for white bread, adapted from the Russian word bulka

Cambará—major tributary of the Krauel settled mostly by Mennonites in 1930 as an extension to Witmarsum.

cará—starchy tuber that becomes sticky (slimy) when ground up, used as a binding agent in corn flour.

Catangara—major tributary of the Krauel where Mennonites settled as an extension of the village Gnadental.

enxada—a heavy Brazilian hoe used for a variety of manual tasks on the roça.

facão—a typical Brazilian bush knife, usually carried on the left side in a thick leather sheath hanging from a person's belt.

Faspa—(LG) leisurely afternoon tea or coffee with some baked goods enjoyed on Saturdays in the family, on Sundays with guests, or at weddings and other celebrations.

Feistel—LG for the Brazilian foice.

Feliz—small tributary of the Krauel settled by Mennonites as part of Gnadental.

foice—(P) indispensable tool used to clear jungle underbrush.

GULAG—Russian acronym for Chief Administration of Correctional Labor Camps.

Hamidje-Wilhelmina—German settlement in Palestine (Israel) where a number of Mennonite families from Russia migrated in the late nineteenth century.

Hamonia—original name of the town in Brazil where the Hanseatic Land Association had its headquarters. Renamed Ibirama

Ibirama—see Hamonia.

Jacabemba—small tributary of the Krauel settled by two or three Mennonite families, belonging to Gnadental.

Jreewischmolt— (LG) ground pork cracklings or greaves used as spread on bread.

kolkhoz—(R) collective farm during Soviet times.

Krauel—name of the river as well as of the Mennonite Colony with three villages—Witmarsum, Waldheim, Gnadental—established along the river in 1930.

Krauel, Richard—German diplomat and explorer in Brazil in whose honor Rio dos Indios was renamed "Krauel" in 1903.

kulak—(R) fist; during the Stalinist era anyone with property or hired help.

mandioca—see aipim.

Meddag—(LG) noon meal.

NEP—New Economic Policy introduced by Lenin to reform the existing economy from private to collective farming.

Oberschulze—(G) authoritative leader of a Mennonite colony in Russia as well as in Brazil. See Schulze.

Peatjhilfleesch—LG for raw pig meat preserved in pure, course salt.

picada—(P) a narrow path for one person cut through the jungle with a facão; also a path in thick underbrush leading to a brook where wild animals go for water.

picadão – (P) same as picada, but wider.

pinhão—(P) seed (edible nut) of the pinheiro.

pinheiro—(P) umbrella pine of the araucária family plentiful in Paraná and Santa Catarina of SE Brazil.

Plumiplautz—(LG) Mennonite plum cake baked in a large flat pan.

poço—(P) water well; also calm and deceptively deep water holes often found in otherwise shallow streams like the Krauel.

Rio Krauel—Krauel River, originally known as Rio dos Indios, a tributary of Rio Hercilio. See Krauel.

roça—(P) a plot of jungle land cleared for planting and harvesting; a farmer's field.

roçar mato—(P) razing or clearing jungle as the first step to making a roça.

Schulze—German designation used by Mennonites for village leader (mayor) in Russia as well as in Brazil.
Schwienstjhast—(LG) colloquial expression describing a traditional custom of butchering a pig in a Mennonite village in Santa Catarina.
serra—(P) a serrated mountain range typical in SE Brazil.
Sildfleesch—(LG) ears, feet, nose, tongue, and heart of a pig cooked, then pickled in brine and eaten cold with bread or potatoes in Russia and with corn bread or aipim in Brazil.
Sildtjhees—(LG) same parts of the pig as in Sildfleesch, but ground up and pressed, spiced and sliced to be eaten either cold or hot.
Tjharpswrenj—(LG) squash jam.
Tjielktje—(LG) typical Mennonite homemade pasta.
Tucaninho—tributary of the Krauel settled by German Lutherans and Catholics as part of the village Witmarsum.
Tucanoboia (Tucano Boi; Boi)—small tributary of the Krauel forming part of the village Waldheim.
Tweeback—(LG) typical Russian-Mennonite baked two-layered bun made of yeast dough. Origin is unknown.
Zwieback—(G) not to be confused with the German Zwieback (twice baked) wheaten rusk toasted yellow after baking. The German Zwieback is entirely different from Mennonite Tweeback or Zwieback.

General Index

Acts 2:38 169
Adrian, Victor 319
Advent 149, 150
aipím (see mandioca) 80-82, 349, 351
Alexandrovka 6-7, 16, 107, 339
Alexey Rykov (ship) 34, 35
Altenau (Itoupava Secca) 54, 231, 349
American Consulate 182-183
Anabaptist/Mennonite 287, 289, 301-302, 313, 315, 334, 339
Anglo American Mennonites 158
Angst 13, 16
Annual prayer week 154
Anteater 129-130
Arentz, Frederico 182-183
Argentina Marú 242-244
Army ants 118-119
Ascension Day 149, 155
Associação Menonita Beneficente 100
Atlantic (Ocean) 43-45, 49, 51-52, 61, 71, 140, 159, 183, 223, 232, 242-243
Augsburger, Myron 198, 271
Auhagen (Stolzplateau) 68, 160
Auhagen, Otto 26, 30, 39, 68
Aurich, Johannes 55

Baake, Wolfgang 291, 309
Bad Lebenzell (Mission) 335
Baerg, William G. and Margaret 197
Baker, DeWitt 268
Balzer, Gerhard 228
Bamboo (blooming) 83-85
Banman, Peter 206
Bärg, Anna 88
Barnaul xiii, 4-7

Bedbugs 22, 32, 117
Bender, Harold S. 63
Bengel's "golden rule" 341
Berlin 30, 33, 39, 40, 309
Bibeldramen Klopstocks 264
Bibelheim am Klosterberg 336-338
Bibelseminar Bonn 334
Bible Memorization 269
Bible school ix, xvi, 124, 162, 174-176, 181, 184, 191-194, 196-198, 200-203, 205-210, 212-213, 216-217, 220, 229, 234, 236-237, 239, 246, 248, 250, 267, 292, 301, 322
Blum, Fritz 137-138
Blumenau (boat) 52
Blumenau (church; city) 51, 52, 72, 129, 196, 217-227, 229-242, 246, 252, 278-279, 319, 322
Blumenau, Hermann Bruno Otto 218
Board of Foreign Missions 216, 246, 250-251
Board of General Welfare 215, 220, 221, 225-226, 242, 246, 249, 250, 251, 253
Board of Missions and Services 278, 280-283, 297, 300, 309, 311, 313, 326
Bolshevik(s), Bolshevism 11, 13, 18, 21, 40, 49
Boldt, Jasch 181
Boldt, John 195, 197
Bosch, David Jacobus and Annemarie 304-308, 312
Boschmann, Peter 159
Botocudos (see Xokleng) 98-100
Botswana 307
"Boy from Brazil" 207-208

Braun, B. J. 242, 251
Braun, Jake 205
Brazilian Consulate 216,219, 220
Brazilian government 97, 100, 162
Brazilian MB Conference 242
Brown, Peter 200-201
Brunner, Fred and Annie, Edeltraud, Horst 232, 235-238
Budenny, Symyon 13
Buhler (Kansas) 88
Bullfrog(s) 79, 123
Bull Prinz 132-133
Butterflies 75, 125-130, 230

Cachorro do mato 92, 104, 121-124
Canadian Consulate (Embassy) 26, 244
Canadian Government (see Ottawa)
Cancer, 106, 158, 241-242, 245, 250, 253, 266, 315
Carrots 112-113
Centro Nova Vida (Brazil) 322
Christian discipleship 77, 171, 339-340
Christian mystics 265
Christmas 37=38, 89, 93-94, 140, 149-152, 190, 195, 202-203, 209, 230, 232, 259-260, 274, 299, 313, 323, 335
Circuit preacher (Lincolnville, Lost Springs, Tampa) 252
Church Mission Institute 281
Clearing the jungle 79-82, 91
Collectivism; collectivization 10-11
Colônia Nova 68, 134, 160, 181, 215, 220, 222, 225, 228, 231, 240, 242, 280, 319
Communism, Communist 10, 13, 23. 29
Conference of MB Churches in Brazil 239-240, 281
Conversion 163-168, 170-172, 196, 235, 280, 315-316, 339
Convocation on Evangelism 277
Cossack Yermack 3

Cultural; culture xviii, 19, 37, 68, 77, 100, 140, 142-144, 147, 149, 151, 155, 158, 162, 179, 182, 190-191, 198, 206, 225, 236, 240, 249-251, 255, 264, 273, 281-282, 284, 287, 292, 307, 313-314, 316, 321, 330, 338, 340-341
Curitiba 29, 56, 69, 100, 116, 128, 177, 180-181, 185, 226-229, 236, 239-242, 279-280, 319-320, 335, 339
"Curitiba 1988" MB world mission convention 319-320
Customs 51, 95, 139-140, 185, 288, 308, 314, 317
Cuxhaven 44, 338
Czar Nikolas II 5, 8, 30

"Decade of Enlargement" 266, 276
DeFehr, C. A. and Elizabeth 226
Dekulakization 10-11, 13
Detour in Academia 248-249, 270, 297, 341
Deutsche Indianer Pionier Mission 56, 100, 336
Dias, Antonio Gonçalves 179-180
Dick, Heinrich 112-113
Digging sweet potatoes 106-107
Diller, Edward 267
Diphtheria 8, 36, 107
Dogs and cats 120ff.
Dormitory life 203-204
Driedger, Jake and Mary 209, 221, 251, 333
Dueck, Abraham and Helene 242
Dueck, Henry and Helen 280
Dueck, Henry 212
Dyck, Annie E. 197
Dyck, Dr. Peter (and Mrs. Dyck) 106, 114-116
Dyck, John R. 206

East Chilliwack Bible School 216, 220, 229
Easter 68, 149, 154-156

Ekk, Kornelius 102
Elbe River 43-44
Engagement (preengagement) 209
Enns-Rempel, Kevin xiii
Epiphany Day 149, 154
Epp, Frank 10, 40
Esau, Bernhard 22, 69, 93-94, 109, 112, 128, 144
Evangelism-in-Depth 273, 278, 282
Evangelistic services 238-239,
Ewert, David and Lena ix, xiv-xvii, 149, 214, 269-270

Farewell 17, 19, 42, 46, 146-147, 177, 179-181, 183, 185, 193, 221, 242, 306, 325-327, 334-335, 337
Fargo, N. D. (car accident) 205
Fast, Franz 174
Fast, Gerhard, 4, 13
Fast, Karl 9
Favorita shoes 136-137
Fehdrau, Agnes 181
Felix Dzerzhinsky (ship) 30
Festschrift x, xi, 304, 317, 335
First house (our) 66-67
Fleas 22, 32, 117
Frankenthal Mennoniten Brüdergemeinde 336-338
Freie Theologische Akademie xi, xiv, 315, 327, 328, 332, 334, 338
Fresno Pacific College ix, 272-273, 292, 313
Friesen, Abe and Erna 189
Friesen, Dan 203
Friesen, Heinrich 228
Friesen, Irwin and Lydia (in Botswana) 307-308
Friesen, Jake 217
Friesen, Peter 29-30, 55-57
Froese, Abe 192
Fuller Theological Seminary xii, 138, 258, 286, 290, 297, 304
Funeral (Warkentin) 168-169

Funk, Betty and Louise Oppel (Kinshasa) 308-309
Funk, C. J. 194
Funk, Kornelius and Susanna (Alice, Arthur, Dorothea, Toni) 17, 41, 87, 93-94, 157, 158, 162

Gates of Moscow 20-21, 25-26, 28, 40, 65
Gauche, Harry and Amanda 229, 232, 237
Gebhardt, Ernst 48
Gerhard, Paul 44
Genre xvi-xviii, 264-265
German Consulate 33
German Embassy 26
German government 30, 33, 36, 39-40, 55, 61, 85, 141, 159
Germany, developments in 35-42
Giesbrecht, Gerhard 171, 176, 222
Glasser, Arthur F. 286, 287, 288-290, 304
Glover, Robert Hall 197
Gnadental 64, 67, 69
Goethe, Johann Wolfgang 25, 120
Goldsmith, Oliver 13
Good Friday 149, 154
Gorkii, Maxim 24-25
Görtz, Hansi 279
Görtzen, Peter 111
Group of Kiel 23, 27-32, 35, 39
Gunther, Wesley and Beverly 329-330

Haak, Karl and Adelina 224, 225
Hamburg 28, 35, 37, 43-44, 96, 265
Hamburg Süd xiii
Hamm, Peter 227, 311
Hammerstein 35-38, 41
Hamonia (see Ibirama) 54
Hanseatic Land Association 39, 46, 49, 55-57, 61, 68, 85-86, 96-97, 158
Harder, Heinrich 121
Harvest Thanksgiving 6, 11-12, 83, 300

Heart surgery (first) 313; (second) 328-329
Heier, John 202
Heim; Heimat; Heimatland; Heimweh 19, 48, 73, 178-180, 188, 190,
Heimann, Ullrich 41-42
Heinrichs, Franz 238
Henry, Bill 244
Hiebert, Clarence 256
Hiebert, D. Edmond x, 304
Hiebert, Lando 250, 252
Hiebert, Paul 273-274, 306, 311
Hiebert, P. C. 160-161; (Widow of) 252
Hiebert, Waldo 242, 251, 266
High German 78, 140-142, 150,199, 225, 267
Hillsboro (Kansas) 215, 246, 251-252, 257, 282, 300-301, 319
High school 171, 200, 206, 208-209, 250, 253, 258, 267, 270, 278, 290
Hindenburg, Paul von 40
Holthaus, Stephan 334-335
Hopp, Günther 291
Holtschlorre 136
Hübert, Franz 112, 175
Hübert, Lena 93-94, 145
Hübert, Willi 112, 145, 176
Huntington College 259, 268, 271-272

Ibirama (see Hamonia) 51, 54, 55, 66, 68, 86, 129, 144
Iguaçú 53, 282
Institute of Church Growth 258, 285
Instituto Biblico Asunción 282, 296, 313
Iron horse 54
Irtysch (river) 3, 5
Isaak, Peter xvi, 104, 171, 181
Itajaí (city, harbor, river) 49, 51-52, 61, 71, 181, 218, 231
Itoupava Secca (Altenau) 51- 55, 231

Jacobs, Donald R. 187, 271, 284

Janitorial work 213-214
Jantz, Gerhard 215
Janz, B. B. 26
Janz, Hugo 301
Janzen, Edmund 272, 276-277
Janzen, A. E. 252
Janzen, H. H. 213-214
Janzen, Johannes 40
Janzen, John 193, 203-206
Janzen, Mimi 181
Janzen, Wanj 157, 171
Johnson, Orval and Bertha 258, 268
Jungle; jungle land 1, 3, 18-19, 39, 43,47, 50, 53-57, 59, 63, 66, 71-87, 89, 91-92, 94-96, 98-99, 104, 109, 111, 115, 118, 120, 124, 126, 129, 131, 134, 136, 151, 155, 166, 168, 170, 193, 253, 306, 322, 339, 343

Kaganovich, Lazar Moiseyevich 11
Kahle, Maria 73
Kaingáng 98-100, 336
Kalinin, Mikhail I. 20-21, 23-25, 34
Kasdorf, David iv, xiv, 226, 232, 243, 246, 251-253, 269, 279, 290-291, 314, 335
Kasdorf, Julia xiii-xiv, 314, 335
Kasdorf, Peter and Mary 206
Kaufman, John 175
Kgakge, Nightingale 307
Kirov, Sergei 11
Klassen, A. J. 275, 282, 297, 313
Klassen, C. F. 26
Klassen, John N. and Mary 322
Klassen, Peter, P. 39, 73
Klaube, Manfred 5
Kliewer, Jakob 45, 145
Klopstock, Friedrich Gottlieb 264-265
Koettker, Wilhelm 220, 225-226, 228, 234
Konrad, George, 273, 297
Kratz, Henry 265

Krauel Colony 40, 51, 55, 64, 68-69, 72, 77, 114, 169, 178, 218
Krauel, Richard (German diplomat) 61
Krauel River als Rio Krauel) 39, 51, 61, 69, 71, 97, 133
Krauel Valley 67-68, 97, 158, 175, 177, 193, 201
Kremlin 11, 16, 23-24
Kroeker, A. A. 197
Kroeker, J. A. 194
Kroeker, M. A. 252
Kröker, Abram 175
Kröker, Grandfather and Grandmother 6
Kröker, Johannes 190
Kröker, Maria (Bärg) 88
Kröker, Waldemar 189-190
Kruger National Park, visit to 306
Krüger, Johann 164
Krüger, Peter 145
Kulak 9, 10-11, 13, 29
Kulunda Steppe 4-5, 18-19, 43, 50, 81

Lake Kulunda 5
Lalla 121-124, 127
Land debt 86
Lange, Friedrich 39, 46, 55
Lange, P. R. 203
Learning English 200
Leary, Timothy 263-264
Lehmann, Arno 289-290
Lengthening service cords 284
Lenin (Vladimir Ilych Ulyanov) 10,11, 21
Leningrad 27-35, 235
Lenzmann, Herman 209-210, 217
Leppmann, Wolfgang 260, 264
Levá, Dianne xiv, 220, 232, 243, 246, 251-252, 279, 290, 299, 314-315, 330, 335
Levá, Steve xiv, 314-315, 335
Lewis, C. S. ix, xviii, 76, 136-137, 171 203, 257

Lice 22, 32, 117
Life (leaking out in blood) 134-135
Lightning 48, 57, 72, 75, 87, 124, 164, 166-168
Loewen, Donald (Don) xiv, 314, 316, 319, 335
Loewen, Evelyn xiv, 245-246, 252, 297, 282, 290-292, 314, 316, 335
Loewen, Henry 209
Loewen, Howard 312
Loewen, Jacob A. 250-251, 255
Loewen, Melvin 270, 273
Loneliness 19, 189-191, 314
Longfellow, Henry W. 203, 330, 332
Lopau (archivist) 37
Löwen, Abram 32, 35
Low German 18, 23, 117, 136, 140-142, 150, 153, 156, 162, 199, 202
Lowie, Robert 99
Lutheran(s) xviii, 9, 17, 39, 68, 171, 218, 227, 231, 238, 242, 289, 315-316
Luther Bible 63, 169

Mandioca (see Aipím) 56, 80, 82, 96, 106, 126, 152, 156, 181
Marburg (er) 291, 309
— Brüderhaus Tabor, in 291
— Marburger Mission 56, 100, 336
Martens, Abrão 160
Martens, Elmer xvii, 297-298, 311-312, 326
Martens, Jakob 181
Martens, Phyllis xiii
Martens, Wilfred xiii, 272
Martin, Loyal 277
Martins, Heinrich 23, 27-29, 39, 44, 48, 141
Max (ship) 47, 48-49, 52
Mayer, Thomas iv, xiii
McGavran, Donald A. 258, 287
McGregor, Bede 399
Mekien (Meckien), Bruno 46, 49, 53, 64, 66, 144

Mennonite Brethren Bible College (MBBC) ix, 212-215, 219, 250, 270
Mennonite Brethren Biblical Seminary (MBBS) ix, 251, 271, 273, 287, 289, 292, 297, 298, 301, 311-312, 319, 321 327, 334, 327, 341
— Decade of Mission 311-315, 317, 319-320
— Department of World Mission 300, 312, 327-328, 332, 334
— Vision Statement 311-312
Mennonite Central Committee (MCC) 38-39, 160, 175,182, 208-209, 216, 232, 242
Mennonite Exodus 10, 40
Mennonite Historical Society, German 321
Menno Simons 64, 284
Missiology, missiological ix, xiv, 197, 249-250, 258, 265, 267, 270, 273-274, 276, 284-289, 292, 295, 297 -306, 311-312, 315-316, 319, 328-329, 332-334
Mission(s) x-xii, 30, 56, 63, 72, 100, 138, 167, 180, 185, 187-188, 191, 196- 197, 214-215, 226, 228, 234, 237, 241-246, 248-252, 263, 265-266, 271-274, 277-279, 281-290, 292, 295, 297-303, 305-307, 309-315, 317, 319-324, 327-328, 332-336, 341
— Africa Inter-Mennonite 307
— mission as a task 285
— missions as agencies 285
Mission interrupted 241-246
Modersohn, Ernst 171
Mölln xvi, 23, 28, 37-39, 41-43, 46-47, 158
Moll, Günther and Rosemarie 41, 292, 338
Monte Olivia (ship) xiii, 43-44, 46, 67
Molotov, Vyacheslav 20
Monolingualism 142
Morgan, Robert J. 178

Mormon Temple 255-256
Moscow 10, 13, 15-19, 20-27, 28-34, 35, 38-41, 55, 65, 68-69, 83, 158, 219, 335
Mowry, George 263
Müller, Klaus W. xii, xiv, 317, 322, 334

Neufeld Brothers, Menno and Walter 210
Neufeld, William 277
Neu Breslau (Presidente Getulio) 68
New Economic Policy (NEP) 10
"New Germany" 158, 161
New Year 94, 149, 152-154, 165, 204, 259, 323, 335
Nickel, Arnold xvi, 88, 94-96
Nickel, Jakob (and Anna) xvi, 88-92
Nickel, Katherine xvi, 202-203
Nikkel, David 141
Nordmeyer, Heinrich 265
Northwest Christian College 257-258
Nova Esperança (Neuhoffnung) 68, 109

Old (family) letters xvi, 16, 88-96
Oma and Opa Reimer 232, 279
Omsk 2, 4- 5, 44
Oppel, Louise (and Betty Funk) 308
Ordination 227-229
Orenburg 44
Orr, J. Edwin 287, 297, 298, 304
Ott, Gerhard 173
Ott, Kornelius 172-173
Ottawa 25-26, 33, 35, 39
Owen, Dr. William (cardiologist) 299, 329

Pacific College (Fresno Pacific College; Fresno Pacific University) ix, 268-277, 284-287, 290-292, 297-298, 313
Pacific District Conference 266, 276-277
Pamplona, Orlando 162

Painting elevators 206
Panama Canal 243
Pão de Açucar 45
Paraguay 38-40, 47, 69, 98, 100, 142, 160, 175, 216, 228, 229, 239, 240, 249, 251, 279-282, 296, 301, 313, 335-336
Paraná 62, 68, 71, 98, 100, 116, 177, 181, 239
Parasites (pests) 74, 114-117, 128
Parrots 89, 126-128, 135
Pauls, Alvin and Lona 108, 329
Pauls, Peter xvi, 48, 64, 100, 126, 147
Pavlodar 2, 4-5, 17
Paxson, Ruth 202
Peasant(s); peasantry 4, 10-13, 20, 24, 31, 52, 56, 70, 81-82, 85, 90
Penner, Jacob G. 280-281
Penner, Peter and Elvira 238
Penner, Peter and Justina xvi, 40, 185, 205
Penner, Peter and Katharina 323
Pentecost 68, 93, 149, 155-156
Perlovka 21, 31
Peschkova-Vinivar,Yekaterina Pavlovna 24-25
Peter the Great 3
Peters, C. C. 212, 216, 220
Peters, F. C. 311
Peters, G. W. and Susan 235, 315, 317, 334
Pflaum, Lienhard 288, 322
picada; picadão 55, 66, 68, 74, 109, 112, 129, 135
Pig butchering 142-144
Pigs on a leash 109-110
Pilgrim xvii-xviii, 38, 49, 50, 54, 57, 72, 248, 295, 343
pinhão; pinheiro 76, 86, 99, 126-127
Pioneer, pioneering xvi, 6, 12, 56, 63, 66, 78-88, 116, 128, 178, 196, 218, 265, 282, 288, 295, 309
Plautdietsch (Low German)140-142

Poland 28, 34
Port of Swinemünde 27, 28, 34, 35
Prayer; praying xvii, xix, 10, 12, 17, 18, 22, 24, 27, 29, 32, 48-49, 65, 67, 80, 83, 90, 93, 101-104, 141, 151-154, 165-166, 170, 172-173, 180, 190, 192, 198, 200, 206, 208-210, 215, 219, 224, 228, 231, 233, 236-238, 240-242, 246, 248, 252-253, 258, 263, 266, 270, 274, 278-280, 286, 290, 292, 297-300, 303, 305, 311, 318-320, 323, 326-329, 344
Prenzlau 36-38, 41
Pries, George D. xvii, 193, 195-196
Providence xvii, 1, 25, 138, 162, 173, 207-208, 219, 257-258, 266, 344
Prussia 28, 34, 140, 182

Quest for holiness, piety 202
Quiring, Jake 214
Quiring, Walter 32, 40, 159-160

Radio ministry 237-238, 246
Radzinsky, Edvard 4, 8-11, 16, 21, 24
Rahn, Peter 3
Railroad, Trans-Siberian 4-5
Redekop, H. H. 194, 196, 201, 204, 208
Redekopp, I. W. 197
Reflections xvii, 56, 300, 325, 327, 339-344
Refugees 20-26, 29-30, 33, 36-42, 44, 52, 56, 69, 199, 218
Regier, Jakob 173-174
Regier, Johann 102
Reimer, Dalton 268-269, 293
Reimer, Dave 199, 212
Reimer, David 192
Reimer, Johannes and Cornelia 253-254, 317
Reimer, Nick 244-245
Reimer, Nickolai (Father, Mother) 208, 210, 216, 232, 233, 245
Retirement (rite of passage) xv, 271, 315, 322, 325-331, 334, 341

Revelation 3:20 169-170
Revolution 6, 8-9, 24-25, 275
Rio de Janeiro 39, 46, 51, 180, 182-183, 190, 221-222, 232-233
Rio dos Indios 61
Rio Grande do Sul 62, 68, 71, 134, 181, 225, 239
Rio Itajaí 52, 61, 71
Rio Krauel 39, 51, 61, 69, 98, 133
roça (rossa) 78-87, 89, 91-92, 102-104, 112-113, 121-122, 126, 128, 131-132
"Rogate" conference center 335-336
Rosenfeld, Gerhard 174-175, 227-228, 233, 239
Rousseau, Jean-Jacques 202
Russian Orthodox Church 154-155
Rutter, August 225
Rykov, Alexey 34-35

Santa Catarina 39, 46, 51, 62-63, 68, 71-73, 84, 94, 98, 116-117, 220, 225, 279, 322
São Paulo 46, 51, 177, 180, 181-183, 227, 232-233, 238, 242-244, 279-280, 319
Schartner, David 13, 45-46, 57, 145
Schartner, Gerhard 173, 215
Schmidt, Henry, 281, 312
School of World Mission xii, 138, 258, 286-288, 290, 306
Schroeder, Harold and Susan 257
Schwing, Eide and Helga 309
Scoll (brothers)Farm 188, 190, 204-205
Seibel, R. C. and Anna 175-176, 229, 290
Service, Robert 4, 10
serra(s) 39, 52-53, 57, 61, 67-73, 81, 84, 107, 109, 112, 123-124, 129, 134-135, 140, 157, 158, 164, 166, 180-181, 190,193, 201, 223
Sheldon, Charles M. 174
Siberia xiii, xv-xvii, 3-7, 9-10, 12-13, 16-20, 22, 24-27, 29-31, 33, 38, 41, 43, 47, 50, 61, 63, 67, 73, 78, 81, 63, 90, 95, 101, 106-107, 136, 140, 164, 170, 178, 191, 339
Siberian Steppe (s) 1, 3-5, 43, 57, 63, 140, 170, 191
Sidler, Werner 138
Silvio, Coelho dos Santos 99
Slavgorod xiii-xiv, 3-7, 11, 13-19, 35, 44, 49, 55, 63, 65, 106
Snakes 79, 85, 114, 120-123, 230, 233
"Sodom and Gomorrah" 190
Solzhenitsyn, Aleksandr 4, 14
Sommerkamp Barracks 55, 57, 66
South American District Conference 239, 242
Stadelmann, Helge 315, 328, 334
Stalin (Dzhugashvili) Joseph 4, 9-13, 16, 20, 21, 23-25, 29, 162
Strachan, R. Kenneth 273-274
Suderman, Jake 199, 204, 212
Sunday school (my first) 111-112
Surveyors (Dudi and Weber) 55, 57
Swinemünde Transport 27-28, 31, 33, 35

Tabor College 246, 248, 250-252, 255-256, 282
Teichrieb, Johann 134
Thanksgiving 6, 8, 11-12, 40, 68, 82-83, 103, 145, 152, 299, 314, 322
Theological Education by Extension 282, 301, 313
Theological Workers Course 296-297
Thielmann, George 217, 229
Thiesen, John 161
Thiessen, Erwin 228
Thiessen, Jakob G. 196
Thrust Evangelism 278-280
Thunder (storm) 48, 57, 72, 79, 95, 124, 164, 166, 169
Tippett, Alan R, 258, 285, 287
Tobolsk 3
Toews, C. D. 210
Toews, J. A. 214, 216, 269, 270, 301

Toews, J. B. 203, 251, 271, 273, 275, 289-290
Toews, J. J. 271, 280
Toews, John E. 312
Toews, Paul xiii
Töws, David 26
Tolstoy(ans) 23, 24
Trans-Siberian Railroad 4-5
Triebel, Johannes 315
Tsebe, Rev. and Mrs. John B. K. of Atterigeville 308-309
turma 97
Tweeback 6, 17-18, 145-146, 189
Two are better...207-211

Ukraine; Ukrainians 9, 63, 73, 88
University of Aberdeen 316
University of Edinburgh 316-317
University of Halle 287, 289
University of Oregon 248, 255-261, 267-269, 272-273
University of South Africa 298, 304, 312
University of Wisconsin 250
Unrau, David and Mary 189, 192
Unruh, Abram A. and Annie 197
Unruh, A. H. 214
Unruh, Benjamin H. 26, 30, 39
Unruh, Jacob and Anna 106
Uruguay xiii, 216, 238-240, 242, 249, 279-281, 313

Vargas, Getulio 137, 161
Vathayanon, Dr, Sathaporn (heart surgeon) 299, 329
Volkogonov, Dmitri 4
Voroshilov, Kliment 13. 20
Voth, H. S. 196
Voth, Kornelius 239

Wagner, Charlie, Mildred 268-269
Wagner Hans 288

Waldheim 44, 64, 67, 82, 89, 111, 115, 160-161, 164, 173-174, 176, 227
Walldorf, Friedemann 333-334
Walls, Andrew 316
Warkentin, Elmo 266
Warkentin (funeral) 167-169
Warkentin, H. K. 238
Warneck, Gustav xi, 287-289
Warneck, Johannes, xii, 288
Wedding(s) 47 89-90, 93, 144-148, 209-210, 213, 314, 323, 338
Western Washington State College 250
Wiebe, Arthur, 268
Wiebe, Elias, 268
Wiebe, John F. 250
Wiebe, Orlando 273
Wiebe, Peter J. xvi, 6, 185, 189
Wiebe, Vernon 250, 280, 300, 311
Wiens, H. R. 251-252
Wiens, Johann G. 196
Willems, Johann (family) 69
Winkler Bible School ix, xiii, 175-176, 192-198, 201, 208, 210, 212-213, 248
Winkler Collegiate 200-201, 203
Winter, Roberta 299
Witmarsum xvi, 44, 64, 67-69, 82, 93, 100, 116, 159-160, 168, 181, 238, 240, 242, 319
Wittke, Ingrid and Hans xiii,338
Wold schloane 78-79
Wolff, Gerd 37
Wölk, Gerhard and Hilda 336
Wood of worth and wonder 85-86
World War I 8, 21, 34, 37, 41, 101, 225
World War II 86, 137, 141-142, 161, 235, 258, 277, 283,

Xokleng (see Botokudos) 98-100, 336

Zagradovka 4, 49, 63, 88
Zinoviev, Grigorii 11, 21, 23
"Zion and Jerusalem" 190

Motivating Generation X

THE POTENTIAL OF GENERATION X
AS A CHALLENGE FOR CHRISTIANS AND FOR MISSIONS

by
JÜRG PFISTER

I am really praying that many people will read this futuristic, cutting-edge, strategic book. Let's make sure this book gets wide circulation.
George Verwer
Founder of Operation Mobilisation (OM)

Hope and help: such can I best describe the book "Motivating Generation X" by Jürg Pfister. I hope that "Motivating Generation X" will be read by responsible members of congregations and missions boards, that it will be heard and that its corresponding initiatives will be implemented.
Thomas Bucher
President of the Evangelical Alliance of Switzerland

Once I had begun to read Jürg Pfister's book, I could not put it down.
Dr. Roland Werner, Germany

Paperback · 150 pp. · $12,99 / £10,95 / €12,80
ISBN 3-937965-06-8

VTR Publications
vtr@compuserve.com
http://www.vtr-online.de

FORM AND FREEDOM

WHAT THE NEW TESTAMENT TEACHES ABOUT
CHURCH GOVERNMENT AND CHURCH LEADERSHIP

by
JEFF BROWN

In a day when churches are forsaking biblical distinctives, this book provides a clear call back to the New Testament church polity and practice. The material in this book will provide encouragement to those who desire a biblical model for their local church, and pause for those who are looking for guidance beyond the Text to current culture. In Short, Jeff Brown's book is a must read.

Daniel K. Davey, Th.D.
Pastor, Colonial Baptist Church, Virginia Beach, Virginia

"Jeff Brown has written a very fine volume by building a solid case for his work, not by simply comparing various systems and traditions, but by going directly to the inspired text. I heartily commend it to all who are interested in learning more about God's intention for the governing process of the church."

Earl D. Radmacher, M.A., Th.M, Th.D
President and Distinguished Professor of
Systematic Theology Emeritus
Western Conservative Baptist Seminary Portland, Oregon

Paperback · 150 pp. · $12,99/£10,95/€12,80
ISBN 3-937965-06-8

VTR Publications
vtr@compuserve.com
http://www.vtr-online.de

www.ingramcontent.com/pod-product-compliance
Lightning Source LLC
Chambersburg PA
CBHW020633230426
43665CB00008B/155